ONE HOT SUMMER

ONE HOT SUMMER

Dickens, Darwin, Disraeli,
and the Great Stink of 1858

Rosemary Ashton

YALE UNIVERSITY PRESS
NEW HAVEN AND LONDON

For information about this and other Yale University Press publications, please contact:
U.S. Office: sales.press@yale.edu   yalebooks.com
Europe Office: sales@yaleup.co.uk   yalebooks.co.uk

Set in Adobe Garamond Pro by IDSUK (DataConnection) Ltd
Printed in Great Britain by TJ International Ltd, Padstow, Cornwall

Library of Congress Control Number: 2017936996

ISBN 978-0-300-22726-0

A catalogue record for this book is available from the British Library.

10 9 8 7 6 5 4 3 2

Contents

Illustrations

Prologue

WHAT WAS IT LIKE to live in London through one of the hottest summers on record, with the Thames emitting a sickening smell as a result of the sewage of over two million inhabitants being discharged into the river? How did people cope with the extraordinary heat leading up to the hottest recorded day, Wednesday, 16 June 1858? What did those living or working near the Thames – including at the Houses of Parliament and the law courts in Westminster Hall – do when they found their circumstances intolerable? What did the newspapers say?

The summer of 1858 was remarkable for the adoption of the engineer Joseph Bazalgette's major civil engineering plan to embank the Thames and convey the capital's waste in intercepting sewers to outfalls east of London. Though the transmission of diseases like cholera, which had afflicted London in a series of outbreaks, most recently in 1854, was generally misunderstood to be airborne rather than waterborne, it was clear to all that the state of the Thames was dangerous to the health of Londoners.

Newspapers, which had increased hugely in number since the progressive repeal of taxes on paper and stamp duty up to 1855, were more than ever before a vital source of information and opinion for the population. From the long-established and respectable *Times* down to new arrivals such as the gossipy *Reynolds's Newspaper*, founded in 1850, the press kept up constant pressure on the authorities to 'do something'. The solving of the problem of the Thames, begun in the summer of 1858, was a major feat of engineering with lasting influence on the health of London's population, on the city's traffic flow, and on its appearance, once it had been adorned with its grand embankments, the Victoria, the Albert, and the Chelsea, as well as new streets and parks, all part of the Bazalgette scheme to improve London. Other important advances were made, or at least got under way, in that hot summer. The *Great Eastern*, Isambard Kingdom Brunel's huge iron-hulled ship, by far the largest built to date, was launched and sat at Deptford on the stinking river awaiting financial support before it could set out on its ambitious voyages. Two other ships, the *Niagara* and the *Agamemnon*, joined their telegraph cables in the middle of the Atlantic in August, enabling instant communication between Britain and America.

Engineering was not the only branch of science to flourish in summer 1858. One event which was to change the prevailing opinion on the nature of evolution, the publication in November 1859 of Darwin's groundbreaking *Origin of Species*, had its catalyst in June 1858. That was when Darwin, working away slowly at proving and illustrating the theory of natural selection which he had formed over the twenty years since his voyage on the *Beagle*, received out of the blue a letter and brief essay from a fellow scientist, Alfred Russel Wallace. The essay shocked him; he thought he might be forestalled, might lose precedence, by continuing to delay publication of his painstaking researches. Darwin was galvanised into writing up his findings quickly and having them published in one readable volume. As he later freely admitted when looking back at this time in his life, the longer, more detailed book he planned would not have reached a general readership or had the immediate impact of the one volume of 1859 with its winning combination of careful scholarship and infectious enthusiasm. To follow Darwin through weeks of trauma – family troubles, health problems, as well as the fright he got over his life's work – is to see how in his case the summer of 1858 was crucial, a period of crisis (though not at that time visibly so outside the small circle of Darwin's family and a few faithful friends). Undoubtedly for Darwin, summer 1858, when he was forty-nine, was one of the most pivotal moments of his career.

Two other important figures who experienced crisis and triumph that summer were Dickens and Disraeli. Like Darwin, each is recognised for his tremendous achievements in his own field of endeavour. Science, literature, and politics were lit up by these three men, all of whom came to be seen as representative of the best of the Victorian age. For Dickens the summer of 1858 was one of horror. Aged forty-six and already the famous author of several successful novels, he lost his head and publicly advertised his separation from Catherine, his wife of twenty-two years and the mother of his nine surviving children, while disclaiming rumours of a relationship with either his sister-in-law or an actress aged nineteen, the same age as his own second daughter Katey. He acted impulsively and brutally, losing friends, dismissing his publishers, causing anguish to his wife and children, as well as getting foolishly entangled in a dispute with Thackeray over a storm in a teacup at the Garrick Club, of which they were both members. The two novelists, rivals for public esteem and never close, had hitherto been on amicable terms (while their daughters were good friends), but now they became permanently estranged. Heads were hot in Clubland in summer 1858; a number of young writers and lawyers, many of them acolytes and imitators of either Dickens or Thackeray, became embroiled in the so-called 'Garrick Club affair', which newspapers followed avidly on behalf of their readers. Dickens's fiction-writing dried up temporarily; that summer he turned in desperation to a new venture, for the first time travelling the length and breadth of the country giving dramatic – and exhausting – public readings from his works. He came within a whisker of losing the admiration of his readers, as well as his friends, but his tremendous determination and the power of his personality, whether speaking, acting, or writing, carried him through his crisis. He returned to novel-writing with *A Tale of Two Cities*, which was published in 1859, and his great imaginative investigations of guilt and shame, *Great Expectations* (1860) and *Our Mutual Friend* (1864–5).

As for Disraeli, he was fifty-three in 1858, but only just making his mark in office. He had been in opposition for almost all his political career since being elected to parliament in 1837, but now he was chancellor of the Exchequer in Lord Derby's reforming Tory government. As leader of the House of Commons, he was responsible for pushing through a number of important pieces of legislation as parliament sat on through the horrible heat and the smell of the Thames just under its collective nose until all its bills were passed on 2 August. A number of these bills would have far-reaching effects on British life. Most notable among them was the act for cleansing the Thames, the so-called 'Thames Purification Bill', which Disraeli got through a disputatious parliament in the gruelling heat of June and July by the sheer force of his rhetoric and his clever management of awkward MPs determined to question or delay every suggestion for improvement. Disraeli's letters to friends and colleagues give a lively sense of his activities. Those to Queen Victoria, telling her the results of each debate in the 'field of battle', quite won her over to a politician whom she, along with Prince Albert, most members of parliament, the newspapers, and even his boss Lord Derby, had distrusted as flashy, reckless, and disloyal. Disraeli also played a major role in the efforts of the Whig Lord John Russell to pass an act which would allow the Jewish MP Lionel de Rothschild to take his seat in the House of Commons without having to swear 'on the true faith of a Christian'. (Disraeli, though Jewish, had been confirmed in the Church of England as a teenager.)

Another of the far-reaching successes for the Derby–Disraeli government that summer was the Medical Act, which founded the Medical Register and the General Medical Council in an important move to regularise a hitherto chaotic, unequal, and unprofessional occupation. Also vital for the future direction of social policy were the discussion of and amendment to the Divorce Act, which had come into force on 1 January 1858. During the following summer a particularly difficult and scandalous case filled the columns of the newspapers. *Robinson v. Robinson and Lane* lasted several months and the country's best legal minds were required to work out how to amend the new act in order to resolve the problems raised. Darwin was aghast to read the reports of his friend Dr Edward Lane's alleged adultery with his patient Isabella Robinson, which were printed day after day for several weeks. Dickens had a nasty moment in June when he feared that he himself might feature in the Divorce Court, with all the attendant adverse publicity that would attract. Meanwhile Disraeli worried that the public scandal concerning the marriage of his close friend and cabinet colleague Sir Edward Bulwer Lytton, also taking up column inches in the press during June and July, would drag down not only Bulwer Lytton, but also Disraeli himself, and possibly the vulnerable Tory government too.

With the recent digitisation of *The Times* and the large mass of nineteenth-century newspapers held by the British Library, it has become possible to delve deeply into the news and current affairs of a specific period of time. So much material relating to the Victorian period is now available in searchable databases that we are able as never before to get a feel for the fabric and structure of daily life. Not only newspapers, periodicals, and magazines, but parliamentary debates, committee minutes, and law court cases can be accessed digitally. We can therefore study in detail the lives of Darwin, Dickens, Disraeli, and others, both as they were experienced and described in their letters and journals, and also as they were viewed by their contemporaries, from friends and colleagues to the host of writers working for the daily and weekly press, in newspaper articles conservative and radical, serious and trivial, friendly and hostile. Hitherto obscure individuals, or those once celebrated – or notorious – but now forgotten, whose experiences contribute to the picture of the time, can be resurrected from the newspaper reports which gave them their moment of fame. Among these are Edwin James, the successful but dubious lawyer known to Dickens; Edmund Yates, the young journalist who unthinkingly and unintentionally caused the Garrick Club affair and the consequent rift between Dickens and Thackeray; the engineers, like Goldsworthy Gurney, who offered solutions to the Thames problem but were *not* engaged to solve it; and the unsung partners and financial backers of Brunel in his pioneering shipbuilding venture.

Microhistory, the study in depth and detail of historical phenomena, can uncover hitherto hidden connections, patterns, and structures. Some events and incidents are revealed over time to have been life changing or nation building. Examples from 1858 are the tackling of London's sewage and the resultant improvement of public health, Brunel's engineering feats, the initial laying of the Atlantic telegraph cable, the beginnings of a long process of attaining justice and equality in the matter of marriage and divorce, and the transformation of a miscellaneous medical practice into a proper profession. Other phenomena prove to have been less momentous, though they formed a living part of the culture of the time. Fashion fads like the mania for the crinoline beloved of the satirical magazine *Punch*; sports events like the Derby horse race; the annual exhibition of painting at the Royal Academy; plays and pantomimes performed in the ever-growing number of theatres, both in the West End and in small venues next to pubs in poorer districts of London; sensational attractions such as the Christy Minstrels or James Rarey, the 'Great American Horse Tamer': all belong to the rich medium of life in Britain, and particularly in London, in summer 1858.

Hitherto unnoticed or undervalued connections can be unearthed between individuals: Darwin and Dr Lane of the famous divorce case; Dickens and the ambitious lawyer Edwin James; Disraeli and Sir Edward Bulwer Lytton, who invited notoriety and provided newspapers with sensational headlines in June–July 1858 by putting his estranged wife Rosina in a lunatic asylum. Paths meet, cross, and converge, and patterns emerge – some intended, others accidental – when a limited period of time is taken and observed in depth. The summer of 1858 offers riches galore for those interested in the life and achievements of Darwin, Dickens, Disraeli, and a wide range of friends, family, observers, critics, and rivals, as well as ordinary people managing their lives as best they could, such as the man sent home on an extremely hot day to get a coat by a magistrate who would not deal with his case if he did not dress 'appropriately'.

A deep delving into lives as they were lived, in the thick of it, in those hot summer days offers insights which full-length biographies and wider-ranging histories are naturally unable to provide, given the requirement to cover whole lives and whole historical periods. Small-scale studies may do for history what Virginia Woolf, in her essay 'Modern Fiction', suggested the novel should attempt, namely as far as possible to 'record the atoms as they fall', and to 'trace the pattern, however disconnected and incoherent in appearance, which each sight or incident scores upon the conscious-ness'. In this way a comparatively neglected time in Disraeli's career can be shown to have been remarkably important in bringing him to prominence. The attention of historians and biographers has focused hitherto on his reckless youth, his racy novels, his controversial journalism, and his late-won success from 1868, when he finally became prime minister. His hard work in the parliamentary session of 1858, particularly in the hectic weeks before the summer break beginning on 2 August, and his success in turning round a hostile press and distrustful colleagues by his efforts, deserve to be acknowledged. In Dickens's case his painful and self-exposing actions in connection with his failed marriage have been fully discussed, but no detailed account exists of the day-to-day struggles he faced in the long summer which followed his catastrophic error of judgment in advertising his separation from his wife in the early days of June. As for Darwin, though much has been written about his abrupt shock and change of plans on receiving in mid-June Wallace's letter outlining natural selection, little attention has been paid to the interaction between his family life and his scientific work in summer 1858. Intense scrutiny of the lives of these men over a short period of a few months allows us to make fresh threads of connection between each of them and the larger society in which they lived, all at a time of public events which proved to be of lasting national importance.

In addition to having access to online databases of newspapers, parliamentary papers, and law courts, I have made use of various archives of unpublished material. My thanks go to librarians, curators, and trustees of manuscripts at the following institutions: the Beinecke Rare Book and Manuscript Library, Yale University; the British Library; Bromley Local Studies Library; the Garrick Club; Lambeth Palace Library; National Meteorological Library and Archive; National Library of Scotland; V&A Theatre and Performance Archive. Individuals who have helped me with information and encouragement, and to whom I express my gratitude, are: Berry Chevasco, Gregory Dart, Mike Dilke, Lindsay Duguid, Nicholas Jacobs, Bill Long, Fred Schwarzbach, Michael Slater, John Sutherland, Jean Sykes, Lorna Unwin, Enrica Villari, René Weis. My thanks also go to my literary agent Victoria Hobbs and my editors at Yale University Press, Heather McCallum and Rachael Lonsdale.

CHAPTER ONE

1858 in History

Moments of consequence

The thermometer had been at 90° all day, and you may imagine what the effect of wax candles, steaming dishes, and a parboiled dozen or two of human creatures must have been. For my own feelings I can only say that St Lawrence on his gridiron was an emblem of cool comfort in comparison.[1]

So wrote the American historian John Lothrop Motley after attending a London dinner party on 16 June 1858, the hottest day of what was proving to be one of the hottest summers thus far recorded. The year 1858, not generally known as a particularly significant year in history, with the exception of its broiling summer, the intolerable stink on and around the Thames, and the decision of parliament to cleanse the river by taking sewage out of London in tunnels under new embankments, was in fact a year of turning points leading to often unforeseen consequences, both for individuals and for the nation as a whole. For ordinary people, and for the rich, the famous, and the powerful, the summer of 1858 was in one way or another a summer of consequence.

When thinking about the past, we often use the shorthand of a single year to represent moments or longer passages of time when events occurred which have subsequently come to be seen as significant in public life, in private life, or in both. In looking for a landmark date for public phenomena we generally refer to the most dramatic discernible moment of some great upheaval or major change, whether social, political, cultural, or ideological. We use 1789 for the event known as 'the French Revolution', and we concentrate our sense of that complicated set of circumstances on the day of the fall of the Bastille. 1914 is forever associated with the declaration and first military actions of the First World War. And 1859, the year of publication of Charles Darwin's *Origin of Species*, does duty as the moment when an irreversible change occurred in humanity's outlook on the natural world and its history. All the while we know that the true beginnings of an event lie half hidden in earlier movements, so that the visible starting point is in fact a culmination of forces which pre-dated its appearance.

Historians spend their time looking back, unearthing and interpreting elements leading up to the iconic moment or year itself. The first great Reform Act of 1832, which gives that year its importance in British history, was a long time coming from the point of view of those agitators, inside and perforce outside parliament, who fought for many years to remove corruption from the election process and to widen representation beyond the tiny minority of the privileged who hitherto held all the political power. 1848 lives in the memory as the 'year of revolutions' in Europe, and indeed armed rebellions occurred in many capital cities, beginning, naturally, with Paris. The year was significant for the domino effect from one country to another, and its events certainly paved the way for progress towards European democracy, but strictly speaking it should be remembered as a year of *failed* revolutions, since autocratic governments were restored throughout the continent within the year and universal representation of peoples had to wait for many more decades. As the historian G.M. Trevelyan put it, 'The year 1848 was the turning-point at which modern history failed to turn.'[2] 1848 was also the year in which Karl Marx published his internationally influential pamphlet, *The Communist Manifesto*, but the work spawned no immediate intellectual or practical revolution; its significance was not recognised anywhere for many years to come.

Often, therefore, a particular year, month, or day which becomes celebrated as significant has been long prepared for. 1859 is a prime example.

In November of that year Darwin's *On the Origin of Species by Means of Natural Selection, or the Preservation of Favoured Races in the Struggle for Life*, to give the book its full, and important, title, was published. It is a work which finally expressed the result of over twenty years of research since Darwin returned from his voyage on the *Beagle*. A hint that the work was truly revolutionary is contained in the unwieldy subtitle, which finds in 'natural selection' the all-important, hitherto elusive, but eventually widely accepted mechanism of evolution. The concept of evolution itself was far from new, as Darwin acknowledged in 'An Historical Sketch of the Progress of Opinion on the Origin of Species', which he added for the third edition of his book, published in April 1861. Here he surveyed the subject from Aristotle via Buffon, his own grandfather Erasmus Darwin, Étienne Geoffroy Saint-Hilaire, the anonymous author of the publishing sensation of 1844, *Vestiges of Creation* (known to the initiated to be the work of the Edinburgh publisher Robert Chambers), and Darwin's rival-cum-enemy Professor Richard Owen, to Alfred Russel Wallace's and his own discovery of natural selection as the explanation for the variation and preservation of species.[3] *On the Origin of Species* was the result of many forces and circumstances in the world of science and in Darwin's own life; it was at one and the same time a culmination and a beginning, since outside the circle of scientific experimenters with whom Darwin corresponded and exchanged papers, the wider non-scientific community was shocked and in some cases repelled by the inferences which now had to be drawn, particularly in the sphere of religious belief. Though 1859 was the year in which Darwin's work met its public, the previous year was for him in a sense more momentous, since it was in the steamy June of 1858 that he received the greatest shock of his life – and the stimulus to complete his great work – in the form of a communication from his fellow naturalist Alfred Russel Wallace, deep in his fieldwork in the Malay Archipelago.

In the autobiography which Darwin wrote late in life for his children he looked back at his career, making the point that 'small circumstances' and hidden causes can lead to great things. He noted that the voyage of the *Beagle* from 1831 to 1836 was 'by far the most important event in my life and has determined my whole career, yet it depended on so small a circumstance as my uncle offering to drive me 30 miles to Shrewsbury, which few uncles would have done, and on such a trifle as the shape of my nose'.[4] This droll observation refers to the fact that young Charles Darwin's father objected to his leaving Cambridge, where he was supposed to be studying to become a clergyman after having given up his medical studies at Edinburgh, in order to travel as unpaid naturalist on the voyage of the *Beagle* to chart the seas of South America. Charles's uncle Josiah Wedgwood interceded with his brother-in-law. The second 'circumstance' was the irascible and unstable nature of the captain of the ship, Robert FitzRoy, later the first official meteorologist when the precursor of the modern Meteorological Society was founded in 1854. FitzRoy agreed to take Darwin on, despite apparently distrusting the shape of his nose. 'He was an ardent disciple of Lavater', wrote Darwin, 'and was convinced that he could judge a man's character by the outline of his features; and he doubted whether anyone with my nose could possess sufficient energy and determination for the voyage.' With a characteristic combination of confidence and modesty, Darwin concludes, 'But I think he was afterwards well-satisfied that my nose had spoken falsely!'[5]

Though Darwin did not achieve wide fame until late in 1859 with the publication of his book, the hot summer of 1858 was the time of crisis for him, as it was, for different reasons, for his close contemporaries Dickens and Disraeli. Other Victorians of lasting fame, and some whose notoriety did not outlast the stifling summer heat, found themselves intricately involved in political, social, or cultural events of national importance during the short four-month period from May to August 1858. Several far-reaching acts of parliament were debated and passed: on the governance of India, Jewish representation in parliament, the medical profession, marriage and divorce, and – most visibly and nauseatingly – the 'Great Stink' for which 1858 is best known. That record-breaking summer the pollution of the Thames by untreated sewage reached the point where a reluctant parliament and a recalcitrant set of local councils, vestries, and water companies finally had to agree with what *The Times* and other newspapers had been arguing for years, namely that 'something must be done'. An act of parliament was swiftly passed for the cleansing and embanking of the Thames, with Joseph Bazalgette put in charge of the efforts.

1858 was thus the year in which Bazalgette began his task of innovative engineering, described by the *Observer* in April 1861 as 'the most extensive and wonderful work of modern times'. The great Thames embankments were the result. The sewage was conducted in intercepting sewers to outfalls east of London at Barking on the north side of the river and Crossness in the south, road congestion on the Strand running parallel to the river was relieved, part of the first underground railway network in London and the world was conveyed through the tunnel in 1864, and London was provided with a grand river promenade such as already enhanced many other European capitals.[6]

Several important inventions and innovations came into being, or prominence, in the summer of 1858. Brunel's *Great Eastern* was a visitor attraction, despite the stink, at its mooring on the Thames at Deptford, prior to beginning its first long voyage. Even Queen Victoria braved the heat and stench to go on board at the end of June as the ship, double-skinned, with two sets of steam engines and capable of travelling to Australia without refuelling, awaited further financial support to complete its fitting-out.[7] As it transpired, the *Great Eastern* was too advanced to be a complete success; very few harbours in the world were big enough or deep enough to allow it to dock. It achieved usefulness only in 1866, when it served to complete successfully that other feat of technical ingenuity which first came to public attention in the summer of 1858, namely the laying of the Atlantic Cable, the two parts of which came together for long enough on 16 August to enable Queen Victoria and President James Buchanan to exchange brief messages before the signals became faint and disappeared. Efforts were postponed until more money and greater technical expertise were acquired; a new company was formed to lay a new cable, and the *Great Eastern*, in laying it in 1866, finally achieved deserved, if unexpected, success.[8]

Significant advances were made in 1858 in the science of photography, so much so that in the early autumn of the year the very first photograph of a comet was taken. Donati's Comet, first seen telescopically in Florence in June by Giovanni Battista Donati, was sighted in the south of England in September, and photographed on the 27th of the month by William Usherwood in Reigate, Surrey.[9] The trade pages of *Kelly's Post Office London Directory* first listed 'Photographic Artists' and 'Photographic Apparatus

Manufacturers' in its 1858 edition, and G.A. Sala, in his topical newspaper column 'Twice Round the Clock', noted in July 1858 that 'of late days, photographers have hung out their signs and set up their lenses in New Street' (in London's Covent Garden). According to Sala's colourful account, if you passed 'through the street' in the afternoon, 'you [ran] great risks of being forcibly dragged into the hole tenanted by a photographic "artist", and "focussed", willy-nilly'.[10]

Two plays put on in the spring of 1858 incorporated the newly popular art of photography. The Royal Lyceum Theatre presented John Hollingshead's 'domestic sketch', *The Birthplace of Podgers*, in March. Its cast included two 'photographic artists' who are intent on immortalising the house where the 'great literary man' Podgers was said to have been born. In April a comic sketch in one act by two young members of the Dramatic Authors' Society, N.H. Harrington and Edmund Yates, was presented at the nearby Strand Theatre. Entitled *Your Likeness – One Shilling!*, it took place entirely in a photographer's studio at the top of a house with a glass roof.[11] That photography had by now, since its introduction in 1839, advanced sufficiently for the lay person to choose it as a hobby is made clear by a sixpenny tract published in June 1858 by Edward Copland. Part of a series called *Manuals for the Many*, this illustrated work of thirty-two pages had the cumbersome but informative title:

> Photography for the Many: containing Practical Directions for the Production of Photographic Pictures on Glass and Paper, with details of the most approved Processes, including Negative and Positive Collodion; the Dry Collodion for Tourists; Stereoscopics with One Camera; and the Whole Art of Printing from Negatives on Glass or Paper; with Particulars of the Cost of the Apparatus and Chemicals for each Process. With Twenty Illustrations by Edward A. Copland, Author of 'The Aquarium and its Lessons'.

Copland recognised that some enthusiasts would wish to develop their photographs on the move; he explained how to do it by the dry negative collodion process. He also pointed out the usefulness of the new technique to 'architects, engineers, &c., whose time is precious'.[12]

That year's president of the British Association for the Advancement of Science, Richard Owen, when summing up in September 1858 the year's achievements in every branch of science, took the opportunity to praise recent advances in photographic technology, and to assess its importance in relation to other sciences and to ordinary lives. He saw that photography would make far-reaching and permanent changes to the way lives were lived and knowledge gained. 'Photography', he said, was 'now a constant and indispensable servant in certain important meteorological records.' It supplied the botanist and the zoologist with data for judging the rate of growth of plants and animals. Moreover, the 'engineer at home' could ascertain 'by photographs transmitted by successive mails the weekly progress, brick by brick, board by board, nail by nail, of the most complex works on the Indian or other remote rail-roads', and the 'humblest emigrant' could take with him images of 'scenes and persons' from the home he had left.[13]

Professor Owen, Britain's leading comparative anatomist and palaeontologist and the superintendent of the British Museum's natural history departments, closed his wide-ranging presidential address to the Leeds meeting of the British Association for the Advancement of Science in September 1858 with an account of the progress of two emergent branches of science, statistical and sanitary science. The two were linked by their importance to 'the prosperity of nations and the well-being of mankind'. Hitherto the official response to plague, fever, and – as recently as 1854 – a countrywide epidemic of cholera had been chiefly reactive. Isolation and quarantine were employed, whereas what were needed were proactive preventive measures in the interests of public health. The recently developed science of statistics, which promoted the study of the comparative rates of mortality in different districts, the investigation of conditions, and the search for causes of disease, showed the way forward. Owen praised the dedicated sanitary reformer Edwin Chadwick, whose *Report on the Sanitary Condition of the Labouring Population of Great Britain* of 1842 had connected contagious diseases with the inadequate sanitary conditions of cities, including London, which had doubled in size and population in the first half of the nineteenth century.[14]

By 1858 Chadwick's star was waning; he had antagonised politicians, engineers, and civil servants alike with his arrogance and obstinacy, and was forcibly retired in 1854 on a generous pension of £1,000 per annum.[15] Though he was removed from his official position, his sincerely held but mistaken views on how to solve the urgent problems of urban living were shared by most people. They did not foresee the catastrophic effects of his well-meaning efforts to alleviate filthy conditions in overcrowded areas of London and other cities. He advocated the extension of the use of water closets by individual households to replace the existing method of collecting effluent in cesspools which were regularly emptied by so-called 'nightsoil men', who sold the contents as fertiliser to farmers outside the metropolis.[16] Chadwick's intervention made things worse, as the sewers, originally built to carry rainwater into the Thames, now held raw sewage from water closets; the resulting mixture was then extracted by water companies to be drunk by their customers.[17] The Thames, swelled further by effluent from its many tributaries, flowed to and from the sea without getting rid of its toxic load. The problem, clear for all to see (and smell) in the summer of 1858, had to be solved.

The study of public health which Chadwick had pioneered was now in the hands of other reformers, medical men like John Snow and John Simon, and engineers like Bazalgette, rather than civil servants like Chadwick. Many of them, along with Owen and most public officials, shared Chadwick's mistaken 'miasma' theory, the view that the transmission of cholera and other contagious diseases was airborne, when the true source of infection was waterborne bacteria. In Britain only Dr John Snow worked it out; during the 1854 cholera epidemic he famously traced the exceptionally high incidence of death in a particular area of Soho to the Broad Street pump from which inhabitants drew their (untreated) drinking water. In his lifetime Snow was celebrated as an early advocate of anaesthesia – he used chloroform for the births of two of Queen Victoria's children – but his truly pioneering theory of waterborne disease was not accepted by his colleagues until long after his untimely death at the age of forty-five. By one of those quirks of history he died of a stroke on 16 June 1858, the hottest day hitherto recorded. Though some of Snow's colleagues began to accept his theory in the 1860s, it was not until some years after

Robert Koch had identified the bacterial cause of cholera in 1883 that Snow's work became generally recognised.[18]

Meanwhile Professor Owen in September 1858 spoke, like everyone else, of the 'atmospheric impurity' and 'noxious and morbific power' of the sewage-filled Thames which became critical 'summer after summer'. While he believed in the miasmic theory of disease, Owen nonetheless recognised the need for efficient drainage and, at the end of this summer to end all summers, he hoped that the 'skill of our engineers' would 'meet the call, and leave nothing but the rainfall of the metropolis to seek its natural receptacle – the Thames'.[19] Though not an expert in sanitary matters, and disinclined to make political points in this scientific forum, Owen permitted himself some criticism of the authorities. The fact that we pollute by our household waste products 'the noble river bisecting the metropolis and washing the very walls of our Houses of Parliament' was a 'flagrant sign of the desert and uncultivated state of a field where science and practice have still to cooperate for the public benefit'.[20] This was true, despite the fact that four years earlier John Snow had produced statistically drawn evidence from the Broad Street pump and elsewhere and had stated in clear terms the connection between contaminated water and disease. Snow could not have made his point more clearly than he did in a letter to *The Times* in June 1856 entitled 'Cholera and the Water Supply', in which he described his own inquiries during the 1854 cholera outbreak into the water supplies of two of London's water companies, the Southwark and Vauxhall Company and the Lambeth Company. The former supplied impure water, he wrote, the latter pure, and the ratio of deaths from cholera of recipients of water from the two companies was six to one. A brief report of his findings, he said, had been published in the *Medical Times* in September and October 1854. He finished his letter with the opinion that 'many other diseases, besides cholera, can be shown to be aggravated by water containing sewage'.[21]

Though Snow's arguments were ignored, the sewage problem insisted on being tackled in 1858, when the summer reached a sustained level of heat which surpassed the previous hottest recorded summers, those of 1846 and of the immediately previous year, 1857.[22] By the time Owen added his voice in September 1858 to those of newspapers from *The Times* to the specialist paper the *Builder* and a number of dogged parliamentarians who had been raising the question of the filthy Thames every summer for at least ten years, legislation was in place. Bazalgette, who himself had offered plans and detailed suggestions for improvements on several occasions in previous years, was at last given the go-ahead – and the required finance – to build his intercepting sewers.

In January 1856 Bazalgette had been appointed chief engineer to the newly formed Metropolitan Board of Works, and he had begun immediately to suggest a drainage system to take sewage out of London to the north and south of the Thames, but was met with obstruction. Though everyone could see that something had to be done, there was little agreement, even among engineers, let alone politicians and civil servants, about how to set about solving the drainage problem. Worse than that was the intransigence and resistance to spending money among the many vested interests which were inevitably involved: vestries, local paving boards, private water companies, Commissioners of Sewers, MPs anxious not to burden their constituents with the cost of improvements.[23] Even now, in summer 1858, when at last something *was* going to be done, debates went on in the unbearably hot chambers of Westminster about who should pay – just Londoners or all of Britain? – and which of several engineering plans under consideration should be adopted.

While newspaper editors fumed about politicians' time-wasting and hair-splitting and people who lived near the offensive Thames fled their homes, if they could – Dante Gabriel Rossetti left his rooms near Blackfriars Bridge to take refuge from 'the river stink' at the home of his friend William Morris in Red Lion Square[24] – the issue was forced on 30 June 1858. On that day, after a whole month of unusually high temperatures, parliament itself could stand the heat and stench no longer. For weeks debates and committee meetings had taken place in horrendous conditions, but everyone had persevered, no doubt because the two Houses of Parliament were trying to complete the legislative programme for the session, which was due to end by the beginning of August at the latest. On Wednesday, 30 June, with the noon temperature recorded in Hyde Park as 75 °F (24 °C), by no means the hottest of the month, but following on from four weeks of even hotter days, one roomful of conscientious committee members admitted defeat. As *The Times* recorded with undisguised glee on the following Saturday, the committee inquiring into the Bank Acts gave up:

> A sudden rush from the room took place, foremost among them being the Chancellor of the Exchequer [Disraeli], who, with a mass of papers in one hand and with his pocket handkerchief clutched in the other, and applied closely to his nose, with body half bent, hastened in dismay from the pestilential odour, followed closely by Sir James Graham, who seemed to be attacked by a sudden fit of expectoration; Mr Gladstone also paid particular attention to his nose . . . The other members of the committee also precipitately quitted the pestilential apartment, the disordered state of their papers, which they carried in their hands, showing how imperatively they had received notice to quit.[25]

All the newspapers noted in the following days and weeks that it had taken impossible conditions on their own doorstep to galvanise politicians into action. The result was indeed speedily arrived at. Disraeli as chancellor of the Exchequer and leader of the House of Commons – the prime minister, Lord Derby, being a member of the House of Lords – brought in a bill for cleansing the Thames on 15 July; it rattled through committee and was passed into law on 2 August, the last day of the session. Disraeli became the hero of the hour, though it was noted that his and his government's energies were called into action only when they were themselves inconvenienced beyond bearing. In an article ironically entitled 'The Silver Thames', Edwin Lankester, a medical reformer who had helped John Snow a few years earlier by examining his water samples under a microscope, wrote in the weekly journal the *Athenaeum* on 17 July, two days after Disraeli's bill was introduced:

> London suffers the worst evils of a double government. With a municipality on the one hand, having no power or influence over nine-tenths of the inhabitants, and an imperial legislature on the other hand, composed, for the most part, of persons who know little, and care less, about London, it is no wonder that this great city lacks that supervision

which its health demands. But the time has come when the state of the Thames threatens even the existence of the legislature on its banks; and we may have to thank the accident of the locality of the Houses of Parliament for the suppression of the foulest nuisance that ever disgraced the annals of a nation.

Lankester goes on to remark that the only remedy is to divert the sewage away from London, no matter what it costs.[26]

Disraeli announced that, after much debate, it had been decided that Londoners would bear the cost, estimated at £3 million, through the levy of a special tax over forty years at the rate of not more than three pence in the pound, the whole to be guaranteed by the government; the work was to take about five years. MPs immediately raised questions about the details; many were doubtful about the competence of the Metropolitan Board of Works, which was tasked with taking the project forward. In the end, however, after speedy readings in the two Houses of Parliament, Disraeli's bill was passed and work could begin.

A critical and still sceptical press followed every step taken. On Saturday, 24 July the satirical magazine *Punch*, which had already carried lurid caricatures of Old Father Thames as a skeleton, gloomily prophesied that the venture would more likely take ten years and cost £10 million.[27] *The Times*, after constant agitation for action, praised the government for at last making a move, though its editorial on 21 July reminded readers that the newspaper had been complaining for ten years about the state of the Thames, particularly in summer, and had been critical of the slow reaction of the authorities and the constant disagreements among engineers and other so-called experts. Thank goodness, wrote the editor of *The Times*, for the particularly hot fortnight in June which 'did for the administration of the metropolis what the Bengal mutinies did for the administration of India'.[28] The reference was to another bill making progress – in this case rather slow progress – through parliament, namely the India Bill which, following the Sepoy rebellion against the British army of 1857–8, was to remove the administration of India from the East India Company and bring it under the direct rule of the British government. The first India Bill had been brought in by the Whig prime minister Lord Palmerston in February 1858.

After the unexpected advent of Lord Derby's Tory government at the end of February, Disraeli took on the task of getting it through parliament.

The rise of Disraeli

Disraeli had tasted power only once, and that briefly, when he was appointed chancellor of the Exchequer by the Tory leader Edward Stanley, 14th earl of Derby, in the ten-month administration of 1852. His budget was poorly received, and contributed to his and Derby's swift fall from power. At the beginning of 1858 the popular elder statesman Lord Palmerston led a Liberal administration which had been in charge since 1855. Palmerston was an experienced politician, an easy-going aristocrat who had served in many administrations, most successfully as a patriotic foreign secretary. This was his first stint as premier; in 1858 he was a large, energetic man of seventy-two. He had his critics in the press. He was known for giving jobs to his relations, and also for his slack sexual mores. There was a carelessness about him which could charm but also irritate observers. One person who studied him closely was Karl Marx, living in political exile in north London. At the end of 1853 Marx wrote a series of articles on Palmerston, which were published in England in the *People's Paper*, the Chartist newspaper owned and edited by Ernest Jones, and in America by Horace Greeley's liberal paper the *New York Daily Tribune*.

Marx, who subjected the politics of Britain and Europe to forensic scrutiny in his regular articles for these newspapers, opened his series on Palmerston with a striking allusion to *Orlando Furioso*, Ariosto's sixteenth-century epic poem, in which the young man Ruggiero falls for the wiles of the sorceress Alcina. Palmerston, though in opposition at the time, had become a favourite of the people once more and looked likely to return to power:

> Ruggiero is again and again fascinated by the false charms of Alcina, which he knows to disguise an old witch . . . and the knight errant cannot withstand falling in love with her anew whom he knows to have transmuted all her former adorers into asses and other beasts. The English public is another Ruggiero, and Palmerston is another Alcina.[29]

Though he was not far off seventy years of age and had been on the 'public stage', as Marx said, since 1807, Palmerston was irrepressible:

> He succeeds in the comic as in the heroic . . . in the tragedy as in the farce: although the latter may be more congenial to his feelings. He is no first class orator. But he is an accomplished debater. Possessed of a wonderful memory, of great experience, of a consummate tact, of a never-failing *presence d'esprit*, of a gentlemanlike versatility, of the most minute knowledge of parliamentary tricks, intrigues, parties, and men, he handles difficult cases in an admirable manner and with a pleasant volubility . . . secured from any surprise by his cynic impudence, from any self-confession by his selfish dexterity, from running into a passion by his profound frivolity, his perfect indifference, and his aristocratic contempt. Being an exceedingly happy joker, he ingratiates himself with everybody.[30]

Dickens, too, though less forensic than Marx, noted critically in a speech of June 1855 that Palmerston, now prime minister for the first time at the age of seventy, had a habit of joking his way through opposition and objections. Dickens was speaking at Drury Lane Theatre in favour of the recently founded Administrative Reform Association, which agitated in the wake of the Crimean War for reform of the army, the navy, and the civil service. Palmerston had already replied flippantly in parliament to the association's accusation that he regularly 'sacrificed' merit to 'party and family influences' when making political appointments. He laughed at the 'Drury Lane private theatricals', by which he meant the meetings of the association. Dickens addressed the third of its meetings on 27 June 1855, rebuking Palmerston for 'officially and habitually' joking 'at a time when this country was plunged in deep disgrace and distress'. He also punished Palmerston for his slighting reference to the theatre. Dickens, famous for directing and acting in private theatricals, often before the queen, turned the insult against its author. He extended the theatrical metaphor to include an allusion to Palmerston's well-known acts of nepotism:

> I have some slight acquaintance with theatricals, private and public . . .
> I will not say that if I wanted to form a company of Her Majesty's

servants, I think I should know where to put my hand on 'the comic old gentleman'; nor, that if I wanted to get up a pantomime, I fancy I should know what establishment to go to for tricks and changes ... The public theatricals which the noble lord is so condescending as to manage, are so intolerably bad, the machinery is so cumbrous, the parts so ill distributed, the company so full of 'walking gentlemen', the managers have such large families, and are so bent upon putting those families into what is theatrically called 'first business' — not because of their aptitude for it, but because they *are* their families, that we find ourselves obliged to organize an opposition. We have seen the *Comedy of Errors* played so dismally like a tragedy that we cannot bear it. We are, therefore, making bold to get up the *School of Reform* [a play of 1805 by Thomas Morton], and we hope, before the play is out, to improve that noble lord by our performance very considerably.[31]

Late in 1857 Palmerston raised eyebrows by appointing to his cabinet the marquess of Clanricarde, who had been named in an Irish court case in 1855 involving a possible illegitimate son and underhand dealings over his inheritance.[32] *Punch*, always quick to sniff out scandal, printed a large cartoon on 23 January 1858 showing Palmerston in a carriage with Clanricarde on the back; the caption read 'Premier's New Cab-Boy – with *such* a character'.[33] A month later Palmerston was out of power, brought down partly by the Clanricarde business; he had 'grown giddy' in making appointments which were an abuse of power, said the *Illustrated London News* on 27 February.[34] When Prince Albert reviewed the parliamentary session in September 1858 he marvelled at the suddenness of Palmerston's fall. The man who was previously 'stamped the only *English* statesman, the champion of liberty, the man of the people, etc., etc.', was now 'frequently received with hooting' and was hated on all sides, including his own. Albert also noted Palmerston's calm manner: 'He remains, outwardly at least, quite cheerful, and seems to care very little about his reverses.'[35]

The main cause of Palmerston's downfall was the public perception that he failed in his patriotic duty as an English statesman in his response to French outrage about the attempted assassination in Paris of the emperor, Napoleon III, on 14 January 1858. The perpetrators were Italian nationalists, led by Felice Orsini, who had used grenades made in England and had been helped by French and English sympathisers with the cause of Italian independence from foreign rule. Pressure was put on Palmerston's government by the French, and a Conspiracy to Murder Bill was brought before parliament early in February. The bill was unpopular with the press and public; as Marx observed in an article in the *New York Daily Tribune* on 22 February, Palmerston's bill 'will only contribute to exasperate the already wounded pride of John Bull'.[36] It was not supported by many of Palmerston's colleagues either, including his bitter rival for leadership of the Liberals, Lord John Russell, who objected to a bill coming forward apparently in response to the demands of a foreign despot. (Louis Napoleon, nephew of the great Napoleon, had been elected president of the Republic in 1848, but when blocked by the constitution from running for a second term, had declared himself emperor in December 1852 and set about imposing censorship and repressive measures.)

Palmerston's home secretary, Sir George Grey, wrote to Russell on 2 February to persuade him to support the bill. He understood that 'we cannot of course listen to any proposal to expel refugees or foreigners on mere suspicion', but 'the law with respect to the crime of conspiracy to murder is in an uncertain and unsatisfactory state'. As an offence under common law, it was currently punishable only by a fine or imprisonment, whereas in Ireland the same offence was 'a capital felony'. The government thought a general act should be passed 'making conspiracy to murder, whether in this country or abroad, a felony punishable by penal servitude'.[37] This may have been a sensible idea, but as another of Palmerston's colleagues, Sir James Graham, pointed out, in terms similar to Marx's, it would not wash with the great British public. 'John Bull is a strange animal. If you goad him, his courage rises.' Besides, 'all Europe would laugh at our degradation' in dancing to a tune set by the self-styled emperor of the French.[38] The vote was lost, and on 19 February Palmerston's administration resigned, whereupon a surprised and reluctant Lord Derby took over with a minority Conservative government. His only hope of this spell in government lasting longer than the previous one in 1852 was that the opposition was divided and Palmerston, round whom many different factions had previously gathered, was no longer supported by many on his own side. As *Bentley's Miscellany* pointed out in April 1858, Palmerston was 'hoist with his own petard'; he relied on mass popularity because of his rugged English patriotism, and was undone when he brought in his bill apparently at the behest of a foreign nation.[39]

Derby appointed Disraeli once more as his chancellor of the Exchequer, though he probably still had some doubts about his colleague's suitability for office. Disraeli presented a risk, with his unorthodox background and demeanour, his Jewishness – though he had been baptised as a youth – his lack of a university education, his authorship of racy novels in his twenties, his frequenting of 'fast' circles composed of scandalous aristocrats, from whom he borrowed large amounts of money and on whose patronage he depended, and his sexual ambiguity. Derby's son Lord Stanley certainly distrusted Disraeli, noting in his journal at the time of his father's accession to power that, 'able as he is, this man will never command public confidence'.[40] No one ever knew quite how seriously to take Disraeli.[41] He was clever, cynical, mocking, and at the same time romantic and exotic in language and behaviour. In his diary in 1833, when he was having an affair with the politically influential Lady Henrietta Sykes, he wrote, apparently seriously: 'My life has been a struggle, with moments of rapture – a storm and dashes of Moonlight, Love, and Poetry.'[42] As Derby was trying to put together a cabinet in 1858, Disraeli wrote to him on 22 February, expressing in fulsome terms his sorrow that Stanley was resisting an appointment (though he presumably did not know that this was partly because of Stanley's disapproval of *him*): 'It draws tears from my eyes, & from yr heart, I am sure, drops of blood.'[43] The stolid Derby is unlikely to have recognised this florid diagnosis of his fatherly feelings.

Despite the difference in their backgrounds and personalities, Derby and Disraeli made a good team. They were fortunate that the support for Palmerston had collapsed, so that many Liberals were prepared to work with them on their legislative programme, which in any case began as a continuation of that of their predecessors. Derby was inclined to favour political reform, as was Disraeli, and they took parliament with them.[44] In particular, they continued with Palmerston's plan to put through an India Bill transferring the government of India from the East India Company to the British government. All sides agreed, particularly in the aftermath of the Sepoy rebellion (known at the time as the Indian Mutiny), that it was unsustainable for the East India Company, a commercial institution, to continue to run India as if it were an arm of government. As Joseph Irving, author of an account of the public events of the year 1858, pointed out, the East India Company by this time 'carried on political functions without ministerial responsibility'. There was 'no responsibility to Parliament, to public opinion, or to the Crown', he wrote, and the 'persons enjoying these functions . . . were elected by bodies and gentlemen who knew nothing about India, and yet the Company had the power of removing the Governor-General at any moment'.[45]

Though there was general agreement about this change of governance, the debates on India were hard fought in relation to administrative detail and took up several months of the parliamentary session. Arguments over competitive entry for civil servants dealing with India under the proposed constitution, and, from the bishops in the House of Lords, a strong desire to impose Christianity on India, held up the passing of the bill until the end of July 1858, but as Disraeli told the queen in one of his almost daily reports to her, the heat and stench hampering parliament were in his favour with regard to getting it through. On 24 June he wrote in the familiar style in which he had begun, with her encouragement, on his ministerial appointment at the end of February, to send her his 'rough notes, written on the field of battle':

The Cr of the Exr with his humble duty to Yr Majesty: The India Bill was read a second time without a division. Lord Stanley [who was soon to be appointed the first secretary of state for India] made a clear & vigorous exposition of its spirit & provisions . . . No serious opposition apprehended in Committee . . . He [Disraeli] proposes to proceed with no other business, until it is concluded. When the Bill has passed, the temper of the House, & its sanitary state, will assist him in passing the remaining estimates with rapidity, & he contemplates an early conclusion of the Session.[46]

Knowing how to flatter Victoria, who had come to like him after having first distrusted him, Disraeli dangled before her an influential future as empress of India: 'It is, the Cr of the Er really thinks, a wise & well digested measure, ripe with the experience of the last five months of discussion: but it is only the ante-chamber of an imperial Palace; & Yr Majesty would do well to deign to consider the steps, [which] are now necessary to influence the opinions, & affect the imagination, of the Indian populations.' He wound up his letter with the reassurance that 'notwithstanding the Thames, I continue very well'.[47] The new dispensation for India was to prove momentous for Victoria, for Disraeli's reputation, and for India itself.

In its summary of the parliamentary session on 1 August 1858, the *Era* singled out the Derby government's achievements in getting through parliament the Thames Purification Bill, for which the nation would be eternally grateful; the India Bill, 'the work of the session, in labour and anxiety'; and a third bill, the Oath of Abjuration Bill, better known, as the session wore on, as the 'Jew Bill', since the main point of contention was the passage to allow Jews to sit in parliament without swearing 'on the true faith of a Christian'.[48] Bills had been brought forward by both Liberals and Conservatives year after year, ostensibly to remove absurd outdated clauses in the parliamentary oath such as that abjuring allegiance to the descendants of James II (whose line had long since become extinct), but in fact in order to remove the 'true faith of a Christian' clause. Time and again the motion was passed by the House of Commons but defeated by the bishops and others in the House of Lords, out of plain religious bigotry in many cases, and a worry about Jews being allowed to legislate on matters relating to the established church. The prominent Whig Lord John Russell, prime minister from 1846 to 1851, brought in the first of his bills in 1849 in order to permit Lionel de Rothschild to sit in the House of Commons. Baron de Rothschild (his title was an Austrian one) had been elected a member for the City of London in June 1847 but could not take his seat. Like its many successors, this first bill was passed by the Commons but failed in the Lords. In 1858 Disraeli discussed a possible compromise with Russell. The outcome, after much toing and froing, was that the Commons once again passed the bill with a large majority and the Lords, on 1 July, permitted the Commons to pass a resolution admitting Jews to their own house, while remaining stalwart against having Jews in the Lords.[49] The awkward compromise allowed Rothschild to take his seat in the Commons on 26 July by swearing on the Old Testament alone.

Medicine and marriage

When the parliamentary session closed on 2 August, it was the job of the lord chancellor Lord Chelmsford – one of the most vehement opponents of the measure to allow Jewish representation in parliament – to read out the Queen's Speech in the House of Lords to members of both houses. He announced that the queen was especially pleased by the India Act, which promised 'a just and impartial administration of the law' and the sympathetic promotion of the welfare of the Indian people; she also welcomed the act to purify 'that noble river', the Thames, 'the present state of which is little creditable to a great country, and seriously prejudicial to the health and comfort of the inhabitants of the metropolis'.[50] The list of other bills passed into law included several relating to local land and railway business, the Atlantic Telegraph Company Bill, and two important pieces of national legislation, the Medical Practitioners Bill and an amendment to the recently implemented Divorce and Matrimonial Causes Act. Both had far-reaching consequences for British life.

Medical reform was much needed. Medical education, and the qualifications bestowed on medical students, varied, as did the subsequent right to practise. Graduates of the medical schools of Scottish universities could not practise in England. The qualifications offered by the universities and the long-established London medical schools were different from those granted by the Royal College of Physicians and the Royal College of Surgeons, both of which had their origins in the reign of Henry VIII. By the Apothecaries' Act of 1815, apothecaries were permitted to practise medicine in England; from this act came the new term 'general practitioner', a growing body looked down on by members of the two royal colleges. In addition, there was nothing to stop anyone, whether medically trained or not, from setting up a practice in homeopathy, hydropathy, or mesmerism, all of which alternative medical practices were well established by the 1850s. Jealousies raged between the different interests. As physicians had been historically the only ones required to have a university degree, they were considered to be at the top of the hierarchy, with the surgeons next, and general practitioners at the bottom of the ranks of legitimate doctors. However, the development of medical schools attached to hospitals, and the introduction of anaesthetics in surgery in the late 1840s, changed the dynamics between the different branches.[51] Scrutiny came, too, from the *Lancet*, the medical journal founded in 1823 by Thomas Wakley, a qualified surgeon and from 1835 a Radical MP. Wakley made it his mission to expose inequalities and bad practice and to lobby for reform of the two royal colleges in particular and of medical education in general.[52] Meanwhile the growing body of general practitioners became increasingly rebellious in the face of obstruction and snobbery from the royal colleges.

Wakley and others set about moving for legislative reform. Between 1840 and 1858 no fewer than seventeen different medical bills were introduced in the House of Commons; early in 1858 three separate bills were being considered simultaneously.[53] The bills failed because of the power in political circles of members of the royal colleges, and also because of a lack of unity among the reformers and differing ideas of what the reforms should be. Some prioritised the removal of outdated privileges from the royal colleges, others stressed the need for a single standard of medical education and qualification for all doctors, of whatever specialism, and still others wanted first and foremost to bolster the status of qualified doctors by imposing sanctions on alternative practitioners and other 'quacks'. As *Punch* noticed in an article entitled 'The Doctors and their Bills', printed in June 1858 while the final bill was going through parliament, disagreement among doctors was endangering yet another effort at medical reform. If, because of this quarrelling, the 'entire measure' could not be passed, could we not, asked *Punch*, tongue in cheek, have it homeopathically, 'contenting ourselves with a small draft' until the whole could be swallowed.[54]

In the end, a compromise act was passed. The chief medical officer of health, the reforming John Simon, was responsible for drawing up the bill. It was brought to the Commons by William Cowper, Palmerston's stepson (and probably biological son, since Lady Cowper had been Palmerston's lover for years before she married him), who was president of the Board of Health until the fall of Palmerston's administration in February 1858. As drafted, it restricted the powers and exclusivity of the royal colleges and made provision for all doctors to take the same qualifying examinations; it also set up for the first time a Medical Register, which would be published annually and exclude unqualified practitioners, and established the General Medical Council to oversee all administration of medical matters. In Simon's draft version the council would be made up of members of the royal colleges, of the universities, and of general practitioners. While the bill was going through its readings in May–June 1858, however, the home secretary Spencer Walpole was lobbied hard by the colleges, so that the final bill retained some of their privileges. General practitioners were therefore excluded from membership of the Medical Council. (It was not until the passing of the Medical Act of 1886 that they were granted representation.) The reformers were disappointed, but, as if taking Mr Punch's advice, they accepted the bill as an important step towards full equality within the profession. The main advances made by the act when it came into effect on 1 October 1858 were the creation of the register to keep quacks out, the forming of the Medical Council to oversee matters, and the unification of medical examinations for students of all branches of medicine.[55] Though imperfect, the act was an important milestone in regularising a profession which had become, as Palmerston had said in parliament in 1853, 'a labyrinth and a chaos', adding frankly that, as home secretary at that time, he had 'no hopes of being able to bring forward a measure'.[56]

If it took many years of trying before an acceptable Medical Act was passed, the journey to completion of the Divorce and Matrimonial Causes Act was somewhat shorter, but no less troublesome. Bills to make divorce more accessible were introduced and failed in 1854 and 1856, in the latter case due to lack of debating time, though the fierce opposition on the part of many politicians and churchmen to making divorce available to anyone other than the very rich was the real obstacle to progress. Dickens wrote scathingly in *Household Words* in October 1856 about the failure to push through an act:

> The Law of Divorce is in such condition that from the tie of marriage there is no escape to be had, no absolution to be got, except under certain proved circumstances not necessary to enter upon here, and

then only on payment of an enormous sum of money. Ferocity, drunk-
enness, flight, felony, madness, none of these will break the chain,
without the enormous sum of money. The husband, who, after years of
outrage, has abandoned his wife, may at any time claim her for his
property and seize the earnings on which she subsists. The most profligate of women, an intolerable torment, torture, and shame to her
husband, may nevertheless, unless he be a very rich man, insist on
remaining handcuffed to him, and dragging him away from any
happier alliance, from youth to old age and death . . .

It is proposed [in the recent bill introduced in parliament] a little to
relax the severity of a thraldom prolonged beyond the bounds of
morality, justice, and sense, and to modify the law. Instantly the singing
of paeans begins . . . Authorities, lay and clerical, rise in their parliamentary places to deliver panegyrics on Marriage as an Institution
(which nobody disputes to be just); they have much to relate concerning
what the Fathers thought of it, and what was written, said, and done
about it hundreds of years before these evils were; they set up their
fancy whipping-tops, and whip away; they utter homilies without end
upon the good side of the question, which is in no want of them, but
. . . the tortures and wrongs of the sufferer have no place in their
speeches.[57]

When the 1856 bill came again before parliament in the session of
1857, it was touch and go whether there would not be a further delay in
passing the measure, but thanks to the then prime minister Lord
Palmerston's boldness and determination – cheek, even – the new Divorce
and Matrimonial Causes Act was passed in August 1857, to take effect on
1 January 1858.

As Dickens noted, until the passing of the act, divorce was for most
people well-nigh impossible to obtain. It required three cumbersome,
lengthy, and expensive stages to be gone through. Changing this would
make a huge difference to large numbers of people, as the anonymous
author of *A Handy Book on the New Law of Divorce and Matrimonial
Causes, and the Practice of the Divorce Court* declared in his enthusiastic
little book welcoming the new legislation in 1860. 'A more important

Statute' than this 'never was passed by the Legislature; or one better calculated "to elevate the character, and promote, and secure, the morality and
happiness of a people"'. At a stroke it did away with a legal absurdity that
had existed for nearly two centuries, during which time it had been necessary 'first, to obtain in an Ecclesiastical Court a divorce *a mensa et thoro*',
that is, for the couple to live separately but still be man and wife, with no
permission for the petitioner to remarry. Secondly, the petitioner was
required to take action before a jury in a court of law for damages for adultery, or 'criminal conversation', as it was called. Thirdly, to obtain a full
divorce, an act of parliament had to be passed granting divorce *a vinculo*,
that is, declaring the marriage void from the beginning and allowing the
petitioner to remarry.[58]

A man had to prove adultery on the part of his wife in order to receive
a full divorce. For a wife seeking a divorce, the required level of proof was
much higher. Adultery must be aggravated by some other offence. In all
cases, hardly anyone could afford to go through these procedures. According
to figures declared in the House of Lords debate on the matter in May
1857, the average number of full divorces granted in the years 1800 to
1850 was two per annum.[59] The total number of *women* granted a divorce
over the past 150 years was said in the 1856 debate to be four.[60] It was
pointed out that English laws were particularly strict; Scottish, Prussian,
and other European laws were more liberal. In 1839 a newspaper dedicated
to discussing the salacious details of divorce cases, the *Crim. Con. Gazette*,
summed up the disadvantaged position of an Englishman (an Englishwoman
having virtually no opportunity at all of getting a divorce):

> A man with a very large sum of money may get a divorce from the
> Houses of Parliament and may marry again. A man with a smaller but
> considerable sum of money may get from the Ecclesiastical Courts a
> half divorce which relieves him merely from his wife's debts but does
> not enable him to enter into another matrimonial connection. A man
> with no money, or an insufficient income, can have no divorce at all.[61]

In Scotland women had equal rights with men in the matter of divorce,
and in Prussia it was realised that adultery need not be the only cause – there

a divorce could be obtained by mutual consent or on the ground of incompatibility of temper.[62]

The most absurd element of the status quo before the passing of the new act was the recourse to the Ecclesiastical Court in Doctors' Commons, a college of lawyers founded in the thirteenth century and occupying a hidden corner near St Paul's Cathedral, as the young Charles Dickens described it in one of his 'Sketches by Boz' in the *Morning Chronicle* in 1836. Ecclesiastical matters were heard here in the Court of Arches; here too Admiralty questions were settled, and wills were proved and probate granted in the Prerogative Office. The 'doctors' were lawyers holding degrees in civil law (based on Roman law) from Oxford or Cambridge, who acted as both judges and advocates in these courts. Dickens, who had himself recently been required to visit Doctors' Commons to obtain a special licence in order to marry Catherine Hogarth, since she was under twenty-one at the time of their union in 1836,[63] described the dozen or so self-important 'solemn-looking gentlemen' in crimson gowns and wigs to be found in the 'old quaint-looking apartment'. Officers of the court wore 'black gown, black kid gloves, knee shorts, and silks', while 'the counsel wore red gowns, and the proctors fur collars', and the business conducted was so outmoded that 'half-obsolete' statutes hundreds of years old were invoked.[64]

Dickens had another tilt at these archaic and complicated arrangements, and the snobbery of the participants, in *David Copperfield* (1850). He puts his criticisms into the sneering mouth of David's older school friend, Steerforth, who answers David's question, 'What *is* a proctor?' thus:

'Why, he is a sort of monkish attorney', replied Steerforth. 'He is, to some faded courts held in Doctors' Commons – a lazy old nook near St Paul's churchyard – what solicitors are to the courts of law and equity. He is a functionary whose existence, in the natural course of things, would have terminated about two hundred years ago. I can tell you best what he is, by telling you what Doctors' Commons is. It's a little out-of-the-way place, where they administer what is called ecclesiastical law, and play all kinds of tricks with obsolete old monsters of acts of Parliament, which three-fourths of the world know nothing about, and the other fourth supposes to have been dug up, in a fossil state, in the days of the Edwards. It's a place that has an ancient monopoly in suits about people's wills and people's marriages, and disputes among ships and boats.'

'Nonsense, Steerforth!' I exclaimed. 'You don't mean to say that there is any affinity between nautical matters and ecclesiastical matters?'

'I don't, indeed, my dear boy', he returned; 'but I mean to say that they are managed and decided by the same set of people, down in that same Doctors' Commons . . . The proctors employ the advocates. Both get very comfortable fees, and altogether they make a mighty snug little party.'[65]

In spite of the obvious need for reform to such procedures, the debates in parliament were complex, robust, and lengthy. Some feared an avalanche of divorce petitions and a loosening of the religious dimension of marriage; questions of women's rights, property, and inheritance loomed large, since on marriage a woman became – along with her money, belongings, assets, and in due course her children – the property of her husband. The disadvantage of marriage to her was that she had no individual rights apart from her husband; the disadvantage to the husband was that he became liable for any debts she might incur. If a couple separated, the father was usually given custody of the children. A large part in the preparatory efforts at improving the chances of both men and women getting a just divorce and making provision for women who were abandoned, treated violently, or deprived of their children by a cruel husband was played by the celebrated, or infamous, Caroline Norton. The witty, beautiful and flirtatious grand-daughter of the playwright Richard Brinsley Sheridan (and thus from a prominent – though impecunious – Whig family), she had married George Norton, a Tory MP who was mean with money and physically violent towards her. In 1836 he brought a case against her of criminal conversa-tion with the former Whig prime minister, Lord Melbourne. Though the case failed and no divorce ensued, mud stuck to Caroline, both because of her behaviour and because of Melbourne's reputation as a womaniser. Her husband removed her three sons from her care, and she embarked on a campaign to improve women's rights in marriage.

Caroline wrote autobiographical novels on the subject, printed pamphlets, and persuaded sympathetic politicians to take up her case in parliament. In June 1855 she published *A Letter to the Queen on Lord Chancellor Cranworth's Marriage and Divorce Bill*, in which she wrote passionately, boldly, at length, and in knowledgeable detail about the then lord chancellor's bill of 1854, which had been withdrawn in the face of firm opposition in the House of Lords. Playing repeatedly on the paradox that the reigning monarch was a woman and a wife, she argued both from her own case and on behalf of all women that the right to property for divorced and separated women should be established. The queen was reminded frankly and dramatically at every turn that though she was the most powerful woman in the land, she too was a married woman with no individual rights at all. Finally Caroline laid down a challenge to her husband with respect to her literary earnings: 'My husband has a legal lien [right] . . . on the copyright of my works. Let him claim copyright of THIS.'[66]

The Divorce and Matrimonial Causes Bill was eventually passed late in August 1857, thanks to Palmerston's determination. All summer the same old arguments were rehearsed at length, with many members of both houses, led in the Lords by Samuel Wilberforce, the bishop of Oxford, arguing for the indissolubility of marriage in the eyes of God. Others feared an embarrassing rush to achieve separations, especially among the poorer classes, who had been obliged to remain married up to now (though of course there was nothing to stop them leaving their spouses and co-habiting with a preferred partner in defiance of the law). Amendments were passed between the two houses, with votes won and lost by narrow margins. By 4 August 1857 members were pleading fatigue and begging Lord Palmerston to bring the session to a close and postpone further discussion to the autumn. The prime minister (aged seventy-two) and his chief ally in supporting the bill, Lord Lyndhurst (aged eighty-five), would have none of it. Palmerston said he was of a sanguine disposition, 'not at all accustomed to flounder in the Slough of Despond'; he was 'ready to sit there as long as necessary'. On 21 August 1857 Palmerston declared that he was prepared to sit till September. Three days later the amended bill was passed by forty-six votes to forty-four (the Tory opposition having largely melted away to their country homes after wilting in the London heat).[67]

The act which thus scraped through a fractious parliament in oppressive heat offered justice to people of little or no means, and gave some protection to women, though they still had to prove not only adultery against their husbands but also cruelty, or incest, or rape, or sodomy, or bestiality, or abandonment without cause for two years or more, while a man had only to prove his wife's adultery. In parliament a social comedy was played out, since many of those deciding on the morality of divorce were, as the wife of one of them, Rosina Bulwer Lytton, never tired of pointing out in public, well-known rakes and adulterers themselves (not least Palmerston and Lyndhurst).[68] The answer to the question, raised so often during the debates, of whether the new act would cause the moral downfall of a nation or bring much-needed relief to the minority of aggrieved spouses who would seek to use it, was not given until the even hotter summer of 1858, when the first batch of divorce cases came to their conclusions.

The Divorce Act of 1857 swept away the Ecclesiastical and Probate courts, creating the new Divorce Court, which met for the first time on 16 January 1858. The place chosen for the new court was Westminster Hall, to the relief of the *Morning Chronicle*, which expressed its pleasure that Doctors' Commons had not been chosen, given its history and its location 'within the antiquated and most inconvenient precincts of the Ecclesiastical Court'.[69] On 9 January *Punch* carried a poem, 'Chant of the Expiring Ecclesiastical Court', in which the ancient court mourned its own passing while taking comfort in the financial compensation allowed to its functionaries. Later in the year, at the start of the legal Michaelmas Term in November, the magazine carried an illustration of two shadowy figures – the proctors about whom David Copperfield had innocently asked – haunting the old Doctors' Commons building.[70] The correspondence of the progressive bishop of London, Archibald Tait, who alone among the bishops in the House of Lords had voted for all the clauses in the Divorce Act (he had argued boldly that a 'whole string of the [Church] Fathers' could be quoted on either side of the religious question about whether marriage was indissoluble[71]), contains letters of protest from Dr John Lee of the College of Doctors' Commons, complaining of the removal of responsibilities from his colleagues and saying that the teachers of Roman law at Oxford and Cambridge were unhappy about the changes too.[72]

As with all major changes, there were winners and losers once the new Divorce Act became a fact of life. Dickens had a moment's frantic fear in early June that his wife's family might persuade her to sue for divorce on grounds of his adultery. And Darwin found himself following with particular interest one of the first divorce cases, and the one which made the greatest splash in the newspapers as it followed its tortuous course in the very hottest days of June. This was the case against Dr Edward Lane, a qualified doctor who ran a successful hydropathic retreat in Surrey, to which Darwin escaped several times, including in the spring of 1858, in an ultimately unsuccessful effort to cure his mysterious symptoms of vomiting and diarrhoea. The case brought against Lane by the husband of one of his patients, Isabella Robinson, puzzled the judges, who deferred judgment until they had taken further advice and instigated an amendment to the act itself in order to solve the case of *Robinson v. Robinson and Lane*.[73] Allegations of insanity against Mrs Robinson (who as a defendant could not be questioned in court) linked marriage and divorce closely to matters of mental health. The question of a wife's sanity was publicly posed in the same weeks through the unwise commitment of Rosina Bulwer Lytton to a lunatic asylum by her equally unstable husband, Sir Edward Bulwer Lytton, parliamentary ally and colleague of Disraeli and friend and fellow novelist of Dickens. Rosina loudly attacked both of these friends of her husband, with Disraeli in particular being threatened with the exposure of his past sexual exploits at the very moment when he was enjoying political power and prominence for the first time.

Literature and art

Almost for the first year since his debut as a writer in 1833 Dickens produced no novel or story in 1858. He was not even working on the manuscript of a piece of fiction, though he told his friend John Forster in January 1858 that if he could

discipline my thoughts into the channel of a story, I have made up my mind to get to work on one: always supposing that I find myself, on the trial, able to do well. Nothing whatever will do me the least 'good' in the way of shaking the one strong passion of change impending over us that every day makes stronger; but if I could work on with some approach to steadiness, through the summer, the anxious toil of a new book would have its neck well broken before beginning to publish, next October or November.[74]

The novel in question was, or would be, *A Tale of Two Cities*, but Dickens could not discipline his wild thoughts or work through the coming hot summer with any steadiness at all, and the novel was not begun until February 1859.

All Dickens's manic energy went into two causes in summer 1858: attempting to resolve his marital problems and embarking on a new career of giving readings from his works for money. While losing his head over the first of these, he also unaccountably antagonised his main rival among fiction writers, Thackeray, by involving himself in a dispute at the Garrick Club, of which both novelists were members. Thackeray, too, seems to have been affected by the heat; he made the foolish mistake of taking umbrage at a snide article by the young penny-a-liner Edmund Yates (co-author of *Your Likeness – One Shilling!*), which accused him of cynicism and hypocrisy. Thackeray stood on his dignity as a 'gentleman' and demanded punishment for Yates, who was publicly defended by Dickens, always aware that Thackeray and his friends looked down on him as vulgar, notwithstanding his literary genius. The so-called 'Garrick Club affair' burst into life in the hottest June days of 1858; its participants fanned the flames for months, and a resolution of sorts was eventually arrived at, though not until the following spring. As it happens, Thackeray, like Dickens, was particularly thin-skinned during the summer of 1858. The novel he was publishing in monthly parts, *The Virginians*, was not meeting with critical success, especially in America, where his portrayal of George Washington was considered too negative, and he confessed to his friends that he was finding it difficult to keep up the momentum. Sometimes he was scarcely able to complete a part in time for publication on the first of each month.[75]

In fact, 1858 was not a good year for novels. Trollope's offering, *Doctor Thorne*, published at the end of May, was coolly received. The critic in the

Athenaeum hit the mark when he praised the 'shrewd good nature' of Trollope the narrator, but declared, reasonably, that the reader was not likely to care much for the eponymous doctor, and that the book was too long by at least a third. The *Spectator* reviewer thought the satire of jealousies among the medical profession was aimed at 'a rather worn matter' which had been dealt with many times before in fiction, and in the *Saturday Review* the story was described as careless and languid.[76] The real literary 'find' of 1858 was George Eliot, whose first attempt at fiction was published by John Blackwood in January 1858 to high praise from Dickens, among others. This was *Scenes of Clerical Life*, three novellas about Midlands life in the early years of the century. Though *Scenes* was well received, it was but a taster for the debut novel that would take the world by storm the following year, *Adam Bede*. As was the case with Darwin, the summer of 1858 was full of significance for George Eliot; she spent it writing the work which would make her name and announce her as a new and worthy rival to Dickens and Thackeray.

What was truly new about the work of George Eliot – really Marian Evans, living with G.H. Lewes as his wife, and therefore unwilling to use her own name on the title-page – was its utterly convincing combination of a realistic portrayal of the day-to-day lives of ordinary people with imagination, wit, romance, and literary pattern and structure.[77] It was not as yet clear that the 'Dutch realism' in art which the narrator of *Adam Bede* praises when defending the novel's less than ideal protagonists would set a standard aimed at by novelists who followed her, not least Henry James. Yet Blackwood boasted to Thackeray that with *Scenes of Clerical Life* he had found a new 'first-class' author, and Dickens not only wrote warmly to the unknown George Eliot on receiving his copy of the work, but told his friend John Forster to read the stories as they first came out serially in *Blackwood's Magazine* during 1857: 'Do read them. They are the best things I have seen since I began my course.'[78]

What we might call the drama and symbolism of everyday life was also evident in certain art works on show at the Royal Academy exhibition of 1858, which opened at the beginning of May. As a commentary on unhappy marriages, Augustus Egg's untitled triptych, known informally as *Past and Present*, attracted attention. The story it tells in its three pictures is the tragedy of a family. The first scene shows a middle-class husband's discovery of his wife's adultery; he is reading a letter revealing her secret while she lies inconsolable on the floor and the couple's two daughters play cards across the room. The scene is reminiscent of those portrayed in seventeenth-century Dutch paintings of domestic life. Though the representation is realistic – a solid family room with heavily draped tables and curtains – the symbols are many. The wife's bracelets have snake motifs; one painting on the wall represents the expulsion of Adam and Eve from Eden, while another, showing a storm-tossed boat at sea, is entitled *The Abandoned*; and the children's house of cards, propped on a book by Balzac, doyen of French fiction with its sexual liaisons and fallen women, is collapsing. The other two scenes represent the fallout from the discovery. One shows the daughters, after their father's death, living in genteel poverty in a garret, while the other features the destitute mother taking refuge under one of the Adelphi arches by the Thames, a well-known haunt of prostitutes, criminals, and suicides. Though Egg gave the piece no title, it was exhibited with an explanatory description: 'August the 4th – Have just heard that B— has been dead more than a fortnight, so his poor children have now lost both parents. I hear she was seen on Friday last near the Strand, evidently without a place to lay her head. What a fall hers has been!'[79]

Egg's painting attracted a lot of critical attention, some of it suggesting that the subject was too painful for art. Another contemporary interior of the Dutch type also caught the eye, though this time it was a representation of a real couple in their own home. Robert Tait's *A Chelsea Interior* is a small but remarkably detailed portrait of Thomas Carlyle and his wife Jane in their modest house in Chelsea. Both Carlyles commented on the progress of the painting over the year prior to its exhibition, Carlyle complaining of Tait 'steaming about all day' in the 'intolerable' heat of July 1857 with his 'photographing (very malodorous) apparatus', and remarking six months later that the artist had borrowed his dressing gown and shoes to paint in his studio. For her part, Jane marvelled that Tait took a whole day to paint her workbox and seemed determined to represent everything in her drawing room with 'Vandyke fidelity'.[80] As the Carlyles were the most famous literary couple in London, the painting did not need to name them in its title. An irony only fully revealed to the public after both their deaths was that their marriage was not a happy one; indeed Jane's letters and private journal reveal that she had recently suffered a sort of break-down brought about by chronic ill health, resentment at Carlyle's spending all his time in his study writing his multi-volume history of Frederick the Great of Prussia, and most of all by her obsessive jealousy of Carlyle's chivalrous attentions to Lady Ashburton, who indulged Carlyle while neglecting Jane's feelings.[81]

The most celebrated painting in the exhibition in 1858 was another work presenting a portrait of the times in minute, almost photographic, detail. William Powell Frith's huge panorama *The Derby Day*, which, like Egg's triptych, is now in the Tate collection (*A Chelsea Interior* hangs appropriately in the Carlyles' drawing room in their house in Cheyne Row, now a museum), caused such a sensation that a barrier had to be put round it and a policeman set to guard it from the press of visitors. Taking a favourite subject of the British people, particularly the inhabitants of London, who flocked in their thousands to Epsom races for the Derby each summer, Frith captured the 'bustle and life' of the great event, as the *Annual Register* noted in its round-up of 1858. *Bentley's Miscellany* consoled those who were not actually going to the Derby that year – the race was held on Wednesday, 19 May – by assuring them that they 'may remain at home content if they pay their shilling to see this wonderful picture – and succeed in getting near enough to see it'.[82] Frith made a large amount of money from engravings and subsequent showings of this famous painting, the first since David Wilkie's *Chelsea Pensioners* of 1822 to require a railing for protection.[83]

All human life was in *The Derby Day*, just as it was at the event itself. The toffs attended annually in their carriages, parliament regularly took the day off, the middle classes borrowed or rented coaches and cabs, or in recent years came by train, and the lower classes walked, camping overnight beside the racecourse. Gypsies, sellers of everything from cool drinks to flowers, acrobats, clowns, and conmen converged on Epsom Downs in Surrey every year for the big race. Frith's painting shows a man whose watch has just been stolen by someone behind him and a group being conned by a thimble-rigger, a common trickster at fairgrounds and outdoor fêtes. The painting, like the verbal descriptions of the occasion in newspapers, adopts an inclusive, if not indulgent, attitude towards the criminal element present at the great occasion.[84] G.A. Sala, ever with his journalist's finger on the pulse of daily life, described in 1859 with consciously Dickensian plenitude how *everybody*, from the top to the bottom of society, goes to the Derby:

> Everybody there, on the rail and on the road, on the Derby Day. The House of Lords, and the House of Commons, the Bar, the Bench, the Army, the Navy, and the Desk; May Fair and Rag Fair, Park Lane and Petticoat Lane, the Chapel Royal and Whitechapel, Saint James's and Saint Giles's. Give me a pen plucked from the wing of a roc (the most gigantic bird known, I think); give me a scroll of papyrus as long as the documents in a Chancery suit; give me a river for an ink-bottle, and then I should be scant of space to describe the road that leads to the course, the hill, the grand stand, the gipsies, the Ethiopian serenaders, the clouds of horsemen, like Bedouins of the desert, flying towards Tattenham Corner [a famous part of Epsom Downs racecourse]; the correct cards that never are correct; the dog that always gets on the course and never can get off again, and that creates as much amusement in his agony as though he had been Mr Merryman [an allusion to a recently published 'magazine of miscellaneous mirth'].[85] The all-absorbing, thrilling, soul-riveting race.[86]

Derby Day in 1858 attracted even more attention than usual; all the newspapers grasped with gratitude the possibilities for puns and jokes and connections between sport and politics, since the new prime minister, arrived in power at the end of February after the surprise fall of Palmerston, was the horse-mad scion of the horse-mad family which had inaugurated the race in 1780.[87] Would Lord Derby's horse Toxopholite, the bookmakers' favourite, win this year's race at a crucial time for its owner's career, while the India Bill and other tricky legislation were passing through parliament? Derby had no majority and, as it happened, was facing a serious motion of censure over India just at the time of the great race. Would his government survive? And would Disraeli, finally making it up the 'greasy pole' as far as chancellor of the Exchequer, be more than a flash in the pan as part of a government which was likely to be short-lived? What would the two unlikely allies, the quiet aristocrat and the flamboyant middle-class chancer, achieve as this hottest summer reached its peak?

All three main protagonists in this story of the hot summer of 1858 were middle-aged. Two of them, Darwin and Disraeli, were late developers in terms of achievements in their chosen fields, while Dickens had known roaring success with his early work *Pickwick Papers*, published in 1837, when he was twenty-five. In 1858 he reached a crossroads, when he nearly became unhinged and feared losing the good will of the public. He and Disraeli were constantly in the public eye during the summer of 1858, while Darwin, going through as violent a whirlwind of emotions as either of the other two, lived in quiet obscurity outside London, though only a short train ride away from the sweltering capital.

None of the three met during 1858. Disraeli and Dickens had met in the past; they both took part in a fundraising event in Manchester in October 1843, chaired by Dickens.[88] In his few recorded references to Disraeli in his correspondence Dickens was less than complimentary; he disapproved of Disraeli's abandonment of Sir Robert Peel during the debates on the repeal of the Corn Laws in 1846, and he offered only faint praise of Disraeli's voting with Lord John Russell on one of the failed motions to allow Rothschild to take his seat. 'It delights me that D'Israeli has done such justice to his conscience-less self, in regard of the Jews', he wrote in July 1849.[89] For his part Disraeli, in an effort to avoid replying directly to a correspondent's request in 1857 for an opinion on Dickens's *Little Dorrit*, claimed that he had lost all zest for fiction, either reading or writing it.[90] He had earlier enjoyed applying names from *Pickwick Papers* and *Oliver Twist* to acquaintances. He told his sister Sarah in 1838 that Sir Charles Grey was called 'Mr Pickwick' in the House of Commons, 'being in his appearance, spectacles, and style of oratory, the "very prototype" '.[91] The following year he described a conversation with Sir Edward Bulwer Lytton on leaving parliament one day; discussing the less reputable publishing firms in London, the two friends 'settled [Richard] Bentley was Fagin; [Henry] Colburn the artful Dodger; S[aunders] and Otley, Claypole'.[92]

Neither Dickens nor Disraeli seems to have been aware of Darwin and his work, even after the publication of *On the Origin of Species* in 1859; certainly their surviving letters make no mention of Darwin. He knew the novels of the other two. He liked reading fiction, and especially admired George Eliot's *Adam Bede* and *Silas Marner*.[93] Like Disraeli he referred in passing to some of the characters Dickens's early fiction had made legendary; Mr Pickwick's idiosyncratic servant Sam Weller is mentioned or quoted, as are *Sketches by Boz* and Mr Snagsby from *Bleak House*.[94] And he remembered in 1864 how one of Disraeli's novels had featured 'some splendid sneers at us transmutationists; a young lady saying "oh it is proved by geology" that we came from crows or something of the kind'.[95] The novel he had in mind was *Tancred* (1847), in which Lady Constance Rawleigh recommends that a friend read *The Revelations of Chaos* (a knowing reference to Robert Chambers's sensational *Vestiges of Creation*), in which, she says, everything is proved by geology: 'We were fishes and I believe we shall be crows.'[96]

Darwin and Dickens, though neither knew it, had shared a moment in June 1838, when they were both elected to the Athenaeum Club, founded in 1824 to celebrate intellectual and literary attainments. The club building on Pall Mall was undergoing renovation in 1838, and the committee decided to elect forty new members at once in order to finance the work.[97] Dickens was an obvious choice, with *Pickwick Papers* behind him and *Oliver Twist* appearing serially in *Bentley's Magazine* in 1838. Darwin, not long back from his voyage on the *Beagle* and not yet well known even in the scientific world, owed his election to one of those serendipitous 'accidental fatalities' which he liked to trace with hindsight as he looked back on his career. Just as he delighted in the unexpectedly fateful connection between his uncle Josiah Wedgwood's generous intervention with his father and his own success in overcoming the distrust of the eccentric Captain FitzRoy about the shape of his nose, so he spelt out the connection between his father's dislike of cheese and his own election to the Athenaeum. His autobiography tells that his father, Dr Robert Darwin, had attended years earlier to the 1st marquess of Lansdowne and disclosed his aversion to cheese, after which the Lansdowne family took an interest in Dr Darwin's family, with the result that a later Lord Lansdowne proposed Charles for membership in 1838:

When forty new members (the forty thieves as they were called) were added to the Athenaeum Club, there was much canvassing to be one of them; and without my having asked any one, Lord Lansdowne proposed me and got me elected. If I am right in my supposition, it was a queer concatenation of events that my father not eating cheese half-a-century before in Holland led to my election as a member of the Athenaeum.[98]

(Disraeli's rather different experience with the Athenaeum was to be black-balled in 1832, after trying very hard to get elected, and again in 1835. He met antagonism from those he had attacked or ridiculed in his novels and journalism, and suffered from a general belief that he was unscrupulous and not respectable, despite his sober, scholarly father Isaac having been a founder member of the club. Only in 1866, after nearly thirty years of political service, at the age of sixty-one, did Disraeli find the doors of the club open to him.[99])

Despite having the luck to be elected before he had achieved anything, Darwin paid little attention to London Clubland. Unlike Dickens and Disraeli, he did not frequent literary or political parties or make speeches on public stages, even in the realm of science. He was retiring by nature and because of his ill health and obsessive working practices had become almost a recluse in his house in the village of Down, in Kent. Although he had scientific friends in London and was a member of various scientific societies which met in the city, he did not attend many meetings and seldom spent more than a few days away from home. He owed his London friends a recognised debt of gratitude for keeping him informed of progress and for ensuring that he gained the credit for the discovery of natural selection; alone, he would not have battled for fame and recognition.

The connections – albeit indirect – that can be discerned between the life experiences of these three great Victorians emerge in rich detail in the context of the lives of other Londoners during the hot summer, of men sitting in stifling chambers deciding on legislation, on costs, on cases of divorce and lunacy, on membership of an exclusive club, on methods of improving public health, on curing diseases, on the value of technical advances or scientific papers, on the topic of the next day's front page and editorial; also men and women involved in religious controversy, entertainment, fashion, literature, and art. Connections, sometimes passing and contingent, sometimes fundamental and vital, exist between the most unlikely people and things. What do Disraeli and Brunel have in common? Or Disraeli and Karl Marx, living in exile in north London and commenting on the affairs of the day in German and American newspapers? Frith's *Derby Day* and Brunel's *Great Eastern*? That ship's construction, the Robinson divorce case, and the promotion of contraception? The plot to assassinate Napoleon III, a Dickensian character, and the Garrick Club affair? Derby Day and the writing of *Adam Bede*? A meeting of the Linnaean Society and the death of Darwin's youngest child? India and the Thames? The Divorce Act and James Rarey, the 'Great American Horse Tamer'? As they negotiated their lives day by day, Darwin, Dickens, Disraeli, and their contemporaries had no certain sense of how their circumstances might change or their problems be resolved, while we can make use of the historian's gift of hindsight to 'trace the pattern' of the 'atoms' as they fell on the protagonists in the hot months of 1858.

CHAPTER TWO

May 1858

Dickens in distress

The inauguration of the Annual Exhibition of Pictures and Sculpture at the Royal Academy of Arts was celebrated on Saturday by the usual anniversary festival. It was attended with befitting pomp and circumstance. Ministers of State, legislators, chiefs of the army and navy, dignitaries of the Church, the judicial Bench, the representatives of literature, science, commerce, and manufactures, all assembled on the occasion to pay their common tribute of homage to art in its own chosen temple.[1]

WITH THIS RHETORICAL FLOURISH *The Times* of Monday, 3 May 1858 began its account of the grand banquet held on 1 May at the Royal Academy, then located in the National Gallery building in Trafalgar Square. Dinner commenced at 6 p.m., chaired by the president of the Royal Academy, Sir Charles Eastlake, and the roll call of those present was indeed prestigious. The prime minister, Lord Derby, was there, along with his son Lord Stanley; the chancellor of the Exchequer, Disraeli; the home secretary, Spencer Walpole; the lord chief justice, Lord Campbell (the leading judge in the newly operative Divorce Court); and the lord chancellor, Lord Chelmsford, intransigent opponent of the bill to allow Jewish representation in parliament. Also present were the chief members of the

Liberal opposition, Lord Palmerston, Lord John Russell, and William Gladstone. David Salomons attended in his capacity as lord mayor of London, the first Jewish holder of the position; like his cousin by marriage Lionel de Rothschild, he had been elected to parliament but could not represent his constituents in Greenwich because of the requirement to take the Christian oath. (When, some months after this dinner, the law was changed and Rothschild was able to take his seat, Salomons stood again in Greenwich and was elected in 1859.[2])

Others present were Archibald Tait, the progressive bishop of London, and Samuel Wilberforce, the ultra-conservative bishop of Oxford. The duke of Cambridge made a speech on behalf of the army, Professor Michael Faraday represented the scientific community, and the presidents of the royal colleges of physicians and surgeons were there in their representative capacity too. Those two giants of fiction, Dickens and Thackeray, attended on behalf of literature. Both responded to the toast raised in their honour. Dickens declared that literature, 'your sister, whom I represent, is strong and healthy [here *The Times* reports 'a laugh']; she has a strong affection for and an undying interest in you; and it is always a very great gratification to her to see herself so well remembered within these walls, and to know that she is an honoured guest at your hospitable board (Cheers and laughter)'. Thackeray followed, with a more personal reply, in which he talked warmly of his 'friend' Dickens, telling his audience that if it had not been for Dickens, 'I should most likely never have been included in the toast which you have been pleased to drink':

> I should have tried to be, not a writer, but a painter, or designer of pictures. That was the object of my early ambition, and I can remember when Mr Dickens was a very young man, and commenced delighting the world with some charming humorous works of which I cannot mention the name (laughter), but which were coloured light green, and came out once a month (a laugh), that this young man wanted an artist to illustrate his writings, and I recollect walking up to his chambers with two or three drawings in my hand, which, strange to say, he did not find suitable. (Laughter.) But for that unfortunate blight which came over my artistical existence, it would have been my pride and my

pleasure to have endeavoured one day to find a place on these walls for one of my performances. This disappointment caused me to direct my attention to a different walk of art . . . [and I] shall always be happy to receive your welcome and partake of your hospitality.[3]

This was a characteristically gallant reference to a man with whom Thackeray never felt completely at ease. Though he was seven months older than his admired rival, he had, as he indicates in his speech, turned to writing much later than Dickens, who made his name overnight in 1836 with the early monthly numbers of *Pickwick Papers*, the work to which Thackeray refers here. Thackeray had applied to illustrate it in April 1836, just after the publication of its first number and the unfortunate suicide of the original illustrator, Robert Seymour. Hablot Knight Browne, known as 'Phiz', was chosen as Seymour's replacement.[4] Only with the publication of *Vanity Fair* in monthly numbers in 1847–8 did Thackeray achieve, at the age of thirty-six, the kind of sudden success Dickens had enjoyed at twenty-four.

Though Dickens paid no compliment to Thackeray at this dinner, he had recently addressed him at another function to which both novelists were invited, a dinner held at the end of March to raise money for the Royal General Theatrical Fund. On that occasion Dickens described his fellow novelist as 'a gentleman who is an honour to literature, and in whom literature is honoured'. Thackeray's works were full of wit and wisdom; they held a 'great mirror' up to nature.[5] On Sunday, 9 May Thackeray hosted a dinner to which Dickens and the painters Daniel Maclise and Edwin Landseer were invited.[6] Thackeray's two daughters were friendly with Dickens's girls, and Charles Dickens Jr moved in Thackeray's *Punch* circle, but things were about to change. Barely a month after the Royal Academy dinner, with the temperature outside rising steeply and causing universal comment, both men would behave recklessly, becoming embroiled in rows and rumours, and their erstwhile polite, if awkward, friendship would come to a premature end.

The Royal Academy exhibition, formally opened by Queen Victoria on Thursday, 29 April, allowed 'the great public' to 'rush in', as the *Athenaeum* reported, on Monday, 3 May. Opinions in the press were divided about the merits of the pictures. More than one critic noted that there were no Pre-Raphaelite paintings on show this year, but there was Frith's acclaimed *Derby Day*, Egg's controversial triptych, admired by some as Hogarthian but condemned as ugly by others, and Tait's *Chelsea Interior* with its 'faithful' representation of the literary giant of the age and his wife, both known for their sharp, witty conversation.[7] Not many other pictures found favour, and Dante Gabriel Rossetti, who did not exhibit in 1858, described the exhibition as 'frightfully seedy', containing 'not a picture which is not done in prose', as he told his fellow painter William Bell Scott in June;[8] this is hardly true of Egg's work, which many found melodramatic in the extreme.

Equally melodramatic was Dickens's behaviour, in public and in private. The public manifestation was hailed as a marvellous success. On Thursday, 29 April 1858 Dickens gave his first public reading for money. He had long been in demand by charities and philanthropic institutions to give readings from his works to raise money for their endeavours. In February he made a stirring speech at a dinner at Freemasons' Hall in aid of the Hospital for Sick Children in Great Ormond Street, helping to raise over £3,000 to extend the building. He was made an honorary governor of the hospital and asked to give a public reading to raise more money.[9] He duly read from *A Christmas Carol* at St Martin's Hall on 15 April. A year earlier he had read from the same story to an ecstatic audience of 2,000 to help the widow and children of his friend Douglas Jerrold. Now with this reading for the benefit of the hospital, he carefully let it be known that he would henceforth lecture for his own benefit, an undertaking which he knew was risky and against which his friend John Forster had strongly argued, fearing that Dickens's honour as a writer might be endangered by his earning money as a public performer.[10]

Dickens had, along with Forster, Augustus Egg, and many other friends, often acted with his own amateur theatre company, but had done so either in his own or others' houses or in public places for good causes.[11] Never one to do things by halves, he had a private theatre built at the back of Tavistock House, his large house in Bloomsbury. According to Francesco Berger, the young composer commissioned by Dickens to write overture and incidental music for some of these performances, this little theatre was 'complete in every point', with 'proper footlights, proper scenery [designed by the famous theatrical scene painter Clarkson Stanfield], proper curtain', dresses made by the tailor from the Adelphi Theatre, wigs by 'Wilson of the Strand', and properties by 'Ireland of the Adelphi'.[12] In July 1857, as part of his effort on behalf of Jerrold's family, Dickens had arranged a private performance for members of the royal family of Wilkie Collins's melodrama of male rivalry and sacrifice, *The Frozen Deep*. Dickens played the part of the fellow intent on murdering his love-rival who instead saves his enemy's life at the expense of his own, a role he would give in slightly modified form to Sydney Carton in his next novel, *A Tale of Two Cities*, published in 1859. Berger noted that in the crucial scene in which Dickens's character, alone on the stage, is faced with his moral decision, Dickens's acting was at its best: 'Anything more powerful, more pathetic, more enthralling, I have never seen.'[13]

Dickens's son Charley, daughters Mamie and Katey, sister-in-law Helen Hogarth, and friends including Augustus Egg, John Forster, and Mark Lemon, the editor of *Punch*, were among the members of the cast who played at the Gallery of Illustration on Regent Street before Victoria and Albert and their guests, King Leopold of the Belgians and his children. Victoria noted in her journal on 4 July 1857:

> At 9 went with dear Uncle [Leopold], our other guests, & 4 eldest children, to the Gallery of Illustration, to see an amateur performance of a Play, a romantic Melodrama in 3 acts, by Wilkie Collins, called 'The Frozen Deep', – a tale of the Northern Arctic Expedition, – most interesting, intensely dramatic, & most touching & moving, at the end. The Play was admirably acted by *Charles Dickens* (whose representation of Richard Wardour was beyond all praise & not to be surpassed) . . . We were all kept in breathless suspense, & much impressed.[14]

Dickens was fully aware of his tremendous success as an actor-director with all kinds of audiences, and he decided in the spring of 1858 that he could make a lot of money performing scenes from his novels in halls first in London, then on a tour of the whole kingdom, and later in America, where he reckoned he could earn £10,000 from readings.[15] From 1858 until his death in 1870, which may have been hastened by his insistence on continuing his public readings at home and abroad in spite of poor health, Dickens put on an energetic one-man show. He designed his own low table at which he would stand in front of a specially lit screen, and revelled in doing the various voices of his characters in the most comic and tragic scenes from his fiction. The most notable and dramatic reading of all was the rendering of the vicious murder of Nancy by Bill Sikes in *Oliver Twist*, which Dickens acted out physically as well as verbally.[16] He had always sought the love of his reading public, but now at the darkest time in his personal life he needed their adoration more than ever.

Anxious not to spoil his reputation or to be seen as a mere showman – and thus not a gentleman – Dickens alerted *The Times* to his new plan, due to commence in the late spring of 1858. On 16 April the newspaper raved about his final amateur performance the previous night in aid of sick children. Not only is Dickens described as an actor 'of such proficiency that he is hardly to be termed an amateur at all', but his readings from his books are said to give 'additional colouring to his already highly elaborated work'. 'Such was the assembled multitude' at St Martin's Hall, the review continues, 'that the sum produced must have been sufficient to physic all the sick children in the United Kingdom'. The paper welcomes the announcement that 'the benevolent "reader" is at last about to employ his elocutionary talents for his own advantage' on Thursday evenings, beginning on 29 April.[17] However positive this sounds, there is still an awkwardness about the plain truth that a man already made rich and famous by his writings intended to become even more so by performing before audiences of up to 3,000 in St Martin's Hall, a huge mock-Tudor building on Long Acre, Covent Garden, before travelling the country addressing his adoring audience. It was the aspect of Dickens that Thackeray and his circle found vulgar. Forster was aware of this and warned his friend, and Dickens knew it too, but was impelled to make the attempt, partly for the money's sake but much more for the sake of gaining and keeping the love of the multitude.

Dickens could not resist explaining his reasoning when he gave his first reading for his own financial gain on Thursday, 29 April. A few days later the *Era* printed his speech in full and without criticism. It is hardly Dickens at his best, with its courteous defiance and false consciousness in claiming moral responsibility as his chief motive for the new venture:

> Ladies and gentlemen, it may perhaps be known to you that for a few years past I have been accustomed occasionally to read some of my shorter books to various audiences in aid of a variety of good objects, and at some charge to myself both in time and money. It having at length become impossible in any reason to comply with these always accumulating demands, I have had definitively to choose between now and then reading on my own account as one of my recognised occupations, or not reading at all. I have had little or no difficulty in deciding on the former course. (Cheers.)[18]

While it is reasonable enough for Dickens to mention his longstanding generosity in lending his name and his time to charity, and utterly believable that he is finding it increasingly difficult to say yes to the many appeals to him, it is hardly logical to claim that the only answer is to go on giving readings, but only for financial gain. Sensitive to the charge of demeaning his profession, he states that he has thought long and hard and has decided that the new plan 'can involve no possible compromise of the credit and independence of Literature'. 'Whatever brings a public man and his public face to face, on terms of mutual confidence and respect, is a good thing.' He may even claim a 'personal friendship, which it is my great privilege and pride, as it is my great responsibility, to hold with a multitude of persons who will never hear my voice or see my face'.[19] This elaborate explanation was no doubt partly forced on Dickens by the snobbery that still existed in some quarters about the 'profession' of writing and in even wider circles about the 'profession' of acting, but much of the forcefulness is likely to have come from Dickens's own need to assert himself at a time when he was struggling with misery and guilt in his personal relations.

On 9 May 1858, the day he dined with Thackeray, Dickens wrote a truly terrible letter to his friend and fellow philanthropist, the banking heiress Angela Burdett-Coutts. It began:

My Dear Miss Coutts,

You have been too near and dear a friend to me for many years, and I am bound to you by too many ties of grateful and affectionate regard, to admit of any longer keeping silence to you on a sad domestic topic . . . I believe my marriage has been for years and years as miserable a one as ever was made. I believe that no two people were ever created, with such an impossibility of interest, sympathy, confidence, sentiment, tender union of any kind between them, as there is between my wife and me. It is an immense misfortune to her – it is an immense misfortune to me – but Nature has put an insurmountable barrier between us, which never in this world can be thrown down.[20]

Dickens goes on to claim that the children – there were nine surviving out of ten born between 1837 and 1852 – did not love Catherine. 'She has never attached one of them to herself, never played with them in their infancy, never attracted their confidence as they have grown older, never presented herself before them in the aspect of a mother.' The children themselves in later years, and many friends including Miss Coutts, rejected this cruel and sweeping opinion of the woman Katey called her 'poor, poor mother'.[21] That Catherine was rather slow and clumsy beside her mercurial, energetic husband is undeniable, and that she was helped in bringing up her large family by her unmarried sister, Georgina Hogarth, whom Dickens constantly praised for her domestic talents, is also true. Georgina had lived with them since 1842, when she was fifteen, and when the bitter separation came in 1858, she sided with Dickens and chose to live with him and look after the eight children he kept with him, from twenty-year-old Mamie down to 6-year-old Edward – all of them, that is, except the eldest, Charles Jr, who was by now twenty-one and could make up his own mind in any case. He did; he chose to stay with his mother.[22]

Miss Coutts was told that Forster was trying to make arrangements for Catherine, who was to leave Tavistock House, the family home in Bloomsbury, where so many amateur theatrical performances had been held, with the whole family, including Catherine, involved. Dickens, meanwhile, was staying overnight at the office of his weekly paper, *Household Words*, in Wellington Street, off the Strand.[23] Though Dickens undertook the upbringing of his younger children, all boys, in fact they were sent away to school at the age of eight or nine, and most were destined by their father to make their careers abroad: Frank (born in 1844) left for India in 1863, Alfred (born in 1845) went to Australia in 1864, Sydney (born in 1847) joined the navy in 1859, and the youngest, Edward, emigrated to Australia in 1868. Only Henry, born in 1849, was kept in England; he read mathematics at Cambridge and became a barrister. Walter, born in 1841, was serving in the army in India in 1858; he died in Calcutta in December 1863, aged twenty-two. Frank returned to see his mother in 1871 (Dickens having died the previous year); neither parent saw the others again after they left Britain as teenagers.[24]

The decision to separate was not merely the result of the extreme incompatibility Dickens described to Miss Coutts. He had been contemplating the break for almost a year, and his acting hobby was intimately involved in his reasons. Though his female relatives and friends took on parts when his company was performing in private or for the queen, he always hired professional actresses for engagements in theatres. This was partly because he felt his womenfolk might not be able to project their voices sufficiently and lacked the required physical presence for such performances, and partly because, despite the efforts of his friend William Charles Macready and other leading actor-managers, it was still generally felt that acting was unbecoming for a woman, and at worst connected with prostitution; this lingering suspicion dated from the time when assignations were made in and around theatres, before Macready in particular sought to clean up the theatrical environment in the 1830s and 1840s.[25]

By the 1850s the chief theatres were respectable spaces, but actresses still had to be especially careful of their reputations. This was true of the family of female actors with whom Dickens became acquainted in the summer of 1857 when planning to put on *The Frozen Deep* in Manchester. On 2 August 1857 Dickens wrote to Wilkie Collins that he had arranged to stage his friend's play in the city's Free Trade Hall. 'It is *an immense place*', he wrote, 'and we shall be obliged to have actresses'.[26] He met and engaged Frances Ternan, an actress in her fifties whose actor-manager husband had died of syphilis in an insane asylum in Bethnal Green in 1845, and two of her three daughters, Maria, who took the main female role in the drama, and Ellen, also known as Nelly, who was given a smaller part.[27] Dickens described in detail to Miss Coutts in September how moved he had been by the 20-year-old Maria Ternan's complete immersion in the sentiment of her part. As she knelt over the dying Richard Wardour (Dickens), 'the tears streamed out of her eyes into his mouth, down his beard, all over his rags – down his arms as he held her by the hair', and she 'sobbed as if she were breaking her heart and was quite convulsed with grief'.[28]

After returning from the triumph in Manchester on 25 August, Dickens could not settle. He described to Collins 'the grim despair and restlessness of this subsidence from excitement' after *The Frozen Deep* and confessed, 'I want to escape from myself'. 'When I *do* start up and stare myself seedily in the face, as happens to be my case at present, my blankness is inconceivable – indescribable – my misery, amazing.'[29] He arranged to go on a walking holiday with Collins, ostensibly in order to co-write a piece for *Household Words* entitled 'The Lazy Tour of Two Idle Apprentices', which duly appeared in October. The real reason was his burning desire to see the younger Ternan sister, 18-year-old Ellen, with whom he had fallen in love. He chose Collins as his companion and confidant; Collins was thirty-four, eleven years younger than Dickens, and had a mistress, Caroline Graves, with whom he lived without ever marrying her. He was racy, a keen visitor to disreputable haunts in London and Paris.[30] Dickens knew that his older, more staid friend John Forster, whom he still relied on to help manage problems with publishers and who would soon undertake negotiations with Catherine's family, would not approve of his taking up with a girl the same age as his own daughter Katey (Nelly was born in March 1839 and Katey in January of the same year), any more than he approved of the plan hatched a few months later to give public readings for profit. To Forster Dickens wrote early in September 1857 that 'poor Catherine and I are not made for each other, and there is no help for it'. He told Forster that the realisation was not new. 'What is now befalling me I have seen steadily coming, ever since the days you remember when Mary was born.' Mary, known as Mamie, was Dickens's second child, born in 1838, two years after his marriage. This declaration was nothing but obfuscation and self-delusion. In fact Dickens had only begun to hint to

Forster in 1854 that his domestic life was no longer happy.[31]

Dickens alone seemed to believe, as was convenient to his sense of his own honour, that the marriage had been disastrous more or less from the start, and this became the refrain of his letters to close friends over the next few months. To one or two female correspondents he spun a strange fairy tale which surely stems from his excitement about *The Frozen Deep* and his overwhelming feelings for Ellen. In December 1857 he addressed the widow of his friend Richard Watson, telling her that he was 'the most restless of created Beings':

> I wish I had been born in the days of Ogres and Dragon-guarded Castles. I wish an Ogre with seven heads (and no particular evidence of brains in the whole lot of them) had taken the Princess whom I adore – you have no idea how intensely I love her! – to his stronghold at the top of a high series of Mountains, and there tied her up by the hair. Nothing would suit me half so well this day, as climbing after her, sword in hand, and either winning her or being killed. – *There's* a state of mind for you, in 1857.[32]

After the excitement of Manchester he and Collins made a tour of the north of England, walking in the Lake District, visiting Carlisle and Lancaster, and fetching up in Doncaster in mid-September 1857, where the Ternan sisters were acting in a number of plays. Dickens and Collins attracted the attention of the local press when they attended a performance; their alibi was their walking tour and the comic piece they were to write about it.[33] The two idle apprentices visit Doncaster races, as Dickens did with Ellen. In the final chapter of their account of their rambles, published on 31 October in *Household Words*, Dickens, Francis Goodchild to Collins's Thomas Idle, 'is suspected by Mr Idle to have fallen into a dreadful state concerning a pair of little lilac gloves and a little bonnet that he saw there', together with the 'golden hair' under the bonnet.[34]

From now until May 1858, Dickens wrote obsessively to his correspondents about his incurable restlessness. In March he confessed to Collins, who knew more than anyone else about his troubles, 'the Doncaster unhappiness remains so strong upon me that I can't write, and (waking)

can't rest, one minute'. He recognises that the idea of reading to the public
is directly connected with his state of mind: 'I have never known a
moment's peace or content, since the last night of the Frozen Deep. I do
suppose that there never was a Man so seized and rended by one Spirit. In
this condition, though nothing can alter or soften it, I have a turning
notion that the mere physical effort and change of the readings would be
good, as another means of bearing it.'[35] He dropped heavy hints to his
closest friends about his intention to separate from Catherine; only Collins,
Forster, and in due course W.H. Wills, his right-hand man at the office of
Household Words, seem to have been informed by Dickens himself about
Ellen, though many others heard rumours and indulged in gossip.

By 19 May 1858, Derby Day, Dickens knew that Miss Coutts wished
to intervene on Catherine's behalf. He wrote to her that day saying that 'no
consideration, human or Divine, can move me from the resolution I have
taken'.[36] Catherine wrote on the same day, thanking Miss Coutts 'for your
true kindness in doing what I asked'. 'I have now – God help me – only
one course to pursue. One day though not now I may be able to tell you
how hardly I have been used.'[37] Dickens was outraged by the rumours
about him he believed Catherine's 'wicked mother' had set going, calling
her 'that woman' in his letter to Miss Coutts. In a second note to the same
correspondent on the same day, he vented his annoyance with his son
Charley for attending the Derby, complaining: 'He might have let the
Race pass him at such a time.'[38] A week later he told Macready that he
did not wish to go into 'what is past and gone', but 'steadily desire[d] to
dismiss it'.[39]

It is likely that Catherine's family, upset by his treatment of her,
were stoking the fire by discussing Dickens's relations with his wife
outside the family. In any case, if Dickens believed that he could keep the
secret from the world in general, he was deluded.[40] A few days later it came
to Dickens's attention that his affairs were being discussed by Thackeray
in the clubs and societies which, as a virtual bachelor – his insane wife
being permanently lodged with a kind housekeeper in Camberwell in
southeast London and his daughters mostly living with their grandmother
in Paris – he naturally frequented. This was one reason for the impending
rift between the two men. Others, too, were soon talking about Dickens's

marriage troubles, and before long he found himself trying to manage the newspaper accounts which inevitably multiplied during May and June. Thackeray first heard the rumours while attending the races at Epsom in Derby week, 17–21 May, and became unintentionally if carelessly involved in spreading them at the Garrick Club, as he told his mother early in June:

> Well, what to say? Here is sad news in the literary world – no less than a separation between Mr and Mrs Dickens – with all sorts of horrible stories buzzing about. The worst is that I'm in a manner dragged in for one. Last week in going into the Garrick I heard that D is separated from his wife on account of an intrigue with his sister in law [Georgina]. No says I no such thing – its [sic] with an actress – and the other story had not got to Dickens's ears but this had – and he fancies that I am going about abusing him! We shall never be allowed to be friends that's clear. I had mine from a man at Epsom, the first I ever heard of the matter, but I should have said nothing about it but that I heard the other much worse story whereupon I told mine to counteract it.[41]

Derby Day

Wednesday, 19 May dawned brightly on the Epsom Downs. After rain the previous day, the weather was mainly fine, and, at around 60 °F (16 °C), relatively warm for the time of year. (Some weeks later *The Times* reported that the weather for the whole of May had been about 6 °F warmer than average, but the really hot weather began only at the end of the month.[42]) All the newspapers, both sporting and general, anticipated the event on the preceding days, called the odds, described the crowds on the day, and gave the result. 'All London seems under the influence of a great mania', according to *The Times* on 20 May. Like every other journalist writing his piece about the Derby, *The Times*'s writer gasps at the numbers and the cheerful rubbing shoulders of all classes, from aristocrats to petty criminals: 'The Downs on a Derby day stand alone as a spectacle, and there is nothing else on earth with which one can compare them.' The betting at the start of the race is given: Lord Derby's horse Toxopholite, the favourite, ran at '10 to 3 against', with Beadsman, the eventual winner, running at 10 to 1.[43]

This Derby Day was of special interest, firstly because the prime minister's horse was in the race, and secondly because the government was facing a motion of no confidence over its recent handling of Indian affairs. Some observers tut-tutted about the time-honoured adjournment of parliament to allow members to attend the race. *The Times* and others noted that Lord Derby seemed to be keener on the progress of his stables than that of his government, while newspapers more sympathetic to the prime minister insisted that the great English tradition of giving politicians a half-day holiday for the race need not be broken over a mere ministerial crisis. The *Racing Times* and the ultra-conservative *St James's Chronicle* both ridiculed the notion that Lord Derby was more interested in horse races than politics, or that it was irresponsible for parliament to take time off in the midst of the India debate.[44] Others revelled in the opportunity to link politics with sport. One prolific writer of popular books about contemporary London, J. Ewing Ritchie, captured the exciting possibilities of this particular Derby Day:

> That man with spectacles and long black stock [a high stiff collar] . . . is England's Premier, whose horse is the favourite – who has never yet won the Derby – who, it is said, would rather do so than have a parliamentary success – and who, it is also said, has offered his jockey £50 a-year for life should he win this race . . . And now, amidst a whirlwind of shouting and hurrahing, the race is over; and in two minutes and fifty-four seconds Sir Joseph Hawley, a Whig baronet, beats Lord Derby, the Conservative Premier, clears £50,000, while his jockey, for that short ride, earns as much as you or me, my good sir, may win by the labour of many a long year. Pigeons fly off with the result. The telegraph is at work . . . and many a man goes home with a heavy heart, for some are hit very hard.[45]

All the newspapers, of whatever political persuasion, had taken the opportunity to combine speculation about the Derby winner with discussion of the chances of the government surviving. The odds were called jokily on both. On 16 May the *Era*, a Sunday paper which specialised in art, entertainment, and sport, and which supported Derby's politics, carried a poem by 'Baptiste' entitled 'The Derby Alphabet 1858'. The writer ran through the names of the horses alphabetically, noting that Beadsman was a good bet, and finishing with a message of good luck to Lord Derby:

> . . . without going further the alphabet through,
> To Lord Derby I give the Turf's riband of blue;
> And long may he flourish successful and great
> In affairs of the Turf as in those of the State.[46]

The *Racing Times* printed a long poem two days before the race, playing on the name Toxopholite (a variation on 'toxophilite', or lover of archery):

> Toxopholite, whom no one *talks of* lightly,
> I'm not the one to fancy him but slightly.
> He will be very near the mark – they say
> They've had no horse like him for many a day;
> And that Lord Derby, minister or not,
> With this Toxopholite will hit the spot.[47]

Of all the comments on Derby politics, *Punch* came up with the most elaborate on the Saturday after the race. Dealing with the politicians as if they were horses, it gave the 'closing prices' for each when the India debate resumed the following week, including:

> 9 to 7 Lord Ellenborough's Scapegoat
> 15 to 12 Lord Stanley's Adhesion
> 20 to 19 The Dizzy Lot (taken)
> 99 to 1 Lord Chelmsford's Anti-Jew-Mania
> 300 to 20 Lord John's Finality (offered)
> 1,000 to 1 Pam and Lord John Russell coupled (take 10,000,000 to 1)
> 6 to 5 against Lord Derby's Dissolution (offered)
> 6 to 5 Lord Palmerston's Succession (taken).[48]

Roughly interpreted, this suggests that *Punch*, at least, believed that Derby and Disraeli ('Dizzy') were likely to survive narrowly, and that if they did not, Palmerston ('Pam') would probably come back in at the head of a Whig ministry. The chances of Palmerston and his colleague Lord John Russell, the two feuding leaders of the opposition, agreeing on a strategy were extremely slim – a thousand or even ten million to one, according to *Punch* – and, for good measure, the fanatical anti-Jewish Lord Chelmsford had very little chance of winning the ongoing parliamentary debate about the Oaths Bill.

Lord Ellenborough, president of the Board of Control, was, as *Punch* put it directly, the scapegoat of a bad diplomatic mistake over India which had brought about the current crisis.[49]

The Sepoy rebellion against the British army in May 1857 had led to massacres of Europeans in various places and to the fall of the British garrison at Lucknow, the capital of the province of Oudh. There was cruelty on both sides until Sir Colin Campbell, the chief of the army in India, succeeded in lifting the siege of Lucknow on 19 March 1858. The news of the massacre of British women and children shocked and enraged the British public. Dickens wrote to Miss Coutts in October 1857 that he wished he were commander in chief in India: 'I should do my utmost to exterminate the Race upon whom the stain of the late cruelties rested.'[50] His bellicose reaction is perhaps partly explained by the fact that 16-year-old Walter, his second son, was serving with the 42nd Highlanders in India; he was, as Dickens told a correspondent in February 1858, 'in the thick of the Indian tussle'.[51] Thomas Carlyle, on the other hand, responded with withering criticism to reports of cruelty on the part of the British army, which included strapping rebels to the muzzle of a gun and firing it:

I cannot bear to read those inhuman details in the newspapers, nor do I love in the least the spirit in wh[ich] the English People mainly have taken it up. To punish the Sepoys, and mince them all to pieces &c &c: it were far better if the English People thought of punishing themselves for the very great folly they have manifested there . . . whereby such results have become possible, and become inevitable.[52]

(Karl Marx made much the same point in a series of articles on the subject in the *New York Daily Tribune* in September 1857; he wrote of the Sepoy cruelty being atrocious, but also a 'reflex' of England's conduct in India.[53])

The governor-general of India, Lord Canning, made a punitive proclamation in March 1858, taking the property of Oudh into British possession. William Howard Russell, the India correspondent of *The Times*, who sent admirably informed reports back to London from Sir Colin Campbell's headquarters, confided frankly to his diary on Sunday, 21 March that the sermon he had just heard in the mess tent, by the Scottish Presbyterian preacher, the Rev. McKay, was 'eloquent but illogical'. McKay 'sought to prove that England would not share the fate common to all the great empires of the world hitherto, because she was Christian and carried the ark of the covenant, whereas they had been heathen'. 'I believe', Russell continued, 'that we permit things in India which we would not permit to be done in Europe, or could not hope to effect without public reprobation; and that our Christian character in Europe . . . will not atone for usurpation and annexation in Hindostan, or for violence and fraud in the Upper Provinces of India.'[54]

Russell was not the only onlooker who disapproved of Canning's action. The chief commissioner of Oudh, Sir James Outram, objected to the severity of the terms, and persuaded Canning to soften them in order not to insult and enrage the local inhabitants by confiscating their lands wholesale. At home in London, Lord Ellenborough sided with Outram; without knowing that the terms had been made less provocative to the inhabitants of Oudh, he sent a dispatch to Canning censuring him. The language of the dispatch was uncompromising:

> We cannot but express to you our apprehension that this decree, pronouncing the disinherison of a people, will throw difficulties almost insurmountable in the way of the re-establishment of peace . . . Other conquerors, when they have succeeded in overcoming resistance . . . have, with a generous policy, extended their clemency to the great body of the people. You have acted upon a different principle . . . We desire that you will mitigate, in practice, the stringent severity of the decree of confiscation you have issued against the landowners of Oude. We desire

to see British authority in India rest upon the willing obedience of a contented people. There cannot be contentment where there is general confiscation. Government cannot long be maintained by any force in a country where the whole is rendered hostile by a sense of wrong; and if it were possible so to maintain it, it would not be a consummation to be desired.[55]

The dispatch was leaked at home before it reached Canning, and the embarrassed government was attacked on all sides for undermining him. Ellenborough resigned on 10 May in order to avert the fall of Derby's ministry, writing on the same day to the queen to tender his resignation, but also to explain that he had intended to make it 'unmistakably evident to the Governor as well as to the governed in India that your Majesty was resolved to temper Justice with Clemency, and would not sanction any measure which did not seem to conduce to the establishment of permanent peace'.[56] Ellenborough's honourable resignation did not stop Palmerston from planning a motion of censure which might easily bring down Derby's minority government. His colleague Edward Cardwell was tasked with bringing the censure motion in the House of Commons, which he did on Thursday, 13 May, and Lord Shaftesbury brought it in the House of Lords on 14 May.

Derby and Disraeli thought their number was up. The following week was Epsom week, and they did not expect to survive it. On Sunday, 16 May Lord Derby told the queen and Prince Albert that he expected the censure debate to last another week and that he would be 'beaten by from 15 to 35 votes'.[57] The newspapers mainly predicted defeat on the return from the Derby but Disraeli was able to report triumphantly to the queen on Friday, 21 May that the motion had been withdrawn. The opposition was, as ever, disunited, despite the so-called 'Cambridge House Plot', a meeting of opposition MPs held by Palmerston at his London residence on Piccadilly on the Friday before the Derby in an attempt to rally enough support for him to form a government if asked. For the debate on 21 May, as Disraeli reported to the queen, the House of Commons was full; 620 members were present and 'it was supposed we sh[oul]d have divided at 3 o'c[loc]k in the morning'. 'Very great excitement; when there occurred a scene perhaps unprecedented in Parl[ia]m[en]t.' One after another, opposition members got up to ask Cardwell to withdraw his resolution; Cardwell and Palmerston retired from the chamber, then Palmerston reappeared, 'embarrassed, with a faint smile', and announced the withdrawal of the motion of censure. 'It has revealed complete anarchy in the ranks' of the opposition, Disraeli declared.[58] He described the scene with gleeful hyperbole a few days later when speaking at a public dinner given for him at Slough in his Buckinghamshire constituency. There he compared the collapse of the previously confident opposition to an earthquake which started with 'a rumbling murmur', then a groan, a shriek, 'a sound of distant thunder', 'a rent, a fissure in the ground, and then a village disappeared, then a tall tower toppled down, and the whole of the Opposition benches became one great dissolving view of anarchy'.[59]

Even Derby, described by Disraeli in his reminiscences as a man without imagination,[60] was moved to use a dramatic metaphor in his own unusually loquacious account to the queen on Sunday, 23 May:

> Your Majesty can hardly be expected to estimate, at a distance from the immediate scene of action, the effect of the event of that evening. It was the utter explosion of a well-constructed mine, under the feet, not of the assailed, but of the assailants; and the effect has been the greater from the immense attendance in London of Members of the House of Commons. No effort had been spared. Lord Castlerosse, only just married, had been sent for from Italy – but Lord Derby hopes that he had not been induced to come – for nothing. It is said that of the 654 Members of whom the House is composed, 626 were actually in London. The Government could rely on 304 to 308, and the whole question turned on the absence, or the conversion, of a small number of 'Liberal' Members.[61]

After this excitement, Disraeli and Derby patiently steered their India Bill through parliament. They had seen off the two 'Artful Dodgers', Palmerston and Russell, who had looked as if they would bury their differences and unite to bring down the government as soon as an opportunity arose.[62] Disraeli wrote to Sarah Brydges Willyams, an elderly friend and later benefactor, of his relief and pleasure at the passing of the danger. He and Derby already had experience of short-lived power; their minority administration of 1852 had been even more precarious than this one, falling after only a few months.[63] Now, as he told Mrs Brydges Willyams, 'the country is with us'. Not only was his April 1858 budget a 'complete success', as he boasted to the queen at the time,[64] but he and Derby had survived a very close call over India. 'Never was a party in such a humiliating plight, as the great Whig Coalition', he exulted, one 'that was to have devoured Her Majesty's Government, as an ogre does a child.'[65]

As well as the public, a large part of the press supported the Derby–Disraeli government, with many commentators expressing surprise both at the unexpected co-operation between the aristocrat, the fourteenth of his noble line, and the parvenu, and at their success in pushing through a number of important reforms despite their precarious position. Though Disraeli was often ridiculed for his flamboyance in dress, manner, and speech, his hard work and cleverness won him praise, especially for guiding the India Bill to completion, for his widely acclaimed budget, and for his swift management of the bill to clean up the Thames. In July 1858 the monthly literary journal *Bentley's Miscellany* compared Disraeli favourably to his predecessor, the Whig George Cornewall Lewis, 'whose soporific periods emptied the House of all who were not too sleepy to rise'. It praised 'Mr Disraeli, the writer, the eloquent debater, the thorough man of business, whose genius, courage, sagacity, and aptitude have placed him in the foremost rank of modern politicians'.[66]

His speeches were certainly the opposite of soporific. In the speech of 26 May to the Conservative electors of Slough in his constituency, in addition to dramatically retelling the story of the collapse of the Cardwell censure motion, he replied with relish to the toast to 'Her Majesty's Ministers' by going on the attack against the opposition. He told the audience, to cheers and laughter, that his government, on coming into power after the unexpected fall of Palmerston's ministry in February, had been told that they 'were a weak government, and had done nothing'. 'Why, they had vindicated the honour of England – they had preserved peace'; they had made up 'an immense deficiency in the finances, and reduced taxation'. They had 'laid down principles for the reconstruction of the

Indian Empire which England approved, which Europe admired, and which, if acted upon', would enhance 'the greatness and glory of their country'. All this had been achieved in three short months and against an unscrupulous opposition, for there existed 'at this moment that which has not existed in England since the days of Charles II', namely 'a cabal which has no other object but to upset the Government of the Queen, and to obtain its own ends in a manner the most reckless but the most determined'.[67] Disraeli here rehearsed the ill-fated 'Cambridge House Plot' which only a week earlier he and Derby had feared would force their resignation.

So outrageous were his claims that the opposition – foolishly – took the matter up in parliament. On 30 May Lord John Russell told the House of Commons that the country was by no means in a poor state when Derby took over, and the following day Lord Palmerston attacked the government as 'factious'. Disraeli outperformed both these formidable speakers. He concentrated on Palmerston's objection to his making his claims in a public speech. 'The noble Lord is quite horrified that I should have spoken in a booth on matters of State policy.' Did Palmerston think that his own way of doing parliamentary business over a drink at his club was more appropriate? That 'special announcements on matters of State . . . should be at a carousel in a club-room . . . in what is styled (though not by me) an inebriated assembly'?[68] In the House of Lords on 31 May Lord Clarendon announced that he intended to bring up the Slough speech in the house the following day, with particular reference to remarks made about himself when he had been in office. Lord Derby's reply shows that he could learn impudence from his irrepressible colleague; he raised a laugh by thanking Lord Clarendon for giving notice of his intention, 'for I shall have an opportunity of reading before to-morrow evening my right hon. friend's speech'.[69] When the matter was discussed on 1 June Derby declared Disraeli's Slough speech to be amusing and entertaining, and truthful too. It simply brought back to him 'the matchless scene' in parliament on the day the motion of censure collapsed, a scene which he would remember till the last day of his life.[70]

In the ongoing tug of war between the two best parliamentary insulters, Disraeli and Palmerston, Disraeli won this battle. He had learned how to turn Palmerston's haughty put-downs back on to him. When Palmerston accused him of vaunting ambition and hypocrisy, Disraeli proved that these adjectives fitted his older, more experienced, aristocratic opponent like a glove.[71] A reluctantly admiring Lord John Russell told the American visitor John Motley at a breakfast party on Tuesday, 1 June that at Slough Disraeli had 'delivered to the farmers and graziers and gentlemen there assembled one of the cleverest, wittiest, most mendacious, most audacious, most besotted speeches that was ever made'.[72]

Disraeli's success as a politician came to him relatively late. Up to now he had been better known as the author of striking, rhetorically ornate novels, including *Sybil, or the Two Nations*, published in 1845 as a rallying cry for the 'Young England' movement with which he was associated, a call for a re-energised Toryism which would attempt to resolve the problems of poverty and working-class despair associated with rapid industrialisation. In the novel the author steps out from the story on several occasions to give his view of the state of the nation and the inadequacy of the day's Tory government, led by Sir Robert Peel. Disraeli was himself a Tory MP at the time, but opposed Peel, whom he would help to bring down the following year, partly out of pique at not having been given a government post. In *Sybil*, as in his parliamentary speeches, he turned disloyalty to his leader into a bold claim on the moral high ground of a better, more compassionate conservatism. An example comes in the middle of the novel:

> In a parliamentary sense, that great party [the Tory party] has ceased to exist; but I will believe it still lives in the thought and sentiment and consecrated memory of the English nation. It has its origin in great principles and in noble instincts; it sympathises with the lowly, it looks up to the Most High . . . Even now it is not dead, but sleepeth; and in an age of political materialism, of confused purposes and perplexed intelligence, that aspires only to wealth because it has faith in no other accomplishment, as men rifle cargoes on the verge of a shipwreck, Toryism will yet rise from the tomb . . . to bring back strength to the Crown, liberty to the Subject, and to announce that power has only one duty – to secure the social welfare of the PEOPLE.[73]

His speeches in the House of Commons were like this too. Yet, divisive and risk-taking though he was, he gained both power and respect during the early summer of 1858, his first real chance to flourish as a minister and to show the qualities which would eventually see him become a successful prime minister in 1868, aged sixty-three. Like Dickens, he dazzled with his verbal energy, his ambition and determination. Like Dickens, as a young man he dressed in dandyish clothes, wore his curly hair long, and exuded a confidence which disguised an unpromising background. Like Dickens, he did not go to university; though more securely middle class than Dickens – who suffered from the ignominy of his father's short stay in debtor's prison when he was a child – Disraeli, the son of the respected scholar Isaac D'Israeli, faced casual as well as vituperative anti-Semitism, such as *Punch*'s frequent representation of him as Fagin.[74] While it allowed him to become an MP, the fact that he had been baptised into the Church of England as a teenager (his father having been advised by non-Jewish friends to baptise his children in order to spare them discrimination) was no security against *ad hominem* attacks.

Disraeli's response to his Jewishness was to claim, falsely, an exotic and romantic family history of Sephardic aristocracy, and to introduce in his novels the Jewish character Sidonia, an idealistic, if sarcastic, creation modelled on his author. At the same time, he took every opportunity to praise true English aristocracy; like Carlyle in his hugely influential study of the ills of contemporary society, *Past and Present* (1843), Disraeli idealised the medieval past for the benevolent patriarchy of the upper class.

Not only was Disraeli – unlike Derby (or Palmerston, or Lord John Russell) – not born with a silver spoon in his mouth, he had to fight hard to gain entrance to public life. It took him many attempts during the 1830s to get into parliament. He succeeded in 1837 through the patronage of the ageing roué Lord Lyndhurst and the woman they shared, Lady Henrietta Sykes. He took risks, such as lying in parliament when he knew he might be found out, telling the House of Commons in a debate in May 1846 that he, Disraeli, had never asked Peel for a job, when Peel had a letter from him written in 1841 doing exactly that. Peel was too gentlemanly to expose his adversary and colleague, and Disraeli got away with it. Equally daringly, he lived in a constant state of debt, despite marrying in

1839 a wealthy widow twelve years his senior, who paid off those debts he chose to tell her about. Disraeli was always on the edge of disaster, on the verge of being found out. Since 1848 he had owed £25,000 (well over £1 million in today's money) to the family of Lord George Bentinck, with whom he was closely associated in parliament; it had helped pay for his great country house, Hughenden Manor. George's elder brother called in the loan suddenly in June 1857, and Disraeli, not for the first or last time, resorted to moneylenders.[75] He was known in certain circles to have enjoyed homosexual relationships, usually with young aristocrats; indeed, many of his novels contained risqué scenes and the semi-obscured vocabulary of homosexuality, with references to 'Greek' love, to Hyacinth, beloved of Apollo in Greek myth, to dandies and effeminate-looking boys. In the vital summer of 1858 he was called a sodomite repeatedly in the letters, private and printed, of Rosina Bulwer Lytton, his friend Sir Edward Bulwer Lytton's estranged wife.[76]

While Dickens tried that summer, not altogether successfully, to protect his reputation as a respectable writer, social critic, husband, and father, Disraeli – just as much in the public eye as Dickens – continued to act recklessly with regard to money, which was still mysteriously lacking, despite his government position, his wife's fortune, and repeated help from friends. As for his dandyism, like Dickens he had toned that down, though he still wore his hair in ringlets, and his wife Mary Anne regularly dyed it black for him.[77] Still, he was not quite such a vision as that described by an American journalist who knew him in the 1830s. Nathaniel Parker Willis, having met Disraeli in various upper-class salons in London, told his reading public in 1852 about the 'gorgeous gold flowers' on the younger Disraeli's 'splendidly embroidered waistcoat', his 'patent leather pumps', and 'a quantity of chains about his neck', all of which made him 'rather a conspicuous object':

He is lividly pale, and but for the energy of his action and the strength of his lungs, would seem a victim to consumption. His eye is black as Erebus, and has the most mocking and lying-in-wait sort of expression conceivable. His mouth is alive with a kind of working and impatient nervousness, and when he has burst forth, as he does constantly, with a particularly successful cataract of expression, it assumes a curl of triumphant scorn that would be worthy of a Mephistopheles.[78]

Descriptions of his exotic appearance in his twenties and thirties abound. He was seen wearing purple trousers with a scarlet waistcoat and white gloves with several rings worn on the outside, or he sported 'fancy-pattern pantaloons' with 'glittering chains' and a 'dark bottle-green frock-coat'.[79] In 1858 he was still known, by acquaintances and strangers alike, as a dandy and an attention-seeker. On 5 May 1858 the Russian novelist Ivan Turgenev attended a dinner at the Freemasons' Hall in Covent Garden, in aid of the Royal Literary Fund, which gave money to impoverished writers and their families. Turgenev described the occasion in an article in a Russian journal in January 1859. He wrote that while Lord Palmerston, who presided at the dinner, looked elegant and aristocratic, Disraeli (who was not at this dinner, but whom Turgenev saw elsewhere on the London circuit) looked like a 'performer and popinjay'.[80]

Yet somehow, in spite of his Jewishness, his eccentricities, and the disreputable aspects of his career and private life, Disraeli managed to thrive in 1858. He arrived properly on the public stage, succeeded, against the odds, in persuading Lord Derby, Queen Victoria, and Prince Albert of his value, and worked harder than anyone to get important reforming legislation through two hostile Houses of Parliament.

Marriage mischief

One piece of legislation for which Disraeli was not responsible, and in which he had no personal interest, was the Divorce Act, which Palmerston's government had pushed through the previous year and which was now being tested in suits brought before the new Divorce Court during the spring and early summer of 1858. Though he was not always a faithful husband, Disraeli was happily married to his Mary Anne, defending her against those who found her silly and vulgar, prone to indiscreet remarks. She was as flamboyant in her dress as he was; she wore pink satin and lots of diamonds at the age of nearly fifty, and was described by her friend Charlotte de Rothschild in the 1860s, when she was over seventy, as wearing a wig 'adorned with sky blue velvet folds and gold butterflies'.[81] In 1871, when she was almost seventy-nine, she appeared in 'youthful muslins, profusely decorated with blue and yellow ribbons', while Disraeli, himself now aged sixty-six, appeared in 'a suit of pearl grey, a soft hat, a new set of teeth and a new collection of curls'.[82] The Disraelis made a devoted couple.

Less devoted couples presented petitions for divorce in the new court from 16 January, but because the early cases brought under the new act were often continuations of petitions previously being heard in the now defunct Court of Arches, or required the judges to send them away to rethink their suit, and because it was agreed on all hands that the judges in the new court would be engaged initially in 'setting principles and forming a practice', as *The Times* put it on 12 January 1858, the first cases to be fully tried and decided under the new act did not reach their conclusions until May of that year.[83] The three judges appointed to sit in the court were the improbably named Sir Cresswell Cresswell, a bachelor of sixty-four, cautious and occasionally irascible, but fair-minded and respected, who presided over the court until his death in 1863; Sir William Wightman, a married man of seventy-two; and the chief justice of the Court of Common Pleas, Sir Alexander Cockburn, the third-highest-ranked judge in England. He was fifty-five, a bachelor like Cresswell, but unlike his colleague he was well known as a limelight-loving socialite and was the father of two illegitimate children in their teens.[84] It is not recorded that Cockburn felt embarrassment about deciding on the sexual morality of the individuals who came before the court, any more than did many of those MPs and peers with interesting private lives who had spoken loudly, at length, and in great heat in the divorce debates of the parliamentary session of 1857. Cresswell, on the other hand, was noted for his even-handedness towards women and for the seriousness with which he took his job; he called in a jury when he felt it necessary, and in his six years in the post oversaw more than a thousand cases in the Divorce Court in Westminster Hall.[85]

A landmark case was that of *Tomkins v. Tomkins*, which was decided on Tuesday, 4 May 1858. The suit was brought by the wife, who had to prove not only adultery, but also cruelty. Her husband, a potato salesman in Farringdon market, beat her, and also had a mistress. Lord Cresswell told the court that this was the first time he had sworn in a jury to hear the case with him. The jury found in favour of the wife and a judicial separation was granted. This was a fine example of the progressive nature of the new act. Since the petitioner was both a woman and a member of the working class, she could only now under the new law hope to gain a divorce. The spectators in court seemed to recognise this; they burst into applause when the verdict was given.[86] Suits now began to be granted in numbers. The newspapers reported on them, and most welcomed the speed and justice with which they were decided, whether brought by husbands or wives. The *Manchester Times* of Saturday, 15 May noted that most of the cases heard so far had been undefended and therefore speedily resolved, and that 'already several injured wives have come forward to obtain the redress to which they were obviously entitled'.[87]

By the end of the year 244 cases had been heard, and the general opinion, at least as represented in newspapers of every political hue, was voiced early on that the new law was a roaring success.[88] The lord chief justice, Lord Campbell, certainly thought so. The *Era* of Sunday, 16 May reported him stating, after the successful conclusion of eight cases in two days on 11 May, that these cases were evidence of the efficiency of the new law. Most had concerned people in a 'humble station in life', who would have stood no chance of gaining relief under the old expensive, lengthy system; the new act offered the same remedy to the poor as to the rich.[89]

Anyone reading a newspaper in the middle of May would find side by side reports from the Divorce Court, stories about the Derby, praise for Dickens's Thursday evening readings, speculation and daily updating of the ministerial crisis over the India Bill, and discussion of the cabinet reshuffle which was forced on Lord Derby by Ellenborough's resignation. On 13 May, three days after the resignation, *The Times* declared that Derby's son Lord Stanley would replace Ellenborough as president of the Board of Control, while Sir Edward Bulwer Lytton was likely to be made colonial secretary, 'the difficulty of securing his return for Hertfordshire being averted by his advancement to the Peerage'.[90] The problem alluded to here was that in order to take up a cabinet place, Bulwer Lytton would have to stand for re-election in his constituency, and, as *The Times* said, he could not be at all sure of succeeding, having won his seat only narrowly in 1852.[91] Hence the suggestion that he might be made a peer and sit in the House of Lords instead of the Commons. As the newspaper knew (Disraeli was in the habit of sending political news in advance to the editor John Delane in letters marked 'confidential'[92]), Bulwer Lytton had already been offered the same cabinet post when Lord Derby took office at the end of February, but had refused unless it was accompanied by a peerage. Derby had been annoyed at this, telling Disraeli on 25 February that he would not give in – 'If he is to be of *any* use, it must be in the H. of Commons' – and asking Disraeli to 'call on our refractory friend, and get him straight again'.[93] Disraeli tried, but Bulwer Lytton again refused, to his friend's annoyance.[94] When the question arose again in May, Bulwer Lytton was prevailed upon to accept the post, thus bringing down on himself, not for the first time, the wrath of his estranged wife Rosina. Disraeli did not escape unscathed by Rosina's righteous venom. Mingling with news in the papers every day about marriage and divorce were reports of abuses of the lunatic asylum system by spouses with a grievance, abetted by unscrupulous doctors willing to sign certificates of insanity for money. Sensational headlines on these topics appeared all summer, and, to Disraeli's chagrin and discomfort, the Lyttons supplied a large proportion of them.

The marriage between Bulwer Lytton and Rosina Wheeler, contracted in 1827, was a disaster from the start. Both were excitable and unstable; he was dependent financially and emotionally on a bullying mother, while she was the socially and sexually reckless daughter of an impoverished Irish upper-class family. They married against the wishes of both families, and Bulwer, as he was then known, had his generous allowance cut off by his furious mother. That did not stop the young couple from setting up house in Mayfair in 1830 and living well beyond their means.[95] He had affairs with both men and women and neglected his wife and their two unfortunate children, Emily and Robert. She responded by taking lovers of her own, and by 1836 the pair were not only separated but implacable enemies. Both husband and wife were unstoppable self-publicists. Bulwer wrote novels of aristocracy and romance in the short-lived genre known as the 'silver-fork school' of fiction. In 1828 his second effort, *Pelham, or, The Adventures of a Gentleman*, the story of an aristocratic dandy, became a bestseller: the protagonist Henry Pelham's penchant for wearing black for dinner gave rise to the fashion for evening dress – the 'dinner jacket' – which persists today. The novel aroused the ire of Thomas Carlyle, who published *Sartor Resartus* in 1833–4 in part to counteract the irresponsible and uncaring dandyism of the English aristocracy as represented in Bulwer's novel.

Rosina also wrote novels, though she gained only infamy, not fame, from her writings. In them she poured out, at length, her grievances against a husband who had neglected and on at least one occasion beaten her, and who, on separating, took advantage of the law to keep her children from her. Their daughter Emily died in 1848 aged nineteen, without her mother being able to see her before her death; thereafter Rosina lobbied politicians, lawyers, and the general reading public in letters, pamphlets, and autobiographical novels drawing attention to the injustice of the law towards women. Unlike Caroline Norton, however, Rosina cared little for the plight of others or for the woman question in principle; all her considerable powers of verbal insult went into advertising her own case and attacking her husband, along with his many friends, from Dickens to Disraeli and other Conservative politicians.

There is no doubt that Bulwer Lytton was a monstrous husband and father, and there is no doubt, either, that Rosina was obsessed to the point of insanity in her pursuit of him. In the spring of 1858 she was preparing to bring out her novel, *The World and his Wife: or, A Person of Consequence*, a lengthy story in three volumes, published at the end of May, with a minimal plot and an emphasis on lampooning the aristocracy, in particular in the person of Sir Hubert de Vere, a not even thinly veiled portrait of her hated husband. This preposterous figure is introduced in the second chapter, with Rosina alluding to her husband's extreme pride in his ability to trace his provenance to the time of William the Conqueror and in his family name; after his mother's death in 1843 he had added her surname Lytton to his previous name Edward Lytton Bulwer, thus becoming, to the amusement of his many hostile critics, Edward George Earle Lytton Bulwer Lytton. Other easy targets for Rosina were his ambition to reach even greater heights in the ranks of the nobility, his personal vanity, and his influence over the press, especially *The Times*:

Hubert de Vere, Earl of Portarjis, Viscount Clanhaven, and Baron Derrersley, in the peerage of the United Kingdom, a Count of the Holy Roman Empire, a Baronet of Nova Scotia, and a Knight of the Garter, was, what in England was emphatically called, a clever man; that is, he parcelled out his existence into two distinct and separate portions of small vices, and great talents; the latter were duly burnished, gilt, and emblazoned for the public service, and, unlike the apartments at Windsor, and Buckingham Palace, were open *to the public* and the newspaper press *all* the year round; while the former were thrust into a private reservoir as concerning no one but himself: a wise precaution, in general use among clever men, for . . . no man likes to subject that which he most cherishes to any severe censure.[96]

Lord Portarjis neglects his wife and laughs at the idea some people have that his friend Lord Lyncius (a portrait of Lord Lyndhurst), in promoting the new Divorce Act, had justice towards women in mind. 'As if any one cared how the deuce' women were treated, says Portarjis; 'after all, confound it, a man *has* a right to use his own wife as he pleases'.[97] Rosina, who knew that her husband was hoping for a cabinet post in Derby's new government, pestered her publisher for months in order to get the book published at the optimum time to do him harm.[98] Her most recent novel, *Very Successful!*, had been printed in the usual three volumes in 1856 with a preface bemoaning the fact that she was publishing it herself in Taunton, in Somerset, where she was then living, because she could not find a publisher in London to take it on. The reason for this was that her husband used his influence against her, and that she had no 'Fudgester' (Bulwer Lytton's friend and adviser John Forster) to support her.[99] Throughout the novel she attacks her husband and his friends; Dickens is sarcastically said to be ready to be made 'Lord Bleedingheartcourt, Lord Fleetditch, Lord Froth de Pewter', while Carlyle, not a close friend of Bulwer Lytton but a good target for her practice of insulting name-calling, is to be created 'Lord Göethecant [*sic*], Lord Haggis, Lord Ursa Major, Lord Fitz Flunkey'. Other victims are *The Times* ('The Weekly Thunderer'), Sir Janus Allpuff (Bulwer Lytton under yet another name), and Disraeli, who appears as Mr Jericho Jabber.[100]

Bulwer Lytton and Disraeli are presented as bosom buddies both in the field of literature and in politics under Lord Derby ('Lord Oakes' in reference to another famous horse race, the Oaks, inaugurated by Derby's ancestor). Their dandyism is also mocked. One character asks another 'who those two ill-looking fellows opposite to us are',

'. . . the one with black ringlets, that look as if they were made out of snakes and leeches, and the other with a head of light hair and moustaches, like a distaff gone mad, and the lines in both their faces giving one the idea of the devil having ridden rough-shod over them, and indented the hoof of every vice into them?'

'Oh! those,' laughed Mr Bouverie, 'are Mr Jericho Jabber and Sir Janus Allpuff, my Lord Oakes's two leading acrobats. Theirs is one of the chief trained bands of our Metropolitan cliques, of which what is called "society" in London has some half-dozen . . .'

'Good heavens! how can Lord Oakes think of balancing his political ladder on the chins of two such mountebanks? 'Pon my life! their hair alone is worth paying a shilling to see . . .'[101]

Jabber, described as 'our friend the *Jew d'esprit*', holds forth on the question of allowing Jews to sit in parliament, while his colleague Lord Lyncius [Lyndhurst] is one of the 'set of superannuated adulterers' in the House of Lords supporting Caroline Norton's 'hocus-pocussed emancipation', a reference to Lyndhurst's efforts to pass laws giving more freedoms to married women.[102] Rosina, though an ill-used wife herself, was fiercely hostile to Caroline Norton's campaigns, and thought all the divorce debates in 1856 and 1857 were nothing but a 'job', with no real intention on the part of parliament to give equality to women.

Rosina, after reading in *The Times* in February 1858 that Bulwer Lytton might be given a cabinet position in the Colonial Office, wrote an extraordinary letter to Lord Derby:

My Lord
　　Every one is aware that it is a matter of very little import whether the manure on the political Dunghill be labelled 'Whig' or 'Tory'[,]

'Conservative' or 'Radical' as the *one* thing needful – the amount of *corruption* is sure to be the same. The dear Whigs once had a ministry nick-named 'All the Talents'[;] yours just formed is far more appropriately named 'All the Blackguards' – Knowing that your Chancellor of the Exchequer has long since paid his *Thirty pieces of silver*[,] people only shrug their shoulders at that act of your New Farce 'The Follies of a Night' and pass on; but in appointing a Liar, a Coward, a Swindler, and a Blackguard *to* the Colonies instead of sending him to *them*! you commit at starting a blunder so ridiculous! that you will make your administration not only the contempt but the laughing stock of the world. And indeed if you would study the propensities of your loathsome Colonial Secretary, and Chancellor of the Exchequer you would make one King of Sodom, and the other King of Gomorrah, they having run the gauntlet of *every vice*.

One comfort is, that your Tickets of leave will as speedily expire *now* as they did the last time.

I remain, My Lord, with every species of contempt for you, and your gang[,] your Colonial Secretaries [*sic*] Hunted, and starving Legal Victim

Rosina Bulwer Lytton

alas![103]

It is not recorded what Derby felt on reading this fearless document, with its reference to Disraeli's debts and dubious financial dealings, and to his and Bulwer Lytton's homosexual activities, possibly with one another, as well as the swipe aimed at Derby himself and the short length of his only previous experience as prime minister.

Not content with confronting Derby, Rosina wrote a week later to his son Lord Stanley and to Lord Lyndhurst. Once more, she did not mince her words. Stanley, who was hesitating about taking a cabinet post, in part because of his distrust of Disraeli, received Rosina's congratulations on 23 February:

It is much to your credit, that you would not sit in the same cabinet with such a revolting incarnation of *every pollution* as Sir Liar Coward

Bulwer Lytton. Surely in point of utter, and shameless want of principle Disraeli! is quite enough to leaven with corruption 50 administrations, *even* in England! . . . when next My Lord Derby blasphemes in the House of Lords about 'transporting adulterers!!' (and except with the variation of Fornicators – what are *both* Houses composed of *but* adulterers?) pray let him put my Lord Lyndhurst . . . at the head of those Legions of Derby Deportees![104]

To Lyndhurst himself she wrote on the same day, reminding him of his sexually adventurous life and his advancing age (he was almost eighty-six and now completely blind):

My Lord

That a superannuated adulterer like yourself! who could not be made Lord Chancellor till your own *crim.con* [*sic*] damages in the affair of my Lady Sykes were paid! should keep the unities[,] by at the dregs of your profligate career jobbing a blasphemous swindle of a bill through Parliament for an old Messalina [i.e. a loose woman] like Mrs Norton . . . is all very natural . . . and you should remember old man, how soon you will have to appear before a Tribunal far other, than the House of Lords! where no blasphemous humbug will avail.[105]

Lyndhurst was a rake; even Disraeli described him in his reminiscences as 'notorious' for his 'susceptibility to the sex'. But he also remembered his friend's lucid mind and 'sweet disposition'.[106] In truth, Lyndhurst did contribute to the improvement of women's lot. He helped Caroline Norton with her successful attempts to change the law of infant custody in 1839, and his interventions in the long debates of 1856 and 1857 on the Divorce Bill were remarkable for their insistence on giving women parity, wherever possible, with men. He succeeded in passing an amendment to the 1857 act promoting the rights to property of divorced women.[107]

Disraeli said he knew 'three great men who rouged', namely Lyndhurst, Palmerston, and Bulwer Lytton, and the vainest of these was Bulwer Lytton.[108] Rosina was not alone in ridiculing her husband's vanity, his love of his hair, his use of make-up, and his habit of wearing corsets to improve his figure. *Fraser's Magazine* carried a cartoon of him looking in a mirror in August 1832; six years later it printed Thackeray's verbal and pictorial sketch of Bulwer Lytton as a lisping dandy sporting a fine head of hair, 'a hook nose', a pale face, a tight coat, and a wig, and introducing himself 'in a thick, gobbling kind of voice' as '*Mistaw*edwadLyttnBulwig'.[109] When Bulwer Lytton foolishly attacked Tennyson in an anonymous long poem of 1846, *The New Timon: A Romance of London*, calling him 'School-Miss Alfred' and parodying refrains from Tennyson's poem 'Mariana', Tennyson responded immediately with a poem printed in *Punch* on 28 February 1846. Entitled 'The New Timon, and the Poets', it describes Bulwer Lytton as 'the padded man – that wears the stays'. Tennyson also spoke of Bulwer Lytton putting 'three inches of cork' in his shoes, which had 'pink chamois tips to them'.[110] Disraeli, an often exasperated friend, recalled his pomposity, eccentricity, and raving ambition, especially in the spring of 1858:

> He wanted to be a popular author, a distinguished orator, & a Baronet of the Kingdom of Heaven – with Knebworth Park [Bulwer Lytton's country house] to boot! He very truly said to me on a memorable occasion, when he wanted me to make him a Peer, & I wished to make him a Secretary of State 'Remember this my dear friend; I speak to you solemnly; you are dealing now with the vainest man that perhaps ever existed.'[111]

Disraeli also noted that Bulwer Lytton, though friendly with Dickens, was 'dying all the time of jealousy & envy' of his fellow novelist.[112]

Rosina turned out spirited and antagonistic prose about Bulwer Lytton and his friends by the yard in her letters and novels. At first she believed, as she boasted to her friend Rebecca Ryves in early March 1858, that it was her intervention with Lord Derby which stopped Bulwer Lytton from being appointed to the cabinet at that time.[113] When she discovered a couple of months later that he was after all prepared to stand for re-election in his Hertfordshire constituency in order to take up the post of colonial secretary, she took her revenge in the full glare of publicity, ensuring that her story filled the newspapers. Things took an unexpected turn in June, with rumours of lunacy and a brief incarceration in the hottest days of the year, before the Lyttons receded from the headlines.

The provisions of the new divorce laws were of no use to Rosina or Edward. Neither could risk petitioning for divorce, as the considerable dirty linen of both would be revealed in court, and no judge or jury would be likely to find in favour of either.

A moment of fear about divorce assailed Dickens, however. He had long sympathised with his friend Bulwer Lytton's marital difficulties, commiserating in 1851 about Rosina, 'the misfortune of your life', when she threatened to turn up at a performance before the duke of Devonshire of Bulwer Lytton's play *Not So Bad as We Seem*, which Dickens was directing.[114] A threat to his control of his own marital arrangements came at the end of May 1858, as he was inducing Catherine to sign a separation agreement which ensured that she was looked after financially and also, importantly for him, that he would face no blame in the matter. The brief but shuddering shock took the form of a possible rebellion by Catherine's family, particularly his hated mother-in-law and her daughter, Catherine's younger sister Helen Hogarth, whom Dickens already suspected of spreading rumours.

A rapid exchange of letters between Dickens, Forster, who was acting for him in negotiating the settlement, Dickens's solicitor Frederic Ouvry, and Mark Lemon, acting for Catherine together with her solicitor, George Frederick Smith, suggests that the Hogarths were hinting that they would encourage Catherine to take Dickens to the Divorce Court. It seems unlikely that they would actually have pursued this course, since Catherine would have had to prove not only adultery but also cruelty or incest or desertion by Dickens – all of which would be difficult, not to mention distasteful to Catherine, who was no seeker of the limelight. Divorce cases depended, inevitably, on the sometimes lurid and often dubious testimony of observers – friends, servants, coachmen, hotel staff, and the like – giving details of adulterous encounters. If, as one of the rumours doing the rounds had it, Dickens's affair was with his sister-in-law Georgina Hogarth, that would legally count as incest (though of course Dickens and Georgina were not blood relations), and so could have constituted a case for divorce.

It stretches credulity, however, that the Hogarth family, no matter how angry they were at Dickens's treatment of their daughter Catherine, would go to court to point to their other daughter Georgina as the guilty party in an adulterous affair.

Nonetheless, Dickens was in such a state of anger and anxiety, writing to correspondents near and far about the 'smashing slanders' of his wicked female in-laws (Catherine's father, George Hogarth, seems to have kept as far out of the controversy as he could), that he believed them capable of fouling their own nest in this way.[115] He indicated as much to his friend Macready, telling him that the Hogarth women's 'wickedness' had led them to the idea of going to court, 'though I warned them in the strongest manner'. Catherine's aunt Helen Thomson later suggested that the family had indeed raised the possibility of taking legal action.[116] Certainly Forster, who like Dickens was inclined to melodrama, wrote urgently to Ouvry on 21 May about the need to get the Hogarths' agreement to the terms of the separation deed Dickens had drawn up 'by 3 o'clock today'. He refers to the Divorce Act as a threat to the agreement, and asks Ouvry to meet him before 3 p.m. and again between 4.30 and 5 p.m. '*with Dickens*'.[117]

However real the threat was, the danger was averted and things went relatively smoothly from then on. Catherine's father signed a legal document denying, on behalf of his family, that any of them had 'stated or insinuated that any impropriety of conduct had taken place between my daughter Georgiana [*sic*] and her Brother in Law Mr Charles Dickens'.[118] After a few more skirmishes, with Dickens insisting on his wife's family signing the statement he had drafted for them, the settlement was finalised – Catherine was to have £600 a year and unlimited access to her children – though not before Dickens had written down a particularly unkind account of Catherine's character and entrusted it to Arthur Smith, the friend who managed his public readings and who would go on his reading tour with him during the summer. Dickens sent it to Smith on 25 May, permitting him to show it to 'any one who wishes to do me right, or to any one who may have been misled into doing me wrong'.[119] Smith obviously did show the letter in certain circles, for it made a very public appearance a few months later, when the great Dickens scandal, which its subject had taken such pains to squash, reared up afresh.

While Dickens was involved in this flurry of manic activity, he was continuing his public readings at St Martin's Hall every Thursday evening, corresponding with friends, and engaging the well-known London photographer Herbert Watkins to take a photograph of him that he could send to a friend in Italy.[120] By this time the great heat of the summer had begun; *The Times* recorded 84 °F (29 °C) in the shade for Monday, 31 May.[121] Queen Victoria, who had turned thirty-nine the previous Monday, noted the change to 'beautiful weather' in her journal that week. 'Another wonderfully fine & hot day', she wrote on 31 May, adding, 'Rather vexed to hear that Sir E. Lytton *has* accepted Office!!'[122] Bulwer Lytton had that day finally taken up Derby's offer, after angling once more unsuccessfully for the desired peerage.[123] The heat was becoming a familiar topic; the *Era*, in its review on Sunday, 30 May of the Royal Academy exhibition, complained of the vast number of exhibits – between 1,100 and 1,200 paintings and nearly 260 sculptures – and of the difficulty of assessing them 'in the midst of heat and dust, and a crush of crinolines'.[124] Crinoline mania had been developing for a few years; it hit new heights – or reached new widths – in this hot summer, as *Punch* and other commentators pointed out incessantly.

Among the news at the end of the month was that Brunel and Russell's great ship, the *Great Eastern*, sometimes called the *Leviathan*, was now open to the public to visit. This 'wonder of the engineering world', as the *Era* called it, broke all records for size and capacity, but was in need of at least £200,000 to complete her fitting-out and get her ready to go to sea. Optimistically, the paper predicted commercial success for the vessel.[125] Hopes were high on several fronts. The other promising engineering feat of the year, the Atlantic Cable, underwent a rehearsal on 29 May, when a squadron left Portsmouth on an experimental trip to test the machinery in preparation for the summer's attempt at laying it and joining it in the middle of the Atlantic.[126] Derby's government had survived its crisis and looked likely to achieve some important legislation before the session ended. Disraeli was riding high in spite of his troublesome friend Bulwer Lytton, Dickens was surviving – just – the greatest crisis of his life.

Meanwhile, 20 miles away at his home in Kent, Darwin was working quietly away, writing to correspondents all over the world to compare notes on various species, studying bees' cells in his garden, and noting down the habits of rare slave-making ants. These last he spotted while on a visit to Dr Edward Lane's hydropathic establishment at Moor Park in late April and early May, and he deemed them interesting enough to include in *On the Origin of Species*.[127] The next few weeks would bring unexpected urgency to his plans for publication.

June was to be a busy month for Darwin, Dickens, and Disraeli, as the summer heat mounted, records were broken, and important decisions had to be made both on the national stage and in private studies and drawing rooms.

CHAPTER THREE

June 1858, Part I

Darwin and the pursuit of science

ON 3 JUNE 1858 Darwin wrote to his best friend, the botanist Joseph Hooker, at that time assistant director of Kew Gardens, asking his advice. He had been elected a few months earlier to the German Academy of Naturalists and was now being asked to pay for the printing of his diploma. 'I am utterly perplexed what to send', he wrote. 'Do for Heaven-sake aid me with one line soon. I do not want to give more than proper, but I am far from wanting to be shabby.'[1] Living in domestic bliss and relative seclusion in his village in Kent, steadily going on with his study of species – from books, from his own notes dating back to the *Beagle* voyage, from correspondence with other scientists – and patiently observing animal life in his own garden, he relied on his London friends for advice and support. Chief among them were Hooker and Sir Charles Lyell, Britain's leading geologist. Darwin's current study being of bees' cells, he corresponded with a number of friends and fellow scientists to compare notes and ask for help on that subject. His older brother Erasmus Alvey Darwin responded to a question about the cells' construction by sending him diagrams, and William Tegetmeier, a London teacher who shared both Darwin's interest in bees and his passion for breeding pigeons, was quizzed for advice on 5 June.[2]

Though Darwin was known and appreciated among his fellow scientists at this time, he was hardly known at all to the public at large.[3] Between 1839 and 1854 he had written or edited various volumes reporting the zoological and geological findings of the *Beagle* voyage, with particular emphasis on coral reefs, fossils, and barnacles, but these reached only a specialist readership. The secret of his achieving eventual recognition as a scientific author of originality and international significance was, in the first place, his extraordinary thoroughness, determination, and patience in carrying out his observations and studies, and, secondly, his way of attaching people to him, which was vital for a scientist who was not in daily face-to-face contact with fellow researchers. His letters give abundant evidence of his charm as a friend and colleague. He had a natural gift for flattering his correspondents while assiduously extracting information from them, and it is clear from the number of scientific men who called him their friend that he was as generous towards them as he expected them to be towards him in the matter of sharing information and insights. He took enormous time and trouble over his chosen life's work, and was a fine communicator of his curiosity, his excitement, his disappointments, his puzzlement, and sometimes his amusement at the results he arrived at and the route taken to get there. A light-hearted example comes in a letter written from the Isle of Wight in August 1858 to Hooker, advising his friend to take his holiday somewhere on the coast:

> If you go to Broadstairs, when there is a strong wind from [the] coast of France & fine dry warm weather, look out & you will *probably* (!) see thistleseeds blown across the channel. The other day, I saw one blown right inland, & then in a few minutes a second & then a third; so I said to myself God bless me how many thistles there must be in France; & I wrote a letter in imagination to you. But I then looked at *low* clouds & noticed that they were not coming inland, so I feared a screw was loose, I then walked beyond a headland & found the wind parallel to coast, & on this very headland a noble bed of thistles, which by very wide eddy were blown far out to sea & then came right in at right angle to shore! One day such a number of insects were washed up by tide, & I brought to life 13 species of Coleoptera [beetles]; not that I suppose

these came from France. But do you watch for thistle seed, as you saunter along the coast.[4]

Hooker and Darwin had met as young men in 1839 and had become friends; it was to Hooker that Darwin first divulged in 1844 his conviction, in defiance of scientific and religious orthodoxy, that species were not immutable, and created so by God. 'At last gleams of light have come', he wrote, 'and I am almost convinced (quite contrary to [the] opinion I started with) that species are not (it is like committing a murder) immutable.'[5] The work he was still pursuing in 1858 as he toiled towards eventual publication was the painstaking checking and working out of his theory that species changed through time, and that they did so by means of natural selection. Asa Gray, professor of botany at Harvard University, was the recipient of a paper he wrote in September 1857 entitled 'Natural Selection'.[6] This was to be Darwin's distinctive contribution to species theory, as he knew, but he was not yet ready to divulge it to the public at large.

Darwin's correspondents lived and worked all over the world. In the first couple of months of 1858 alone, Darwin begged for information about bees, ants, and various plant species from correspondents in Ceylon (George Thwaites, curator of the Botanic Garden of Ceylon), Central Africa (William Baikie, a naval surgeon exploring the River Niger), America (Asa Gray), as well as experts in the natural history departments of the British Museum.[7] His poor health, an innate diffidence, his hatred of living in London and dislike of socialising combined to keep him in Down, where he relied on friends to send him the information he would otherwise have to seek by undertaking more exploratory voyages to distant places or working in a laboratory. Hooker regularly sent parcels of books from the Linnaean Society library and botanic samples from Kew to his friend in Kent. According to Hooker's early biographer, Leonard Huxley (son of Thomas Henry Huxley), parcels from Kew generally went 'to the Nag's Head in Borough [near London Bridge railway station], the head-quarters of the Down carrier', though 'in the case of a rare orchid in flower, Parslow, the immemorial butler, would travel to Kew and carry it back in his own safe hands'.[8] Items might also travel by train, as Down was close to the town of Bromley, which was soon served by two railway companies from London; one of them, the Crystal Palace and West End Railway, opened on 3 May 1858, and the other, the Mid-Kent Railway, operated to and from London Bridge from 5 July.[9] As for Darwin's correspondence, it was dispatched with impressive frequency. According to the local monthly newspaper, the *Bromley Record*, which was launched on 1 June 1858, mail went in both directions between Bromley and London four times every weekday and once on Sundays.[10]

Darwin's life of study was smoothed by the presence of his loving wife Emma and eight children, and by his servants, including Parslow the butler, who lived with the family from 1839 to 1876. Also in the household were Mrs Davies the cook, successive governesses, footmen, coachmen, and various maids and boys who helped with the large house and surrounding land, where cows and chickens were reared. Since much of Darwin's work consisted of experimenting on seeds and worms in his garden, and on exotic plants in his greenhouse, he employed two gardeners, William Brooks and Henry Lettington, who spent their whole working lives at Down House.[11]

With all this support and, thanks to inherited family money, no need to earn a living, Darwin knew he was lucky in comparison with some of his younger colleagues. Thomas Henry Huxley, by contrast, had to write scientific columns in the press and give lectures in various institutions across London while he fought for one of the few permanent scientific posts available, and was obliged to wait eight years before he could afford in 1855 to bring his fiancée over from Australia, where he had met her on his own youthful voyage, in his case on the *Rattlesnake*, which set out on a four-year trip in December 1846 to study the Great Barrier Reef.[12] Huxley was thirty-three to Darwin's forty-nine in the summer of 1858; though he, too, became famous, he continued to teach and examine at various institutions as well as writing scientific papers and journalism, and never became financially secure. Darwin, in his autobiography, praised Huxley's mind – 'as quick as a flash of lightning and as sharp as a razor' – and regretted that his friend had not enjoyed the leisure to write more: 'Much splendid work he has done in Zoology', he wrote, but he would have done much more if his time had not been 'so largely consumed by official and literary work', by which Darwin meant editing and writing for periodicals.[13]

The geologist Sir Charles Lyell, now aged sixty and living a celebrated and comfortable life, mixing with aristocracy and royalty (he was 'very fond of society, especially of eminent men, and of persons high in rank', Darwin noted in his autobiography[14]), also observed with regret Huxley's prodigious work rate. He wrote to Darwin in 1863:

> If he had leisure like you and me; – and the vigour and logic of the lectures, and his address to the Geological Society, and half a dozen other recent works (letters to the 'Times' on Darwin, &c.), been all in one book, what a position he would occupy! I entreated him not to undertake the 'Natural History Review' before it began. The responsibility all falls on the man of chief energy and talent; it is a quarterly mischief, and will end in knocking him up.[15]

Lyell's prediction came true in 1873, when Huxley suffered a breakdown from overwork. The Darwins helped by raising money to allow him to take some time off and by looking after the Huxley children at Down while he recuperated in the Auvergne.[16]

The precariousness of a life in science is illustrated not only by Huxley's example, but also by that of another young scientist working in the field of evolution, Alfred Russel Wallace, aged thirty-five in 1858. Though both Huxley and Wallace were born to middle-class parents, Huxley's father being a maths teacher and Wallace's a solicitor, neither family had enough money to support their son through university. Huxley got his education in science and medicine by taking classes here and there, while earning money as he could; he won scholarships and medals at the University of London, but after spending four years as an assistant surgeon on the *Rattlesnake* as it surveyed the Great Barrier Reef and New Guinea, he sailed home in 1850, engaged but unable to marry, owing £100, and not knowing what to do next. Despite being elected a fellow of the Royal Society in 1851 – the youngest candidate in his year – he could not obtain either a university post or a government grant for more research.[17]

Wallace's father lost money through imprudent investments, and Alfred had to leave school at thirteen to join his older brother in learning the surveying trade in London. He educated himself by reading books and attending evening lectures for working men, some of them politically and religiously radical, at the Hall of Science near Tottenham Court Road.[18] In 1848, having read Darwin's *Journal* of his researches on the *Beagle* and Robert Chambers's *Vestiges of Creation*, he was encouraged to set off with an entomologist friend, Henry Bates, to sail down the Amazon, returning four years later with a huge collection of insects and butterflies. (Wallace's younger brother Herbert had joined them in 1849 only to die of yellow fever in Brazil.[19]) He earned a modest living by sending and bringing home specimens to one of London's specialist scientific agents, Samuel Stevens, who sold them to museums and wealthy private collectors. Wallace met and admired Huxley at evening meetings of the Zoological Society, where he was struck by the fact that Huxley was two years his junior and yet already had a 'wonderful power of making a difficult and rather complex subject perfectly intelligible and extremely interesting to persons who, like myself, were absolutely ignorant' of the subject under discussion, in this case the liver of a zebra which had died in London Zoo.[20]

In 1854, having published an account of his and Bates's travels on the Amazon, he was given a grant by the Royal Geographical Society to sail to Singapore and on to the Malay Archipelago, where he spent the next eight years travelling between the numerous islands, observing and collecting specimens to send back to Stevens, who sold them and posted funds back to Wallace to allow him to extend his stay. As Darwin did with reference to his experience on the *Beagle*, so Wallace described his eight years of 'wandering' in Malaysia as 'the central and controlling incident of my life'. Though he took Charles Allen, a 16-year-old boy from London, with him, after eighteen months he was alone, studying and describing in his journals, letters, and scientific papers, often for the first time, hundreds of species of beetles, insects and birds, orang-utan skins and skeletons, and – most exotic and prized of all – 'the rare red bird of paradise'. He traversed the sea between islands, covering 14,000 miles in locally built boats, often seasick; he was sometimes seriously short of food; he caught fevers and sweated them out in solitary home-made huts, dosing himself with quinine got from government doctors in Singapore and elsewhere.[21] During his time in Malaysia he collected over 100,000 specimens of plants and animals, and with his discovery that animal species differed on either side of an invisible oceanic line within the Malay Archipelago, he made an early contribution to zoogeography. This boundary was named the Wallace Line by Huxley in 1868.[22]

Wallace met some European travellers and local government officials from time to time. He told his friend Bates in a letter of 4 January 1858 that he had spent twenty days collecting in Amboyna, where he talked to entomologists and doctors, a German collector, and a Hungarian 'who studied a year in the Vienna Museum'.[23] Three weeks later he wrote to Bates from Ternate, cheerfully saying that he planned 'to stay in this place 2 or 3 years, as it is the centre of a most interesting & unknown region'. He added that a Dutch steamer arrived once a month bringing 'letters from England in about 10 weeks which makes the place convenient & there are plenty of small schooners & native Prows by which the surrounding islands can be visited'.[24] To his agent Stevens he had written in May 1857 in high spirits from the Arru Islands. He had found some glorious birds of paradise, which he intended to mount properly, unlike the specimens mounted by the locals, which were 'miserable' and not indicative of the birds' 'true attitude when displaying their plumes'. In a rare moment of boasting, he added:

> I believe I am the only Englishman who has ever shot and skinned (and ate) birds of Paradise, and the first European who has done so alive, and at his own risk and expense: and I deserve to reap the reward, if any reward is ever to be reaped by the exploring collector . . . I am now, and have been a whole month, confined to the house, owing to inflammation and sores on the legs, produced by hosts of insect bites. Confinement has brought on an attack of fever, which I am now getting over. My insect collecting has suffered dreadfully by this loss of time.[25]

Though Darwin had suffered illness and discomfort on his own voyage of discovery as a young man, he expressed frank admiration of Wallace's sticking power in his often solitary existence in remote regions full of dangers, from unseaworthy vessels to wild creatures, severe deprivation of food and water, and malarial fevers. The two men were not close

acquaintances, but each knew the other's published papers and they corresponded from time to time. While in Sarawak near the beginning of his
eight-year sojourn Wallace wrote an article which, as he says in his autobiography, formed his first contribution to the question of the origin of
species. He sent it to the *Annals and Magazine of Natural History*, where it
appeared in September 1855. With characteristic scrupulousness and lack
of egotism, Wallace adds in his memoir:

> Its title was 'On the Law which has regulated the Introduction of New
> Species', which law was briefly stated (at the end) as follows: '*Every
> species has come into existence coincident both in space and time with a
> pre-existing closely-allied species.*' This clearly pointed to some kind of
> evolution. It suggested the *when* and the *where* of its occurrence, and
> that it could only be through natural generation, as was also suggested
> in the 'Vestiges' [by Chambers]; but the *how* was still a secret only to be
> penetrated some years later.[26]

Darwin read and annotated Wallace's 1855 paper, and, knowing that
Wallace was on his travels, included him in a long list of colleagues working
abroad in India, Antigua, Panama, Natal, the Cape of Good Hope, Hong
Kong, The Gambia, Tunis, South America, Angola, and Jamaica from
whom he requested 'Pigeon and Poultry Skins'.[27] He wrote to Wallace on
1 May 1857, acknowledging that from reading Wallace's paper he could
'plainly see that we have thought much alike & to a certain extent have
come to similar conclusions'. He continued with a feeling remark: 'I
daresay that you will agree with me that it is very rare to find oneself
agreeing pretty closely with any theoretical paper; for it is lamentable
how each man draws his own different conclusions from the very
same fact.'[28]

What Darwin has in mind here is the to him disappointing fact that
even his best friend Hooker did not yet share his increasing certainty that
natural selection was the mechanism (the *how*, in Wallace's word) of evolution, let alone Lyell, who never quite accepted it. Nor did the doyen of
British natural history Richard Owen, nor Darwin's old teacher at
Cambridge, the geology professor Adam Sedgwick (who on reading *On the*

Origin of Species was aghast at the consequences for religious belief), nor, beyond these scientific great men, a multitude of readers of Darwin's work when it was finally published for the general public. Here in his letter to Wallace he recognises a kindred spirit and expresses his gratitude. At the same time, we can perhaps detect some anxiety in Darwin that his theory, already fully worked out in his mind but not yet presented in its fullness to the world, might just have been 'discovered' independently by another. And that this other might well be the young scientific explorer with only a small amount of published work to his credit so far, Alfred Russel Wallace. For Darwin follows his remark allying himself with Wallace against the rest with a careful observation – one which he makes to a number of his correspondents at around this time – that he has been working on this particular question for a long time: 'This summer will make the 20th year (!) since I opened my first note-book, on the question how & in what way do species & varieties differ from each other. I am now preparing my work for publication, but I find the subject so very large, that though I have written many chapters, I do not suppose I shall go to press for two years.'[29] Wallace, having presumably received Darwin's letter some time in August 1857, replied on 27 September, answering Darwin's question about how long he intended to stay in the Malay Archipelago and expressing his pleasure at Darwin's agreement with his paper, which is, he says, only a preliminary piece; he envisages having to spend much time on his return, doing research 'in English libraries & collections'.[30]

Darwin replied on 22 December 1857, reassuring Wallace that his paper had not been ignored by the scientific community at home; 'two very good men', Lyell and Edward Blyth at Calcutta, had drawn Darwin's attention to it. He hopes to read Wallace's more recent notes on the distribution of animals in the Arru Islands, though he thinks Wallace is 'inclined to go *much* further than I am in regard to the former connections of oceanic islands with continent'. As for his own work, he repeats that he has been at it for twenty years now, estimates that he has written about half his book, and confesses that he is getting on 'very slowly, partly from ill-health, partly from being a very slow worker'. 'I have now been three whole months on one chapter on Hybridism!' Finally, he expresses his astonishment that Wallace expects to 'remain out 3 or 4 years more':

What a wonderful deal you will have seen: & what interesting areas, the grand Malay Archipelago & the richest parts of S. America! I infinitely admire & honour your zeal & courage in the good cause of Natural Science; & you have my very sincere & cordial good wishes for success of all kinds; & may all your theories succeed, except that on oceanic islands; on which subject I will do battle to the death.[31]

This letter is one of many, to Wallace and others, which show the combination in Darwin of openness, courteousness, generosity, modesty, and humour, married to an intellectual toughness, a strong sense of his own worth, and a not quite concealed determination to be credited with originality in his chosen field. He is transparent and apparently guileless, while expertly slipping in claims to precedence. These claims were helpful to him when he received Wallace's next communication, a letter and short paper, now lost, written in February 1858 and arriving in Down in mid-June, which gave Darwin the fright of his life.

In the early days of June 1858 he was not yet ready to declare his findings beyond his close circle of scientific acquaintances. On 18 May he had written to Syms Covington, his erstwhile assistant and secretary, and before that his servant aboard the *Beagle*, telling his old friend, now living in Australia, about his work and plans and reiterating the remark about the length of time he had been researching his book:

My health has been very indifferent of late, owing to my working too hard. I have for some years been preparing a work for publication which I commenced 20 years ago, and for which I sometimes find extracts in your handwriting! This work will be my biggest; it treats on the origin of varieties of our domestic animals and plants, and on the origin of species in a state of nature. I have to discuss every branch of natural history, and the work is beyond my strength and tries me sorely.[32]

At this point Darwin still considered publication to be a few years away and expected to produce several volumes of his great work.[33]

His health, with distressing symptoms of vomiting and diarrhoea, had caused him, not for the first time, to seek a cure at one of the now fashionable hydropathic resorts. He told Covington that he had just got back from a 'water-cure establishment, where I bathe thrice a day, and loiter about all day doing nothing, and for the time it does me wonderful good'. He had returned home on 4 May after spending two weeks at Dr Edward Lane's establishment at Moor Park, in Surrey, a fine old house with extensive grounds. Darwin was much taken with the young doctor and his family, and admired Lane's recent book *Hydropathy: or the Natural System of Medical Treatment. An Explanatory Essay* (1857).[34] Less than six weeks after his return from Moor Park, he watched in sorrow as Lane attracted unwanted notoriety in newspaper reports from the Divorce Court.

Meanwhile, as the temperature in London and the surrounding area continued in the high 70s and low 80s °F (between 24 and 28 °C), Darwin worked on, telling Hooker on 8 June that he was 'confined to sofa with Boil', and was having to reply in pencil to Hooker's note approving of a paper on genera which Darwin had sent him. 'I had the *firmest* conviction that you would say all my M.S. was bosh'; 'if you condemned that you w[oul]d condemn all – my life's work – & that I confess made me a little low'. He hoped to write next on 'the "principle of Divergence", which with "Natural Selection" is the key-stone of my Book'.[35]

On Thursday, 10 June an event occurred which, along with the arrival a week later of Wallace's letter and its enclosure, was to have an unexpected effect on Darwin's plans. The 84-year-old Robert Brown, keeper of botany at the British Museum and former president of the Linnaean Society, the oldest biological society in the world, died. Hooker and Darwin were both members of the society, which was due to hold its last meeting of the year on 17 June, before the long summer break. Brown's death meant that the meeting was postponed till 1 July so that a new committee member could be elected in Brown's place. The delay made a difference to Darwin's publication plans which he could not have foreseen.

Dickens dissolves his marriage

On that same Thursday, 10 June, Dickens's public reading centred on the pathetic description of the death of little Paul Dombey, aged eight; it was to become a favourite of audiences everywhere. Dickens himself reported his great success the next day to his friend Daniel Maclise: 'We had an amazing scene of weeping and cheering, at St Martin's Hall, last night. I read the Life and Death of Little Dombey; and certainly I never saw a crowd so resolved into one creature before, or so stirred by any thing.'[36]

The *Illustrated London News* declared later in the summer that Dickens had 'invented a new medium for amusing the English audience, and merits the gratitude of an intelligent public'; alongside the article is a sketch of a fraught-looking Dickens standing on the stage in St Martin's Hall, clearly moved by his own prose.[37] Dickens had put a huge effort into preparing for the first reading of the 'Little Dombey' passage on 10 June; he had extracted various pages from his novel *Dombey and Son* (1846–8), made additions and deletions, and had the resulting extract printed in large type with wide margins for his use.[38] The reading lasted two hours, and covered Paul's birth, painful episodes in his short life, his illness, and the death which takes up a whole chapter in the novel and dares to be insistently sentimental, with its repetition of the idea of waves over-taking the child under a streaming golden light and the narrator's cry at the end.[39]

It was important to Dickens that this reading in particular should be welcomed by an adoring audience, for he had just made a significant move in the ongoing saga of his separation and the management (mismanage-ment, we might rather say) of the publicity which was inevitable in the case of such a public figure. He asked Delane, the editor of *The Times*, to carry a statement about his separation from Catherine; it appeared on Monday, 7 June, followed on Saturday, 12 June by publication of the same statement in Dickens's own paper, *Household Words*, as well as in innumer-able newspapers up and down the country. A great many people read and commented on the announcement. In particular there was much critical comment from a grateful, and in some cases gleeful, set of journalists writing for daily, weekly, and evening papers, fortnightly and monthly magazines, and – troublesomely for Dickens – the scurrilous penny papers which were making their appearance in large numbers in the years following the repeal of the last tax on newspapers in 1855.[40]

Dickens wrote as follows:

Three-and-twenty years have passed since I entered on my present relations with the public . . .

Through all that time I have tried to be as faithful to the public as they have been to me. It was my duty never to trifle with them or to deceive them . . .

My conspicuous position has often made me the subject of fabulous stories and unaccountable statements. Occasionally such things have chafed me, or even wounded me, but I have always accepted them as the shadows inseparable from the light of my notoriety and success . . .

For the first time in my life, and I believe for the last, I now deviate from the principle I have so long observed, by presenting myself in my own journal in my own private character, and entreating all my brethren . . . to lend their aid to the dissemination of my present words.

Some domestic trouble of mine of long standing, on which I will make no further remark than that it claims to be respected as being of a sacredly private nature, has lately been brought to an arrangement which involves no anger or ill-will of any kind . . .

By some means, arising out of wickedness, or out of folly, or out of inconceivable wild chance, or out of all three, this trouble has been made the occasion of misrepresentations, most grossly false, most monstrous, and most cruel – involving not only me, but innocent persons dear to my heart, and innocent persons of whom I have no knowledge, if, indeed, they have any existence – and so widely spread that I doubt if one reader in a thousand will peruse these lines by whom some touch of the breath of these slanders will not have passed like an unwholesome air.

Those who know me and my nature need no assurance under my hand that such calumnies are as irreconcileable [*sic*] with me as they are, in their frantic incoherence, with one another. But there is a great multitude who know me through my writings, and who do not know me otherwise; and I cannot bear that one of them should be left in doubt, or hazard of doubt, through my poorly shrinking from taking the unusual means to which I now resort of circulating the truth.

I most solemnly declare, then – and this I do, both in my own name and in my wife's – that all the lately whispered rumours touching the trouble at which I have glanced are abominably false, and that whoever repeats one of them after this denial will lie as wilfully and as foully as it is possible for any false witness to lie before Heaven and earth.[41]

Unsurprisingly, Dickens had been advised against making this statement by his friends, especially Forster, who offered 'strenuous resistance' to the idea, though equally unsurprisingly the *Times* editor had encouraged him to go ahead.[42] Dickens surely strikes the wrong note altogether in his feverish desire to put himself out of reach of the rumours – about both Ellen and Georgina, as he now knew, partly thanks to Thackeray – by appealing to his undoubtedly large public. He cannot avoid seeming boastful when he writes of the 'faith' of his readers – his 'brethren' – over many years. He contradicts himself by claiming at once that he is a public man and yet that his private life is no one else's business, then compounds the contradiction by voluntarily referring to that private life, thus making it everyone's business. By alluding to 'grossly false', 'monstrous', and 'cruel' slanders while not saying directly what they are, and by talking mysteriously of 'innocent persons', some known to him and others perhaps imagined (who? and by whom?), he invites the interested but not initiated reader – in other words everyone outside the small circle of his friends and family and London's journalists and clubmen – to ask what the terrible slanders are and who the innocent persons could be. He insists most vehemently on his truthfulness just where he is being most untruthful, but no doubt he speaks truly when he says he 'cannot bear' for even one of his readers or admirers to think badly of him.

Dickens himself had given good advice to the artist William Holman Hunt only two months earlier. Hunt had written to complain of a story printed in *Household Words* in April which he asserted was a disgraceful libel on himself, since it concerned an artist (unnamed, but clearly meant to represent Hunt) who is suspected of having a sexual liaison with his model. Dickens replied, expressing his astonishment that Hunt should think the artist in the story (by Robert Brough) was a portrait of him and urging Hunt not to insist on Dickens inserting an assurance in the paper that Hunt was not the original. Employing the logic he was subsequently unable to bring to his own case, he told Hunt on 20 April that he had 'not a doubt' that such an insertion 'would suggest to the public what they have not the faintest idea of, and that its effect would be exactly the reverse of your desire'.[43] Wise words. Dickens, the all-powerful editor of *Household Words*, had the last word in the case of Hunt; he saved him embarrassment by not including an explanation.

Many of the newspapers that carried Dickens's statement in the days after 7 June simply printed it, as did *The Times*, without comment. Some, like the *St James's Chronicle*, expressed sympathy with him. 'We welcome his authoritative and touching denial', it said on 8 June, which 'will be accepted as a sufficient vindication of the honour of his untarnished name.'[44] The *Era*, though declaring its warmth towards Dickens, expresses the very opinion Dickens had offered Hunt, saying that it was a mistake for him to bring his private business before the public. At the same time it indicates that, as a metropolitan newspaper with its finger on the pulse, it knows about the stories in circulation, for good measure making it clear that it dislikes his assumption of his own supreme importance in the world:

> In our judgment, the scandal was not so widely spread as Mr Dickens has been led to believe. Not one in a hundred of those who admire his works have ever heard of the reports in question. They have been confined mainly to the literary world in which Mr Dickens lives, and therefore have appeared to him to be more general than they were . . . Unfortunately, Mr Dickens has fallen into the common error of little minds, in thinking that he is of much more consequence in the world than he really is, and that his whereabouts, his social and domestic proceedings, are events in which the public feels an absorbing interest.[45]

Much worse for Dickens was his treatment at the hands of two of the gutter press weekly newspapers, the cheekily titled *Court Circular* of Saturday, 12 June and *Reynolds's Newspaper* of Sunday, 13 June. Both filled in the gaps in Dickens's account, the former going straight for 'the story in circulation' that Mrs Dickens has left the marital home 'on account of that talented gentleman's preference of his wife's sister to herself', warning

Dickens that he is 'in a fair way to figure in the new Matrimonial Court, and in a mode which will add little to his laurels'. Not to be outdone, *Reynolds's* affirms that the rumours alluded to in Dickens's statement 'have, indeed, been widely circulated, and generally credited in literary and artistic circles'. 'We trust', it continues mock-sonorously, that

> they are, as he alleges, nothing but calumnies. The names of a female relative and of a professional young lady, have both been, of late, so intimately associated with that of Mr Dickens, as to excite suspicion and surprise in the minds of those who had hitherto looked upon the popular novelist as a very Joseph in all that regards morality, chastity, and decorum . . . Mr Dickens has been ill-advised. He should either have left the 'calumnies' to die a natural death, or have explained them away in a style less ambiguous and stilted than that he has adopted in the above letter [i.e. the *Household Words* statement].[46]

Though Dickens got his *Household Words* colleague Wills to ask his solicitor Ouvry if 'it would be expedient to move for a Criminal Information' against the proprietor of the *Court Circular* and possibly the proprietor of *Reynolds's* too, common sense prevailed in this case, and Dickens dropped the idea of prosecuting his tormentors.[47] (G.W.M. Reynolds had long been a thorn in Dickens's side. A radical, impulsive, often insolvent journalist and writer of potboiling fiction, he had quickly cashed in on Dickens's success with his suggestive fictional 'guide' to Paris, *Pickwick Abroad, or, the Tour in France* (1837–8). As if to irritate Dickens further, Reynolds's newspaper office was at No. 7 Wellington Street North, off the Strand, while Dickens's *Household Words* office was diagonally opposite at No. 16.[48])

Dickens survived this mainly metropolitan literary gossip. The young men about town, both those who idolised and openly imitated Dickens in their fiction and journalism, like G.A. Sala and Edmund Yates, and those who looked down on him for not having been to one of the two ancient universities, such as Thackeray and some of his fellow *Punch* writers, talked in club rooms, supper rooms, theatres, and at horse races. Other members of the literati discussed the affair too, including Dickens's friend Carlyle, to whom in 1859 *A Tale of Two Cities* was dedicated in homage to Carlyle's vibrant history of the French Revolution (1837). Carlyle attempted to dampen speculation even while he shared it. He wrote to Ralph Waldo Emerson in America, telling him on 2 June – a few days *before* Dickens's statement in *The Times* – that the newspapers 'will babble to you about Dickens: "Separation from Wife" &c &c: fact of Separat[io]n (Lawyer's *Deed* &c) I believe is true; but all the rest is mere lies and nonsense. No crime or misdemeanour specifiable on either side: *unhappy* together these good many years past, and they at length end it.'[49] If Carlyle knew about the impending separation a week before it was announced, another member of London's literary world had heard the news a week before *that*. Edward Leman Blanchard, one of the most successful writers of burlesques and pantomimes for the theatres, noted in his diary on Wednesday, 26 May, 'Hear of Charles Dickens's separation from his wife on Saturday!'[50]

While Carlyle was content to take Dickens at his word on the nature of the separation, others shook their heads. Thackeray, telling his mother early in June about the gossip, added that he felt sorry for Catherine, mother of nine children and blameless, having to leave her marital home: 'To think of the poor matron after 22 years of marriage going away out of her house!'[51] Marian Evans and G.H. Lewes, who were spending the summer months in Germany, learned about the separation while in Munich. They knew all about the unpleasantness and damaging gossip that awaited those who embraced unorthodoxy or irregularity in their personal lives. They had suffered when they began to live together openly in 1854 (also in Germany) after the breakdown of Lewes's marriage and the birth of two children to his wife Agnes by another man. Their chosen path was different from the one Dickens was about to go down; they continued their devoted partnership, accepting that some friends might cut off ties completely, as Marian's brother Isaac did. One thing they refused to do was to join in tittle-tattle about the affairs of others. Lewes merely noted sadly in his journal on 14 June that on visiting the famous chemist Justus von Liebig after dinner that night, 'we spoke sorrowfully of Dickens's public separation from his wife, which is making a scandal here as in England.'[52]

Dickens busied himself with his Thursday evening readings and prepared to flee London, which had got too hot for him, both literally and metaphorically. He went off with his shrewd manager Arthur Smith on his reading tour from 2 August to 13 November, starting in Bristol and finishing in Brighton, after taking in towns in every part of England, Scotland, and Ireland.[53] He had some more bad moments to negotiate, but for now he was relieved that Catherine had signed the deed of separation on 4 June and was preparing to move, with Charley, to Gloucester Crescent, near Regent's Park. Dickens himself would henceforth spend most of his time between the office of *Household Words* and his country home, Gad's Hill in Kent. Tavistock House, the family home for almost a decade, complete with its private theatre, was soon given up as the Dickens family split for ever.

Midsummer madness

The hot weather began in the last days of May and continued to increase through the first week of June. Queen Victoria's journal records it as 'stiflingly hot' in London on Friday, 4 June, 'steamy & heavy' the next day after a thunderstorm, and 'oppressive' on the following days.[54] On Monday, 7 June, the same day on which it printed Dickens's statement, *The Times*, in its notice of the long-running entertainment, *The Ascent of Mont Blanc*, by Arthur Smith's better-known brother Albert, added that in this hot weather 'Mr Albert Smith places filters of iced water in different parts of the Egyptian-hall at the service of his audience'.[55] Smith was an entrepreneur, loud and bohemian; he had climbed Mont Blanc in 1851 and opened his show at the Egyptian Hall in Piccadilly the following year. It consisted of a moving panorama of the ascent of the mountain complemented by Smith's topical songs and humour. Smith finally closed the show on 6 July 1858 after the 2,000th performance.[56] Meanwhile his brother Arthur, who had managed Albert's performances, turned to helping Dickens arrange his readings outside London over the summer.

Among those bothered by the extreme heat in this first week of June was Disraeli. On the same Monday, 7 June, when the temperature reached 75 °F (24 °C) in the shade, he wrote a brief note from the House of Commons to his wife in Buckinghamshire asking her to send him 'a pair of boots for my feet are quite damp in these varnished [patent leather] ones'.[57] *The Times* was receiving letters from correspondents about the heat (and soon about the smell in London); on 11 June the paper printed a letter from someone in Fareham, Hampshire, declaring that on Tuesday, 8 June,

> the heat was at one time so intense at this place that my thermometer, at 1 p.m., showed 136 deg. [well over 50 °C] of heat in the sun. I never observed during last year [the previous record breaker] a greater degree of heat than 123 [about 50 °C] in the sun. I write this, as doubtless you will give us from some of your numerous scientific correspondents some interesting statistics.[58]

Tuesday, 8 June was hot in Hertford, 30 miles north of London, too, where Bulwer Lytton was obliged to seek re-election in order to take up his cabinet appointment. His fears of being beaten and losing his seat were eased when it became clear that the Liberal opposition would not, after all, put up a candidate against him.[59] This was good news, but not so the fact that he was dramatically denounced, as he gave his speech to the voters, by his furious wife, Rosina, who travelled to Hertford from her home in Somerset to placard the town and embarrass him at the hustings. Disraeli wrote urgently to his colleague about her renewed bout of letter-writing in advance of the election:

> My dear Bulwer,
>
> I thought you had tamed the tigress of Taunton – but, unhappily, this is not the case.
>
> She is writing letters to your colleagues, & friends, of an atrocious description, such as, I thought, no woman could have penned, accusing you of nameless crimes, at least wh[ich] can only be named by her, & threatening aggravated hostilities.
>
> This is not very pleasant to your friends: I should think hardly, to yourself.
>
> What can be the explanation? Is it possible, that your agent has been so negligent, or so imprudent, as to leave her allowance in arrear?[60]

The friend to whom Rosina's activities were particularly unpleasant was Disraeli himself, since she was freely naming him in her letters as not only a crony of Bulwer Lytton's, but also a fellow sodomite; hence his sharpness with his friend here. As Bulwer Lytton was notoriously stingy – Rosina constantly complained that her allowance from him was mean and often not paid on time – it is likely that Disraeli's question at the end was intended as a rebuke. If Bulwer Lytton would only increase her allowance and in that way buy her off, or at least remove that motive for her aggression, it would be better for Bulwer Lytton and Disraeli alike.

On that hot Tuesday Bulwer Lytton was staggered to find himself interrupted by his estranged wife as he spoke in a field outside Hertford. Rosina shouted that he had murdered their daughter Emily through neglect, and declared, echoing her remarks in her letters to Lord Derby and his colleagues, that instead of being appointed secretary for the colonies, he should be transported there for his crimes. The details of her ambush vary according to the source. Rosina herself wrote letters to her friend Miss Ryves; she also, through supporters in Taunton, fed juicy morsels to local Somerset and Hertfordshire newspapers. Much later she wrote a gaudy account in her vituperative autobiography, *A Blighted Life*, which was printed in a swiftly suppressed edition in 1867, before being eventually published in 1880, some years after Bulwer Lytton's death and the deaths of many others who were libelled in the book.[61] It was generally agreed that when Bulwer Lytton saw Rosina approaching, he almost fainted off the platform and made a hasty retreat through a nearby garden, while she harangued the crowd about the misdemeanours of 'Sir Liar'.[62] Carlyle, having escaped the London heat to stay with his sister in Dumfriesshire, heard from the newspapers some weeks later about 'the furious Lady's spring up upon the Public Stage, and clutching her Phantasm Husband in sight of the world, at some sublime acme of his Harangue', as he put it with his usual brightly coloured verbal portraiture.[63]

Rosina soon set about getting her denunciation published, but it took several weeks before any national newspaper would oblige her. The Bulwer Lytton-friendly *Times* – she called it 'that beastly National Typographic Weathercock' – reported his successful re-election on 9 June. The paper quotes sycophantic speeches by his supporters, followed by Bulwer Lytton's own speech, which reveals that Rosina's parodies were by no means excessive; he apparently began by claiming that an ancestor of his 'somewhere between 300 and 400 years ago . . . held a considerable station in the council of Henry VII'.[64] There is no mention in *The Times*'s report of Rosina's interruption. Bulwer Lytton's influence in high places seems to have kept the news of his humiliation out of the national press for a while. But by his own desperate actions a few weeks later, he ensured that by the beginning of July the story was being run day after day across the country.

The letters Rosina wrote to her friend Rebecca Ryves in the days following 8 June reveal that she told the electors of Hertford that her husband was plotting to make her out to be mad. He was. In March 1858 he had asked six doctors for their written opinions on her sanity, but though they supported his view that she was insane, he did not take action at that time.[65] His friend John Forster, busy enough acting for Dickens over his separation from Catherine, was called in to help here too. Forster, known in literary and journalistic circles as 'the beadle of the universe', had acted for Bulwer Lytton when he separated from Rosina in 1836 and had even spied on her for his friend in 1839.[66] He was also, since January 1856, secretary to the Lunacy Commission, a body which had come into existence after the passing of the Lunacy Act of 1845, with powers to inspect and regulate asylums. In October 1857 Forster had advised Bulwer Lytton not to incarcerate Rosina; though he agreed that she was mad, he believed it would be difficult to persuade doctors to certify her.[67] But Bulwer Lytton was determined to frighten Rosina into silence by threatening to commit her to a madhouse. On 12 June 1858, back in Taunton, she was visited by two doctors and a woman from a local lunatic asylum who attempted to dissuade her from publishing her accusations about her husband. According to her hectic account to Miss Ryves, Dr Hale Thomson, sent up from London by Bulwer Lytton, said to her:

'But *surely*, Lady Lytton, you *dont* [sic] mean to give lectures through the Kingdom, – narrate your own history, and read out all Sir E's letters?' Don't I? – as there is a god in Heaven I'll do it; unless he pays what I owe, and gives me at least an adequate – and above all a *clear* unmortgaged allowance . . . I then wrote that if he would pledge himself to . . . pay the £2,500 of debt his 26 years persecution had entailed on me, and settle £500 a year on me for *my* life, not *his*, as his beggarly £400 is now settled – I would pledge myself never to mention his name, which indeed I should be only too glad to forget.[68]

Such an agreement to pay her debts and improve her settlement might have brought the episode to a reasonable conclusion, but neither Rosina nor her husband could do the sensible thing. She continued to send furious letters to his supporters, and began threatening to turn up in London, where he 'may chance to find the *Colonial* office *rather* too hot to hold him'.[69] Before the end of the month the full-blown scandal Disraeli feared for his friend (and himself) had materialised.

Stories of incarcerations in lunatic asylums were among the hot topics of the day. Sometimes they related to husbands locking up inconvenient wives on the pretext that they were mad. It only took two corrupt medical men to sign a statement, and scandals were beginning to erupt over conspiracies between unscrupulous husbands who paid unscrupulous doctors, who in turn referred the 'patients' to the unscrupulous owners of private asylums. There were cases where husbands, not wives, were wrongly locked up, and others which involved parents and children, or other relatives who resorted to desperate measures in order to gain a disputed inheritance.[70] The most publicised case concerned a man who everyone agreed was insane, but whose wife was in dispute with his three sisters over who should gain from his enormous wealth when he died. The question at issue over nine 'very exceedingly hot days' in June 1858, as *The Times* reported at the end of the case, was whether the unfortunate lunatic had been mad when he made a codicil to his will the previous year, leaving everything to his young wife and nothing to his sisters, or only became mad subsequently. In other words, was the new will valid or not?[71]

The lunacy trial, held in the Thatched House Tavern on St James's Street, off Piccadilly, was that of the fabulously wealthy Sir Henry Meux, a member of a famous brewing family, and, along with Bulwer Lytton, one of the three Conservative MPs for Hertfordshire. At the general election in April 1857 Bulwer Lytton and his colleagues had tried to persuade Meux to stand down, since he could not speak coherently. Though on that occasion Meux 'presented a most pitiable sight', appearing 'haggard, worn, and distressed', and taking 'no notice of what was going on', he remained as a candidate.[72] He therefore continued as an MP, though an inactive and incapacitated one, until the general election of May 1859, which saw Derby's government thrown out and Palmerston's ushered back in. The lunacy case attracted huge attention because of the stakes; during the trial, brought by the disinherited sisters, it became clear that Meux's estate was worth more than £600,000 (approximately £60 million today[73]). The proceedings began on Tuesday, 8 June 1858, the same day as Bulwer Lytton's troubles occurred at Hertford, and lasted till Thursday, 17 June, when the jury, exhausted by the heat – which had reached the record of 94.5 °F (35 °C) in the shade on 16 June – and the complications of the case, declared that it could not say precisely *when* Sir Henry had become insane in law, and therefore could not find in favour of either the greedy sisters or the apparently gold-digging young wife. The case was dismissed without resolution, and against all odds Sir Henry lived on until 1883, though in a hopeless state.[74]

The counsel acting for Lady Meux was Edwin James, who specialised in lunacy and other headline-hitting cases; in fact, he was becoming well known for taking on difficult briefs, often defending the indefensible. In the Meux case he made the court laugh, despite the uncomfortable heat, when he addressed the jury. According to the *People's Paper* of 19 June, he 'went into a minute analysis of the evidence, and was extremely humorous in his attempts to laugh out of court the various acts of delusion which were ascribed to Sir Henry Meux', declaring that 'if he was insane at the time contended for, he was also equally insane when he advanced . . . sums to his relatives'.[75]

One person who followed the case with eagle eyes was the indefatigable Rosina, who, in the midst of her own fight against being branded a lunatic, wrote to Miss Ryves on 11 June: 'As they are having an inquiry about Sir Henry Meux's state of mind, I think they had better have one about Sir Liars [*sic*] who is much the madder brute of the two.'[76]

As the middle of the month approached, and with it the hottest day, complaints abounded about the heat in parliament, in theatres, and in people's homes. By 12 June Carlyle had abandoned his study at the top of his Chelsea house to work on Frederick the Great under an awning in the garden. A few days later he had finished his book and was planning his getaway to Scotland, while worrying that his horse (called Fritz in honour of Carlyle's subject) was 'not quite himself' at present, 'owing to his hot stable' nearby.[77] He gave Forster a vivid account of his own state of mind and body: 'I am just out, half-alive, from the Slough of Despond, temperature 82° in the shade: Thames River with a Stink worse than Acheron [one of the five rivers of Hades]; a gilt Old-Clothes man [a disparaging reference to Disraeli's Jewishness] ruling the Empire of Britain; and Beelzebub, so to speak, doing his will on earth, with a clear working majority.'[78]

At Buckingham Palace Queen Victoria groaned about the blazing heat.[79] Lord Derby fell ill and could not attend parliament. Disraeli told his friend Mrs Brydges Willyams that his 'chief & colleague' was suffering from 'a raging fit of the gout, wh[ich] terribly disconcerts me'. 'Fortunately, we are now, generally speaking, on velvet; but, unhappily, all the measures, wh[ich] I have carried thro' the House of Commons, will soon be going to the Upper House, & he will be required to advocate & conduct them.'[30] These included India and the tricky question, being batted to and fro between Lords and Commons at this time, of the Oaths Bill and Rothschild's position.

The House of Lords had debated the Oaths Bill on 31 May, with Lord Lucan attempting to 'restore harmony between the two houses' by reminding peers that the question had been appearing before parliament since the 1830s. He begged the House of Lords to stop blocking the legislation, insisting that 'the exclusion of the Jews was both impolitic and inexpedient'.[81] Lucan was answered with objections by the lord chancellor, Lord Chelmsford, an 'able lawyer and eager partisan', according to a contemporary, and noted for being implacably opposed to having Jews in parliament.[82] Lord Lyndhurst offered to present a compromise amendment to the bill which would allow each house to decide separately what to do about Jewish representation. 'The days of Jewish disabilities are numbered', said the *Liverpool Mercury* on 2 June, since 'Lord Lyndhurst is to prepare the anodyne for the Peers.'[83] On 9 June Lord Derby wrote a 'Confidential Circular' from his London home in St James's Square to his young Tory colleague Lord Carnarvon, among other peers, expressing his

unease about the embarrassing difference between the two houses. He
believed the efforts by Lord Lucan and Lord Lyndhurst to reach a compromise should be accepted, and wished to know the opinion of his correspondents and whether they would send a proxy if they were unable to
attend the vote. 'I fear that on this occasion', he wrote courteously, 'I may
differ from many of those with whom I generally agree.' As an incentive he
points out that if each house were to pass a resolution, it would be, 'unlike
an Act of Parliament', 'only binding on the House which passes it; and, on
that, only during the Parliament in which it is passed'. In other words, if
the opponents of Jewish representation really wished to bring the subject
up again, they could do so in the next parliament.[84] The juggling and toing
and froing were coming to an end at last.

During June the Thames got ever smellier. On Monday, 14 June the
lord mayor told an audience at Mansion House that he had received several
complaints about the state of the river. His speech was reported in the
Weekly Chronicle the following Saturday: 'It might be beneficial to notice
publicly a statement to the truth of which he could bear testimony himself,
having been amongst hundreds of witnesses on the steam-boat passage
from London-bridge to Westminster a day or two ago. Certainly no stench
that ever he had encountered was comparable with that which assailed the
passengers on that occasion. He would not try the experiment again.'[85]

People's livelihoods were suffering, as pleasure boats, having no takers,
ceased to travel along the stinking river.[86] The *People's Paper* noted that by
the end of June those who 'look forward to this time of year to make a little
harvest by the letting of boats are completely at a standstill', and 'the only
trade which is flourishing on the river is carried on in the cabins, where
drops of brandy are in constant request'.[87] The theatres found attendance
decreasing, so oppressive was the heat; the critic of the *Theatrical Journal*
sat out the performance of *Othello* at the Soho Theatre on 16 June, but
could not bear to stay for the two short pieces which were to follow: 'The
heat of the theatre was so great, that we left the house at half-past eleven
o'clock.'[88] On that very hottest day in the Court of the Exchequer in
Westminster Hall, one of the lawyers asked permission of the lord chief
baron, Sir Frederick Pollock, 'to dispense with his wig during this very hot
weather'. Permission was granted, with jokes being exchanged about the

weather in London as compared with hot countries, where wigs tended not to be worn.[89]

Meltdown in Clubland

Among the gossipy newspapers which fell greedily upon political and social events in the summer of 1858, from Disraeli's flamboyant politics and Derby's precarious position as prime minister to Dickens's predicament, not to mention the state of the Thames and the constant news from the new Divorce Court and the Lunacy Commission, were two new weeklies. Both papers were started on 1 May and both featured the writing of young men about town who emulated Dickens and Thackeray in their journalism. Dickens was imitated sometimes for the righteous anger he expressed in his novels and in *Household Words* against social deprivation and the do-nothingism of the institutions which ought to be acting against it – from parliament to law court to church – though more often for the power of his satirical rhetoric when attacking the objects of his scorn. Thackeray, less of a radical social critic than Dickens, aimed his satire at class snobbery (while consciously sharing it himself) and in particular hypocrisy. His rather cynical view of mankind was taken up by the two new papers, the *Welcome Guest* and *Town Talk*, the latter in particular setting out to be offensive and notorious under its proprietor, the publisher John Maxwell. Two young men, G.A. Sala and Edmund Yates, leapt to relative prominence as they burned the midnight oil turning out copy by the yard for these papers.[90]

Sala, a bibulous and irrepressible bohemian, wrote for *Household Words*, persuading Dickens to pay for him to visit Russia in 1856 in return for sending back accounts of his adventures there. He was unreliable and often late with copy, and made the mistake of quarrelling with Dickens over the money he felt was owed to him. Dickens sacked him in 1857. Sala worked for an extraordinary number of papers, including the anti-establishment penny paper the *Daily Telegraph*, and he was engaged by the bohemian publisher Henry Vizetelly to write for a number of cheap papers that Vizetelly started up in the years after the repeal of newspaper taxes.[91]

One such paper, launched in May 1858, was *Welcome Guest*, a penny weekly which carried a successful series of sketches by Sala of London life, a racier version of Dickens's early *Sketches by Boz*. Entitled 'Twice Round the Clock', the sketches take the reader into the streets and buildings of London by day and by night, sticking closely to the actual calendar, so that when London boils in June and July 1858, Sala gives a vivid sense of the discomfort experienced by many Londoners as they go about their business and pleasure. The 'Twice Round the Clock' pieces describe the morning activities in stuffy law courts and in parliament. The author drops in on the Court of the Queen's Bench in Westminster Hall at 10 a.m. on a hot June morning and sees the jurymen 'wiping their foreheads with blue cotton pocket handkerchiefs' as they puzzle over the rhetoric of the counsels on both sides in the hot, cramped room. From that historic venue with its medieval carved roof and recent adornments of brass and stained glass by Sir Charles Barry, Sala moves dramatically to the contrasting Prison of the Queen's Bench on the south of the Thames. Drawing cheekily on Dickens's descriptions of the Marshalsea debtors' prison in *Little Dorrit* (1855–7), he gives a picture of this place where prisoners are confined yet free to walk about and even conduct business within the walls:

> I am standing in the centre of a vast gravelled area, bounded on the south side by a brick wall of tremendous height . . . To the north there is a range of ordinary-looking houses . . . There are no barred windows, no bolts, bars, or grim chains apparent . . . The guardians themselves are ruddy men with very big keys; but they seem on the very best terms with the gentlemen whose intended exercise outside the walls they feel compelled . . . to debar . . . And what of the collegians [Dickens's word in *Little Dorrit*] – the prisoners – themselves? It is ten o'clock in the morning, and they are sauntering about in every variety of shabby dishabille, smoking pipes . . .[92]

(Sala was soon to see the inside of the Queen's Bench Prison himself, and not as an amused visitor. Having failed to gamble his way out of debt at the roulette tables on a visit to Homburg with Vizetelly and another penny-a-liner and writer of topical fiction, Augustus Mayhew, in September

1858, he got even deeper into trouble and in December found himself spending a couple of weeks in the prison. He wrote from there to his friend Yates at three in the morning, sending him a piece of writing for publication in one of the papers they both wrote for. Yates, who frequently lent his friend money, may well have paid his debts once more to get him out.[93])

This is how Sala goes on, filling his pages with easy chit-chat and keeping his eye all the while on London life, reckoning – correctly – that there is a large readership for this new kind of journalism, adding to Dickens's reportage a careless, jaunty air of the *flâneur* while at the same time giving an accurate view of London's social geography. He flits around, noticing in July a scene of fashionable afternoon shopping in Regent Street with its carriages and crinolines ('Dulcinea in a hoop petticoat'). Evening adventures include visits to uncomfortable theatres, concert halls, and rooms where 'scientific conversazioni' are being held. The night-time life of London is portrayed too. Famous late-night resorts for men of a bohemian tendency around the Strand and Covent Garden, like Evans's Supper Rooms, are name-checked by Sala, who alludes to Thackeray's frequent presence there and his portrait of the place as the 'Cave of Harmony' in *The Newcomes* (1853–5). He also visits the porters in Billingsgate fish market and in Covent Garden fruit market in the early hours, then at 5 a.m. looks into the offices of *The Times*, quoting from a famous passage in Thackeray's novel *Pendennis* (1850), in which the young hero walks the streets at night and observes the brightly lit offices of a national newspaper in the small hours as it prepares to give the world's news to the reading public next morning.[94]

In Sala's amusing if unreliable memoirs of 1895, *The Life and Adventures of George Augustus Sala, Written by Himself*, he claimed that long ago he had been told the 'secret' of Dickens's 'matrimonial troubles', but that he would not reveal it. As far as he knew, apart from the Dickens family, only Wilkie Collins and Edmund Yates, both now dead, had been told.[95] No doubt it was his close friend Yates, who almost certainly did know all about it in 1858, who had disclosed the not-so-secret secret of Dickens's relationship with Ellen Ternan. Yates was friendly with Dickens. Like Sala, he came from an acting family with whom Dickens was familiar; unlike Sala, he had not fallen out with his older friend. It was the pair's other literary hero, Thackeray, with whom Yates fell out in the summer of 1858. While Sala was probably the roguish author of a ditty making fun of Dickens's marital situation in the ever-annoying *Reynolds's Newspaper* on 20 June – 'With tongue and pen, none can like Dickens fudge; / But now in vain in virtue's cause he pleads; / Henceforth the public will his virtues judge, / Not by his "Household Words", but household deeds'[96] – Yates was supporting Dickens in print wherever he could. In another of Vizetelly's papers, the twopenny *Illustrated Times*, he rushed to defend Dickens's statement to the press. Writing as 'The Lounger at the Clubs' in the paper, he declared on 12 June that the rumours concerning Dickens's domestic affairs were 'absurd and mischievous'.[97]

In the following weeks he and Dickens supported one another in the scandals that each faced. For it was precisely because of Yates's lounging in clubs that he got into trouble. Yates had been allowed to become a member of the Garrick Club in 1848, six months before his eighteenth birthday, on account of his parents' profession.[98] In June 1858, he was about to turn twenty-seven. The club, located in Covent Garden, had been founded in 1831 for people associated with the nearby theatres, and for literary men, though it also had members from other professions, particularly politics and the law.[99] Both Dickens and Thackeray were members, but while Dickens scarcely ever went there, except when attending meetings of the committee, of which he was a member, Thackeray used the club as a home from home. Yates, who had admired *Pendennis* above all other novels and claimed to have been inspired by it to become a journalist and writer,[100] wrote a foolish article on Thackeray which was printed on Saturday, 12 June, the day Dickens's separation statement was widely published. Thackeray had a rush of blood to the head in response, and Dickens, already unhappy to know that Thackeray was gossiping about his marital difficulties, became unnecessarily involved.

Having written a portrait of Dickens in the new penny weekly *Town Talk* the previous Saturday, Yates had now set about doing the same for Thackeray. The article begins with a description of Thackeray's appearance which starts neutrally and gradually builds up to unpleasantness:

Mr Thackeray is forty-six years old, though from the silvery whiteness
of his hair he appears somewhat older. He is very tall, standing upwards
of six feet two inches, and as he walks erect his height makes him
conspicuous in every assembly. His face is bloodless, and not particularly expressive, but remarkable for the fracture of the bridge of the
nose, the result of an accident in youth . . . No one meeting him could
fail to recognise in him a gentleman; his bearing is cold and uninviting,
his style of conversation either openly cynical, or affectedly good-
natured and benevolent; his *bonhomie* is forced, his wit biting, his pride
easily touched – but his appearance is invariably that of the cool, *suave*,
well-bred gentleman, who, whatever may be rankling within, suffers no
surface display of his emotion.[101]

So much for Thackeray's physical appearance and social demeanour.
Yates turns next to his career, praising his witty contributions to *Punch* and
his *Book of Snobs*, which began life as essays in *Punch* in 1846 under the title
'The Snobs of England, by One of Themselves', though Yates does not
acknowledge the self-deprecation of the title in his piece. As for the novels,
Yates notes that Thackeray first achieved proper fame with *Vanity Fair* and
its successor *Pendennis*. 'Then came *Esmond*, which fell almost still-born
from the press; and then the *Newcomes*, perhaps the best of all.' Yates goes on
to touch a raw nerve: 'The *Virginians*, now publishing, though admirably
written, lacks interest of plot, and is proportionately unsuccessful.' Thackeray
was only too aware of the truth of this, as he battled on to write his monthly
instalments. He had told an American friend in April that he had only just
written that month's number in time, adding, 'The book's clever, but stupid,
thats [*sic*] the fact . . . Here is a third of a great story done equal to two thirds
of an ordinary novel – and nothing actually has happened, except that a
young gentleman has come from America to England.'[102]

Yates ends his article with a paragraph accusing Thackeray of flattering
the aristocracy in his 'Lectures on the English Humorists of the Eighteenth
Century', which were 'attended by all the court and fashion of London',
then going to America and attacking the British monarchy while praising
George Washington. 'Our own opinion is that his success is on the wane',
writes the young upstart. Finally, 'there is a want of heart in all he writes,

which is to be balanced by the most brilliant sarcasm and the most perfect knowledge of the workings of the human heart.'[103] On this note, half censorious, half eulogising, Yates finishes his dashed-off piece of page-filling about a novelist he mainly admired. Of course, he may have had reason to feel, as Dickens keenly did, that Thackeray was inclined to look down on the likes of him from his public-schooled, university-educated gentlemanly height. Still it seems likely that Yates's motivation for writing the piece was, as he later claimed, the necessity for writing articles at speed to keep his family comfortably off (he was married with three young children and had a regular job as a clerk at the General Post Office). Perhaps he was also influenced by the atmosphere of flippant, careless, and uncaring journalism in which he worked.[104]

If Yates's attack was unnecessary and perhaps even only half felt, Thackeray's response was thunderous. He was often unwell at this time (his diary frequently records 'spasms', and he had to cancel engagements because of indisposition[105]), and struggling with his writing.

It is not known whether Thackeray sought advice from anyone, but given that he wrote to Yates on Sunday, 13 June, the day after the offending article appeared, it is likely that he did not. Someone had drawn his attention to Yates's piece, as well as to a remark made in *Town Talk* the previous Saturday, also by Yates, to the effect that Thackeray was being paid £200 a month by his publishers Bradbury and Evans for the foot-dragging serialisation of *The Virginians*. Thackeray allows that Yates is entitled to his opinion of his works, 'wh[ich] of course you are at liberty to praise or condemn as a literary critic'. His objection is to the ungentlemanly mention of his financial arrangements with his publisher and the accusation of hypocrisy in both his private conversation and his public lecturing:

> As I understand your phrases, you impute insincerity to me when I speak good-naturedly in private; assign dishonourable motives to me for sentiments wh[ich] I have delivered in public, and charge me with advancing sentiments wh[ich] I have never delivered at all.
>
> Had your remarks been written by a person unknown to me, I should have noticed them no more than other calumnies: but as we have shaken hands more than once, and met hitherto on friendly terms

. . . I am obliged to take notice of articles wh[ich] I consider to be, not offensive & unfriendly merely, but slanderous and untrue.

We meet at a Club where, before you were born I believe, I and other gentlemen have been in the habit of talking, without any idea that our conversation would supply paragraphs for professional vendors of 'Literary Talk', and I don't remember that out of that Club I ever exchanged 6 words with you. Allow me to inform you that the talk wh[ich] you may have heard there is not intended for newspaper remark; & to beg, as I have a right to do, that you will refrain from printing comments upon my private conversation; that you will forgo discussions however blundering, on my private affairs; & that you will henceforth please to consider any question of my personal truth & sincerity as quite out of the province of your criticism.[106]

That Thackeray spent some time wondering how best to respond is shown by the fact that he wrote at least three drafts of this letter, in one case referring to Yates's comments about some of his works being failures.[107] He clearly decided, sensibly, to concentrate on the attacks on his personal morality rather than those on his books. However, his tone is haughty; he mentions Yates's youth (and therefore junior position in relation to himself), and makes rather a meal out of the breach of club rules, of gentlemanly behaviour, which he thinks Yates has committed. He also overreacts by calling Yates's remarks slanderous. Though Yates does refer to Thackeray's conversation in his article, he gives no examples of it, so cannot really be said to have broken the unspoken rule about not quoting from someone's club conversation.

While Thackeray received, or took, no calming advice, Yates approached his mentor Dickens for help in responding in his turn. In a self-excusing passage in his *Recollections and Experiences*, published in 1884, he recalls drafting an inflammatory reply before sending a note to Dickens on Tuesday, 15 June asking if he could visit him later that day for advice.[108] Dickens, godfather since 1855 to one of Yates's twin sons, and admirer of his young friend's actress mother, was close to Yates at this time, addressing him as 'my dear Edmund' in some of his letters. He replied immediately on 15 June, telling Yates to come before 6 p.m.; 'I needn't tell you that you

may in all things count upon / Yours Ever / CD.'[109] Dickens persuaded
Yates to tone down his intended reply, though not enough to put an end
to the silly spat. It is hard not to suppose that Dickens, in his current state
of mind, was inclined to find Thackeray particularly irritating, no doubt
because he could imagine Thackeray making jokes about his alleged relationship with an actress, and because he knew that Thackeray believed
himself Dickens's social superior. Here he was, yet again harping on about
what was, or was not, 'gentlemanly' or permitted in a club frequented by
'gentlemen'.

After the consultation with Dickens, the reply Yates sent that very
evening was far from humble or appeasing. It matches Thackeray's outrage,
pointing out that 'it is absurd to suppose me bound to accept your angry
"understanding" of my "phrases"; I do not accept it in the least; I altogether reject it.' He goes so far as to fling Thackeray's adjectives 'slanderous
and untrue' back at him, saying the words describe Thackeray's angry letter
to Yates as much as they do Yates's article in *Town Talk*. He finishes his
short reply: 'Your letter being what it is, I have nothing to add to my
present reply.'[110] All in all, the letter is not particularly offensive, though it
is defiant. The first draft, as described by Yates after all the people involved
were long dead, would certainly have raised the stakes much higher, yet
oddly it might have stopped Thackeray in his tracks, since it pointed out
some undeniable and provable truths about Thackeray's own practice of
insulting others in his journalism, and using his club membership in the
process. Yates remembered how he 'sat down at once' on receiving
Thackeray's complaint and 'took the liberty of reminding him of some past
errors of his own – rather strong errors of a similar kind as to taste':

> I reminded him how, in his *Yellowplush Correspondence* [in *Fraser's
> Magazine*, 1837–8], he had described [Bulwer Lytton as] 'Mistaw
> Edwad Lytton Bulwig' [*sic*] . . .
>
> In regard to the Garrick Club, I called Mr Thackeray's attention to
> the fact that he had not merely, in his *Book of Snobs*, and under the
> pseudonym of Captain Shandy, given an exact sketch of a former
> member, Mr Stephen Price, reproducing Mr Price's frequent and well-
> known phrases . . . he had not merely, in *Pendennis*, made a sketch of a

former member, Captain Granby Calcraft, under the name of Captain Granby Tiptoff, but in the same book, under the name of Foker, he had most offensively, though amusingly, reproduced every characteristic, in language, manner, and gesture, of our fellow-member, Mr Andrew Arcedeckne, and had gone so far as to give an exact woodcut portrait of him, to Mr Arcedeckne's intense annoyance.

With hindsight, Yates thinks, he should probably have sent this, for if he had, he 'might have heard no more of Mr Thackeray or his outraged sensitiveness'.[111] Certainly, Thackeray could not have denied the charge. Indeed, he had written to Bulwer Lytton in 1853 apologising for the *Yellowplush* satire and saying that he now wondered 'at the recklessness of the young man who could fancy such satire was harmless jocularity, and never calculate that it might give pain'.[112] The wording could not have been more appropriate to Yates's silly article about him.

Thackeray made the further mistake of referring the matter to the committee of the Garrick Club, writing on 19 June to express his hope that the committee would agree with him that 'the practice of publishing such articles as that which I enclose will . . . be fatal to the comfort of the Club, and is . . . intolerable in a Society of Gentlemen'.[113] This ensured that the business rolled on for many more months and, as collateral damage, put an unbridgeable distance between himself and Dickens. Another action of his at this time would have exacerbated the rift, if Dickens had heard of it; on 15 June Thackeray wrote to Charley Dickens, now living with his mother in Regent's Park, inviting him to a dinner the following Sunday, 20 June. Several others were coming, he wrote, adding: 'Is your mother in town, and would she care to come and meet old friends, who will be very happy indeed to see her?' 'The girls', he said (his daughters Anny and Minny, now aged twenty-one and eighteen), 'send their very best regards to her.'[114]

Saturday, 12 June was a busy day for newspapers reporting scandal. In addition to *Household Words* and Dickens, *Town Talk* and Thackeray, and the universal coverage of the Meux lunacy case, *Punch* drew attention to the Poisons Bill, introduced by Lord Derby on 4 June, which was intended to tighten up regulations for the sale of poisons. Though the bill was timely following the main scandal of the previous hot summer, the trial during June and July 1857 of Madeleine Smith for poisoning her lover with arsenic,[115] *Punch* was not particularly impressed with the proposed legislation, preferring to turn the conversation towards this year's main scandal:

> It may have a limited beneficial effect, but while Two Millions of people in London are living over a far worse poison than an Apothecary can sell, and are inhaling it day by day until they are killed . . . these tiny measures are child's play. Cleanse the Thames, the stench whereof, this last beautiful week, has been perfectly loathsome, and carry out a system of sewage, and then attack the chemists' shops.[116]

Complaints about the state of the Thames filled the papers for the next few weeks, until it was clear that something was at last going to be done, at which point the papers turned to discussing and criticising the committees empowered to decide what to do.

Meanwhile *The Times* of 12 June became excited by a scandal in a London church. Its editorial declared:

> An extraordinary meeting at St James's-hall yesterday will introduce to our readers for the first time certain ecclesiastical abominations discovered in this metropolis. We have heard a great deal about the Confessional, about priests and prying questions [i.e. in the Roman Catholic Church] . . . Few, however, have suspected that the system so often exposed had charms for any of our own Church . . . It appears that at least one clergyman, connected with the Church of St Barnabas, has been for some time in the habit of inviting and even compelling women of all ages to make confession of their mental habits as well as their actual words and deeds, not merely for some recent period, but for the whole of their lives, as one condition of receiving the Sacrament of Communion . . . There has been an exposure in St James's-hall.[117]

A second article in *The Times* on the subject that same day, 'The Confessional in Belgravia', gave a detailed account of the meeting at

11.30 a.m. on Friday, 11 June in St James's Hall in Piccadilly, which was 'crowded to excess', according to the paper. Lord Shaftesbury, a defender of Anglican evangelical orthodoxy against Anglo-Catholicism, was on the platform alongside 'many other noblemen and gentlemen'. In the body of the hall 'upwards of 50 peers and 200 members of Parliament' were in attendance. The purpose of the meeting was 'to hear certain disclosures respecting the use of the confessional by the Rev. Alfred Poole, late curate of St Barnabas, and others connected with that church'. The bishop of London, Archibald Tait, had suspended Poole pending an explanation of his conduct, and in the absence of such an explanation, had revoked Poole's licence to preach. Queen Victoria read about this in *The Times* and told her daughter Vicky, recently married to Prince Frederick William of Prussia and living in Berlin, to 'be sure and read' the account of the meeting about St Barnabas. 'It will shock you.'[118] *Punch* joked its way through the rest of the year with illustrations and slogans about the confessional, clergymen wearing large crosses, and churches displaying punningly named 'Roman' candles. On 24 July the 'Big Cut' – the main full-page illustration – featured a lady being handed into a carriage by a servant who asks her 'Confession or Cremorne, my lady?' (Cremorne being the famous pleasure garden in Chelsea).[119]

St Barnabas church had been built in 1850 in Pimlico, near Westminster, as a daughter church of the wealthy parish of St Paul's in Knightsbridge, which, according to a book on London's churches published in 1858, had recently become notorious for its 'Catholic' furniture – a screen with a cross, 'costly flowers' wrapped round its pillars, 'painted glass', and a preacher who expatiated on the 'sanctity of the priestly office'.[120] St Barnabas, too, had its screen with a cross and its silver candlesticks. Both churches were suspected of 'Roman' sympathies just at the time of the so-called 'Catholic revival' in England under John Henry Newman and Nicholas Wiseman, the latter having been appointed cardinal-archbishop of Westminster by Pope Pius IX in 1850 to mark the restoration after nearly four centuries of the Catholic hierarchy in England. Lord Shaftesbury spoke warningly of the 'surpliced priests' in 'the gorgeous temple of St Barnabas'.[121] As the prolific Yates wrote in the *Illustrated Times* on 19 June, it was remarkable that so many politicians should have turned up to discuss religious matters in St James's Hall:

The sayings and doings of the Rev. Alfred Poole and his comrades at St Barnabas's have been the theme of constant gossip during the week, and came as a boon to the ever-novelty-hunting quidnuncs [gossips who are always asking 'what now?', like the Lounger himself], whom the hot weather and the lack of excitement were generally exhausting.[122]

There was, as we have seen, plenty of excitement in the press at this time. For good measure, on Monday, 14 June the Divorce Court began hearing the most interesting case of its short existence thus far, that of *Robinson v. Robinson and Lane*. Sir Cresswell Cresswell, Lord Cockburn, and Mr Justice Wightman presided. There were three sets of counsel, one for each of the parties. The case raised legal questions which required amendments to the law to resolve them, and the bulk of the 'evidence' of adultery came from the journals of the accused woman, Isabella Robinson. As the mercury rose, reaching its height two days after the beginning of the case, the story gripped the country, providing the same kind of interest which had been generated by the Madeleine Smith case the year before. At the same time the Garrick Club affair became common knowledge and filled the columns over the summer; Dickens's separation fell out of the news briefly, only to return to the headlines in August; the Lytton fracas continued. And as Darwin received the letter from Alfred Russel Wallace which jolted him out of his quiet routine, Disraeli worked day and night to get his various bills through parliament before the summer recess.

CHAPTER FOUR

June 1858, Part II

The silver Thames

MID-JUNE BROUGHT THE hottest day of this or any previous summer, and with it came letters to *The Times* reporting local temperatures and records. G.J. Symons from Camden, north London, wrote on Tuesday, 15 June:

Sir,

Thinking it probable that many of your readers will be glad to know the exact heat of this 'very hot' day, I beg to forward the annexed observations from instruments tested by the Meteorological Society:

Temperature in the Shade

	Deg.		Deg.		Deg.
9 a.m.	80.3	2 p.m.	87.2	Greatest heat	89.9 or 90.0 [32.5 °C]
11 a.m.	84.4	3 p.m.	88.7	Least heat	61.4 [16.4 °C]
1 p.m.	88.4	5 p.m.	82.5		

The mean temperature has, therefore, notwithstanding a gentle breeze, been nearly 15 degrees above the average.[1]

On the same page the newspaper reported that the two official London measurements for Monday, 14 June, taken at noon in Hyde Park and at the entrance to Brunel's Thames Tunnel in Rotherhithe, on the south bank of the Thames, were 86 and 87 °F respectively (30 and 31 °C). By Wednesday, 16 June the top temperature of 94.5 °F in the shade (35 °C) was reached, and soon people were sending in their observations from all over the southeast of England.[2] Darwin's local journal, the *Bromley Record*, noted on 1 July that the month of June had been 'unusually fine' in that neighbourhood too, with no rain since 5 June; the 'intense heat' had 'reached its height on Wednesday, the 16th, when it was 93 degs. [34 °C] in the shade'.[3] The Rev. W. Adams, who kept 'Charts of Daily Maximum and Minimum Temperature' in nearby Beckenham and sent them to the Royal Meteorological Society in London, recorded 91 °F on the hottest day.[4]

The House of Commons sat until just before 6 p.m. on 16 June debating two bills relating to Scotland, one concerning a church tax imposed on the country in 1634 during the reign of Charles I which a number of Scottish members wished to repeal. At the end of a heroically long discussion it was decided that the bill should be 'put off for six months'.[5] Disraeli wrote to his friend Sarah Brydges Willyams on the same day, telling her that his life 'has been passed in constant combat, but I am glad to add, with respect to all important matters, constant victory'. Waxing dramatic about the weather, he connects it to the ongoing discussion of the India Bill and the last actual skirmishes in India between rebels and Sir Colin Campbell: 'The enemy, however, like the Sepoy, still keep the field, & like Sir Colin, I really have to carry on the campaign under a scorching sky.' He explains that parliament has been holding morning sittings as well as the usual afternoon ones, in order to get through the business before the end of the session. His life is 'engrossed & absorbed' from waking in the morning till 'generally three hours after midnight', the more so as his boss Lord Derby is away with a severe attack of gout.[6]

A notice in *The Times* a few days later recorded the death on 16 June, 'at his residence, 18 Sackville-street, Piccadilly', of 'John Snow, M.D., of apoplexy, aged 45'.[7] On Tuesday, 8 June Snow had attended a meeting of the Royal Medical and Chirurgical Society; on the evening of 9 June he was at a private meeting of fellow doctors discussing chest diseases. On 10 June he collapsed at home, and died of a stroke the following Wednesday.[8] His friend and colleague Benjamin Richardson completed Snow's unfinished work, *On Chloroform and Other Anaesthetics*, later in 1858, writing in his preface of his friend's achievements in the field, and also claiming for him 'the entire originality of the discovery of a connection between impure water supply and choleraic disease'. Snow, he said, had published a work on the subject in 1855 which cost him more than £200 to print and 'realized in return scarcely so many shillings'.[9] Despite Richardson's efforts, Snow's discoveries in the field of public health were largely ignored, both in Britain and abroad.[10] Notices and obituaries for Snow were few. Only the *Builder* gave him credit in its short piece on 26 June for his investigation of cholera and its causes and his pointing out 'the fact that drinking impure water had much to do with it'.[11]

Snow was therefore unable to take any part in the discussions, which now became loud and frequent, about the state of the Thames. Parliament debated it, among other topics, for four hours on 18 June, and a Commission of Sewers also met, but with so many agencies – vestries, City of London companies, water companies – putting their own financial interests first, and the Metropolitan Board of Works paralysed by disagreements about how to proceed, nothing was being decided. *The Times*'s editorial on 18 June was scathing:

As long as the nuisance did not directly affect themselves noble Lords and hon. Gentlemen could afford to disregard the safety and comfort of London; but now that they are fairly driven from their Libraries and committee-rooms – or, better still, forced to remain in them, with a putrid atmosphere around them – they may, perhaps, spare a thought for the Londoners . . . How many years has the subject been under consideration, while the Board of Works has been 'referring' plans and squabbling with the Commissioner for the time being! . . . Shall the sewage be utilised or not? Shall the outfall be at this point or at that? Surely, questions such as these . . . are not impossible of solution. They must be solved at last, and why not now, as well as three years hence? . . . It would not be amiss to deal with the Board of Works as we do with a jury which cannot be brought to hand in a decisive verdict. Let them be confined in a river steamer and compelled to ply, without intermission, between London and Vauxhall bridges until they have agreed upon a plan, or the last man of their number has been summoned away to regions where the stench which they have protected can trouble them no more.[12]

Other papers took up the cry; on Sunday, 20 June the *Era* called the Thames a sewer and noted that the Commission of Sewers would meet every so often, have 'a little discussion' about who is to 'pay the piper', then adjourn without coming to a decision. It noticed that the press had been full during this past week – the hottest – of letters complaining of the 'filthy state of the Thames', and told the authorities that they should be ashamed of themselves.[13] One such letter was sent to *The Times* on 17 June by 'T.S.', a lawyer living in chambers in the Temple, right by the river:

> I am one of those unfortunate lawyers who 'hug the festering shore', and festering it is, indeed, with a vengeance. The stench of the Temple to-day is sickening and nauseous in the extreme; we are enveloped in the foul miasma which spreads on either side of this repository of the filth of nigh three millions of human beings . . . I am being killed by inches . . . I beg, therefore, most emphatically to protest against being poisoned, and I beg further to ask those whose business it is, and who are highly paid to see that I am not poisoned, why it is that I am being poisoned . . . Let the Government bring in a Bill . . . and they will earn for themselves a renown that will not be ephemeral, and upon the next occasion that the present Chancellor addresses the electors of Slough he will be able with good reason to boast that Lord Derby's Government have done good service to the country.[14]

The writer, referring to Disraeli's crowing at the dinner given in his honour in Slough on 26 May after the failure of Palmerston's 'plot' to oust the government over the Oudh proclamation, makes a prophetic point. Derby and Disraeli were indeed to be praised for finally doing something about the Thames. 'T.S.' subscribes, rather luridly, to the common miasmic theory of disease. He was not alone in fearing an epidemic of cholera or some other contagious disease as a direct result of the state of the Thames. The *Illustrated London News* raised the prospect of 'Cholera Morbus', Lord Brougham said in parliament that he feared cholera, and stories went round of people who lived near the river dying in numbers, and of the stench striking men and women down where they stood.[15] In fact, when the statisticians got to work on the numbers, they found that there was no appreciable rise in disease in the summer of 1858; certainly there was no cholera outbreak, a fact which might have convinced people that fetid air was *not* the cause of the disease.[16] It is to be presumed that people stopped drinking Thames water, not because they connected drinking it directly with disease, but because it was so disgusting. At the end of the year the *Annual Register* looked back at the heat the smell, the 'deep blackish-green' colour of the 'once sweet and silver Thames', and marvelled that the health of the population of London had not been seriously affected.[17]

On Monday, 21 June Thomas Carlyle was preparing to escape to cool Scotland in two days' time; he told a friend that he and Jane had more or less given up eating dinner 'in this frightful roasting weather'.[18] Two days later Edward Blanchard noted that his evening walk home to his rooms in Southampton Street, leading from the Thames to the Strand, was unpleasant; he had experienced 'the frightful effects of the black and beastly Thames, about which everyone is now talking'.[19] John Ruskin wrote on 25 June from Bellinzona in Switzerland to his father in south London, congratulating him on living far enough away from the river – 'out of the way of all docks and bridges' – to be spared the suffering of many Londoners. 'I am better off', he wrote, 'even within five miles of the marshes of Ticino.'[20] The American historian John Motley, fitting in as many sociable breakfasts, lunches, and dinners with famous politicians, society ladies, and literary folk as he could during his visit to London, alluded to St Lawrence on his gridiron when attempting to give his wife an idea of the heat in a letter of 20 June. On Monday the 14th he had dined with Darwin's older brother Erasmus on an 'insufferably hot' day, even by American standards. For the whole week, he wrote, it had been 'hotter than any one ever believed it possible to be in England'. 'There was a sense of suffocation in the air, which was intensified by dining in the inevitable white choker [tight collar] in close rooms. For once in my life I have known the weather too warm for my taste.'[21]

On 21 June *The Times* printed a long letter from 'L.G.', who was clearly something of an expert on the matter of the Thames. He realised that part of the problem was the fact of so many interested parties having a role to play and yet being unable to pull in the same direction. 'Father Thames is polluted', he wrote, 'notwithstanding his many sponsors – the City, the Crown, the Metropolitan Board of Works, vested rights, private claims, and a host of technical obstructions.' The ownership of the Thames had long been a bone of contention:

> For two Centuries have the Crown and the Corporation of the city of London disputed their claim to its bed, and it was only last year that 'the Thames Conservancy Act' created a Conservancy Board and regulated the revenues . . . These revenues, however, as at present appropriated, promise but to maintain the *status quo*; there is no fund sufficient to remedy the glaring public evil. That must be done by the public at their own expense.[22]

'L.G.' implores Mr Kendall, chairman of the House of Commons committee newly formed to look into the state of the Thames, to move quickly to cut through the bureaucratic difficulties, accept that the work will be expensive, and listen to engineers like Bazalgette, who laid out a plan for his system of intercepting sewers soon after the Metropolitan Board of Works was formed at the end of 1855. 'L.G.' and the many other voices now clamouring for action were at last heeded, and from mid-June some urgency was brought to the proceedings. Among the most influential voices was that of John Simon, medical officer of the Board of Health, who produced with the help of his medical colleague Edward Greenhow a sanitary report, published in June 1858, entitled *Papers Relating to the Sanitary State of the People of England*. Simon called for public health to be taken seriously and for sanitary measures to be put in place in order to prevent in the future 'the present wasteful expenditure of human life in England'.[23] (A few years later Simon was one of those who came to accept that the miasmic theory of disease, to which he had formerly subscribed, was wrong and that John Snow and his few followers had been right about the role of contaminated water in spreading disease.[24])

The House of Commons committee which was tasked with deciding how to proceed on the sanitary question was composed of thirteen MPs and four members of the House of Lords; it included the two chief opposition politicians, Palmerston and Lord John Russell. Its members met thirteen times in all during June and July, interviewed a large number of engineers and chemists, and finally reported on 19 July. The parliamentary record of select committees shows that most members attended at least twelve of those meetings.[25] Though this was a committee which had clout and clearly meant business, the newspapers continued to keep a close and unforgiving eye on its progress.

By Saturday, 26 June the temperature was reaching the high 70s or low 80s °F daily, and the law courts in Westminster Hall gave up their sittings, wigs or no wigs, while parliament carried on in the unbearable conditions.[26] When Disraeli reported on 24 June to the queen, who was filling her diary every day with comments about the heat ('most stifling, oppressive day', she noted on 23 June[27]), he wrote in high spirits despite the exhaustion of long hours spent in purgatory. He reckoned that the heat was on his side, that 'the temper of the House, & its sanitary state, will assist' in passing the bills still being discussed, in particular the India Bill and the bill on the Thames which he was hoping to introduce in the next few days.[28] On Friday, 25 June he told the House of Commons that, while the government was not responsible for the state of the Thames, it had a moral duty to protect the public health of Londoners, and he intended that the government should act accordingly.[29] The newspapers were filled with remarks, opinions, and statistics about 'the public health', especially at the weekend, when the Saturday and Sunday papers – many of them radical or at least suspicious of a Tory government, however uncharacteristically progressive that government was revealing itself to be – weighed in behind *The Times* with their colourful details and dire warnings. *The Times* itself waxed ironically lyrical on Saturday, 26 June, anticipating many a *Punch* illustration and a host of Thames-themed pantomimes to come at Christmas 1858:

Rivers are poetically supposed to think and talk, to rise from their oozy beds with warnings or predictions, and to lament over national calamities or the deaths of monarchs. If the river god who rules the stream flowing beneath our London bridges possesses the qualities of his brethren in mythical ages, he must exult at the acknowledgements of his might which are being made on every side. The Thames fever is now at its height. Every power, dignity, and institution confesses its alarm. The City Corporation, which is generally unable to detect a fault in anything connected with or subject to itself, admits that the Thames is not exactly in a state of purity. The civic functionaries who found the aroma of Smithfield [London's meat market] dainty and delicate allow that the water which splashes up at Billingsgate [the fish market] is not grateful to the human smell. The Courts of Law have been almost stunk out of Westminster-hall ... The Common Pleas and the Exchequer have both borne witness to the pestiferous exhalations which creep into their courts. Both Houses of Parliament are full of the subject.[30]

The article reports that Goldsworthy Gurney, the engineer appointed to supervise the heating, lighting and ventilation of the new Houses of Parliament recently built by Sir Charles Barry and still undergoing completion and decoration, has written to the speaker of the Commons to say that 'he can no longer be responsible for the health of the House'. Gurney was one of the men interviewed in the coming days by the committee on the Thames; he put forth his own solution, rejected by the select committee, to put slopes in the river and disperse the sewage *in* the Thames itself by directing it below the low water mark, and to burn the gases in sewers.[31] Surely, says *The Times*, there are enough engineers in the House of Commons to take the lead. It should not have 'abandoned' the matter to a 'half-powerless' Board of Works, which has been bedevilled for the last three years by disputes between the board as chaired by John Thwaites and the bogeyman of many commentators, Sir Benjamin Hall.[32] Thwaites had been elected chair of the Board of Works in 1855, and would continue in the post until his death in 1870.[33] Hall had been chief commissioner of works in Palmerston's government, bringing in the bill 'for the better local management of the metropolis', by which the Board of Works was first established. It was this piece of legislation, passed into law in 1855, on which Disraeli was about to build with his Metropolis Local Management Act Amendment Bill, popularly known as the Thames Purification Bill.

Though Hall was quarrelsome and divisive, and was one of those who had previously rejected Bazalgette's plans, he was commemorated in the name 'Big Ben' given to the newly cast bell which was to be hung in the clock tower of the new Palace of Westminster.[34] On 5 June the *People's Paper* had reported the impressive procession as the new Big Ben was transported from the Whitechapel factory where it was cast to its destination in Westminster. 'It was drawn on a truck by ten horses, and had a union jack hoisted on the top of it'; a large crowd accompanied it on its way.[35]

All the weekly newspapers concentrated on the weekend of 26–27 June on the heat, the Thames, and public health. That Saturday Ernest Jones's Radical *People's Paper* carried a short piece entitled 'No Coat, No Justice'. It reported from the Thames Police Court, located in Stepney in the East End of London, that a man waiting to make an application to the court was ordered by the magistrate, Mr Yardley, to return home and put on a jacket: 'I will not hear you without your coat. It is most indecent trim for you to come into this court. I will not hear anyone without his jacket or coat if he has one.' According to the paper, the man left the court without making his application and before he returned the magistrate had left the bench.[36] Not for this working man the courtesy shown to the lawyers in Westminster Hall who had asked on the hottest day if they might remove their wigs.

On the same Saturday, 26 June, *The Times* printed a letter from the surgeon and chemist Alfred Smee, who wrote of having observed the river from a professional point of view for thirty years and never before seeing it like this, 'opaque and black as ink'. Stop the 'twaddling debates', he urged, and give someone the power to get on with improving things. The *Illustrated London News* talked of 'our representatives' heroically sitting, 'both night and morning to be poisoned by the stenches from the River Thames' and yet not being prepared to spend the money to solve the problem. 'Londoners, Look to Your River! The Thames a Deadly Cesspool' cried the *Era* on Sunday, 27 June;[37] the *Era* was one of the papers which raised fears of contagious diseases, stating rather vaguely and without authority that cases of typhus and diarrhoea were increasing among those living near the Thames.[38]

One person whose family was affected by contagious disease, though it was not in this case related to the Thames air or water, was Darwin, who wrote from Down to Charles Lyell on 26 June, telling him that '3 children have died in the village from Scarlet Fever, & others have been at death's door, with terrible suffering'.[39] He told Lyell that he and Emma were frightened, because a few days earlier their 15-year-old daughter Henrietta, known as Etty, had become seriously ill with something like diphtheria, an illness unknown in Britain until an outbreak in 1857. By 25 June the youngest Darwin child, eighteen-month-old Charles Waring, was showing symptoms of what Darwin thought might be scarlet fever.[40]

Queen Victoria groaned almost every day about the heat, but she was impressively active, going to a concert of Beethoven and Mendelssohn music at the Philharmonic Hall on 21 June, to another concert at the Royal Academy the following day, to the Crystal Palace in Sydenham by train with some guests on 25 June, when she suffered from 'a bad head-ache', so could not stay very long. During the hottest two weeks there were royal visits to ballets and operas, including Donizetti's melodramatic opera *Lucrezia Borgia*, and to a performance of the French comic opera *Fra Diavolo* by Daniel Auber at the newly opened Theatre Royal, Covent Garden, in the splendid building (which still stands today) designed by Sir Charles Barry's son Edward.[41] She also hosted dinners which were attended by foreign royalty, Derby, Disraeli, Lord John Russell, Sir Edward Bulwer Lytton, and other public figures.

Queen Victoria, Cruiser, and the *Great Eastern*

On Saturday, 26 June Victoria and Albert went, not for the first time that year, to see the famous American horse tamer, James Rarey, perform his show. Like thousands of others who attended his performances, Victoria marvelled at his ability to tame in front of her eyes various wild horses and other animals. On this occasion, as she recorded in her journal, he first showed us a very wild zebra from the Zoological Gardens, – very wicked & spiteful, which is not yet by any means vanquished but already follows him about, then 'Cruizer' [actually Cruiser], a most vicious stallion, whom no one could go near, & who was, in consequence half starved & shockingly ill used; it has now become like a lamb, & has been taught to do all sorts of tricks. We patted it. After this, Mr Rarey went through the whole process with 'Snipe', one of Albert's horses which furiously resisted, but with which he was also perfectly successful.[42]

Rarey's show, along with his book *The Art of Taming Wild Horses*, was one of the entertainment sensations of the year. Cruiser was a stallion owned by Lord Dorchester, who was one of a number of horse-loving aristocrats from whom Rarey raised subscriptions for his book. The queen, Prince Albert, the prince of Wales, Baron de Rothschild, and Sir Alexander Cockburn of the Divorce Court also subscribed.[43] Rarey provided thrills for the masses and the aristocracy alike, and was also a rich source to be mined by illustrated magazines and by the pantomime writers in the 1858–9 season. In the volume of *Punch* covering January to June 1858 Mr Punch dreams that he is Rarey and can tame all the world's political leaders. The ever-alert Sala jumped on the bandwagon too with his comic story in November 1858, *How I Tamed Mrs Cruiser*, an update for the 1850s of Shakespeare's *The Taming of the Shrew*.[44]

Despite the weather and the stink on the Thames, Victoria braved it all to see another of the popular sights of the summer. She stepped on board Brunel's *Great Eastern*, though she still used the ship's baptismal name, the *Leviathan*. As she told Vicky on 29 June:

We went by land to Deptford yesterday[,] got into boats and rowed along to the Leviathan which is lying there and went on board her; but they can't proceed for want of funds! . . . we were half poisoned by the dreadful smell of the Thames – which is such that I felt quite sick when I came home, and people cannot live in their houses; the House of Commons can hardly sit – and the session will close soon in consequence.[45]

In her journal she described the ship as 'stupendous; 600 ft long, 83 wide, & 58 in depth'.[46]

Punch soon printed a poem commemorating the queen's visit:

What sight was that which loyal eyes
Beheld with horror – not surprise –
   On Thames's filthy tide,
Which bore Victoria, England's Queen,
Who, down the River having been,
   Back to her Palace hied . . .
The Sovereign, as she neared Dog's Isle,
Was fain to hold – nay do not smile –
A bouquet to her nose![47]

The great ship was moored at Deptford on the south side of the river, opposite the Isle of Dogs, where she had been launched initially, and had been open for viewing by the public since the beginning of June. The papers had welcomed the initiative to raise money to fit out this extraordinary ship; they were full of her record-breaking measurements and potential feats. The *Weekly Chronicle* described what readers might see for the cost of half a crown (two shillings and sixpence, or an eighth of a pound): 'Although the mammoth ship is still so far from a state of completion that it is calculated it would take a thousand men five months' unceasing toil day and night to fit her out entirely – there is still, in all conscience, quite enough of her visible to enable any reasonable mortal to arrive at some adequate notion of her matchless magnitude.'[48] There were 30,000 wrought-iron plates, 3,000,000 iron rivets, the shell of the ship weighed 10,000 tons, and she was 700 feet long and 83 feet wide, said the *Chronicle*, adding, 'without her paddle-boxes, she would stick in passing through one of the broadest streets of London – Pall Mall'. 'Supposing the Leviathan to be now upon the eve of her first voyage, she might, in a month, take an army of 10,000 men out to the shores of Hindostan', or carry 4,000 passengers and 18,000 tons of coal and cargo.

This technological wonder, visited by all and sundry during the next few months, was hampered not just by the need for more money, but also by the sheer audaciousness of her proportions. Launching her had proved difficult and dangerous, because she was too long to launch at right angles to the river; she would have almost hit the Deptford shore opposite the huge Millwall Iron Works Company at Masthouse Terrace Pier on the Isle of Dogs where she was built. She had to be launched parallel to the river with the bows pointing out to sea. Two huge timber cradles on a specially designed slipway held the ship until she was ready to slide into the water.[49] (Part of the slipway, together with one of the ship's huge iron chains, can still be seen at Masthouse Terrace Pier.)

As a contemporary engineer, Thomas Wright, wrote in 1867, the Isle of Dogs was the centre of the iron shipbuilding and marine engineering trade, hosting more than a dozen establishments, including the 'gigantic one' which built the *Great Eastern*. The company, owned by John Scott Russell, who collaborated – not always amicably – with the brilliant but prickly Brunel on the great ship, employed, according to Wright, 4,000 men and boys. A number of these, including Russell himself, were Scots who had learned their trade on the great shipbuilding River Clyde in Glasgow.[50] Brunel was irascible and undiplomatic, writing on one occasion in 1855, early in the process, to the placid Russell, who had failed to give him the precise details he wanted about the weight of the ship: 'How the devil can you say you satisfied yourself of the weight of the ship when the figures your Clerk gave you are 1000 tons less than I make it or than you made it a few months ago. For *shame*, if you are satisfied. I am sorry to give you trouble but I think you will thank me for it. I wish you *were* my obedient servant, I should begin by a little flogging.'[51] There were arguments and a brief parting between the two men, but the ship continued to be built. When *The Times* described Russell as the builder in April 1857, he wrote to the paper to demand that Brunel be given his fair share of the praise:

I designed her lines and constructed the iron hull of the ship, and am responsible for her merits or defects as a piece of naval architecture . . . It is, however, to the company's engineer, Mr I.K. Brunel, that the original conception is due of building a steam ship large enough to carry coals sufficient for full steaming on the longest voyage . . . The idea of using two sets of engines and two propellers is original, and was his invention . . . It will be seen that these are the main characteristics which distinguish this from other ships, and these are Mr Brunel's ideas.[52]

The launch was planned for autumn 1857; Brunel was hurried into it by the financial backers, who advertised the launch for 3 November and encouraged paying spectators, to Brunel's annoyance. The attempt failed, as the cradles did not move as planned but jerked, killing one of the workers. Brunel suspended the operation until more trials could be made and advice taken.[53] Everyone watched with interest to see whether the next attempt would be successful. For two weeks in December preparations were made to try again, but once more the launch failed. On 7 December Carlyle told his brother John that 'a terrible tussle is going on, launching that Big Ship'.[54] Brunel despaired; he was tired and ill and worried about money. To his relief success came finally on 31 January 1858, when the ship slid into the river as intended.

The naming of the ship was confusing. She was registered as the *Great Eastern*, but apparently at the first launch attempt on 3 November 1857 a reluctant and infuriated Brunel, when asked to choose a name, snapped that they could call her Tom Thumb for all he cared. The young woman designated to name the ship was Henrietta Hope, the daughter of one of the company's financial backers, Henry Hope, the richest commoner in England and an MP who had supported Disraeli's Young England movement twenty years earlier. She it was who cracked a bottle of champagne over the hull and named the ship *Leviathan*.[55] Though she was finally launched successfully in January 1858, there was no money to complete her or sail her anywhere. Brunel was ill and ordered by doctors to go abroad to rest. The *Leviathan/Great Eastern* sat at Deptford, on display and visitable, until a new company bought her at the end of November 1858. After more delays and anxieties about costs she was ready by September 1859 to make her first voyage, to Liverpool, with the idea that if all went well she would then embark on a proper maiden voyage to New York.[56] Brunel, though very feeble, went on board, but was too ill to travel. The ship set off without him on 7 September; an explosion off the Kent coast killed six sailors on board. Brunel himself died the following week. The *Great Eastern*, as she was now called, sailed on, but the envisaged voyage to

New York was put off for another year.[57] She was ahead of her time and never reached her full potential, though she was to be rightly celebrated as the only ship large enough to carry sufficient cable to complete the Atlantic Cable project in 1866. Brunel died in despair, but his efforts made him a hero. The most famous photographs of him are those taken in 1857–8 on the slipway beside the huge chains of the *Great Eastern*, and later on board his masterpiece. He looks tiny and unwell. (The young photographer who caught these images, Robert Howlett, had been commissioned by W.P. Frith to take pictures of the crowds at Derby Day in May 1856. Frith used them when painting his famous *Derby Day* picture for exhibition in 1858.[58])

The weather stayed hot right till the end of June. Record-keepers varied slightly in their observations and calculations, but it was generally agreed that June 1858 was either the hottest or second-hottest month on record. Joseph Irving, the journalist and antiquary who published a largely accurate account of public events from 1837 to 1871, *The Annals of Our Time*, reported that 'the mean high day temperature' was 76.5 °F (just under 25 °C) – 'or 8.6 above the average'. Wednesday, 16 June hit the heights, reaching an unprecedented 102 °F (39 °C) momentarily at Greenwich, according to Irving.[59] When on the last day of the month Disraeli, Gladstone, and other members of the House of Commons Bank Acts committee were seen rushing from a committee room at two in the afternoon, with handkerchiefs pressed to their noses, the image was seized on to characterise the crisis.[60] The heat and stink were widely compared to the trials faced by the British in India; the Thames was likened to the Ganges, as well as to the fearful rivers of myth, the Lethe and the Styx. The writer for the *Athenaeum* whose misfortune it was to review a matinée concert on Saturday, 26 June wrote of 'crowd, crinoline, *ciarleria* [chatter], and a heat which made one think sympathetically of Lahore and Lucknow'.[61]

Crinolineomania

Contemplating on Saturday, 3 July the previous fortnight's excessive heat, *Punch* offered its readers a survival guide in an article entitled 'Advice in Hot Weather':

Refrain from reading the Debates. Keep as cool as possible . . . Avoid
going near a tallow-chandler's shop . . . Shun public dinners . . . Keep
clear of concerts, classical quartets, *matinées, soirées, réunions, thés
dansantes* or *chantantes*, private parties . . . Walk twice the distance
rather than get *inside* a red-hot oven of an omnibus; in the latter case,
you will infallibly be baked alive . . . Avoid all theological hair-splitting
matters of metaphysical mysticism, . . . parish squabbles, and Puseyite
scandals [a reference to the goings on at St Barnabas], until the cool of
the evening. Wear old boots . . . Tight clothes are a nuisance . . . during
this brain-boiling and all-your-joints-hot-roasting weather.[62]

Though it might seem that the surprisingly long-lasting vogue for
ladies to wear crinoline petticoats under their ever-expanding skirts would
make life doubly unbearable in such hot weather, the reverse was true.
Queen Victoria's daughter Vicky, broiling in a Berlin summer, expressed
her surprise and delight that her mother was wearing 'a cage'; 'what a
comfort they are, so cool and light', she wrote on 24 July.[63] When Darwin's
granddaughter Gwen Raverat wrote down her memories of the family, she
recalled asking her Aunt Etty, Darwin's daughter Henrietta, what it was
like to wear a crinoline. Gwen, born in 1885, suffered through the fashions of the 1890s and 1900s, when women wore floor-length 'heavy tweed
"walking skirts", which kept on catching between the knees', and girls
sweltered in summer in vests, stays, heavy woollen stockings, and overalls
with long sleeves. Aunt Etty told her that it was 'delightful' to wear a
crinoline: 'I've never been so comfortable since they went out [of fashion].
It kept your petticoats away from your legs, and made walking so light
and easy.'[64]

Skirts had been getting progressively fuller for most of the nineteenth
century, and required more and more petticoats underneath them to keep
them from collapsing. The petticoats got stiffer and heavier to accommodate the increasing width. Something was needed to support the yards of
material in skirts without making the whole costume too hot and heavy.
The word 'crinoline', originally denoting a fabric woven with horsehair
(French *crin*) used to stiffen petticoats, came to mean the new type of
petticoat patented in 1856, which allowed skirts to grow in diameter

without weighing down the dress and its wearer. This was the spring-steel hoop, known as a cage because of its shape; it was worn on top of a cotton petticoat, with the dress draped over the cage. The steel solution was found after experiments with rubber, inflatable tubes, whalebone, and cane.[65] The popularity of the crinoline lasted for at least ten years, after which the fullness moved to the back of the skirt in the form of a bustle, before beginning to subside altogether.[66] In May 1865, *Punch*, which constantly lampooned the crinoline, declared that the garment was now 'doomed'. 'Ladies fresh from Paris startle our eyes now-a-days by appearing in what at first sight we might fancy are their night-dresses.'[67] The fashion had come from Paris in the first place. The Empress Eugénie, wife of Napoleon III, had her crinolines made for her by the English couturier Charles Worth.

Thanks to the advent of steel hoops, dresses could become bigger and more elaborate in their decoration without bringing discomfort to the wearer. In April 1856 Disraeli's wife Mary Anne, rather too keen – given her age (she was now sixty-four) – on keeping up with the latest fashion, told her elderly friend Sarah Brydges Willyams that the dresses in London 'this season' were 'vast & grand looking, [with] such an immense quantity of trimming'.[68] That the fashion was new in London and might not yet have reached provincial parts of Britain in 1856 was suggested in a short story by Elizabeth Gaskell, published in Dickens's journal *All the Year Round* in 1863. Called 'The Cage at Cranford' and set in 1856, the story never mentions the word crinoline, but tells of the ladies of Cranford expecting something fashionable from Paris. When they are told it will be a 'cage', they are disappointed, thinking it must be a present for the parrot. The item arrives, and they are puzzled by its lack of top or bottom and try to sew and tie it up in order to put the parrot inside. The maid Fanny shyly suggests it might be a petticoat, and is ridiculed by the ladies, until the local doctor recognises its identity from looking at his wife's fashion magazine.[69]

Punch began its ten-year running commentary on crinolines in the summer of 1856, with pictures of complicated cage structures, including one showing a woman in a very wide dress with the cage worn *outside* her skirt and with a circular platform on top on which her two children play, one spinning a hoop, the other hanging over the bars of the platform. The picture is entitled 'Every Lady her own Perambulator'.[70] By December 1857 'Dr Punch' is shown taking the pulse of a woman wearing a crinoline; the accompanying text, 'Crinolineomania', declares that this is a new female complaint, but it is the husbands who have something to complain about. The contagious disease broke out first in Paris, says *Punch*, starting with the empress and soon spreading alarmingly to Britain. 'Like other insane people', goes the article, 'the Crinolineomaniac is difficult to approach – indeed it may be said that even her nearest relatives have to stand some distance off her', with even her husband being compelled to keep at arm's length. Dr Punch's advice is to keep away from illustrated books of fashion and from Regent Street, where the most up-to-date cages can be bought. Husbands should put their patients 'on a low diet of pin-money' and try laughing them out of their insanity. To help them Dr Punch 'will continue to dispense this wholesome medicine [i.e. ridicule], in weekly doses, at the small charge of threepence'.[71]

Punch was as good as its word. All through 1857 and 1858 the magazine commented on the disadvantages of the crinoline craze. In February 1857 it said with authority that ladies were now complaining that they received fewer invitations to parties, because rooms which used to accommodate fifty ladies now only had space for fifteen. In May it suggested that many paintings sent in for the annual Royal Academy exhibition would take up too much room, as they depict life-size ladies wearing crinolines.[72] In February 1858 two ladies in huge dresses are shown trying to get through a narrow church door; in July a short article entitled 'Crinoline in the Slums' describes the scrum at the old clothes market held on Sundays in the appropriately named Petticoat Lane, where servants and the working-class women of Houndsditch now buy crinolines discarded by the ladies of Belgravia; and in October the magazine declares a 'New Omnibus Regulation', namely that ladies must now hang their hoops on the outside of the vehicle so as not to take up too much space inside.[73]

Most surprisingly, but in fact truthfully, *Punch* pointed out on 29 May 1858 that Edward Barry's new Covent Garden Theatre, recently opened, had taken crinolines into account by making the seats and staircases wider than in the previous building, which had burnt to the ground in 1856:

'*Place aux dames!* To ladies more than ever now must place or space be given' ... It is a new thing to us to say anything in favour of the Crinoline monstrosities, but we must admit that the present width of fashion may, masculinely viewed, be found of some advantage. For instance, thanks to large and lovely woman, Covent Garden is so built that a man may stretch his legs in it ... We gentlemen of England may loll there at our ease, and sit through a whole opera uncramped as to our knees, etc. Decidedly, for this we have to thank the ladies.[74]

The *Builder*, in a long article on 22 May on Barry's sumptuous new building describing the crowds gaping as it emerged from its wrapping to open on 15 May, gave detailed accounts of the increase in dimensions offered by this state-of-the-art edifice.[75] Meanwhile men's fashions had begun to accommodate themselves to the crinoline craze by becoming narrower at the bottom. The so-called 'pegtop' trousers came in from the mid-fifties, making dancing easier.[76]

Though the dangers to women of falling over by catching their hoops on an obstacle, or having their dresses catch fire, were obvious, crinolines came in handy on some occasions. They could keep a drowning woman afloat long enough for her to be saved, for example.[77] In July the *People's Paper* reported a 'Perversion of Crinoline': 'On Tuesday [6 July] a female attired in a most voluminous skirt, was committed by the Liverpool magistrates for pocket picking and shop-lifting. By an ingenious contrivance she had formed her crinoline into an immense receptacle for stolen property. Several shawls and other articles stolen, shortly before her apprehension, were found upon her.'[78]

When the season of pantomime came round in December, crinoline played an important part in the story of Amy Robsart, the heroine of the extravaganza *Kenilworth, or ye Queene, ye Earle, and ye Maydenne* at the Strand Theatre. The historical Amy was the wife of Robert Dudley, earl of Leicester, a favourite of Queen Elizabeth I. While her husband accompanied the queen on her royal progresses through the kingdom, Amy was left alone at home. She died suddenly from falling down a staircase; almost immediately a plot to murder her on the part of her ambitious husband was suspected. This tragic story was turned to 'pun and parody' by the authors of the burlesque, which according to the review in the *Athenaeum* was 'manufactured with some skill'. A happy ending is contrived; Amy Robsart 'is saved from death by her crinoline, which prevents her from falling through the fatal trap'.[79]

Punch and several of the 1858–9 pantomimes punned and joked about the crinoline petticoat by calling it the 'hoop-de-dooden-do'. The originator of this trend was the *Punch* writer Henry Silver, who published a poem in the magazine on 5 June 1858. Called 'Hoop de dooden doo. A fashionable ballad', it drew on an already popular dance song, the *Hoop de dooden do Galop*, by Charles Marriott, first published in 1857 and much reprinted. This in turn seems to have been influenced by a song of the same title performed in New York concert halls by the banjoist and comedian Henry Fox. This song, imitating the voice of a freed slave as he walks along a railway track, begins 'One hundred years ago to-day, / My old massa set me free', and ends every stanza with 'Hoop de dooden do'.[80] Henry Silver combines the minstrel dialect with the idea of a dance; he concentrates on the awkwardness for the male partner caused by the crinoline, or 'hoop de dooden do'. The speaker complains that his dance partner's crinoline trips him up; he addresses young women in general:

Now, gals, if you at parties show,
And in de dance would shake de toe,
Not like balloons but ladies go:
    Hoop de dooden doo.
You tink de Crinnylean de ting,
But your partners it to grief do bring,
It bruise dere leg, it break dere shin –
    Di Hoop de dooden doo.[81]

The hoop joke seems less funny to us now than it apparently did to many Victorians, who enjoyed hearing variations of the ballad throughout the spring and summer of 1858 as part of an entertainment put on in various packed halls, including St James's. The American blackface troupe the Christy Minstrels sang and danced to it as they 'capered' and 'spooned' their 'sentimental airs', as the *Illustrated Times* noted in its review on 26 June.[82]

The crinoline era was a relatively long one in the history of fashion. Women of all classes were keen to get hold of the item. By 1864 many were becoming tired of it, among them Jane Carlyle, though she noted in a letter to her husband in September of that year that her own maids were still going around in 'abominably large Crinolines'.[83]

More marriage troubles

Covent Garden Theatre was not the only building which accommodated the crinoline. Moor Park, Edward Lane's elegant hydropathic establishment in the rolling Surrey hills, was lavishly decorated with pastoral scenes; it had French windows looking out upon a fountain, a river with an island in the middle, and a summerhouse; and it also boasted a 'crinoline staircase', sweeping and curving with iron railings ballooning like a lady's skirts.[84] Lane ran a successful business, attracting wealthy patients, to whom he gave individual care and attention. Darwin was one of them. He sought relief at Moor Park from his chronic nausea, vomiting, headaches, boils, and flatulence, and from working too hard on his 'everlasting species-Book', as he told Charles Lyell.[85] His first visit to Moor Park took place in April 1857. He had already tried the long-established water cure of Dr James Gully in Malvern without success, and he disapproved of Gully's belief in clairvoyance. He was hoping for a better outcome under Dr Lane's care.

At first Darwin thought he had found respite from his chronic ailments. He told Hooker that, after only a week at Moor Park, he could 'walk & eat like a hearty Christian; & even my nights are good', adding humorously that though he had no idea how hydropathy works, 'it dulls one's brain splendidly. I have not thought about a single species of any kind, since leaving home.'[86] To W.D. Fox he wrote even more cheerfully:

I had got very much below par at home, & it is really quite astonishing & utterly unaccountable the good this one week has done me. I like Dr Lane & his wife & her mother, who are the proprietors of this establishment very much. Dr L is too young – that is his only fault – but he is a gentleman & very well read man. And in one respect I like him better than Dr Gully, viz that he does not believe in all the rubbish which Dr G does; nor does he pretend to explain much, which neither he [n]or any doctor can explain . . . I really think I shall make a point of coming here for a fortnight occasionally, as the country is very pleasant for walking . . . I am well convinced that the only thing for Chronic cases is the water-cure.[87]

He visited again several times, despite his disappointment that within a week of getting home in May 1857, 'all the wonderful good which Moor Park did me at the time' had 'gone all away like a flash of lightening [*sic*]', now that he was back at work again.[88]

Edward Lane was thirty-four when Darwin met him for the first time. He had moved south from Edinburgh three years earlier to start his water-cure business, having studied medicine alongside the older of two remarkable brothers, George and Charles Drysdale, in the Scottish capital. The Lane and Drysdale families were neighbours there, and Edward married the brothers' sister Mary in 1847. When he moved to Surrey in March 1854, Mary, their two sons, and Mary's mother, the wealthy Lady Drysdale, came with him.[89]

George and Charles Drysdale often stayed at Moor Park. Both were medical practitioners, though Charles, the younger of the two, had trained first as an engineer and worked for a time on Brunel's *Great Eastern* while employed by John Scott Russell's company in Millwall.[90] The brothers were freethinkers in religion and held unorthodox views in medicine. Charles worked among the poor, supported the movement for medical education for women, and in 1877 helped to found the Malthusian League, an organisation which advocated the use of contraceptives to limit family size on economic, social and medical grounds.[91] He was also, in 1878, one of the first doctors to warn that tobacco was both addictive and dangerous to health.[92]

George, having scooped all the prizes as a student in Edinburgh, in 1855 published, anonymously, *Physical, Sexual, and Natural Religion, by a Student of Medicine*, a frank discussion of sexuality and health, in which he deplores the general public's ignorance of the workings of the body, including the sexual organs, and offers 'a short sketch of these organs and the function of reproduction'.[93] Drysdale's pioneering attempt to educate his readers about sexuality and birth control was clearly welcome, for his book, under the less explosive title *Elements of Social Science*, went through thirty-five editions in the next fifty years, selling 80,000 copies by the end of the century.[94]

Since Drysdale never publicly acknowledged his authorship of this philanthropic but shocking book, it is unlikely that Darwin knew it was his. But Edward Lane and a group of unorthodox Edinburgh friends almost certainly did. Among these were Robert Chambers, the publisher and, like Drysdale, the anonymous author of a notorious book (in his case *Vestiges of Creation*), and his friend George Combe, the leading British advocate of phrenology, the science of reading character through the contours of the head. Combe was consulted by Prince Albert about the education of his unbiddable oldest son, the prince of Wales; in 1850 Albert sent his secretary and son's tutor, Dr Ernest Becker, to Edinburgh to study phrenology with Combe in the hope of learning how to correct the boy's 'violent & selfish dispositions'.[95] Combe was a regular visitor to the water cure at Moor Park. He had befriended not only Edward Lane in Edinburgh, but also the woman who nearly brought Lane to ruin in 1858, Isabella Robinson.

Isabella was an excitable woman, fond of reading poetry and inclined to fall for, and flirt with, younger men, including John Thom, the tutor she engaged for her three sons in 1854.[96] She had been widowed as a young woman and had remarried in 1844, aged thirty-one. Her husband, Henry Robinson, was six years older. He and his brothers were engineers who ran an iron works building steam-powered ships at Millwall. The Robinsons went into business with John Scott Russell in 1848, separating from him four years later. Henry had two illegitimate daughters, and was a mean and inattentive husband, often away on business; Isabella was bored and unhappy.[97] Like Emma Bovary, flawed heroine of Flaubert's notorious novel of 1857, she turned in her boredom to reading romantic literature, dreamed of exciting lovers, and engaged in sexual flirtation outside her disappointing marriage. Isabella kept a journal full of steamy thoughts, and when she began in 1854 to frequent Moor Park as a friend of the

Lanes and Drysdales, and a 'patient' – in the rather vague sense of suffering from loneliness and ennui and needing stimulating company – she focused her emotional and sexual needs on Dr Lane, who was ten years her junior. It was her journal which constituted the bulk of the 'evidence' in the divorce suit Henry Robinson brought against her in the summer of 1858.

The case became headline news from its first day, 14 June 1858. It stood out in two respects. Firstly, Henry, having found Isabella's secret journal in 1856 and read in it of her hatred of him, her passion for Lane, and Lane's reciprocation – as she represented it – of her love, had applied in December 1857 to the Ecclesiastical Court for a judicial separation *a mensa et thoro*. The sleepy old court in Doctors' Commons granted him his separation, as one of the final acts of its existence. Isabella, who had not contested the proceedings, lived apart from Henry from then on. He kept two of their sons with him (along with his illegitimate daughters).[98] When the new Divorce Act came into force in January 1858, Henry decided to apply for a full divorce, which would allow him to marry again. The new proceedings meant that he had to prove adultery against Isabella *and* to name her co-respondent, in this case Edward Lane. The evidence he brought was the journal and the testimony of one former servant of the Lane household. The second remarkable feature of the case was that it proved to be unresolvable by the new act as it stood in the early days, since the co-defendant, Lane, was also – or should have been – a witness, inasmuch as he was the medical attendant on Isabella Robinson, whose physical and mental health were to form a large part of the proceedings, and the chief person who could testify about the contents of the journal as they related to him and his movements. The law as it stood did not allow for Lane to give evidence.

Cresswell, Cockburn, and Wightman presided. Henry Robinson, Isabella, and Edward Lane were each represented by a different counsel. None of the three protagonists was to appear in the witness box, Isabella and Lane being prohibited under the new Divorce Act. Henry's counsel declared that he would prove Isabella's guilt by reference to her journal, but he also said he was 'bound to confess that I entertain some doubt whether your Lordships will consider it sufficient as against Dr Lane'.[99] He meant that in law the journal could be used as evidence of a confession of guilt by

Isabella but not as an accusation against Dr Lane unless he could give evidence in his own defence or there was sufficient evidence in addition to the journal to prove the case against him. Lane's lawyer wished to have the journal ruled out as inadmissible evidence, but this was turned down by the court after the judges had conferred. Isabella's counsel, who had also been hoping that the journal would be dismissed, changed his plan and set about using the journal to prove that his client was a fantasist who filled her diary with imagined sexual encounters, that she was, in short, mentally ill, suffering from the kind of instability associated in many doctors' minds with the menopause. It was a dangerous strategy, and one which Isabella only intermittently agreed to him using. Little wonder that the case became the first in the new Divorce Court to attract widespread public attention.

The case for Henry Robinson soon came to depend on the journal, since his main 'witness' of unseemly goings on between Isabella and Dr Lane, a former stable boy at Moor Park, was shown to be unreliable. In Edward Lane's defence a number of Moor Park's paying guests were brought in to say that though they had often seen Lane and Isabella walking together in the grounds, they had also seen the doctor walking with other female patients in the same way. Lady Drysdale was called on the second day of the trial, 15 June. *The Times* reported her testimony the following day: 'Lady Drysdale, the mother of Mrs Lane, said there had been great intimacy between the families of Dr Lane and Mr Robinson. There was nothing in the conduct of Dr Lane towards Mrs Robinson at all different to his conduct towards other ladies.'[100]

Isabella's counsel Robert Phillimore followed, 'dwelling upon the weakness of the oral evidence' brought against Isabella and Lane, and insisting on the 'fallacious character of journals, as compared with other confessions'. 'This journal had evidently been written by a woman of so flighty, extravagant, excitable, romantic, and irritable a mind as almost to amount to insanity.' It had been written 'under the influence of a disease peculiar to women' – especially menopausal women – 'which had the effect of producing the most extraordinary delusions upon the mind of the patients, and frequently caused them to accuse themselves of the most horrible crimes'.[101] He read out extracts from the journal (which most of the newspapers declined to print verbatim, though they summarised them fairly fully); these were self-accusatory and also referred to Isabella's physical suffering. Her doctor, asked to describe her state of mind, talked of 'morbid depression'. Other medical men renowned for their expertise in female complaints, or insanity, or both, were called to give their opinions, though none had met, let alone examined, Isabella.[102] Phillimore requested leave to examine the co-respondent, Dr Lane, but the judges declared that under the terms of the new act 'no party to a suit in cases of adultery could be examined'.

However, they saw that this was problematic in Dr Lane's case, and adjourned until the next day, Wednesday, 16 June, in order to decide whether he could be called. They were troubled enough to state on that day that they needed to discuss further whether to take the unprecedented step of dismissing Lane as a co-respondent and admitting him as a witness instead. The court was adjourned until Monday, 21 June.[103] In the meantime, the weekend newspapers enjoyed speculating on the outcome. On Saturday, 19 June the *People's Paper* quoted liberally from Isabella's diary as read out in court in an article under the loaded and presumptuous title 'An Unfaithful Wife – A Lady's Extraordinary Diary'.[104] The *Era* for Sunday, 20 June gave its report on the case the enticing title 'Crim. Con. and Hydropathic Love: Exposure of a Lady's Diary'; like the *People's Paper*, it was bold enough to quote from Isabella's journal, including a relatively explicit passage about her relations with Dr Lane during the drive from Moor Park to the local railway station.[105]

When proceedings resumed on the Monday, Cockburn announced that five of the six judges authorised to sit in the Divorce Court had decided that they were unable to dismiss Lane from the suit in order to allow him to be a witness. Mr Justice Wightman alone thought that there was nothing in the wording of the new act to stop them from doing so. Given the majority opinion, Cockburn continued with the case, asking the barristers to sum up. More quotations from the journal were read out to prove that Isabella was fantasising when she wrote of embraces – and more – in the gardens, on coach journeys, and in Edward Lane's study at Moor Park. The journal was the sole 'evidence' of such encounters. The case was further adjourned until Saturday, 3 July for judgment to be pronounced.[106]

The journal entries which were read out to the court related to Isabella's visit to Moor Park in September and October 1854. In them she describes intense discussions with Lane about poetry and philosophy as they walked in the grounds, followed by 'passionate kisses, whispered words, confessions of the past'. One evening they sat alone together in the study, where they enjoyed 'passionate excitement, long and clinging kisses, and nervous sensations'. Fearing interruption, they parted, she having 'smoothed my tumbled hair'. On her final evening at Moor Park, she and Edward were together in the cab taking them to the station, while her 13-year-old son Alfred sat on top with the driver. 'I never spent so blessed an hour as the one that followed', she wrote in the passage quoted by the *Era*. 'I shall not relate ALL that passed, suffice it to say I leaned back at last in silent joy in those arms I had so often dreamed of and kissed the curls and smooth face, so radiant with beauty, that had dazzled my outward and inward vision' at their first meeting in 1850.[107]

The newspapers mostly accepted that these were the ravings of an insane, or at least deluded, woman. The *Daily News* diagnosed 'passionate sentimentalism' in the style of Rousseau and declared Mrs Robinson 'a crazy woman, not far off fifty', who looked likely to 'ruin the rising prospects of this young and meritorious man'.[108] According to the *Saturday Review* of 26 June, the diary 'stands self-convicted of insanity'. While several of the serious papers saw that the case was important for the legal questions it threw up in matters of divorce, the medical journals quickly realised that doctors were especially vulnerable to accusations of impropriety with female patients. Though Lane was a hydropath, and therefore on the unorthodox spectrum often despised by the medical establishment, he was properly qualified and by no means a quack. Indeed, he had been careful to draw attention to his medical qualifications in the first advertisement for Moor Park issued under his management. Having taken over from another prominent hydropathic doctor, Thomas Smethurst, editor of the *Water-Cure Journal*, Lane stressed his credentials in his advertisement in *The Times* in May 1854: 'MOOR-PARK MEDICAL AND HYDROPATHIC ESTABLISHMENT, near Farnham, Surrey. This INSTITUTION is now OPEN for the reception of patients, under the superintendence of Dr Edward W. Lane, A.M., M.D., Edin.'[109]

Edinburgh University had long been famous for the high quality of its medical education. Here, and also in the short work on hydropathy which Lane published in October 1858, he was at pains to point out that he was properly educated in medicine, and was able to add to his hydropathic measures any orthodox treatment he might think appropriate.

The profession's leading periodical, the *British Medical Journal*, while not able to approve of Lane's methods of treatment, was aware of the risk to the profession in general and argued for fair play in Lane's case:

> Of course we cannot be expected to sympathise with hydropaths particularly, but his case may be our own any day. Any of our associates with 'curls and smooth face', and less favoured ones for that matter, may some day find themselves plunged from domestic happiness and pecuniary prosperity into utter ruin . . . The *Times* has come forth very nobly to champion Dr Lane in this crisis of his fortunes . . . It would indeed be cruel to him to defer his acquittal of the heavy charges brought against him until the legislature has repaired the bungling, by which at present an innocent man is not allowed to give evidence in his own defence.[110]

The presumption of Lane's innocence was widespread in the press, partly because of the medical testimony at the trial and the obvious exaggeration and embellishment, at the very least, in Isabella's journal, and partly because Lane had powerful friends who could influence the press, from *The Times* to various provincial newspapers. George Combe, who corresponded with Lane and Isabella in the weeks leading up to the court case, lobbied acquaintances on *The Times* and got Robert Chambers to help too. Lane asked Combe to intervene with the *Scotsman* on his behalf, and he could be sure of support from the *Examiner*, since its editor, Marmion Savage, was a frequent visitor to Moor Park.[111] Combe advised Isabella in letters sent to her early in 1858, after the separation had been granted by the Ecclesiastical Court and when it was becoming clear that Henry Robinson was intent on taking his case to the new Divorce Court. Realising that she felt guilty about the potential effect of the journal on Lane's marriage and career, he pointed out on 23 February: '*If* your Journal contains the descriptions now mentioned, & be *true*, Dr Lane is ruined as a professional man; for no woman of reputation could venture under his roof, with such a stain attaching to him. His poor wife is robbed of his affections, & Lady Drysdale, in her old age, sees the dearest objects of her affections disgraced & ruined.'[112]

In her lengthy reply three days later Isabella blamed her mean hypocrite of a husband, explaining that she turned to her journal as a 'resource' in her loneliness. 'What was my consolation?' she asked, answering, 'solitude & my pen'. 'I dipped my pen but too often in the fairy ink of poesy; – the true & actual, the shadowy & the visionary were too often blended – I had the fatal gift – more curse than boon of giving "to airy nothings, a local habitation and a name".'[113] She agreed with Combe that the only way to repair the damage to Dr Lane was to admit that she was the 'victim temporarily of my own fancies & delusions' and that she had written down as facts 'the wildest imaginings of a mind exhausted with the tyranny of long years'.[114] Since she was not permitted to testify, however, these admissions did not come to court and the case was left to rest on the hope that the divorce court judges would accept that the apparently incriminating journal entries were mere fantasy. As the proceedings unfolded on the hottest days of June it became clear that the case of *Robinson v. Robinson and Lane* required to be adjourned while the judges took further advice on the legal questions raised by its anomalies.

Darwin, liking and trusting Lane, and being adamant that he was not a charlatan – after all, hydropathy had offered Darwin some relief from his chronic symptoms over the years, where orthodox medicine had failed – expressed surprise and sorrow on reading about the case. He wrote to W.D. Fox on 24 June 1858, as the final judgment was awaited, saying that all the people he had asked about the story 'think that Dr L is probably innocent'. He cites in favour of this view the 'absence of all corroborative evidence' and 'the unparalleled fact of a woman detailing her own adultery, which seems to me more improbable than inventing a story prompted by extreme sensuality or hallucination'. But he fears nonetheless that the case 'will ruin him', adding 'I never heard a sensual expression from him.'[115] Like everyone else, Darwin would have to wait until the case was resumed on 3 July. Meanwhile, he was coping with the greatest crisis of his own life.

Darwin's dilemma

Having returned from his latest sojourn at Moor Park in early May 1858, Darwin was working hard at his manuscript, disappointed once more to find that all the good he felt the hydropathic treatment had done him had evaporated as soon as he got back to work. The health of his children worried him too. Etty was ill again, with inflammation of the throat.[116] Darwin had sent her to Moor Park the previous summer, joining her himself for two weeks in June.[117] He told Hooker then that 'Dr Lane & wife & mother-in-law Lady Drysdale are some of the nicest people, I have ever met'.[118] Not only did he like Lane better than the credulous James Gully, but the fact that his beloved 10-year-old daughter Annie had died in Gully's establishment at Malvern in 1851 meant that he could not bear the thought of returning to a place with such sad memories.[119] In October 1857 he described in a letter to W.D. Fox his anxiety about Etty and also his son Leonard, whose pulse was feeble and often irregular, 'like three of our other children'. He found it 'heart-breaking', adding, 'a man ought to be a bachelor, & care for no human being to be happy! or not to be wretched'.[120] (Most of Darwin's children, about whom he and Emma worried so much, were long-lived, not that Darwin could have foreseen this; Etty died in her eighties, and Leonard in his nineties.)

On Friday, 18 June, two days after the summer's hottest day, Darwin wrote to his old friend and mentor Charles Lyell, beginning calmly enough:

> Some year or so ago, you recommended me to read a paper by Wallace in the Annals, which had interested you & as I was writing to him, I knew this would please him much, so I told him. He has to day sent me the enclosed & asked me to forward it to you. It seems to me well worth reading. Your words have come true with a vengeance that I sh[oul]d be forestalled. You said this when I explained to you here very briefly my views of 'Natural Selection' depending on the Struggle for existence. I never saw a more striking coincidence. If Wallace had my M.S. sketch written out in 1842 he could not have made a better short abstract! Even his terms now stand as Heads of my Chapters.

Please return me the M.S. which he does not say he wishes me to publish; but I shall of course at once write & offer to send to any Journal. So all my originality, whatever it may amount to, will be smashed. Though my Book, if it will ever have any value, will not be deteriorated; as all labour consists in the application of the theory.[121]

On reading this, Lyell, himself not lacking in authorial vanity, would understand Darwin's despair. He would also notice the apparently casual mention in Darwin's letter of the unassailable fact of his own precedence, and the underlying hope that because he had shown Lyell and Hooker previous parts of his written conclusions going back to 1842, he could, if required, prove that the concept of 'natural selection', as well as the phrase itself, was originally his. Darwin also points out (in his own favour) that 'all the labour consists in the application of the theory', the task he has been pursuing for years, whereas Wallace's short piece consists of the idea itself, without the voluminous examples required to prove it. Wallace's letter and its vital enclosure are now lost, though the latter has come down to posterity as a result of Lyell's action on receiving this bombshell from his friend.[122]

Darwin waited anxiously for Lyell to reply and advise, for though he had not directly asked for Lyell's help, he clearly hoped that it would be forthcoming, especially in relation to his remark about Wallace not having asked him to publish his piece and his own fair-minded assurance that he would 'of course' offer to send it to a journal for publication. Meanwhile he wrote to his son William, now eighteen and preparing to go to university in Cambridge, informing him about the habits of caterpillars, the progress of William's moths and butterflies in a box at Down, and the news that 'the poor old horse has cut his knee so badly that he never is likely to be good for anything'. He mentions Etty's illness, but not, of course, his own trouble.[123] On 24 June he wrote to W.D. Fox, expressing his belief in Edward Lane's innocence of the charge of adultery and telling him that in addition to Etty's illness, 'last night our Baby commenced with Fever of some kind'.[124] Charles Waring Darwin had been born in December 1856, when Emma was forty-eight.

Darwin wrote again to Lyell on 25 June, apologising for troubling him, and asking his opinion on what to do about Wallace; 'I have entire confidence in your judgment & honour.' He sets out his thoughts:

There is nothing in Wallace's sketch which is not written out much fuller in my sketch copied in 1844, & read by Hooker some dozen years ago. About a year ago I sent a short sketch of which I have a copy of my views . . . to Asa Gray, so that I could most truly say & prove that I take nothing from Wallace. I sh[oul]d be *extremely* glad *now* to publish a sketch of my general views in about a dozen pages or so. But I cannot persuade myself that I can do so honourably. Wallace says nothing about publication . . . But as I had not intended to publish any sketch, can I do so honourably because Wallace has sent me an outline of his doctrine? I would far rather burn my whole book than that he or any man sh[oul]d think that I had behaved in a paltry spirit . . .

If I could honourably publish I would state that I was induced now to publish a sketch . . . from Wallace having sent me an outline of my general conclusions. We differ only, that I was led to my views from what artificial selection had done for domestic animals. I could send Wallace a copy of my letter to Asa Gray to show him that I had not stolen his doctrine. But I cannot tell whether to publish now would not be base & paltry . . .

This is a trumpery affair to trouble you with; but you cannot tell how much obliged I sh[oul]d be for your advice.[125]

Everything Darwin writes here is truthful; many a person would not have worried about the morality of going ahead and publishing manuscript material built up, as he so often told his correspondents, over twenty years of experimenting and reading, comparing and testing. Certainly, most of his fellow scientists would have made sure they got the credit for their work without squirming on the hook of conscience in this way. Jealousy and sharp practice were rife in the small world of science. Richard Owen was not above praising his own works by reviewing them anonymously in the *Edinburgh Review* and comparing them favourably with the work of others; he was to do this in his dismissive review of *Origin of*

1. Augustus Egg, third part of the triptych of adultery and destitution, *Past and Present*, exhibited at the Royal Academy exhibition in summer 1858.

2. W.P. Frith, *The Derby Day*, the most popular painting at that exhibition.

3. Group photograph of the cast of actors in Dickens's amateur production of Wilkie Collins's play *The Frozen Deep*, 1857.

4. Tavistock House, where Dickens and his family lived from 1851 to 1858, when the household split up following Dickens's separation from Catherine.

5. Dickens photographed by Herbert Watkins, 17 June 1858.

6. Catherine Dickens photographed by J.J.E. Mayall, *c.* 1863.

7. Undated photograph of Ellen Ternan.

8. Sir Edward Bulwer Lytton's *carte de visite*, J.J.E. Mayall, 1857.

9. Charles Darwin photographed by Maull & Fox, 1860.

10. Down House and garden illustrated by Alfred Parsons, 1883.

2ème Ordre PASSEREAUX CONIROSTRES.

11. Male greater bird of paradise, from Charles d'Orbigny's *Dictionnaire Universel d'Histoire Naturelle*, 1849.

12. Alfred Russel Wallace photographed in Singapore, 1862.

13. 'Interior of the Court of Queen's Bench', 1858, in G.A. Sala, *Twice Round the Clock*, 1859.

14. Isambard Kingdom Brunel standing beside the launching chains of the *Great Eastern*, photographed by Robert Howlett, 1357–8.

A WHOLESOME CONCLUSION.

15. 'A Wholesome Conclusion', *Punch*, 6 February 1858.

16. Notice of the burial of Charles Waring Darwin, aged eighteen months, in the parish of Downe, Kent, 1 July 1858.

EXTRAORDINARY NARRATIVE
OF AN
OUTRAGEOUS VIOLATION OF LIBERTY AND LAW,
IN THE
Forcible Seizure and Incarceration of Lady Lytton Bulwer,
IN THE GLOOMY CELL OF A MADHOUSE!!!
AND THE PROCEEDINGS TO OBTAIN HER RELEASE.

[Lady Bulwer Lytton's first interview with her Solicitor, in the dismal dungeon of Bedlam.]
WITH EXCLUSIVE DETAILS OF SIR E. B.'S AMOURS IN THE ALBANY—THE
DELICATE DISCOVERY BY HER LADYSHIP,
THE CAUSE OF THE SEPARATION,
With many curious particulars, never before published.
ADDRESS OF LADY BULWER TO THE ELECTORS OF HERTFORDSHIRE.

LONDON: PUBLISHED BY W. JAMES AND CO., 34, BOOKSELLERS-ROW,
ST. CLEMENT'S, STRAND,
AND SOLD BY ALL VENDORS OF NEWSPAPERS, &c.

17. Title page of the pamphlet printed to publicise the incarceration of Lady Bulwer Lytton in a lunatic asylum, July 1858.

18. A photograph of Benjamin Disraeli by W&D Downey.

DIPHTHERIA.   SCROFULA.   CHOLERA.

FATHER THAMES INTRODUCING HIS OFFSPRING TO THE FAIR CITY OF LONDON.

(*A Design for a Fresco in the New Houses of Parliament.*)

19. 'Father Thames Introducing his Offspring to the City of London', *Punch*, 3 July 1858.

20. The Members' Entrance, House of Commons, in the 1850s.

21. Sir John Gilbert's pen and ink drawing of the Smoking Room of the Garrick Club at the time.

22. Dickens reading 'Little Dombey', *Illustrated London News*, 31 July 1858.

23. 'The Smiler with the Knife':
William Makepeace Thackeray's
drawing of Edmund Yates preparing
to stab him at the Garrick Club, 1858.

24. Thackeray photographed by
Ernest Edwards, *c.* 1863.

25. Sir Richard Owen photographed by Maull & Polyblank, *c.* 1855.

26. Thomas Henry Huxley photographed by Maull & Polyblank, 1857.

27. Joseph Bazalgette photographed by George B. Black, 1863.

Species in April 1860, though he always denied being the author, as well he might.[126] Wallace was to some extent an unknown quantity: Darwin and he had corresponded intermittently and cordially for a few years, but they did not really know one another. Would he feel anger if Darwin published now? Would he even come out as a controversialist and accuse Darwin of intellectual theft or dishonesty? Of the men Darwin knew best, Huxley, though as honest a man as himself, would probably have felt less compromised than his friend did; Hooker, too, would not have hesitated to put his own work into the public domain in the knowledge that, however it might seem to others, he did have precedence and was doing nothing wrong in claiming it. But then these active men, living and working in the thick of London professional science, and capable of fighting their corner against prejudice and rivalry, would not have waited so long as Darwin to publish their work, and the current problem would not have arisen.

Darwin felt unready to publish until he had painstakingly covered every possibility that his theory might be disproved; in addition, his miserable health held him back, as did also – importantly – the anxiety of his devout wife Emma about the consequences for religious faith were the theory to be accepted. He had no desire to upset Emma, and beyond her he could imagine a whole community of readers who would balk at taking the step towards agnosticism which he himself had taken without fuss. In his autobiography, written late in life, he described how as a young scientist he could not believe in miracles; nor could he believe in Christianity 'as a divine revelation'. The rate at which he lost his faith was 'very slow' and therefore not distressing,

> and I have never since doubted even for a single second that my conclusion was correct. I can indeed hardly see how anyone ought to wish Christianity to be true; for if so the plain language of the text seems to show that men who do not believe, and this would include my Father, Brother [Erasmus] and almost all my best friends, will be everlastingly punished.
>
> And this is a damnable doctrine . . .
>
> The old argument of design in nature, as given in Paley, which formerly seemed to me so conclusive, fails, now that the law of natural

selection has been discovered. We can no longer argue that, for instance, the beautiful hinge of a bivalve shell must have been made by an intelligent being, like the hinge of a door by man. There seems to be no more design in the variability of organic beings and in the action of natural selection, than in the course which the wind blows.[127]

This is remarkable for its clarity and certainty; in the *Origin* itself he was necessarily more circumspect, leaving readers to draw such conclusions for themselves if they wished. When his son Francis came to print the autobiography in his father's *Life and Letters* in 1887, five years after Darwin's death, Emma vetoed this passage as 'raw', and in deference to her objection it was omitted.[128]

In one of his letters to Darwin from the Malay Archipelago Wallace broached the difficult subject of mankind's place in the new theory of evolution. Darwin wrote to him on 22 December 1857: 'You ask whether I shall discuss "man".' The answer was, 'I think I shall avoid the whole subject, as so surrounded with prejudices, though I fully admit that it is the highest & most interesting problem for the naturalist.'[129] Later he explained in his autobiography his views on the human species and how he came to deal with the problem in *The Descent of Man*, published in 1871, twelve years after *Origin of Species*:

> As soon as I had become, in the year 1837 or 1838, convinced that species were mutable productions, I could not avoid the belief that man must come under the same law. Accordingly I collected notes on the subject for my own satisfaction, and not for a long time with any intention of publishing. Although in the *Origin of Species*, the derivation of any particular species is never discussed, yet I thought it best, in order that no honourable man should accuse me of concealing my views, to add that by the work in question 'light would be thrown on the origin of man and his history'.[130]

In other words, he wished neither to offend religious believers by directly discussing humanity in *Origin* nor to pretend that the human species existed outside the law of evolution. Upsetting his own wife and the many people who still believed in miracles, an afterlife for humanity, heaven and hell, and the immutability of all species created whole and final by God was not something Darwin was in a hurry to do. It was an uncomfortable irony for him that he, the most uncontroversial of men, was required by the workings of his own mind to stand forth in the spotlight of fame and notoriety, for even if he omitted humanity from his work, conclusions contrary to religious beliefs would be drawn. Yet he had a story to tell, and it was only natural that he should wish to receive the acclaim (even if accompanied by hostile criticism) due to him; otherwise what was the point of all his hard work? Against Lyell's advice he had delayed until it might be too late to claim originality in the field in which he had laboured so long and hard. It was to Lyell, to Hooker, and to Huxley that he now turned for reassurance and support. Lyell, he wrote in a postscript to the letter of 25 June, was 'as a Lord Chancellor' to him.[131]

By Tuesday, 29 June Darwin had heard from both Hooker and Lyell. He wrote to the former, thanking him. 'You have acted with more kindness & so has Lyell even than I could have expected from you both most kind as you are.' He added that he could easily get a copy made of the letter outlining his theory which he had written to Asa Gray in America in September 1857, though he worried that it was 'too short'.[132] Lyell and Hooker were planning to solve Darwin's problem by having Wallace's paper and some extracts from Darwin's writings which friends had already read, including the letter to Gray, read out at the impending meeting of the Linnaean Society. They would show that both men had arrived at the theory of natural selection independently, but that Darwin had expressed it first.

By a stroke of luck the death of the former president Robert Brown had induced the society to postpone its summer meeting from 17 June, the day before Darwin received Wallace's letter, to Thursday, 1 July. This meant that Darwin (and Wallace) would not have to wait until September to have their papers made public. The Linnaean Society published its annual proceedings in August. Most importantly, the arrangement satisfied Darwin's honour while ensuring that Wallace, so many thousands of miles from home, ten weeks away from receiving his next letter, and nearly four years from arriving home from the Malay Archipelago, was fairly treated in London. (Wallace announced his arrival in England from the Pavilion Hotel, Folkestone, on 31 March 1862, writing to Philip Sclater, secretary of the Zoological Society, that he was back, bringing with him 3,000 bird skins, 20,000 beetles and butterflies, as well as two of the famous elusive birds of paradise – *live* specimens arriving in Europe for the first time – which were intended for the society.[133])

Lyell and Hooker lost no time. On 30 June they wrote a carefully worded letter to the secretary of the Linnaean Society:

> The accompanying papers, . . . which all relate to the same subject, viz. the Laws which affect the Production of Varieties, Races, and Species, contain the results of the investigations of two indefatigable naturalists, Mr Charles Darwin and Mr Alfred Wallace.
>
> These gentlemen having, independently and unknown to one another, conceived the same very ingenious theory to account for the appearance and perpetuation of varieties and of specific forms on our planet, may both fairly claim the merit of being original thinkers in this important line of inquiry; but neither of them having published his views, though Mr Darwin has for many years past been repeatedly urged by us to do so, and both authors having now unreservedly placed their papers in our hands, we think it would best promote the interests of science that a selection from them should be laid before the Linnaean Society.[134]

The three papers, given in order of composition, were 'Extracts from a M.S. work on Species' by Darwin, sketched in 1839 and copied in 1844, which had been read by Hooker; an abstract of Darwin's letter to Professor Gray of Harvard of September 1857, showing, said Hooker and Lyell, that Darwin's views 'remained unaltered from 1839 to 1857'; and Wallace's essay, 'On the Tendency of Varieties to depart indefinitely from the Original Type', written in Ternate in February 1858 'for the perusal of his friend and correspondent Mr Darwin, and sent to him with the expressed wish that it should be forwarded to Sir Charles Lyell, if Mr Darwin thought it sufficiently novel and interesting'.[135] Thus was Darwin's problem solved; it could be shown that neither he nor Wallace had 'borrowed' ideas from one another, and that he had reached his conclusions several years before Wallace. Darwin was grateful to his friends, but still felt guilty, now also worrying that he was asking too much of them. 'Do not waste much time', he urged Hooker on 29 June. 'It is miserable in me to care at all about priority.'[136] The stage was set for 1 July. What would the society's members make of these short but groundbreaking essays? What, if anything, would the wider public think?

Though Darwin cared very much – too much, he feared – about the effect of his and Wallace's work, he was also coping with family tragedy. In the letter he wrote to Hooker on 29 June thanking him for his kindness he also had cause to add:

> You will, & so will Mrs Hooker, be most sorry for us when you hear that poor Baby died yesterday evening. I hope to God he did not suffer so much as he appeared. He became quite suddenly worse. It was Scarlet-Fever. It was the most blessed relief to see his poor innocent face resume its sweet expression in the sleep of death. Thank God he will never suffer more in this world.[137]

CHAPTER FIVE

July 1858

Darwin in distress

THE REGISTER OF BURIALS 'in the Parish of Downe [*sic*] in the County of Kent in the Year 1858' records the funerals between 7 June and 22 July of three adults and of four children from the village: 13-year-old Amy Parker, 8-year-old Arthur Perceval, 2-year-old George Elliott, and 18-month-old Charles Waring Darwin.[1] Darwin's child was buried at St Mary's church on Thursday, 1 July; his parents' immediate concern was to get their other children away from home as soon as possible. In the few letters Darwin wrote in early July, he told correspondents that all the children except Etty, who was still weak, had gone with their maternal aunt Sarah Elizabeth Wedgwood to her house in Hartfield, on the Kent–Sussex border. He and Emma were staying at home for a few days more until Etty was fit to be moved and the household's nurse and governess, who both showed symptoms of fever, were better. By Tuesday, 6 July the danger was over, and 'we are getting less frightened & in every way, more composed', he told W.D. Fox. Nevertheless, 'I have been much knocked up & so has my poor dear wife'.[2] Three days later he and Emma took Etty to Hartfield, and on 16 July the whole family went on holiday to the Isle of Wight, returning home to Down on 13 August.[3]

The day after the baby's funeral Darwin wrote a short memorial of his tenth and youngest child:

> Our poor Baby was born Dec[embe]r 6th 1856 & died on June 28th 1858, & was therefore above 18 months old. He was small for his age & backward in walking & talking, but intelligent & observant . . . He had never been ill, & cried less than any of our babies. He was of a remarkably sweet, placid & joyful disposition; but had not high spirits, & did not laugh much. He often made strange grimaces & shivered, when excited . . . He was very affectionate, & had a passion for Parslow [the butler] . . . Our poor little darling's short life has been placid innocent & joyful. I think & trust he did not suffer so much at last, as he appeared to do; but the last 36 hours were miserable beyond expression. In the sleep of Death he resumed his placid looks.[4]

It has been suggested by some experts that Charles Waring had Down's syndrome, the condition named after its identification in 1866 by John Langdon Down, superintendent of an asylum, who corresponded with Darwin in the latter's later years about facial features.[5] Etty Darwin later recalled that her baby brother 'never learnt to walk or talk' and was born, she believed, without his 'full share of intelligence'.[6]

With such a sad family event taking place on 1 July (during a brief lull in the hot weather), there was no chance that Darwin would be able to attend the important delayed meeting that evening of the Linnaean Society at Burlington House, Piccadilly, at which his and Wallace's papers were to be read. In truth, Darwin would probably not have gone up to London even without the death and funeral of his child. His last trip to the capital had been on 20 May, when he attended a dinner of the Philosophical Club of the Royal Society in the Thatched House Tavern in St James's, the building in which the notorious nine hottest days of June were spent unfruitfully in an attempt to solve the riddle of exactly when Sir Henry Meux had become insane. Darwin spoke with Hooker at the dinner, and it was the last time he visited London, or saw his close and supportive friends, Hooker, Lyell, and Huxley, for many months to come.[7] The whole business of getting Darwin's and Wallace's work laid before London's scientific experts was done by Hooker and Lyell, for which Darwin was grateful. His letters to these two friends continued to thank them and express his guilt at putting them to trouble and at worrying so much about his own desire to be recognised as the first person to formulate the theory of natural selection. On 5 July he thanked Hooker for sending him an account of the 1 July meeting and for offering to write to Wallace on Darwin's behalf: 'I certainly sh[oul]d much like this, as it would quite exonerate me.' And from his sister-in-law's house in Hartfield he wrote again to Hooker on 13 July, confessing that he had been punished for complacency and lack of self-knowledge: 'I always thought it very possible that I might be forestalled, but I fancied that I had grand enough soul not to care; but I found myself mistaken.'[8]

While Darwin coped with his family's health, his friends acted in his interest at the meeting brought about by the death of Robert Brown, a Scottish botanist who had studied and collected plants on a voyage to Australia from 1801 to 1805. He had been president of the Linnaean Society from 1849 to 1853. Hooker and Darwin, among others, felt that he was rather a drag on the society, an opponent of progress in his field. Darwin recalled visiting Brown often as a young man and wishing that he would publish more and be more generous to his fellow scientists: 'He seemed to me chiefly remarkable for the minuteness of his observations and their perfect accuracy. He never propounded to me any large scientific views in biology. His knowledge was extraordinarily great, and much died with him, owing to his excessive fear of ever making a mistake.' Darwin had observed Brown's jealousy and secretiveness, his refusal to lend specimens of the plants he had collected.[9]

Whatever Darwin and Hooker thought of Brown, his death was, as Hooker recalled at a 'Darwin–Wallace Celebration' at the Linnaean Society fifty years later, 'the direct cause of the Theory of the Origin of the Species being given to the world at least four months earlier than would otherwise have been the case'.[10] He meant the Darwin–Wallace papers, not Darwin's book, but of course it is also true that the whole sequence of events from 18 June, when Darwin received Wallace's letter, to 1 July, when their papers were read, led to the great book itself being published years earlier than Darwin had anticipated and in a form much more adapted to attract universal attention. Since neither Darwin nor Wallace was able to be in London, their papers were read out by the secretary of the Linnaean Society, John Joseph Bennett, preceded by 'a few words to emphasise the importance of the subject' by Hooker and Lyell.[11] Among those present were the current president of the society, the zoologist Thomas Bell, and Brown's replacement as a member of council, the botanist George Bentham. Of the other twenty-five or so members who attended, the best known was W.B. Carpenter, biologist and professor at University College London.[12] On publishing *Origin of Species* the following year, Darwin received an encouraging letter from Carpenter, who, he told Hooker, was 'likely to be a convert', one of the handful of scientists he thought ready to accept the theory of natural selection.[13] After the minutes of the previous meeting were read out, and acknowledgment was made of various books and papers which had been donated to the society, the main business of the meeting was arrived at, namely the three papers presented by Lyell and Hooker and read out by the secretary Bennett. Five short communications from other colleagues brought the occasion to a close.[14]

As Hooker and Lyell had agreed, two of Darwin's pieces of writing were read out before Wallace's paper, on the grounds that they had been written earlier. First came 'An Abstract from a M.S. Work on Species', sketched by Darwin in 1839, 'copied in 1844', and read at that time by Hooker. Second was Darwin's letter to Asa Gray in Boston, dated 5 September 1857; Hooker's wife Frances had kindly made a fair copy for the meeting of this piece, 'my ugly M.S.', as Darwin shamefacedly described it to Hooker on 13 July 1858.[15] The letter to Gray, with a few minor stylistic emendations made for the Linnaean Society meeting, sets out Darwin's belief:

In nature we have some *slight* variation . . . & I think it can be shown that changed conditions of existence is the main cause of the child not exactly resembling its parents; & in nature geology shows us what changes have taken place & are taking place. We have almost unlimited time: no one but a practical geologist can fully appreciate this: think of the Glacial period, during the whole of which the same species of shells at least have existed: there must have been during this period, millions on millions of generations.

I think it can be shown that there is such an unerring power at work on *natural selection* (the title of my Book), which selects exclusively for the good of each organic being . . . I have found it hard constantly to bear in mind that the increase of every single species is checked during some part of its life, or during some shortly recurrent generation. Only a few of those annually born can live to propagate their kind. What a trifling difference must often determine which shall survive & which perish . . . [Organic beings] always seem to branch & sub-branch like a tree from a common trunk; the flourishing twigs destroying the less vigorous, – the dead & lost branches rudely representing extinct genera & families.

In the letter of September 1857 Darwin signs off by telling Gray that 'this sketch is *most* imperfect, but in so short a space I cannot make it better. Your imagination must fill up many wide blanks.' He finishes in a characteristic sentence which Hooker deleted from the version to be read out on 1 July 1858, 'Without some reflexion it will appear all rubbish; perhaps it will appear so after reflexion.'[16]

Here in a scrap barely three pages long is the idea at the heart of Darwin's theory; the phrases about millions of generations, about the small differences which determine the survival or perishing of species, and especially the metaphor of the great tree with its branches and sub-branches to describe evolution, found their way almost unchanged into *On the Origin of Species*, which so shocked those who believed the age of the earth to be counted in thousands, not millions, of years, and who rebelled at the idea of species created by God perishing in such numbers.

Next came Wallace's contribution, 'An Essay on the Tendency of Varieties to depart indefinitely from the Original Type', written in Ternate, an island of eastern Indonesia, in February 1858. This was the longest of the three pieces, though it ran to only eight pages. In his autobiography, written nearly fifty years later, Wallace recalled that at the time he was 'suffering from a sharp attack of intermittent fever'. 'Every day during the cold and succeeding hot fits [I] had to lie down for several hours, during which I had nothing to do but to think over any subjects then particularly interesting to me.'[17] Thomas Malthus's *An Essay on the Principle of*

Population, published anonymously in 1798 and expanded in 1803, came to Wallace's mind. Malthus had written that while population tends to increase in 'geometric ratio', doubling every twenty-five years, food supply grows only in 'arithmetic ratio', so that population and food supply are only kept in balance by 'checks' including wars, famines, plagues, delayed marriages, and prostitution. In the second edition he advocated a positive check for the problem, namely delayed marriage, but only when accompanied by 'moral restraint' both before and during marriage.[18] Though Malthus was controversial in respect of his diagnosis of, and suggestions for the improvement of, the human condition, the idea of checks and balances in the natural world attracted Wallace, as it had Darwin years earlier. In October 1838, as he recalled in his autobiography, Darwin read Malthus 'for amusement', and was struck that in the 'struggle for existence' 'favourable variations would tend to be preserved, and unfavourable ones to be destroyed'. 'Here, then, I had at last got a theory by which to work.'[19]

Wallace, too, felt he had experienced a 'Eureka' moment. 'Why do some die and some live?' he asked. The answer, he recalled in his autobiography,

> was clearly, that on the whole the best fitted live . . . then it suddenly flashed upon me that this self-acting process would necessarily *improve the race*, because in every generation the inferior would inevitably be killed off and the superior would remain – that is, *the fittest would survive* . . . The more I thought it over the more I became convinced that I had at length found the long-sought-for law of nature that solved the problem of the origin of species . . . I waited anxiously for the termination of my fit so that I might at once make notes for a paper on the subject. The same evening I did this pretty fully, and on the two succeeding evenings wrote it out carefully in order to send it to Darwin by the next post, which would leave in a day or two.[20]

The paper he wrote, which first Darwin, then Lyell, then Hooker read, and then about thirty gentlemen of the Linnaean Society heard on 1 July, contained such sentences as the following (many of which, as Darwin had seen in his shock, were almost in the same words as his own bits of writing and thinking): 'The life of wild animals is a struggle for existence'; 'even the least prolific of animals would increase rapidly if unchecked', yet it is clear that 'permanent increase, except in restricted localities, is almost impossible'. Though 'very few birds produce less than two young ones each year, while many have six, eight, or ten', a 'simple calculation' would show that, without checks, 'in fifteen years each pair of birds would have increased to nearly ten millions!'[21] In chapter three of *Origin of Species*, entitled 'Struggle for Existence', Darwin took the most slow-breeding of all species, the elephant, and calculated that in five centuries, without checks, there would be 'fifteen million elephants, descended from the first pair'.[22] Wallace's essay continues with the theme of variation and struggle. Individuals might survive or not according to various differences:

> Even a change of colour might, by rendering them more or less indis-
> tinguishable, affect their safety; a greater or less development of hair
> might modify their habits . . . If, on the other hand, any species should
> produce a variety having slightly increased powers of preserving exist-
> ence, that variety must inevitably in time acquire a superiority in
> numbers . . . All we argue for is, that certain varieties have a tendency
> to maintain their existence longer than the original species, and this
> tendency must make itself felt.[23]

Though Hooker later remembered that the papers caused 'intense interest' in the audience at Burlington House, he also saw that 'the subject was too novel and too ominous for the old school to enter the lists before armouring'.[24] He reported optimistically to both Darwin and Wallace at the time, though the former recalled with amusement in his autobiography that 'our joint productions excited very little attention, and the only published notice of them which I can remember was by Professor Haughton of Dublin', whose 'verdict was that all that was new in them was false, and what was true was old'.[25] (Haughton was not only a biologist but also a minister in the Church of Ireland, who believed in the truth of biblical texts and could therefore not reconcile his views with Darwin's.[26]) Certainly there seems to have been no immediate notice in the press of the Linnaean Society meeting, and at the Leeds meeting of the British Association for the Advancement of Science in September 1858, though the Darwin–

Wallace papers had by this time been published in the Linnaean Society journal, the only mention of them was a brief, grudging, neither welcoming nor dismissing paragraph in the address of the president, Richard Owen, who was to attack Darwin fiercely, though anonymously, in his review of *Origin of Species* in April 1860.

By October 1858 Wallace had received letters from both Darwin and Hooker. He told his mother on 6 October that the letters (now lost) of 'two of the most eminent Naturalists in England' had 'highly gratified' him. On the same day he thanked Hooker for his and Lyell's efforts on behalf of his paper, adding that 'It would have caused me much pain & regret had Mr Darwin's excess of generosity led him to make public my paper unaccompanied by his own much earlier & I doubt not much more complete views on the same subject, & I must again thank you for the course you have adopted, which while strictly just to both parties, is so favourable to myself.'[27]

Darwin and his friends were struck at this time, and later, when Wallace returned to England, by his immediate and full acceptance that Darwin's work took precedence, both in terms of the dates of his discoveries and the fullness of the studies which allowed him to reach his conclusions. As early as January 1858 Wallace had written to Henry Bates, his erstwhile travelling companion, that Darwin was 'preparing for publication his great work on *Species & Varieties*, for which he has been collecting information 20 years'. He added clear-sightedly, 'He may save me the trouble of writing the 2nd part of my hypothesis [as first put forward in his essay from Sarawak, published in *Annals and Magazine of Natural History* in September 1855].'[28] Wallace would accept praise for only one thing. As he wrote in his autobiography, 'I may have the satisfaction of knowing that by writing my article and sending it to Darwin, I was the unconscious means of leading him to concentrate himself on the task of drawing up what he termed "an abstract" of the great work he had in preparation, but which was really a large and carefully written volume – the celebrated "Origin of Species", published in November, 1859.'[29]

Huxley was one friend who delighted in the effect Wallace had on Darwin; he wrote to Hooker in September 1858 expressing his pleasure that 'Wallace's impetus seems to have set Darwin going in earnest, and

I am rejoiced to hear we shall learn his views in full, at last. I look forward to a great revolution being effected.'[30] In the memoir of the reception of *Origin of Species* which he contributed to Frank Darwin's life of his father in 1887, Huxley, while making it clear that Darwin deserved all the credit he got, was commendably scrupulous in noting Wallace's contribution: 'The facts of variability, of the struggle for existence, of adaptation to conditions, were notorious enough; but none of us had suspected that the road to the heart of the species problem lay through them, until Darwin and Wallace dispelled the darkness, and the beacon-fire of the "Origin" guided the benighted.'[31]

As was usual with Darwin, he himself did not immediately spring to the idea that his great work could be completed and published soon. His family problems and continuing wretched health, as well as his self-confessed slow way of working and thinking, meant that he went off for his summer break believing that at most he might work up, as Wallace noted, a longer 'abstract of my Species Theory'.[32] It took him many more months, almost to the point of publication itself, before he was persuaded by his good friends to drop the self-deprecating words 'abstract' or 'essay' from the title.[33] Much later he put down his sense of obligation to Wallace in determining the form of his published work: 'An element in the success of the book was its moderate size; and this I owe to the appearance of Mr Wallace's essay; had I published on the scale in which I began to write in 1856, the book would have been four or five times as large as the *Origin*, and very few would have had the patience to read it.'[34]

Meanwhile he concentrated on his own and his family's health, returning in October 1858 to Moor Park to try Edward Lane's hydropathic treatment once more, and to show solidarity with the young man whom he liked and for whom he felt pity over the ghastly and still unresolved court case of the summer.[35]

'Mad' wives and vengeful husbands

On Saturday, 3 July the judges in the case of *Robinson v. Robinson and Lane* reconvened at Westminster Hall as promised when they adjourned on 21 June. *The Times* reminded its readers on 5 July that on that occasion 'an application to discharge Dr Lane from the suit, as there was no evidence against him, and to admit him as a witness on behalf of Mrs Robinson, had been refused by the Lord Chief Justice and Sir C. Cresswell, after consultation with Lord Campbell, the Lord Chief Baron, and Mr Justice Williams, contrary to the opinion of Mr Justice Wightman'.[36]

At the recommencement of the case the lord chief justice, Sir Alexander Cockburn, announced that he had changed his mind and 'now concurred' in Mr Wightman's doubts about the justice of the decision not to discharge Lane. In addition, he declared, a new factor had entered the equation, namely a bill which 'was now pending before the Legislature, and had passed one House'. This bill, containing a set of amendments to the Divorce Act,

> was intended to introduce a clause for the purpose of solving those doubts, and of enabling the Court . . . to dismiss the co-respondent under such circumstances as those of the present case, and make him admissible as a witness . . . If that clause should become law, as they had every reason to believe it would, the Court would avail themselves of the power that would be given to them and discharge Dr Lane, and allow him to give evidence in the suit . . . [Therefore] the Court thought that the most proper and expedient course to pursue was to adjourn for the present the further consideration of the case.[37]

Everyone connected to the case would now have to wait several months before it could reach its conclusion. Though Cockburn's phrasing gave a strong hint that Dr Lane would be found innocent of adultery, the suit still hung over him with potential hurt to his marriage and damage to his business. Darwin, concerned about the effect of the scandal on Lane's ability to continue at Moor Park, expressed relief to a correspondent from the Isle of Wight on 21 July that Lane's practice did not appear to be suffering: 'Dr Lane has his house full, I am glad to say.'[38] Henry Robinson, meanwhile, got his solicitors to write to *The Times* on 7 July, accusing the paper of bias towards Lane:

> Notwithstanding the decision which you have pronounced on this case [in an article published on 5 July] before the evidence has been

concluded, we earnestly hope that the public will suspend their judgment until Dr Lane has been examined, and the other evidence has been adduced which the petitioner is entitled to call. When this is before the Court the public will be able to judge whether Dr Lane is the innocent individual which you represent, and whether Mrs Robinson is in a sane state of mind or not. We ask this only in justice to the unfortunate petitioner.

We are, Sir, your obedient servants, THE SOLICITORS FOR THE PETITIONER.[39]

The Times had certainly rooted for Lane in its many pieces on the case during June. Parliament passed the required amendment to the Divorce Act early in August, but the Robinsons, the Lanes, and everyone else had to wait until November for the case to reopen with Lane as a witness, and it was not until the following March that judgment was finally given.

While it was in Henry Robinson's interests that his wife be found *not* insane, in order that her journal accounts of adultery could be accepted by the court and Isabella and Dr Lane found guilty, Bulwer Lytton, newly appointed colonial secretary and dealing with important issues to do with Canada, was determined to prove *his* wife insane after the shenanigans at the hustings at Hertford on 8 June. On Thursday, 8 July, when he introduced the Government of New Caledonia Bill for its second reading in the House of Commons (it was later to be renamed the Government of British Columbia Bill, since the French objected to 'New Caledonia' as a name for the new province and Queen Victoria suggested 'British Columbia' instead[40]), he had already arranged for Rosina to be sent to an asylum. Needless to say, she did not go quietly. The whole story became public in the first two weeks of July.

After the hustings fiasco Rosina returned to Taunton in Somerset, where she was visited by doctors sent from London by her husband; she wrote her demands to one of them, Frederick Hale Thomson, on 12 June. To keep silent, she demanded that her allowance be increased from £400 to £500 a year for her lifetime, not Bulwer Lytton's; that her debts of £2,500 be paid off; that her husband should promise not to '*molest*, or *malign*, me, *directly*, or *indirectly*', and 'to leave me perfectly free to live and go, where I liked, and as I liked'.[41] If Bulwer Lytton had taken Disraeli's advice and attended to the money question, he might have been able to put an end to the dispute, though given Rosina's wrath and impulsiveness, it is by no means certain that she would have quietened down. In the event, Rosina got no immediate reply from Thomson, and she raised the stakes in a further letter to him on 15 June, threatening to come up to London to confront Bulwer Lytton at the Colonial Office.[42] Receiving no reply to this or a further letter, she tried again on 20 June, saying that Bulwer Lytton, 'your infamous Employer, My Lord Derby's rotton [*sic*] old dregs of Sodom, and Babylon, converted into a Colonial Secretary', must now 'take the consequences'. These would be that 'despite of universal gagging and purchase of *the* most venal, and corrupt organ in the world, the English Press', her husband's behaviour would become '*publicly* and universally *known*'.[43]

Three days later she was tricked into coming to London, supposedly to discuss her allowance, and was taken from her hotel in Clarges Street, off Piccadilly, to Wyke House in Brentford, just west of London. This was a fine eighteenth-century house used as an asylum by Dr Robert Gardiner Hill, a surgeon who, along with Dr John Conolly, was a pioneer of humane non-restraint for mental patients.[44] Hill and his family lived in nearby Inverness Lodge, where he advertised that ladies 'suffering under any of the milder forms of insanity, could be received into the private family of Mr R. Gardiner Hill'.[45] Rosina duly spent her time while in Hill's care in the family home. According to her account, she was 'abducted' by Hill, accompanied by an apothecary called George Ross, a male assistant, and two asylum nurses, one of them 'a great Flanders mare of six feet high', while Bulwer Lytton looked on.[46] Her friend Rebecca Ryves asked two policemen to intervene, but they were shown certificates signed by Thomson and Ross which gave them the right to remove Rosina to the asylum. Most of the details of her removal, against her will, come from her highly coloured autobiography, *A Blighted Life*, published long after many of the people attacked in it were dead, but others confirmed at least some of the facts.[47] On Tuesday, 29 June Rosina wrote to Rebecca Ryves from Inverness Lodge about Ross and Thomson signing the certificate of her insanity, and on Sunday, 4 July she reported a visit the previous day from some members of the Lunacy Commission, one of them being John Conolly. On 5 July she attacked an old enemy, Bulwer Lytton's friend John Forster, 'that ruffianly blackguard, Sir Liar's oldest, most unscrupulous, and chief doer of dirty work', reminding Rebecca that Forster 'is the *Secretary* to this Farsical [*sic*] Commission of Lunacy'.[48]

By now the press, which Bulwer Lytton had largely succeeded in muzzling over the Hertford incident, had got wind of the new scandal. The whole story started to appear, first in a local newspaper in Somerset, where Miss Ryves and other friends were rallying support for Rosina, then in the national press. Many recited the tale of the hustings as a prelude to telling the story of the 'incarceration' of Rosina. A penny pamphlet appeared, *Extraordinary Narrative of an Outrageous Violation of Liberty and Law, in the Forcible Seizure and Incarceration of Lady Lytton Bulwer, in the Gloomy Cell of a Madhouse!!! and the Proceedings to Obtain her Release.* The title page was decorated with a lurid illustration of 'Lady Bulwer Lytton's first interview with her Solicitor, in the dismal dungeon of Bedlam'. The picture shows a frightened woman in her nightgown on a couch, with a skeleton in an alcove behind her, and a shocked-looking gentleman arriving to help her.[49] A public meeting was held in Taunton on Tuesday, 6 July to offer Rosina support, and by the middle of the month a national paper, the *Daily Telegraph*, had become Rosina's chief cheerleader in the press.[50] The support of the *Telegraph* was vital; founded in 1855 and edited by Joseph Levy, it cost only a penny, while of its rivals, *The Times* cost seven pence, and the *Daily News* and *Morning Post* cost five. By 1856 Levy's paper, which supported liberal and progressive causes such as the campaign against capital punishment and reform of the House of Lords, was outselling the others.[51]

On 13 July alone the story, taken from the *Somerset County Gazette*, was told in the *Morning Chronicle*, the *Birmingham Daily Post*, the *Liverpool Mercury*, the *Leeds Mercury*, and many more daily papers. They made reference to the incarceration, the hustings, the penny pamphlet, the protest meeting in Taunton, and the amount of money Rosina had requested as a settlement. Bulwer Lytton was being assailed on all sides for his inhumanity, and by the infuriated Disraeli – so intimately and embarrassingly connected with his friend in Rosina's telling of the story – for his stupidity and meanness with money. Another deluge of articles appeared on Thursday, 15 July, led by the *Morning Chronicle* with its arresting headline, 'Extraordinary Proceedings. Appeal for Public Justice. Lady Bulwer Lytton in a Lunatic Asylum'.

The *Daily Telegraph* went into battle on Rosina's behalf on 12 July, beginning a merciless series of articles and letters to the editor about the case. Carlyle, escaping the London heat up in Scotland, received the gossip from Jane, who got it from the *Daily Telegraph*, but also directly from John Forster and his wife Eliza. Forster, of course, was closely involved as Bulwer Lytton's agent and adviser and, particularly, as secretary to the Lunacy Commission. The Carlyles knew the Lyttons quite well, especially Rosina, whose side they had always taken in the fights between the couple. Jane sent Carlyle her news on 12 July, starting with the fateful day at the hustings, about which she had some colourful new details to relate:

> Lady B. true to her oath that she 'would oppose "Sir Liar, Coward" at every step of his career' – *rendered* herself, escorted by her Taunton landlady, the evening before his Election. For that night she kept her self *incognita*. But the Town was astonished in the morning, at seeing itself placarded all over with insults to Bulwer.
>
> In *his* absence (for he did not arrive till the business of the day commenced) his son, Robert Lytton, never dreaming who had done this thing, employed people to rush about and tear the placards down.[52]

When Bulwer Lytton and Robert were on the platform at the hustings, Robert heard a commotion and saw 'a prodigiously large woman, dressed entirely in *white*, with a *white* parasol, talking to the people about her'. Robert did not recognise his mother at first, but, as Jane Carlyle recounted, 'at last the idea struck him "like a pistol shot" "*it is my Mother*"! (This was his own account to Mrs Forster).' Robert told his father that Lady Lytton was here; Bulwer Lytton, notoriously deaf, and for that reason an unsuccessful speaker in parliament, did not understand until Robert screamed in his ear, 'Your *Wife* is here!' At this, Jane continues, quoting from the account Eliza Forster had given her,

Sir Liar 'staggered, turned as white as a sheet – cast one wild look at his wife – and rushed down the companion ladder'! – (the platform steps) near the bottom of which, by the kind foresight of somebody, his carriage and servants stood ready! He 'jumped in – fell back almost fainting' – and was gallopped [*sic*] back to Knebworth [his Hertfordshire country seat] – leaving his friends to *speak* for him! – Don't you think the Lady had the best of the day here?

Jane now comes on to more recent events, including 'a report that he inveigled her up to London by the offer of "an amicable arrangement" and increased income – and then handed her over to a *mad doctor* – instead of a *Solicitor*!'[53]

In his reply on 14 July Carlyle entered the excitement fully, calling Dr Thomson a 'Scoundrel Flunkey' and gamely declaring Rosina 'no more *mad* than I am', though certainly 'unwise, ill-guided to a high degree, and plunging wildly under the heavy burden laid on her'. He was critical of Bulwer Lytton's conduct 'in finishing this frightful affair. No man of real humanity, I think, in any case would or could have kept the once Partner of his Life, if he could have possibly helped it, in a state of *poverty*, for one thing.'[54] He wisely adds that he is sure Rosina will get out of the asylum and suggests that the best thing for him and Jane to do is '*not to speak of it*'.

Sure enough, the *Daily Telegraph* begins its article on the subject on 15 July with the remark that 'Sir Edward Bulwer Lytton has succeeded in hushing up the scandal of his wife's arrest and conveyance to a madhouse at Brentford'. However, 'a compromise has been extorted from the Secretary of State':

It is with pleasure that we record that this ignominious family war has been terminated, and the accusation of insanity has been abandoned; that Lady Lytton is confessedly qualified to treat with her husband upon terms of equality . . . [P]opular opinion has driven Lord Derby's choice and brilliant colleague into a virtual surrender. It matters little whether Sir Bulwer Lytton, under cabinet influence, has found it necessary to save the reputation of the government as well as his own, but it is not to be forgotten that he employed attorneys, nurses and policemen to capture his wife; that she was forcibly consigned to a lunatic asylum –

that medical certificates were obtained to prove her insanity, and that now, an explosion of national feeling having taken place, she is to be released and allowed to live in personal independence.[55]

Rosina's friends had suggested an inquiry by the Lunacy Commission, at which point Bulwer Lytton backed down, agreed to Rosina's financial demands, and arranged for her to be released on 17 July and to go abroad for the summer with her luckless son Robert. *The Times*, which as a friend of Bulwer Lytton's had kept silent about the scandal, confined itself to a short piece on 14 July, placed presumably by Bulwer Lytton, saying it was 'requested to state' that 'all matters in reference to this lady' are in process of being 'amicably settled by family arrangements to the satisfaction of all parties concerned'.[56] The Bulwer Lytton camp were so worried and angered by the surge of support in the press for Rosina and the attacks on her husband's behaviour towards her that Robert Lytton was asked to write a letter to *The Times* on 17 July, denying the 'exaggerated and distorted' accounts in the *Daily Telegraph* and other newspapers.

In his letter, Robert could not quite avoid the awkward truth that Rosina had been taken to Hill's asylum against her wishes, but he put as favourable a gloss on his father's actions as possible:

I carried out the injunctions of my father, who confided to me implicitly every arrangement which my affection could suggest, and enjoined me to avail myself of the advice of Lord Shaftesbury [chairman of the Lunacy Commission] in whatever was judged best and kindest to Lady Lytton.

My mother is now with me, free from all restraint, and about, at her own wish, to travel for a short time, in company with myself and a female friend and relation of her own selection.

From the moment my father felt compelled to authorise those steps which have been made the subject of so much misrepresentation, his anxiety was to obtain the opinion of the most experienced and able physicians, in order that my mother should not be subject to restraint for one moment longer than was strictly justifiable.

The certificates given by Dr Forbes Winslow and Dr Conolly are subjoined.[57]

Robert explains that Conolly was consulted at his father's request, while Forbes Winslow, another well-known expert in mental health – he had only recently been giving evidence in the Robinson case, being one of the experts called by the Divorce Court to discuss the connection between uterine disease and mental delusion[58] – had been retained by his mother's legal advisers. Robert had asked 'my friend Mr Edwin James' to 'place himself in communication' with Winslow. Beneath Robert's letter are printed a short letter to James, dated 16 July, in which Forbes Winslow declares that, having examined Lady Lytton that day, his opinion is that her state of mind is 'such as to justify her liberation from restraint'. However, he adds that, having read the medical certificates which allowed her to be restrained in the first place, and wishing to do justice to her husband's actions, he cannot consider Bulwer Lytton's 'painful proceedings' of the past few weeks to have been 'harsh or unjustifiable'. Conolly's letter, addressed to Bulwer Lytton, is even more awkward and contradictory, since he had visited Rosina at the asylum on 3 July and found her insane then. He stresses that though he had felt it his duty, when visiting her 'at the private residence of Mr and Mrs Hill', to express his 'decided opinion' on her state of mind at that time, he now has 'much satisfaction in hearing of the arrangements which have been made for her leaving their family in the society of her son and her female friend'. It is clear from the phrasing of all these letters, and especially from the emphasis on Rosina's being kept in the Hill family home and not in Wyke House itself, that they were the result of careful collaboration with Bulwer Lytton and his advisers.

Among the legion of commentators on the Rosina affair, Karl Marx noted in his article 'Imprisonment of Lady Bulwer-Lytton', written for the *New York Daily Tribune*, that Robert's letter was worded evasively, especially in the 'studiously awkward passage' in which he tried to make out that Bulwer Lytton 'felt the necessity of authoritative medical advice, not for sequestering his wife as insane, but for setting her free as *mentis compos*'. As was his wont, Marx connected the single case to the larger question, namely 'whether, under the cloak of the lunacy act, *lettres de cachet* [warrants for arrest or imprisonment] may be issued by unscrupulous individuals able to pay tempting fees to two hungry practitioners'. He noted that questions had recently been raised in the House of Commons in connection with another case, and that a commission of inquiry into the operation of the Lunacy Act was likely to be demanded early in the next parliamentary session.[59]

Meanwhile Rosina stayed in the south of France with Robert and her friend Rebecca Ryves until she fell out with both. In August she wrote from Bordeaux to Edwin James, thanking him for offering to become one of her trustees in the arrangements being made for her future. 'I do trust you implicitly.'[60] By October she had read Robert's letter to *The Times*, with those of Forbes Winslow and Conolly. She saw that Edwin James, whom she now dubbed the 'Old Bailey Mephistopheles', was employed by her husband; she also suspected 'that viper' Rebecca Ryves of conspiring against her. As for poor Robert, from being her 'Prince Charming' in August, he was now her chief enemy, the tool of his father.[61] On 25 October she addressed a letter to the earl of Shaftesbury in his capacity as chairman of the Lunacy Commission, accusing him of conspiring with Robert and her *soi-disant* friend Rebecca to get her out of England. She now saw the journey to France as a '*compulsory* journey' into which she had been 'half bullied, half cajoled' by Rebecca.[62] Robert, she now believed, had all along taken his father's side, and she 'never desire[d] to see his face again'.

By November she was back in Taunton and Robert was in The Hague, where he held a diplomatic post as attaché to the British embassy. Rosina faded from public view at last, though she published a few more books before her death in 1882, lonely and indebted. Most scandalously, 1880 saw the publication of her unrestrained autobiography, *A Blighted Life*. There she gave her version of the events of the summer of 1858. When discussing her treatment at Dr Hill's hands she is inconsistent, on the one hand complaining of privations, on the other describing delightful walks and carriage journeys with Hill's daughter, with whom she became friendly. She also remembered the great heat, the 'horrible tepid ditchwater' she had to drink in Hill's establishment, and the 'broiling' weather on Saturday, 17 July, the day she was released from Inverness Lodge.[63] (*The Times* recorded the maximum temperature in the shade in the south of England as 82 °F, or 28 °C, on that day.[64])

Dr Hill, who kept notes about Rosina's behaviour in the three weeks she spent with him, noted that she used a lot of rouge (like her husband),

accused Bulwer Lytton of having caused her daughter Emily's death by
neglect, repeated her accusation of sodomy against Disraeli – shouting it
out of a window at the top of her voice – and said that Forster 'was drunk
every day of his life'. Hill thought her delusional.[65] He fell victim to the
press's negative reporting of the story at a time when several Lunacy
Commission cases of false imprisonment were also receiving coverage. The
Dublin newspaper, *Freeman's Journal and Daily Commercial Advertiser*,
printed a letter of complaint from Hill on Friday, 23 July:

> Whilst Lady Bulwer Lytton remained under my care I did not consider
> myself at liberty to reply to the various injurious reports that have been
> circulated respecting my share in the affairs of Sir Edward and Lady
> Lytton, but now that her ladyship is no longer so, having left my home
> on Saturday last to travel with her son, I think it right, for the vindica-
> tion of my own character, to unequivocally contradict that Lady Lytton
> was 'feloniously deprived of her liberty and consigned to a notorious
> madhouse at Brentford, the keeper of which is named Hill' . . . I deny
> that her ladyship was 'forcibly removed by policemen', or that a
> policeman ever touched her . . . I deny that Lady Lytton was 'consigned
> to a madhouse', 'buried in the depths of a lunatic bastille', or 'left alone
> with individuals in a ghastly state of lunacy', or that she was even
> restrained by bolts or bars. Her ladyship had the opportunity of going
> out whenever she thought proper, and there were no locks to prevent
> her. I had no other patient in the house, and Lady Lytton's companions
> were my wife and eldest daughter . . . Now, I challenge any one to say
> that this asylum is otherwise than humanely and respectably conducted.[66]

(It is reasonable to assume that Hill tried to get his letter printed in *The
Times* or another London newspaper; certainly a Dublin newspaper would
not have been his first choice in which to air his complaint.)

Hill suffered at the hands of the Lunacy Commission, which stated in
March 1859 that Inverness Lodge was not a 'suitable abode' for a Mrs
Burkitt. Hill was furious with Forster and Shaftesbury. He claimed his
business was suffering because of the unfair publicity following the Lytton
affair and implicated both Forster and Shaftesbury in the plan to put

Rosina in an asylum in the first place. There was truth in this. Shaftesbury had written to Bulwer Lytton on 29 July 1858 that he was 'quite convinced that your course was just and necessary in placing Lady L. under care and treatment'.[67] Now Forster feared Hill's threat to go to law over the dispute about who was responsible for the apprehension of Rosina, telling Bulwer Lytton on 14 March 1859 that if the true sequence of events were to come to light, 'it would be a momentous scandal, and would require a public inquiry into the lunacy laws and practice'.[68] Shaftesbury and Bulwer Lytton held firm, denying any conspiracy between Bulwer Lytton and the Lunacy Commission, and it was Hill whose business went into decline.

As for Bulwer Lytton, he was already hated and despised by Thackeray, *Fraser's Magazine*, and the *Punch* writers, all of whom made sport of his ridiculous vanity and snobbery. But he survived the onslaught of July 1858, partly because, though the papers supported Rosina's right to a fair hearing, they were quite aware of her outrageous and unbalanced behaviour. Indeed, both husband and wife came in for criticism as incorrigible self-publicists on the edge of insanity. Edmund Yates wrote on 17 July in the *Illustrated Times* that he had heard that 'Lady Bulwer's troubles are to be brought to an "amicable arrangement" ', adding cheekily that 'a rigid abstinence from pen and ink should form part of the conditions, for the public's sake'.[69]

Neither did the Derby government suffer from the general condemnation of Bulwer Lytton's treatment of his wife, though the *Daily Telegraph* constantly reminded its readers that Bulwer Lytton the tyrannical husband was a member of Derby's government. Derby's administration was now popular because it was seen to be tackling the Thames problem, had rectified the troubles in India, and, mainly thanks to Disraeli's energy and determination, was bringing various pieces of legislation to a satisfactory conclusion before the end of the session. Bulwer Lytton himself proved to be a thorough administrator, if a poor orator, making good decisions about the provinces of Australia and Canada, which he was keen to see self-regulating as soon as possible. He told parliament in December 1858 that he favoured 'that safe and gradual independence which should be the last and crowning boon that a colony should receive from a parent state', and in 1860 he displayed prophetic insight when he said that the time would

come when 'these new Colonies will be great States', raising fleets and
armies which would rush to Britain's rescue if need be. 'Across the wide
ocean ships will come thick and fast' to help 'the mother of many free
Commonwealths' in her hour of need.[70]

Nonetheless he did not last long in office. By December 1858 he was
complaining of physical and psychological ailments and begging Derby to
let him resign. He used Disraeli as a go-between, sending him a letter from
his doctor to prove his inability to continue, to which Disraeli replied
brutally, not least because he and Derby were having their reform proposals
blocked by a number of powerful colleagues and feared their administration might fall. Disraeli mixed some flattery with his aggression:

> I have no opinion of Dr Reed, or of any Doctors. In the course of my
> life I have received fifty letters from physicians like that which you
> enclosed to me, and which I return. Had I attended to them, I should
> not be here, Chancellor of the Exchequer, and in robust health . . .
>
> I hope you will reconsider your position, and not sacrifice a political
> career at a public emergency, and when you have gained, on all hands,
> credit for the masterly administration of your Department. It will cause
> you regret hereafter.
>
> I say nothing of the effect on the position of the Government by the
> retirement of any of its members at this moment.[71]

Bulwer Lytton countered with complaints about his deafness, his weak
pulse, his tendency to consumption, and his fear of 'organic heart disease'
and 'sudden paralysis'.[72] Disraeli worked on him and was able to inform
Derby on New Year's Day 1859 that he had persuaded Bulwer Lytton to
stay on in order to avoid a cabinet crisis; he added callously, 'He expects to
die before Easter, but, if so, I have promised him a public funeral.'[73] As the
government valiantly tried to introduce a Reform Bill during the spring of
1859 Bulwer Lytton played his part. Disraeli reported to the queen on 22
March that his irritating friend had just given one of the 'greatest speeches
ever delivered in Parliament', despite his disadvantages: 'Deaf, fantastic,
modulating his voice with difficulty sometimes painful, at first almost
an object of ridicule to the superficial, Lytton occasionally reached even

the sublime, & perfectly enchained his audience. His description of the English Constitution, his analysis of Democracy – as rich & more powerful, than Burke.'[74]

This was generous, but Disraeli bated Bulwer Lytton once too often about his hypochondria. His friend took offence and resigned from the cabinet on 4 April, though the following month he stood for election as an MP once more in Hertford (without a surprise visit from Rosina).[75] In any case, by the end of June 1859 Derby's government had resigned over internal disagreements about its ill-fated Reform Bill. The greatest achievement of the short-lived ministry was the passing, after much wrangling, of the bill to cleanse the Thames. Close attention to Disraeli's tactics and to the response of an alert press reveals his masterly handling of the matter, a moment in his career which has been curiously ignored or undervalued by many historians.[76]

Disraeli tames the Thames

Now that a parliamentary committee had been formed to inquire into the state of the Thames and to come up with a plan to improve it, the papers, led by *The Times*, kept the committee itself under constant review. With its influential members, including Sir Benjamin Hall and Alderman William Cubitt (a member of the great Cubitt architectural and building firm), and various representatives of vestries, not to mention Lord John Russell and Lord Palmerston, it carried a great deal of weight. It also came in for a lot of suspicion and scepticism, since Hall and others had been kicking the topic of metropolitan drainage to and fro for several years. Now, with parliamentary committees fleeing the Houses of Parliament with handkerchiefs to their noses on 30 June, and with Disraeli driving things forward, the committee got to work in earnest. On Thursday, 1 July *The Times* reported in some detail the committee's meeting the previous day.

Parliament's own heating engineer, Goldsworthy Gurney, had been called to give evidence and advice. He outlined his plan to form 'two channels 30 yards wide and three yards deep' in the river, with 'a slope of 1 in 12', by which means he considered 'that the mud which is now cast upon the banks of the river will be removed, and so get rid of the nuisance' within the Thames itself. George Bidder, a civil engineer, followed and made objections to Gurney's plan: the formation of the two channels would be an inconvenience to shipping, he thought, and in any case he did not believe that a slope of 1 in 12 would prevent the deposit of mud in the river. 'I agree with Mr Bazalgette', he said, 'that the sewage lodging on the mud banks is the cause of great evil.' Another expert, James Lawes, gave his opinion that Gurney's plan to send the sewage into the river itself would not work. 'As long as we have a mass of floating sewage in the Thames, Mr Gurney's plan will not remove it. In warm weather there is a great escape of the noxious gases.' But he also thought that if the sewage were to be discharged at Barking Creek (Bazalgette's plan), it would return to London on the tide. The committee more or less agreed that throwing lime into the river to deodorise it would only work in the short term, and would be expensive.[77] More experts were called, and more disagreements among them emerged, over the next week or so, as the committee reconvened again and again.

In its editorial on 1 July *The Times* showed impatience:

Committee after Committee, Commission after Commission, has sat on the question, collecting facts enough to build on them a hundred different systems of drainage . . . They are now doing nothing but throwing a few boatloads of lime into the river, in the vain hope of sweetening the classic shores of Lambeth and Millbank, or pottering somewhere or other with the mouths of the sewers. All that will make mighty little difference this time next year. We want something that will go to the heart of the evil, and that without a day's longer delay than is absolutely necessary.

Changing tack from gloom to national pride, the article exhorts the engineers and politicians to emulate the spirit of those who designed the Crystal Palace in Hyde Park for the Great Exhibition of 1851. That was 'a thing of brick and mortar, an architectural triumph'. Even more impressive was the dismantling of the great glass edifice and the rebuilding of it in Sydenham three years later, a work achieved with 'wonderful cheapness, speed, punctuality', and stability. The key was 'a few iron types'. 'Why cannot the most noxious part of our sewage . . . be conveyed in iron pipes along and just under the banks of the river far enough for the purpose?' the editor asked.[78]

Though none of the newspapers, which all took up the cry in favour of making a decision and going to work on it as soon as possible, had much sympathy for the politicians who were suffering more than anyone from the Great Stink, *The Times* did publish an agonised letter the following day from 'A HARD-WORKED AND NEARLY STIFLED MP', who begged for understanding of his and his colleagues' plight:

> During the whole month of June the condition of the Thames, which rolls its inky waters underneath our windows, has been in the last degree abominable; and yet a very considerable number of members have during that month given an average attendance of from 12 to 15 hours a-day to the business of the House . . . Take, as an illustration, the case of a committee of which I have the honour – certainly not the happiness – to be a member.

He tells of the dilemma in soaring heat between being 'half choked and half poisoned' by the disgusting smell if the windows are kept open and being 'literally baked' if they close the windows and sit in the room 'for six mortal hours' at a time, 'gasping for a mouthful of pure air'. On one occasion the committee members tried opening the door instead of the window, but 'in vain! – the stench was there as well'.

> How long, sir, is this state of things to last? Are we to wait until half-a-dozen peers, including a bishop or two, perish by this living poison? . . . Is it possible that Parliament can sit any longer in London if the Thames is not purified? . . . Unless the remedy be found and applied between this and next session men will not consent to peril their lives by sitting for days and nights by the side of a festering cesspool, and both Houses of Parliament will have to be removed to some salubrious locality – to Edinburgh, to Oxford, or to Dublin.[79]

Another anonymous MP wrote the same day, complaining less and suggesting remedies. A workable scheme should 'contain three objects', he wrote: first 'the purification of the Thames', second 'the embankment of its shores in its course through the metropolis', and third 'the utilization of the vast mass of productive matter that is now worse than wasted'.[80] Of these three objects, the first two were soon to be implemented by Bazalgette.

On Saturday, 3 July the *Illustrated London News* welcomed the 'vigorous measures' at last being put in place, with 200 or more tons of lime being thrown into the Thames near the mouths of the sewers, and, more importantly, the fact that the plan of 'Messrs. Bidder, Hawksley, and Bazalgette' to embank the river looked like being accepted.[81] On the same day the 'Big Cut' in *Punch* was a drawing of 'Father Thames introducing his Offspring to the Fair City of London (A Design for a Fresco in the New Houses of Parliament)', the offspring being Diphtheria, Scrofula, and Cholera.[82] And to drive the point home further, a short poem parodying Tennyson's 'Break, break, break' was printed on 3 July too. Entitled 'To the Thames (After Tennyson)', it begins:

Bake, bake, bake,
O Thames, on thy way to the sea!
And I would that thy stink could poison
A Bishop, Peer, or M.P.[83]

Not to be outdone, the *Era* weighed in on Sunday, 4 July with its demand that action be taken as soon as possible. On the question of who should pay, the paper believed that the whole nation should contribute so that the Thames would no longer be 'a reproach to the capital of the world'. Why waste time by holding endless parliamentary meetings on the subject, when everyone knew that the plan to take the sewage out of London to Kent and Essex must be implemented? The task of Londoners, egged on by their newspapers, was not to trust the Board of Works, but to keep a constant eye on it and chivvy it out of its customary state of apathy. Like all the commentators, this one subscribes to the mistaken airborne theory of infectious disease; the *Era* reported that an 'unfortunate clergyman' at Lambeth had lost his wife and four children that week to the 'noxious miasmata of the Thames'.[84]

More meetings of the parliamentary committee on the Thames, and of the universally maligned Board of Works under its hard-working chairman

John Thwaites, took place as the temperature, having dipped in the first few days of July, rose again to 80 °F (27 °C) and more. Bazalgette was called to give evidence; on 8 July he reported to the board that he had already put in place the temporary measure of deodorising the river by putting lime into the sewers (at a cost of £180 a day), a procedure which would continue as long as the weather remained hot.[85] On Monday, 12 July the parliamentary committee on the Thames was attended by such a large number of its members that, appropriately, 'the heat of the room was almost insupportable', according to *The Times*. The committee was ready to finalise its decision to accept the plan put forward by Bazalgette and his partners to take the sewage out of London by means of intercepting sewers, and to release it far enough from the city to ensure that it would not return on the tide. The idea of using the sewage as fertiliser had been rejected, since, as Thomas Hawksley told the committee, deodorised sewage was no longer useful as a fertiliser, and no one could make a commercial business out of selling it for re-use.[86]

The select committee on the Thames was due to report on its delibera-tions on 19 July. Disraeli had already told Queen Victoria on 8 July that the 'Thames Purification Bill is drawn, & will be introduced probably in a week'.[87] True to his word, he introduced the all-important amendment to the 1855 Metropolis Local Management Act on Thursday, 15 July. His plan was to propose a bill in principle, and not to let MPs get bogged down in detailed discussions of the various projects which it was the committee's duty to compare and assess. He did so with a flourish, beginning by interrupting the business of the House of Commons to bring his bill:

Sir, I took the liberty of moving that the orders of the day should be postponed in order that I might bring under the attention of the House a Bill the object of which is the purification of the river Thames. The condition of the waters of that river has fallen upon the inhabitants of this metropolis, generally speaking, as an unexpected calamity; but I believe there has always been an observant minority in the community which has expected the catastrophe that has recently occurred . . . Sir, all that they then predicted has been more than fulfilled. That noble river, so long the pride and joy of Englishmen, which has hitherto been associated with the noblest feats of our commerce and the most beautiful passages of our poetry, has really become a Stygian pool, reeking with ineffable and intolerable horrors. The public health is at stake; . . . there is a pervading apprehension of pestilence in this great city; and I am sure I am only taking a step that will have been anticipated when I ask leave to introduce a Bill which will attempt – and I trust the attempt will be successful – to terminate a state of affairs so unsatisfactory and fraught with so much danger to the public health.[88]

By 'an observant minority' Disraeli meant not only the newspapers but also experts including Bazalgette and the great scientist and discoverer of electromagnetism Michael Faraday, who had written to *The Times* on 9 July 1855 warning about the state of the Thames in *that* summer's heat. Faraday wrote to the editor saying he had 'traversed this day by steamboat the space between London and Hungerford bridges' between 1.30 and 2 p.m., at low tide. He had been assailed by the foul smell and 'opaque brown fluid' of the river. The river ought not 'to be allowed to become a fermenting sewer'; finally, 'if we neglect this subject, we cannot expect to do so with impunity; nor ought we to be surprised if, ere many years are over, a hot season give us sad proof of the folly of our carelessness'.[89] *Punch* had immediately followed up Faraday's letter with a cartoon showing him on a boat, holding his nose with one hand and handing his card to a filthy Father Thames with the other.

The evil had been unintentionally exacerbated by Edwin Chadwick's mistaken notion in the 1840s that it was better to pour sewage into sewers which emptied into the Thames than to continue to fill – and overfill – the 200,000 cesspools which had accumulated in London.[90] Water usage in London had doubled between 1850 and 1856, and by 1858 the city's population had reached nearly 2.5 million.[91] As the *People's Paper* pointed out on 10 July 1858, the Parisian administration, faced with similar problems of removing sewage safely, wished to 'suppress' its present practice – emptying cesspools into carts to run on rails along the public streets – but was not inclined to follow London's disastrous custom of 'poisoning the sewers' and consequently the Thames.[92]

Disraeli continued, asking the question (already answered in his mind and that of the government) 'Is this a local or a national business?' In other

words, who should pay? The answer was that London should pay. Then
came the fact that though the Metropolitan Board of Works, operative since
early 1856, had not been noticeably successful, it had been considering the
subject over 'a long period of time', and should now be tasked with carrying
forward the scheme to be adopted. The costs were estimated at £3 million,
the term during which a special tax of not more than three pence in the
pound would be levied was to be forty years, and the government would
guarantee both capital and interest. The Board of Works was to be given
'perfect freedom as regards the construction of the works'.[93] As soon as
Disraeli had put the motion, a speaker rose to make a point of order about
the 'rules of the House'; Palmerston came to Disraeli's aid by proposing a
solution to the point of order. Several speakers were determined to dig down
to the details it was Disraeli's intention to avoid. He wisely let them do so
for a while. One speaker gave the house a history lesson about the unpopu-
larity of special taxes among the populace, instancing a Hackney Coach Tax
and a Coal Tax. A Mr John Locke declared that 'the Bill shadowed forth by
the Chancellor of the Exchequer was very much like the play of Hamlet,
with the principal character omitted'. The house was still 'in utter ignorance
whether any plan had been suggested'; and what of the Metropolitan Board
of Works? Did it deserve to be given carte blanche to manage the business,
as Disraeli had announced? Finally: 'What, then, was the meaning of the
present Bill, which had been brought down to the House with such a great
flourish. Nobody understood it. Her Majesty's Government had not
explained what was to be done. All they said was, "We will place unlimited
confidence in a body who have hitherto done nothing."'[94]

This was a veritable hit, but Disraeli did not rise to it. Next, presumably
to Disraeli's consternation, though he did not express it, several members
of the parliamentary committee on the Thames spoke up doubting the
wisdom of handing over power to the board. The committee chairman,
Kendall, said his members 'had suggestions pouring in upon them from
engineers, chemists, and all quarters in England, Ireland, and Scotland',
which they had not yet had time to digest fully. Sir Benjamin Hall went
back in time to explain his own part in the deliberations of the new
Metropolitan Board of Works in 1856; he had been blamed for bickering
about Bazalgette's plan then and causing delays over arguments about who

should foot the bill for any such project.[95] He announced that he thought
intercepting sewers were a good idea, but not sufficient to solve the whole
problem. A 'much greater work must be undertaken', one which should be
financed by the whole country, namely the embankment of the Thames.[96]
Lord John Manners agreed with Disraeli, his friend and fellow Young
Englander in their earlier days, that general principles must be agreed first,
before the house adopted a particular plan. He supported the bill, assuring
his colleagues that they would find it 'carefully and skilfully framed'. Other
members of the committee brought up the usefulness and cost of deodorising with lime. Colonel Sykes declared that 'there have been so many
Thames doctors, with their prescriptions, both in the House and out of the
House', that he had 'hitherto abstained from increasing the list and offering
[his] nostrum'. But now he must speak up in favour of the bill and the
Bazalgette plan to combine drainage of the river with its embankment. He
reminded the house that more than twenty years earlier the historical
painter John Martin had suggested such a plan, but was ignored. [97]

Having let them all have their say, Disraeli summed up in breezy, flattering fashion. He wished to congratulate 'the inhabitants of the metropolis upon the manner in which, generally speaking, the proposition of
the Government has been received'. (How did he know what ordinary
Londoners thought? Those who wrote letters to the newspapers were often
critical of the do-nothingism of parliament on the subject, and who knew
what those who did not write letters thought?) As for the highly unpopular
Board of Works, Disraeli took a risk and boldly declared that 'one result of
the Bill will be to convert' the board into a 'real corporation'. 'I cannot
doubt that a body of Englishmen, elected by a large and enlightened
constituency, like the inhabitants of this great city, will do their duty, and
that their conduct will entitle them to the confidence and respect of their
fellow-citizens.' No one should worry about the money involved, since the
government was prepared to underwrite the expense and at the end of the
operation they should all find themselves 'entirely out of debt'. This calculation, 'made by a person [unnamed] of the highest authority', will 'display
the magic influence of compound interest when applied with prudence
and discretion'.[98] In other words, all would be for the best in the best of all
possible worlds, according to the finance minister (who never in his life got

himself 'entirely out of debt' and who knew precious little about the workings of 'compound interest'). But confidence was all. Disraeli was given
leave to bring in his bill and it passed its first reading.

After further debates and readings, the heat and dust settled, and
Disraeli's bill was passed by the end of the month with very little in the
way of amendments offered by either house. The *Illustrated London News*
celebrated on Saturday, 24 July, noting that the bill for the purification of
the Thames had now gone through and the work was in the hands of the
Metropolitan Board of Works, which, as it remarked, was not a popular
body, being elected by vestries with their narrow local interests.[99] The
paper, though sceptical, realised that Disraeli had played a clever hand:

> When Mr Disraeli introduced [the bill], one suspected, the moment he
> began, that not much in the way of a measure was to be expected, for
> he spoke in his loftiest style, and all his opening sentences were down-
> right blank verse, which was not exactly adapted to a bill which commits
> the metropolis hand and foot to Mr Thwaites and his concentrated
> essence of vestry board, with the dangerous addition of the command
> of three millions of money.[100]

Nevertheless, the uneasiness felt at subsequent readings of the bill was
quelled, according to the *Illustrated London News,* because people seemed
to expect a mess but were ready to let the Metropolitan Board of Works
take the responsibility – and blame – if the plan failed.

Disraeli was therefore triumphant, the consensus being that his Thames
Bill was the best piece of legislation of the parliamentary session. The
newspapers continued to snipe at the Thames committee over the next
weeks, with *Punch* naming a cod 'select body of investigators' on 17 July,
among whom were Mr Crucible the chemist, Mr Meter, 'engineer to the
Economical Gas Company', Mr Puddinghead, Lord Muggins, Professor
Blowpipe, Mr Wiseacre, Mr Sump, and others.[101] But the main thing was
that something – at last – was being done.

If there was an irony in Disraeli, with his extraordinarily chaotic personal
finances, being nominally in charge of the nation's Treasury, a parallel irony

existed in the case of one of his shrewdest observers, the great philosopher-critic of capitalist economics, Karl Marx. On the day Disraeli introduced his Thames Bill, 15 July, Marx wrote the most miserable of many begging letters to his friend Engels in Manchester. Engels was in the habit of sending frequent £5 notes to London to keep the Marx family afloat while Marx spent his days in the reading room of the British Museum preparing his great work on capital and writing copious articles for German and American newspapers. On 29 March 1858 he thanked Engels for the latest £5 and talked of the arrangement to publish his *Contribution to the Critique of Political Economy* in instalments. Joking grimly, he told Engels that he had been ill and taking medicine for his liver, with many relapses 'owing to prolonged work by night, and, by day, a multitude of petty annoyances RESULTING FROM THE ECONOMICAL CONDITIONS OF MY DOMESTICITY'.[102]

On 15 July Marx had reached rock bottom. In a long letter at which he asked Engels 'not to take fright', since it was not intended as an appeal 'to your already unduly overloaded exchequer', he outlined the parlous state of his finances. He could not get on with the work of writing articles, from which he earned small amounts, because he was spending all his time 'running around in fruitless attempts to raise money'. His wife Jenny was ill and a 'nervous wreck'; the family doctor had advised her to go to the seaside to rest, but of course there was no money for that. He had borrowed from friends, from loan societies, from the newspapers he wrote for, yet he had 'not a penny left over even for the most urgent day-to-day expenses'. Enclosing a statement of recent expenditure on rates, gas, baker, butcher, cheesemonger, coalman, and school fees and clothes for his three daughters, he declared that since 17 June there had been *kein pfennig im Hause* ('not a penny in the house'); the current state of his indebtedness amounted to nearly £112, owed to the above-itemised creditors. In his desperation Marx toyed aloud with the idea of moving from north London to Whitechapel in the East End, where he might find a 'working-class lodging', but he could not bring himself to subject his wife and 'growing girls' to such privation. 'I HAVE NOW MADE A CLEAN BREAST OF IT', he told Engels, since 'I must speak my mind to somebody'. He only asked for Engels's advice on 'WHAT TO DO'. 'I would not wish my worst enemy to have to wade through the QUAGMIRE in which I've been trapped for the past two months, fuming the while over the innumerable vexations that are ruining my intellect and destroying my capacity for work.'[103]

So much for Marx's home life during this hot summer. His true-hearted friend Engels replied the next day, offering £30 and suggesting Marx should raise the rest from London friends and the People's Provident Assurance Society, an institution set up in 1853 on socialist principles.[104] All the while Marx, always alert to the political situation in Britain and in the rest of Europe, and with a determination to reach back in history to define causes and their consequences, wrote his series of remarkably knowledgeable articles on politics and economics. He also wrote on popular topics of the day, such as the incarceration of Rosina Bulwer Lytton in Inverness Lodge, which he tackled only a week after his desperate letter to Engels. Despite his poor health and anxiety about money, he managed to write a number of newspaper articles in 1858 which contained detailed historical and statistical analyses for which a good deal of research in parliamentary reports (known as 'Blue Books') and scholarly works lodged in the library of the British Museum was required.

Marx's articles, though relatively brief, differed from the day-to-day accounts of public affairs in newspapers like *The Times*; they resembled rather the long scholarly analytical essays which appeared in the great quarterly reviews, the *Edinburgh Review*, the *Quarterly Review*, and the *Westminster Review*. There was a scornful assessment of the career of 'Mr Pam' in February, when Palmerston lost office after appearing to cave in to French attempts to intervene in British justice over the plot to assassinate Napoleon III; a brief study of Disraeli's budget in April (of which Marx approved); an analysis of Canning's proclamation on Oudh in May; and an informed essay on 'The Increase of Lunacy in Great Britain' in August.[105] Marx's main concern was to write his great work on capital, if he could only regain good health and financial security. Since he lived quietly and did not move in London's fashionable or literary circles, and since his articles were printed in foreign or out-of-the-way newspapers, like the *People's Paper*, which was in constant financial difficulty, Marx's writings remained largely unknown to his British contemporaries. He followed with interest the careers of Dickens and Disraeli – he was an avid reader of Dickens's novels – and after 1859 of Darwin, but none of them followed his.

Rothschild enters the Commons at last

During July 1858 Disraeli was polishing off many pieces of legislation, doing the work of two men while Lord Derby was incapacitated by gout in the early days of the month. Though the *Era* reported on Sunday, 4 July that the prime minister had recovered and was back in the House of Lords, Queen Victoria noted that Derby, who was invited to Buckingham Palace for dinner that day, looked 'much pulled down'.[106] He had rallied by the middle of the month, visiting Victoria and Albert at Osborne House, their residence on the Isle of Wight, when he 'was in great force' and telling jokes, 'though still not quite free from the gout'.[107] Various bills were reaching their last readings and amendments, including the India Bill, which was passed largely thanks to the excellent work of Lord Stanley. Disraeli had assured Derby on 17 June, when the latter was away from parliament because of his gout, that Stanley had 'gained golden opinions' in the House of Commons that day, from the opposition's Lord John Russell, among others. Russell had praised his 'fairness and candour, coupled with an evident determination to apply his high abilities to the consideration of this most important question'.[108] By 8 July, thanks to Disraeli's and Stanley's combined efforts, the India Bill passed 'amid general honour, & congratulations from all sides', as Disraeli told the queen.[109]

The Medical Act was less of a success. Carried through by Lord Cowper as a final effort to achieve some sort of medical reform after years of attempts to shift vested interests, and suffering from lack of vocal support from Derby or Disraeli, whose interests lay with India and the Thames, it passed after its third reading in the House of Commons on 9 July and a quick subsequent passage through the Lords. The act in its final form was much watered down from the revolutionary bill drafted by John Simon and supported by the universities and general practitioners, but even the conservative political influence of the Royal College of Physicians and Royal College of Surgeons could not halt the march of progress completely. At least the Medical Register was set up and measures were put in place to deter unqualified practitioners.[110]

Like the Medical Act, the Oaths Bill, intended to allow Jews elected to parliament – in particular, of course, Lionel de Rothschild – to take their seats without having to swear on the 'true faith of a Christian', had been round the block a few times over the years, and kept popping up in this parliament, supported by Lord John Russell (Rothschild's fellow elected MP for the City of London) and Disraeli, and tolerated as a necessary act of justice by Derby. The Lords blocked every version sent to them by the Commons, and there were a few diehard objectors in the Commons too. The most notable of the latter was Charles Newdigate Newdegate, owner of Arbury Hall in Warwickshire, the estate managed until 1849 by Robert Evans, father of Marian Evans, who had just begun to make her mark as a writer of fiction with *Scenes of Clerical Life*. Newdegate was a Tory traditionalist, an upholder of the Church of England as the national religion, and a fervent opponent of Roman Catholicism and Judaism. He led the opposition to the Oaths Bill, writing letters to the press declaring that Jews had been 'among the office bearers' of the Spanish Inquisition. He was supported by some strongly anti-Semitic rhetoric in the *St James's Chronicle*, which professed to believe that 'the hatred of the Jew towards Christianity' was alive and well. The paper attacked Rothschild directly on 20 May 1858, when the Oaths Bill was being batted to and fro in parliament:

> Baron Rothschild seeking admission to the British Parliament in the nineteenth century, with professions of religious liberalism upon his lips, is playing precisely the same game as the 'gentlemen of the Hebrew persuasion' who, in the fifteenth and sixteenth centuries qualified in Spain as 'familiars of the Holy Office of the Inquisition'. In both cases the object, as well as the result, is the same – to inflict a 'heavy blow and great discouragement' upon the hateful creed of the 'Nazarene'.[111]

Most newspapers supported the bill as a matter of justice to a man who had been elected to parliament several times but was unable to take his seat, though there was a good deal of casual joking about Jewishness. When the Lords finally conceded on 1 July that the Commons could bring in an act to allow Jews to sit in their house, while the House of Lords would remain stubbornly closed to them, the newspapers enjoyed the embarrassment of all sides at such a laborious compromise. The *Era* on Sunday, 11 July toyed with the idea that 'we may one day see a Hebrew Lord

Chancellor', a sly dig at the current lord chancellor, Lord Chelmsford, who, as Sir Frederick Thesiger, had been Newdegate's predecessor as chief gatekeeper against admitting Jews into the House of Commons.[112] *Punch* offered a poem, 'The Triumph of Moses', on the same weekend, which ridiculed the Lords, while reminding them that Rothschild had a foreign baronetcy, not to mention fabulous wealth:

> In the Commons 'tis certain that Moses will meet
> With no opposition in taking his seat,
> Which he'll firmly endeavour with credit to fill,
> For economy, measures, materials, and skill . . .
>
> Then room for Lord Moses, ye proud Barons, yield,
> With his crest on his carriage, and arms on his shield,
> And his pedigree, higher than Normans can run,
> And his business – which he can entail on his son.[113]

Two weeks later *Punch* reported on the further proceedings in parliament which the Lords were inflicting on the Commons before they conceded the point; on 24 July, with an allusion to Walter Scott's *Ivanhoe*, it hailed the 'final triumph of Isaac of York over Front de Boeuf Alamode, and all the rest of the Feudal Lords'.[114] The *Illustrated London News* was scathing about the Lords' apparent terror that a flood of Jews would soon be rushing into parliament; yes, says the paper sarcastically, the number of likely representatives has already doubled from one, Rothschild, to two, with David Salomons likely to be the next Jew to take his seat.[115] (In the general election in summer 1859 Salomons was returned for Greenwich, as before, and Lionel de Rothschild's younger brother Mayer was elected as Liberal MP for Hythe, bringing the total number of Jewish MPs to three.) It was clear by now that the curious compromise bill would pass into law, but its opponents, including most of the bishops in the House of Lords, continued to wrangle until the last moment before the bill finally passed on 21 July and received the royal assent, along with all the other bills, on 2 August.[116] Even on Monday, 26 July, the day Rothschild was introduced to the Commons by Lord John Russell and the Liberal banker John Abel

Smith, there was one last division before he was allowed to take his seat. It was lost by sixty-nine votes to thirty-seven, with Newdegate and the home secretary Spencer Walpole among the dissenters.[117]

Though Disraeli was often treated to anti-Semitic rhetoric and caricature in the press, most of them left him out of the picture when discussing the erratic course of the Oaths Bill, perhaps because he kept a low profile, despite being in constant liaison with the bill's main proposer, Lord John Russell. An exception was the deliberately provocative *Reynolds's Newspaper*, which opened its column 'Gossip of the Week' on Sunday, 1 August with the following clever paragraph, in which Disraeli is credited with (or blamed for) getting the 'Jew Bill' through:

> The Jew egg, which many supposed addled, is at length hatched. Lord John Russell cackles, and fain would crow; which, no doubt, he would, as well and as lustily as an antiquated political capon of his pigmy capacity could, were it not that he is deterred by the very natural terror inspired by the presence of another game bird, of oriental extraction, who wields a fiercer beak and claw, and displays a more gorgeous plumage than the Bedford bantam, even in his palmiest days, could sport. This game bird is not only cock of the walk, but master of the best and richest dungheap in Mr John Bull's farm-yard. We need scarcely say that we allude to Mr Disraeli . . . There can be no doubt that to the more vigorous and skilful incubation of Mr Disraeli is now due the fact that Baron Rothschild is enabled to display his new-fledged senatorial pinions . . . We may be quite certain that if the Derby–Disraelites had been in Opposition the whole session, the Jew Bill had not yet been carried.[118]

The diminutive Russell – his lack of height was the chief detail fixed on in those newspapers which were unsympathetic to his politics – came in for due praise in December in the pantomime *Tit, Tat, Toe*, put on in one of the unofficial theatres, the Effingham Saloon in Whitechapel. Thanks to 'Little Lord John Russell', the Jews, 'once despised of races', will 'prove to brave old England / The right men in the right places', since 'they ever lend a helping hand – don't talk of milk or honey / For many a Sovereign would have lost a Crown / Had it not been for Jewish Money'.[119] The

Illustrated London News for Saturday, 24 July noted that some members of the House of Commons, despite being 'in the last stage of physical exhaustion', fought the battle to the end. Mr Newdegate was particularly 'vigorous' in his opposition, but was being taught a lesson, says the paper, 'in the art of Conservative government on Radical principles'.[120] Rothschild finally took his seat eleven years after first being elected to parliament.

Reynolds's Newspaper and the *Illustrated London News* were not alone in noticing that the Derby–Disraeli administration passed a remarkable number of reforming measures for a Tory government. Derby was praised by a late nineteenth-century historian of his illustrious family for his moderate reformism in addition to his 'matchless eloquence', 'scathing sarcasm', and 'lofty bearing'.[121] Only days after he regained power at the end of February 1858, he spoke in the House of Lords of the need for 'constant progress, improving upon the old system, adapting our institutions to the altered purposes they are intended to serve', and 'judicious changes meeting the demands of society'.[122] One minor piece of reform legislation went through parliament quietly during June 1858 and was given the royal assent on the 28th of that month. This was the Property Qualification Bill, like the Oaths Bill an enabling measure. It abolished the requirement that men standing for parliament had to prove they owned a certain amount of property in money or land. As *The Times* said on 7 June, 'a law that can always be evaded' was 'not worth retaining'.[123] Many a serving MP could be proved to have perjured himself on this point. *The Times* was keen to welcome the abolition of the property law, wondering aloud on 11 June, 'Can we trust the evidence of our senses when we see a Tory millennium inaugurated by the admission of the Jews [and] by the abolition of the Property Qualification? . . . What next?'[124]

CHAPTER SIX

July–August 1858

Hot heads at the Garrick Club

WHEN JOSEPH IRVING CAME to compile *Annals of Our Time* in the 1870s, he noted all the significant public events of 1858: the launch of the *Great Eastern* and the Orsini bomb plot of January; the change of government in February; the Ellenborough crisis over India, the result of the Derby, and Disraeli's famous speech to the electors of Slough in May; the Puseyite scandal of St Barnabas in June; the passing of various pieces of legislation, including the act to purify the Thames, in July. Irving also drew attention to two striking events in the literary world during the hot months. These were not the appearance of a great work of fiction by Dickens, who published nothing in 1858, or Thackeray, whose *Virginians* was limping along its slow serialised way, and not yet George Eliot's runaway success, *Adam Bede*, on which she was working throughout 1858, with publication following early in 1859. The two matters which caused a stir were private problems which became public, and which lingered on for months, to the embarrassment of the protagonists. The first was Dickens's separation from his wife and the statement that announced it to the world; the second was the absurdly magnified rift in the Garrick Club caused by the callow Edmund Yates's casually malicious article on Thackeray. The main event in this saga occurred on 10 July, when the Garrick held a special meeting of its members to decide what to do about Yates. After much ado about not very much during the summer, the chief result, as *Annals* summed it up, was 'the temporary estrangement of Mr Thackeray and Mr Dickens'.[1]

The relationship between Dickens and Thackeray had always been strained, with Thackeray jealous of Dickens's success, and Dickens irritated by his fellow novelist's snobbery. As *Vanity Fair* began its serialisation in January 1847, Thackeray had been well aware of Dickens's established position as the great novelist of the day. In March of that year, with his own novel in the early stages of publication and not yet sure to be a favourite with the reading public, he is said to have gone into the offices of his publisher Bradbury and Evans, holding a copy of the latest number of Dickens's *Dombey and Son* containing the celebrated death of little Paul Dombey, banged it down on the table, and exclaimed, 'There's no writing against such power as this – one has no chance! Read that chapter describing young Paul's death: it is unsurpassed – it is stupendous!'[2] By the time *Vanity Fair* was approaching the end of its serialisation in January 1848, it was beloved of both readers and critics. Thackeray wrote self-consciously to his mother, telling her, 'I am become a sort of great man in my way – all but at the top of the tree: indeed there if the truth were known and having a great fight up there with Dickens.'[3]

As the years went on the two men published their novels serially, and, as it happened, often simultaneously. *David Copperfield* competed with *Pendennis* in 1849–50; both novels contained a large element of autobiography and both were published by Bradbury and Evans. Dickens always edged ahead in the opinion of the public and the majority of critics, but both had their enthusiastic advocates, and it was widely recognised in the literary world that there were two distinct 'factions'. The Dickens faction consisted of the great mass of readers throughout the country and the young Bohemians in London, among them Sala and Yates. On Thackeray's side were readers who admired the knowing satire of human vanity and hypocrisy which his novels shared with those written by Henry Fielding in the previous century, and Thackeray's fellow writers on *Punch*, public school and university-educated men like John Leech and Henry Silver. *Punch* was also published by William Bradbury and Frederick Evans, the two genial hosts of the weekly *Punch* working dinners, where, as Silver recorded in his diary, the talk was frequently of Dickens's vulgarity and lack of 'class'.[4] The critic David Masson wrote about the literary rivalry in his book, *British Novelists and their Styles* (1859), that 'there is no debate more common, wherever literary talk goes on, than the debate as to the respective merits of Dickens and Thackeray'.[5] Thackeray, as the writer who achieved fame a decade after his rival, was much more alert to the competition than Dickens, who did not need to feel threatened, so assured was he of his place in the public's affection. Nevertheless, Dickens felt vulnerable in the summer of 1858. What if his adoring public believed the unwelcome stories in circulation about the breakdown of his marriage? Anxiety about this no doubt drove him to publish his explanatory statement in *Household Words*; it also underlies the audience-orientated rhetoric of the piece.

As regards that statement, Thackeray had tried to be helpful when asked by Dickens in late May 1858 to contradict rumours going round which were, as Thackeray reported to a friend, 'derogatory to the honor [*sic*] of a young lady whose name has been mentioned in connection with his'.[6] Yet Dickens soon heard that Thackeray had been gossiping about the affair at the Garrick Club and elsewhere, a fact confirmed by Thackeray's 21-year-old daughter Anny in a chatty letter later in the year in which she mentioned 'all the stories Papa was telling of Mr Dickens' in the 'smoking room at the G'.[7] When the Garrick Club affair arose out of Yates's foolish article in *Town Talk* on the same date as the personal statement in *Household Words*, Dickens, who had enough on his mind, ought to have kept clear of it, but his state of mental hyperactivity, combined with annoyance at Thackeray's loose talk and his awareness that Thackeray looked down on him as 'not a gentleman', meant that he became unnecessarily involved by taking Yates's part.

Having written his pompous letter to Yates on 13 June and received in return an unrepentant reply on the 15th, Thackeray – as we have seen – hot-headedly sent the correspondence to the committee of the Garrick Club, appealing melodramatically for its concurrence in his opinion that such articles as Yates's were 'intolerable in a Society of Gentlemen'.[8] When Thackeray told him what he had done, Yates in turn addressed the committee in a letter of 19 June, asking its members to 'suspend your judgment until I have consulted my friends, and been able to prepare my own version of the matter for submission to you'.[9] The club's secretary, Alexander Doland, replied immediately, saying that a special meeting of the committee would take place the following Saturday, 26 June, 'to take the subject of Mr Thackeray's complaint into consideration'.[10] The chief friend consulted by Yates was, of course, Dickens, who wrote to Thackeray to suggest that the row was not the business of anyone other than Yates and Thackeray.[11] Whether the great heat of that middle week of June was instrumental in pushing all these men into extreme positions or was merely an appropriate backdrop, there was certainly a general loss of any sense of proportion among them.

Yates appealed once more to the committee, explaining, reasonably enough, that his article, though perhaps written in 'bad taste', did not break the unspoken rules of the club which Thackeray had invoked in his complaint, since it 'makes no reference to the Club, refers to no conversation that took place there, violates no confidence reposed there, either to myself or to anyone else'. (The strong syntax and emphatic repetition of negatives suggest that Dickens may have drafted this sentence.) If Yates had stopped there, he might have won over the committee to his point of view. Instead, he continued by saying that the matter was not an appropriate one for the committee to concern itself with, that to his knowledge club members had in the past made 'very strong remarks' in print about fellow members (he meant Thackeray himself in his satirical writings), and that he owed no apology to Thackeray.[12] This confirmed the committee in its support of Thackeray; the secretary told Yates on 26 June that the committee believed that it *was* the proper forum for considering Thackeray's complaint and that in its opinion 'Mr Yates is bound to make an ample apology to Mr Thackeray, or to retire from the Club'. If Yates refused to apologise, the matter would be discussed further at a general meeting of the whole club on Saturday, 10 July.[13]

The highhanded attitude of the committee can be explained in part by some previous discussions of the leaking of conversations to the burgeoning popular papers, with their 'Gossip of the Week', 'Lounger at the Clubs', and 'Lounger at the Theatre' columns. One such article had appeared in the *Literary Gazette* in March, raising discussion at the committee, which resolved that such writings gave 'offence to members of this Society' and transgressed 'the laws which regulate the social intercourse of gentlemen'.[14] Perhaps emboldened by the knowledge that the committee was on his side, Thackeray aimed a dart at Yates in the ninth number of the *Virginians*, published by Bradbury and Evans on 1 July. There he wrote of 'young Grubstreet, who corresponds with three penny papers and describes the persons and conversation of gentlemen whom he meets at his "clubs" '.[15] Yates read this before writing on the same day to the Garrick declaring that he would not retire from the club and would not apologise to Thackeray.[16]

Since Thackeray was a popular frequenter of the weekly *Punch* dinners, where, according to Henry Silver, the talk was a combination of smut and snobbery, with Thackeray and Leech recounting stories of sexual exploits and dirty jokes at their old school, Charterhouse, it was natural for the magazine to join in on Thackeray's side.[17] On Saturday, 3 July Percival Leigh's parody of Yates's 'Lounger' articles in *Town Talk* appeared, highlighting the kind of gossip about people's appearance and about their earnings from their writings in which Yates had indulged in his piece on Thackeray: 'The popular novelist, Mr Jenkinson, is about five ten or eleven in height; he is stout, has red hair, and green eyes, in one of which he sticks a glass. He receives a thousand pounds a month from his publishers.'[18]

The cheap papers took up the dispute with glee. On the same Saturday the *Critic* enjoyed combining the Garrick row with Dickens's personal statement, deciding that both he and Thackeray had fallen into the trap of believing that their private concerns were of interest to the public at large. (Of course, the papers were banking on the existence of just such an interest when they brought these matters to the attention of their readers.) 'Your literary man gets his head above the soil', wrote the *Critic*'s hack, 'and imagines that the business of mankind mainly consists in looking at him.' Dickens had merely managed to set 'all the old women in the land inquiring what dreadful things the amiable author of "Pickwick" has been doing'.[19]

As the meeting of 10 July loomed, Dickens advised Yates not to attend; he was sure Thackeray would not.[20] On 7 July he filled in his friend in India, W.H. Russell of *The Times*, with the news of recent events, including the unfortunate breaking of the Atlantic telegraph cable, his own public readings from his books, and the latest news of trouble at the Garrick:

The Garrick is in convulsions. The attack is consequent on Thackeray's having complained to the Committee (with an amazing want of discretion, as I think), of an article about him by Edmund Yates, in a thing called Town Talk. The article is in bad taste, no doubt, and would have been infinitely better left alone. But I conceive that the Committee can have nothing earthly, celestial, or infernal, to do with it. Committee thinks otherwise, and calls on E.Y. to apologize or retire. E.Y. can't apologize (Thackeray having written him a letter that really renders it impossible), and won't retire. Committee thereupon call General Meeting, yet pending. Thackeray *thereupon*, by way of shewing what an ill thing it is for writers to attack one another in print, denounces E.Y. (in Virginians) as 'Young Grub Street'. Frightful mess, muddle, complication, and botheration, ensue. Which Witch's broth is now in full boil.[21]

This amused and apparently disinterested account did not stop Dickens from stiffening Yates's elbow in his determination not to give way. The two men met for dinner on 8 July, and Yates wrote to apologise to the Garrick committee on the day of its meeting, but reiterated his decision not to apologise to Thackeray.[22]

The great meeting on Saturday, 10 July was attended by 127 members, among them Dickens, Wilkie Collins, and Forster. Yates's letter was read out, as was one from Thackeray regretting the fact that 'our little Society has been plunged for weeks past in a turmoil' in which he unfortunately had played a part, but still maintaining that Yates's conduct was detrimental to 'our or any Society'.[23] Thackeray, like Yates, had taken soundings among his friends. The Edinburgh publisher John Blackwood, who was bringing out Bulwer Lytton's latest novel *What Will He Do with It?* in the monthly *Blackwood's Magazine*, advised Thackeray to drop the matter.[24] But Thackeray was stubborn. He well knew that he had a propensity to get into petty arguments with friends and acquaintances, most of which he resolved in the end with comic expressions made up of equal amounts of penitence and pride. One such example is his youthful journalism attacking Bulwer Lytton and his letter of apology in June 1853. Another is a spat he had with John Forster in 1847, when he refused to shake hands with him after hearing that Forster had spoken of him being 'as false as hell'. On that occasion Dickens acted as peacemaker, and Thackeray accepted that while 'Forster ought not to have used the words', he himself 'ought not to have taken them up'.[25]

In the Yates affair Thackeray was unable to see the funny side or accept that the offence was trivial. Two of his *Punch* friends later told him he could have been more magnanimous towards a young penny-a-liner. Shirley Brooks thought he should have sent Yates a note saying, 'Dear Yates next time you want a guinea write to me and not of me. Yours etc.'[26] And according to Silver's diary, Horace Mayhew, after drinking a lot at a *Punch* dinner in August 1863, found the courage to remonstrate with Thackeray, saying, 'With your strength you might have been more generous.' At this, according to Silver, Thackeray 'blazes up – and finally bolts'.[27]

At the meeting Dickens, Collins, and Forster spoke up for Yates, but lost the vote by seventy to forty-six in favour of requiring Yates to apologise or be removed from the club.[28] Dickens, in the midst of arranging with his son Charley what should happen about Catherine and her contact with the children, wrote to the Garrick committee on Monday, 12 July, resigning from it (though not from membership of the club) on the grounds that he differed from the majority 'on the whole principle of last Saturday's discussion'.[29] As no apology came from Yates, his name was erased from the club's list of members on Tuesday, 20 July.[30] Thackeray had won the day, but he was unwell and uneasy. His diary in late June records early-morning 'spasms' and 'cold sweats'. By 12 July, with the Garrick meeting – which he had not attended – over, he escaped to the continent, travelling in Germany and Switzerland until 17 August, when he returned home, still suffering from frequent bouts of sickness.[31] His friend and fellow member of the Garrick Frank Fladgate informed him while he was in Lucerne that 'the *matter* has long since ceased as between you and the ex-member'. 'It became a question between *him* and the *Club* only – and it is settled.' Fladgate added a pun at Yates's expense: 'Some one wrote to me the other day "Y's conduct has been very un Y's [*sic*]". I can add nothing to all this.'[32]

The matter might have rested there, though Yates was sore at losing his place in a club which he was proud to have joined at an unusually early age, and Dickens was furious at both Thackeray's snobbery and the subservience of the club to Thackeray's pique. He also had to read in the minutes of the meeting of 20 July which decided to expel Yates that the latter 'had been unfortunate in those whom he had selected as his advisers'.[33] Dickens fanned the flames rather than damping the embers. On 23 July he wrote to a club member who had supported Yates at the meeting, thanking him for his 'generous feeling' and assuring him that he, Dickens, intended to 'render steady, unflinching, and enduring support' of Yates's cause. The committee had 'gone perfectly mad', he said; moreover, he believed that in expelling Yates they had acted illegally. He had recommended Yates 'to ascertain, from good sound legal authority, the exact state of the legality of the question'. 'This he is now doing.'[34] According to Yates, in the self-excusing pamphlet he wrote for private circulation in March 1859, *Mr Thackeray, Mr Yates, and the Garrick Club: The Correspondence and the Facts*, he was told by a legal expert that the committee had no right to eject him and that he should try to gain entry to the Garrick in order to get himself forcibly removed, which he duly did. The secretary, Alexander Doland, refused him entry, which allowed Yates to name him as the defendant in the case he was preparing to bring.[35]

From 28 July to 1 August Dickens was at his house, Gad's Hill, in Kent, getting ready for his three-and-a-half-month reading tour of the country, beginning in Bristol on 2 August.[36] He gave no more thought to Yates's position, except to advise him from his stopover in Liverpool on 21 August that his own solicitor Frederic Ouvry believed it would be best to wait until the end of the long legal vacation before taking the next step of serving a writ on the secretary of the Garrick Club.[37] In the meantime the penny papers had their say. *Reynolds's Newspaper*, having dug the dirt on Dickens after the separation statement, now turned its fire on the Garrick Club and Thackeray's vanity and snobbery. In 'The Garrick Club – Thackeray and Yates – A Tempest in a Teapot' on Sunday, 1 August it described the members of the club as an eclectic mixture of comic authors, Whig journalists, 'fourth-rate artists', 'fast barristers', 'faded dandies', 'unspeakable' MPs, and 'impudent showmen', together with 'a small, miscellaneous shoal of insignificant individuals whose sole title to distinction is that they are inveterate and intense tufthunters'. The story of Yates's article is told, with much quoting of its criticism of Thackeray, with which *Reynolds's* tends to agree; Thackeray, 'this great god of the Garrick', is condemned for his sensitivity and also for hypocrisy, since 'there is no writer living who has indulged more extensively in the practice of giving sketches and caricatures of his friends and acquaintances than Mr Thackeray'. The committee has acted in a 'servile' manner and its rules are silly and snobbish.[38]

Sala, too, in his ongoing column 'Twice Round the Clock' in the *Welcome Guest*, touches on the Garrick affair and the cruel ejection of his friend Yates. Reaching 5 p.m. in his hourly round in the weeks immediately following Yates's expulsion, Sala describes 'The Fashionable Club'. A man, he writes, 'if he be so minded', can 'make his club his home'. But he, Sala, will not give away any secrets: 'Men have been expelled from clubs ere now for talking or writing about another member's whiskers, about the cut of his coat, and the manner in which he eats asparagus. I have no desire for such club-ostracism ... I fear the awful committee that, with a dread complacency, can unclub a man for a few idle words inadvertently spoken, and blast his social position for an act of harmless indiscretion.'[39]

A storm in a teacup it certainly was, but as it concerned Thackeray and – indirectly – Dickens, it attracted much notice in the newspapers. Ruskin even read about it in Turin.[40] Thackeray, half sensitive, half blasé, part amused and part ashamed, wrote to some American friends on 25 August, after his return from Switzerland, telling them that he 'went away having got into trouble with a young fellow who told lies of me in a newspaper, wh[ich] I was obliged to notice as we are acquaintances, and meet together at a little Club'. He went on, quirkily, to refer to the Yates fiasco and the ongoing misery of writing *The Virginians*: 'The little papers are still going on abusing me about it I hear – and don't care as I never read one. The public does not care about the story nor about the Virginians nor I about either.'[41]

Reynolds's Newspaper was not finished with Thackeray. It returned to the Garrick Club affair twice more in August. On the 22nd it became downright abusive. 'We do not believe in the divinity of this bloodless-visaged and broken-nosed god of the Garrick', this 'hideous sycophant of wealth and fashion', and 'Mephistophelian libeller of mankind'. 'We shall next week revert to the subject, as law proceedings have already commenced.' 'The club is in a fix', and has appointed a solicitor, while 'Mr Yates is advised by Messrs Farrer, of Lincoln's-Inn-fields'.[42] Farrer, Ouvry, and Farrer were Dickens's solicitors, though the newspaper does not point this out. It does print on the same day a letter dated 3 August from Farrer,

Ouvry, and Farrer to the secretary of the Garrick Club, declaring that by the action taken against Yates by the committee, 'the powers of the society have been exceeded', and calling on the club to 'rescind their resolution of expulsion'. If they decline to do so, 'Mr Yates is determined to try the question in a court of law'. Doland's reply of 7 August is also printed; he has read the solicitors' letter to the committee, which has in turn put the matter in the hands of its own solicitor.[43] Presumably Yates was the newspaper's source for this correspondence. *Reynolds's* had another go at the subject the following week, telling its readership on 29 August that in its view the club has no case and that its legal advisers will advise them to reinstate Yates, since he breached no rules. It talks of various 'toadies' supporting Thackeray, and finishes with a quote from Dickens – who probably did not appreciate being given prominence by his old adversary Reynolds – to the effect that 'out of the club there is but one opinion' on the matter, 'and that is not on the side of the snobs'.[44]

Though things went quiet for a time, this was not the end. Before the year was out Yates, egged on by Dickens, had hired the flamboyant Edwin James to prosecute his suit against the Garrick in court, and Dickens and Thackeray had comprehensively fallen out. Though both novelists were away from London for most of the summer, Dickens reported to Yates in August that he and Thackeray had met one day 'on the steps of the Reform Club' on Pall Mall. At that point relations between the two men were merely strained; according to Dickens, 'we spoke as if nothing had happened', though Thackeray's companion Fladgate had shown his surprise at the encounter – his 'eyebrows went up into the crown of his head, and he twisted himself into extraordinary forms'.[45]

Dickens on tour

On 7 July 1858 Dickens wrote to his old friend William de Cerjat in Lausanne, bringing him up to date with events personal and public. He wrote from Gad's Hill, near Rochester, describing his 'little Kentish freehold' as

a grave red brick house (Time of George the First, I suppose) which I have added to, and stuck bits upon, in all manner of ways; so that it is pleasantly irregular, and as violently opposed to all architectural ideas, as the most hopeful man could possibly desire. It is on the summit of Gad's Hill. The Robbery [as told in Shakespeare's *Henry IV, Part One*] was committed before the door, on the men with the Treasure, and Falstaff ran away from the identical spot of ground now covered by the room in which I write.[46]

Though he knows that he can 'never hope that anyone out of my house can ever comprehend my domestic story', he 'will not complain'. 'I have been heavily wounded, but I have covered the wound up, and left it to heal.' 'The children are all as happy as children can be', and the girls, Mamie and Katey, 'are happier than they ever were'; they keep house for Dickens at Gad's Hill, helped by their aunt Georgina, 'who is, and always has been, like another sister'. As for other news, 'you will have read in the papers that the Thames at London is most horrible. I have to cross Waterloo or London Bridge to get to the Railroad when I come down' to Gad's Hill, 'and I can certify that the offensive smells, even in that short whiff, have been of a most head-and-stomach distracting nature'. Nobody knows what to do, he adds; 'at least, everybody knows a plan, and everybody else knows it won't do'. He notes that the Atlantic Cable has broken again, 'at which most men are sorry, but very few surprised'.[47]

While he was advising Yates about the Garrick affair at this time, Dickens was also taking further steps about his wife's future. When he had got her to sign the deed of separation on 4 June, it had been, though in effect forced on Catherine, a generous document in financial terms. He had settled on £600 a year, to be paid in quarterly instalments. Dickens also promised Catherine 'free access to all or any of her children at all places' and 'at all times'.[48] He persuaded two reluctant friends, Mark Lemon, the editor of *Punch*, and Frederick Evans, his own and *Punch*'s publisher, to act as Catherine's trustees.

The arrangements about the children were that the two oldest girls, Mamie and Katey, would keep house for him, while the eldest, Charley, moved to the house near Regent's Park with his mother; all the younger boys were to be based in Tavistock House and Gad's Hill with Dickens, though they were often abroad or away at school. Dickens was keen to

assure correspondents that the children were not 'divided' in the sense of
taking sides with one parent or the other. As for his relations with Catherine,
'there is no anger or ill-will between us', he told the novelist Catherine
Gore.[49] To John Leech, *Punch*'s main artist, he insisted that 'Charley's
living with his mother to take care of her, is *my* idea – not his', though the
truth was that Charley, being of age, could decide for himself, and did
make the choice to stay with his mother.[50] He had written to Dickens on
10 May, after being told about the impending separation, which he said
'completely took [him] by surprise', declaring that 'in making my choice I
was [not] actuated by any feeling of preference for my mother to you'.
Charley showed his awareness of his father's raw sensitivities. 'God knows
I love you dearly', he wrote, 'and it will be a hard day for me when I have
to part from you and the girls. But in doing as I have done, I hope I am
doing my duty, and that you will understand it so.'[51] Though Dickens was
civil towards Catherine at the time of the deed, writing on 4 June that he
hoped 'all unkindness is over between you and me', he announced in the
same letter that there were those 'among the living, whom I will never
forgive alive or dead', meaning her sister Helen and her mother.[52]

By early July Dickens's attitude had hardened. With the trouble at the
Garrick, the hostile chatter in the newspapers about the wisdom of the
separation statement, and his suspicions that the Hogarths were talking
about his relationship with Ellen Ternan, together with the reluctance
shown by both Lemon and Evans to get involved in his marriage problems,
he took against these two friends and became more ruthless towards
Catherine too. Around 12 July he wrote to Charley to change the terms of
Catherine's contact with her children. She could still see them, but only
under strict circumstances, which he outlined for Charley to relay to her.
His words were characteristically vehement, and also cruelly inappropriate,
considering that the youngest child, Edward, was just six years old: 'I positively forbid the children ever to utter one word to their grandmother or
to Helen Hogarth. If they are ever brought into the presence of either of
these two, I charge them immediately to leave your mother's house and
come back to me . . . I positively forbid the children ever to see or speak to
[Lemon], and for the same reason I absolutely prohibit their ever being
taken to Mr Evans's house.'[53] Charley, whose engagement to Evans's

daughter made this difficult for him – though as an adult he could not be told by Dickens who to see and who to avoid – passed the message on to his mother on 13 July. He expressed his regret at 'being the medium of the communication I have to make to you', but reminded her on his father's behalf that Dickens, as the children's father, had 'an absolute right to prevent their going into any society which may be distasteful to him'.[54] A few days later Catherine, who had left Tavistock House some weeks earlier and spent two weeks in Brighton with her mother and sister, followed by some days with the Lemons, moved to Gloucester Crescent with Charley.[55]

Having turned against Mark Lemon, whom he apparently did not meet or speak to again until they coincided at a mutual friend's funeral in 1867,[56] Dickens reacted even more violently to Frederick Evans, his old friend and publisher, and father of Bessie, Charley's fiancée. On 22 July he wrote from Gad's Hill in frosty terms:

Dear Sir,

I have had stern occasion to impress upon my children that their father's name is their best possession and that it would indeed be trifled with and wasted by him, if, either through himself or through them, he held any terms with those who have been false to it, in the only great need and under the only great wrong it has ever known. You know very well, why (with hard distress of mind and bitter disappointment), I have been forced to include you in this class. I have no more to say.[57]

Probably Evans was suspected of speaking sympathetically of Catherine or passing on rumours unfavourable to Dickens; Dickens never spoke to him again, and did not attend Charley's wedding to Bessie in November 1861. He soon broke off with the firm of Bradbury and Evans, moving to another publisher. Thursday, 22 July was also the last day of Dickens's readings at St Martin's Hall. Just over a week later he and his manager Arthur Smith were on their way to Bristol to start their gruelling tour of England, Ireland, and Scotland. He also took along a manservant, a special lighting assistant to set up his stages, and a general assistant.[58] Having attracted huge crowds and general adulation in London, he now anticipated that his readings would be a tremendous success the length and breadth of the country.

By the time Dickens left London Ellen had also left; she spent the six-week summer season of July and August in Manchester, acting with the Haymarket company managed by the comic actor John Buckstone. She played mainly minor roles in the comedies and farces in which Buckstone specialised. By the end of August the company, including Ellen, were back in London. Dickens installed her and her sister Maria, who was a member of the Strand Theatre Company, in lodgings in Berners Street, just north of Oxford Street. He also paid for the oldest Ternan sister, Fanny, to go to Florence with her mother to have specialist singing lessons.[59] Dickens was extremely careful to keep his transactions with the Ternans as secret as possible. Only Forster and W.H. Wills, Dickens's trusted assistant editor on *Household Words* and later *All the Year Round,* were informed of his dealings with them; in his business letters to Wills he often enclosed messages to 'my Darling'. Ellen was 'E.T.' in his account at Coutts's bank, and he adopted pseudonyms when taking accommodation for her and her family.[60]

Ellen's acting career, having begun in 1857, was over well before the end of 1859, when she was still only twenty. The *Athenaeum* named her in December 1858 as a member of Buckstone's cast at the Haymarket, acting before a 'fashionable audience' in *The Tide of Time*, a 'conversation-drama' by Bayle Bernard.[61] After that she acted only a few times more before disappearing from public view. The only substantial part she got was as Lady Castlecrag in *The World and the Stage*, performed on 12 March 1859 as a vehicle for one of the most famous actresses of the day, Amy Sedgwick. Ellen's part was that of Lucy, the snobbish wife of an old aristocrat who has compromised herself by corresponding flirtatiously with a rake; her noble sister, played by Sedgwick, sacrifices her own reputation for Lucy's sake. Ellen did not take the role when the play returned for a run on 25 April; though the critic in *The Times* had said of her single performance that the character's 'weak and impulsive nature' was 'very prettily assumed by Miss E. Ternan', the reviewer in the *Era* wrote that, while she 'did her best', the part of Lady Castlecrag was 'rather beyond her reach'.[62] After acting maidservants and governesses intermittently during the spring and summer of 1859, Ellen seems to have made her last appearance in a farce entitled *Out of Sight, Out of Mind,* in which she apparently played a small part for a few nights from 4 August; by 11 August her sister Maria, now also acting in the Haymarket company, had taken over the part.[63] Ellen may have given up the theatre because of her limited success as an actress, or because Dickens did not like her to continue in the public eye, or from a combination of the two.

Off went Dickens on his reading tour with his energetic manager Arthur Smith and his helpers. In the week beginning 2 August 1858 he read in the West Country, beginning with Clifton, just outside Bristol, then on subsequent evenings at Exeter, Plymouth, and Clifton again. His second week was spent in the Midlands and the northwest, with Liverpool enjoying performances on three evenings and one Saturday afternoon. On that Saturday night, 21 August, he made a stormy crossing from Liverpool to Dublin, where he gave five performances, including two on Wednesday, 25 August. Then came Belfast, Cork, and Limerick, and in September northern English cities including Manchester, Leeds, Sheffield and York, followed by five readings in Edinburgh. October saw him in Dundee, Aberdeen, Perth, and Glasgow (for four readings), then back to England with repeat performances in Liverpool and Manchester, followed by towns including Birmingham, Oxford, Southampton, and Portsmouth, finishing on 12 and 13 November in Brighton.[64] Everywhere he went he reported huge success, as did all the local newspapers which reviewed his performances.

He wrote regular accounts of his triumphs to Georgina Hogarth and Mamie Dickens at Gad's Hill. The pieces he had chosen for his London readings were used on the tour, with some new additions. 'The Story of Little Dombey' was the great tear-jerker, while the Christmas stories were favourites too – *A Christmas Carol*, *The Cricket on the Hearth*, and *The Chimes*. He also used other stories from *Household Words* including 'The Poor Traveller' and 'Boots at the Holly-Tree Inn' (especially popular for his assumption of a Cockney accent for Boots), as well as extracting and editing 'Mrs Gamp', a portrait of the grotesque drunken midwife in *Martin Chuzzlewit*. These reading texts were published separately by Bradbury and Evans and taken round the country with him, with Smith selling them to audiences.[65] The whole enterprise was highly professional, and Dickens was keen to keep count of audience numbers, cheers and applause, and guineas. The audience at Exeter, he told Georgina Hogarth on 5 August, was 'the finest Audience I have ever read to'. It was clearly important to him that he had not lost the love and admiration of his readers as a result of the separation statement; 'I never beheld anything like the personal affection which they poured out upon me at the end', he added.[66] If he read the notice in *Chambers's Exeter Journal* on 7 August, he will have felt the glow of approval and adoration expressed there, though no doubt the reference to his marriage troubles will have irritated him: 'We regret to hear that the vile poisonous calumny is continued to be whispered in reference to his domestic affairs, notwithstanding his own manly explanation . . . the reptiles who bite at his heel he can well despise. That he is the greatest author of modern time, all must admit.'[67]

And so it went on. He told Mamie on 7 August about the evening performance the night before, revelling, not for the first or last time, in his manager's manic energy and enthusiasm: 'You will be glad to hear that at Clifton last night, a torrent of five hundred shillings bore Arthur away, pounded him against the wall, flowed on to the seats over his body, scratched him, and damaged his best dress suit. All to his unspeakable joy.'[68]

He found time on 11 August to write to Edmund Yates – 'My Dear Edmund' – from the Swan Hotel at Worcester, arranging to meet him at the office of *Household Words* the following Tuesday, 17 August, when he intended to stop in London briefly to discuss the paper with Wills. He touched lightly, if sharply, on the hated subject of Helen Hogarth: 'What a little serpent, that daughter of poor honest good [George Hogarth].'[69] That same evening he wrote to Wilkie Collins, adopting the man-about-town innuendo he often used with his younger correspondent. Collins had obviously made some suggestive remark about Dickens's freedom to misbehave in various hotels around the country; Dickens turned the joke back on his friend, alluding to the most notorious of all seducers and the naughty exploits of two characters in *Arabian Nights*:

> As to that furtive and Don Giovanni purpose at which you hint – that may well be all very well for *your* violent vigor [*sic*], or that of the companions with whom you may have travelled continentally, or the Caliphs Haroon Alraschid [*sic*; Dickens means Haroon and his grand vizier] with whom you have unbent metropolitanly, but Anchorites who read themselves red hot every night are chaste as Diana (I suppose *she* was, by the bye, but I find I don't quite believe it when I write her name.)[70]

Dickens himself had 'travelled continentally' with Collins, having spent time in Paris with his friend in spring 1856, writing to him at that time with nudge-and-wink references to Collins's mistress Caroline Graves.[71] From his Worcester hotel room in August 1858 he goes on to describe for Collins how his audiences are always surprised to find what a show – with lights and mirrors and props – he puts on for them. 'They don't understand beforehand what it is, I think, and expect a man to be sitting down in some corner, droning away like a mild bagpipe.'[72]

For the first few weeks he claimed not to feel exhausted by his exertions, though he confessed to getting into 'the most violent heats' every night as he performed.[73] After taking a break of two days in London and Gad's Hill, he fell ill with a bad cold, for which he applied mustard poultices to his throat and chest.[74] By Wednesday, 18 August he was in Liverpool, from where he reported that he had enjoyed 'the largest house I have ever had since I first began. 2,300 people. Over £200 in money.' He was not the only one to get excited by this huge success. Georgina was treated on 20 August to a description of the antics of his crew: 'What Arthur's state has been tonight – he, John, Berry, and Boycett, all taking money and going mad together – you cannot imagine. They turned away hundreds, sold all the books, rolled on the ground of my room knee deep in checks [sic], and made a perfect Pantomime of the whole thing.'[75]

Next came Dublin, where he arrived on Sunday, 22 August after a 'very, very nasty' passage. He told Angela Burdett-Coutts of his success and the handsome profits he was making. He also replied to some remark of hers, saying that he understood and appreciated her 'feeling that there must be no reservation between us' over his separation from Catherine, with whom Miss Coutts sympathised. Yet he felt compelled to correct her impression of the state of affairs, especially in regard to Catherine's relations with her children. He repeated his unkind – and untrue – remarks of the terrible letter of 9 May to the same correspondent:

> She does not – and she never did – care for the children; and the children do not – and they never did – care for her. The little play that is acted in your Drawing-room is not the truth, and the less the children play it, the better for themselves, because they know it is not the truth

> . . . As to Mrs Dickens's 'simplicity' in speaking of me and my doings, O my dear Miss Coutts do I not know that the weak hand that never could help or serve my name in the least, has struck at it – in conjunction with the wickedest people, whom I have loaded with benefits! I want to communicate with her no more. I want to forgive and forget her.[76]

How vehement is the apparently emollient phrase 'I want to forgive' when followed by the unforgiving 'and forget her'. And once again, as with his insistence that the children have nothing to do with the Hogarths, the Lemons, or the Evanses, it is his own name and its honour with which he is most concerned.

He was to learn some news in the next few days which would raise the whole question of his treatment of Catherine and give him a nasty shock about the way the honour of his name was now viewed in some circles, but meanwhile the readings in Ireland trumped anything that had gone before. Though he grumbled that one commentator in Cork had said that 'although only forty-six I look like an old man' (Herbert Watkins's photograph of him, taken in that hot and difficult week in the middle of June, shows him looking certainly older than his years[77]), he was delighted with the reception.[78] The crowds trying to get into his performances in Dublin were huge. 'Ladies stood all night with their chins against my platform. Other ladies sat all night upon my steps. You never saw such a sight.'[79]

A letter to Georgina from Morrison's Hotel, Dublin, on 29 August hints at trouble on two fronts. He tells his sister-in-law that she should expect him back at Gad's Hill the following Sunday, 5 September. He has just received 'a very watchful and true and excellent letter from Forster, on a personal matter', relating to his separation from Catherine. The second problem involves his wayward brother Frederick, cast off by Dickens many years earlier for his profligacy and tendency to use his famous brother's name to get credit, just as Dickens's incorrigible father John had done as soon as *Pickwick Papers* brought success. Dickens did not attend Fred's wedding in December 1848, and complained in 1851 that he was 'rasping my very heart just now', though he did pay off Fred's debts from time to time until in 1856 he finally refused to do any more.[80] He was particularly angry that Fred had borrowed money from friends including Wills and

Henry Austin, the sanitary engineer who was married to Dickens's sister Letitia. 'I cannot lend you the £30', he told Fred in February 1857, 'because I cannot trust you, and because your bad faith with Wills and Austin makes the word "lend" an absurdity'.[81] Fred responded on 7 February – Dickens's forty-fifth birthday – with some criticism of his own. His brother was, he said, 'cold & unfeeling':

> It is very easy to sit in Judgment on others – nothing more so – The world fancy from your writings that you are the most Tolerant of Men – let them individually come under your lash – (if one is to judge from your behaviour to your own flesh & blood) & God help them! For a quarter of a century you have had the world at your foot – such a blessing ought at any rate to make you charitable in respect to the shortcomings of others – instead of placing yourself on a Pinnacle upon the assumption that poor human nature is perfection – (or ought to be so -) & you her Judge when e'er she errs!
>
> Yrs affectionately
>
> FREDERICK DICKENS
>
> Many happy returns of the day.[82]

There was truth in this accusation, but Dickens felt righteous, having worked his way to fame and success against the odds, after having been forced to leave school at twelve because of his father's insolvency and made to work in a factory putting labels on bottles, an experience he transmuted into the sensitive narration of young David Copperfield's dreadful childhood. Dickens famously could not bring himself to tell anyone except Catherine and his close friend Forster about his childhood feelings of shame at his lowly situation and burning resentment against his parents. He had hauled himself out of the gutter, and he did not see why others could not do so as well.

Now, in August 1858, he tells Georgina, Fred has turned up in Dublin: 'Fancy FREDERICK presenting himself here, in this house, to me, last Thursday a few minutes before Dinner. I was dreadfully hard with him at first; but relented.'[83] Frederick's troubles were threatening to bring Dickens's name into disrepute for reasons other than his debts. His wife Anna was

about to appeal for a judicial separation under the new Divorce Act on the
grounds of Frederick's desertion of her and adultery with a woman in the
Red Lion Hotel in Dorking in April 1857.[84] On Frederick's surprise visit to
him in Dublin Dickens advised him 'with the greatest emphasis' to make his
wife an allowance, but 'my belief is, that I made no impression upon him
whatever. He left me, declaring that I had made none; and I have not the
faintest reason to suppose that he attached a feather's weight to any thing I
said.'[85] Dickens's gloomy prediction was correct. Though he attempted to
negotiate with Anna Dickens's relatives over the amount she would accept
in the hope that a settlement of 'this wretched business' could be arranged
quietly and without it going to court, Fred had other ideas, not least because
he could not afford to support Anna.[86] (The case was to come to court and
be reported in various newspapers in the early months of 1859.)

     This trouble was nothing, however, to the sudden unwelcome appear-
ance in an American newspaper of the letter Dickens had written to Arthur
Smith on 25 May, at the time of the separation arrangements. Hot-headed
and almost paranoid about the gossip at the Garrick, at Epsom races, and
among the penny newspapers, Dickens had written down his side of the
marriage story and given it to Smith, giving him 'full permission' to show
it to anyone who 'wishes to do me right' or who 'may have been misled
into doing me wrong'.[87] It is unclear how the letter came into the hands of
the *New York Daily Tribune*, which published it on 16 August. Though
Dickens did not blame Smith, he was wholly embarrassed by the publication of the letter, which brought the story of his separation back into the
headlines just as he was feeling hopeful that he could suppress all such talk
by dint of taking Britain's towns by storm with his wonderful readings. He
referred to it as the 'Violated Letter'.[88]

     The text, which was soon taken up and reprinted by the British press, did
not show Dickens at his best. As in his letter of 9 May to Miss Coutts, he
declared that the marriage had been unhappy 'for many years', and that 'no
two people, not vicious in themselves, ever were joined together, who had a
greater difficulty in understanding one another, or who had less in common'.
He even suggested that Anne Cornelius, their long-serving female servant,
could vouch for this. (She certainly knew about the increasing distance
Dickens was putting between himself and Catherine. He had written to Anne

from Gad's Hill in October 1857, while still in a state of excitement about his time with Ellen in Doncaster, instructing her to close off the door connecting his dressing room and Catherine's bedroom in Tavistock House. He wished Anne to be discreet about the arrangements, 'as I would rather not have them talked about'.[89]) In the 'Violated Letter' Georgina Hogarth is praised for her devotion to the children and her excellence as a housekeeper. Dickens even hints at mental illness in Catherine: 'For some years past Mrs Dickens has been in the habit of representing to me that it would be better for her to go away and live apart; that her always increasing estrangement made a mental disorder under which she sometimes labours – more, that she felt herself unfit for the life she had to lead as my wife and that she would be better far away.'[90]

One thing which rings true in this mean-spirited account is that Catherine, so much slower than her whirlwind husband, may have found it difficult to live in the public eye. A disinterested observer, the young Henry Morley, who arrived in London in 1851 to assist Dickens on *Household Words*, described an evening at Tavistock House at that time. He wrote innocently to his fiancée:

> Literary people do not marry learned ladies. Dickens has made evidently a comfortable choice. Mrs Dickens is stout, with a round, very round, rather pretty, very pleasant face, and ringlets on each side of it. One sees in five minutes that she loves her husband and her children, and has a warm heart for anybody who won't be satirical, but meet her on her own good-natured footing.[91]

If it was Dickens's misfortune to have paired himself with an ordinary wife, it was surely Catherine's to have married a manically energetic, quick-tempered, and above all 'satirical' husband.

The embarrassing letter to Smith goes on with a remark which reveals Dickens's anxiety about money and his desire to be seen as generous. (Thackeray and his friends would call this vulgar.) He proclaims 'of the pecuniary part' of the arrangements that 'they are as generous as if Mrs Dickens were a lady of distinction and I a man of fortune'. He adds to the ill-advised hints in his personal statement in *Household Words* a reference to Ellen and an attack on his enemies Mrs Hogarth and Helen:

Two wicked persons who should have spoken very differently of me, in consideration of earned respect and gratitude, have (as I am told, and indeed to my personal knowledge) coupled with this separation the name of a young lady for whom I have a great attachment and regard. I will not repeat her name – I honour it too much. Upon my soul and honour, there is not on this earth a more virtuous and spotless creature than this young lady. I know her to be innocent and pure, and as good as my own dear daughters.[92]

The *New York Daily Tribune* could assume on the part of its American readership an intense interest in the doings of the great English novelist. It printed, in addition to the letter to Smith, the statement Dickens had required Mrs Hogarth and Helen to sign on 29 May, 'solemnly' declaring that 'we now disbelieve' certain accounts which had been circulating about the separation. Dickens's voice can be clearly heard: 'We know that they are not believed by Mrs Dickens, and we pledge ourselves on all occasions to contradict them, as entirely destitute of foundation.'[93] The newspaper was not impressed by Dickens's protestations. Of course rumour was busy with the story, it said; Dickens should have stopped after his denial in *Household Words* and left the subject alone. In these cases the public instinctively side with the wife 'unless she insists on proving herself a vulgar shrew and virago like Lady Bulwer'. If the wife 'maintains perfect silence and the husband issues bulletin after bulletin, he is sure to lose ground with each succeeding hour. One more uncalled-for letter from Mr D. will finish him.'[94] In London the *Morning Star* reprinted the letter on Monday, 30 August, while the *Morning Chronicle* and *Morning Herald* carried it the following day, but luckily for Dickens they made no comment on it. *The Times* left it alone and the *Daily Telegraph*, while not printing it, regretted that the others had done so with the strong suggestion that Dickens had intended it to be circulated.[95] Dickens was worried, though, asking his solicitor Frederic Ouvry to inform Catherine's solicitor that he had no part in the publication of this letter, but was in fact very 'shocked and distressed' by it.[96] To Wilkie Collins he wrote with righteous anger, conveniently forgetting that he had given Smith permission to show the letter to anyone he liked: 'I have been greatly vexed by the wantonness of some of our

English papers in printing what is evidently on the face of it a private document of mine, violated in America and sent home here. But it is one of the penalties and drawbacks of my position.'[97]

Really he got off lightly, considering that he had brought this on himself. Inevitably the letter attracted some attention. Elizabeth Barrett Browning, whom Dickens had met socially during his time in Paris in 1856, reacted critically. She had already commented sharply from her home in Florence on 11 July 1858 on Dickens's separation statement:

> What is this sad story about Dickens and his wife? Incompatibility of temper after twenty-three years of married life? What a plea! – Worse than irregularity of the passions it seems to me. Thinking of my own peace & selfish pleasure, too, I would rather be beaten by my husband once a day than lose my child out of the house – yes, indeed. And the Dickenses have children younger than [her own son] Penini! – Poor woman! She must suffer bitterly – that is sure.[98]

Now she expressed her indignation at the 'Violated Letter', believing, as many did, that Dickens had intended it to be published. In this 'dreadful letter', she said, Dickens was using his genius 'as a cudgel' against his wife, 'taking advantage of his hold with the public to turn public opinion against her. I call it dreadful.'[99]

One person who wrote extensively in response to the publication of the 'Violated Letter' was Catherine's aunt, her mother's sister Helen Thomson. On 30 August she wrote to a friend expressing her understandable anger at Dickens's behaviour, and claiming that Dickens had attempted, like his embarrassing friend Bulwer Lytton, to prove his wife to be of unsound mind. According to her, Dickens 'did indeed endeavour to get the physician who attended her in illness, to sanction such a report, when he sternly refused, saying he considered Mrs Dickens perfectly sound in mind'. It was hardly surprising that Catherine's spirits were low 'considering the manner in which she had been treated'. Helen Thomson assured her correspondent that her niece 'had no desire to leave her home or children so long as that home was endurable to her', and 'not till matters had come to extremity did her father think it right to interfere, and then the affair was brought to a compromise, to avoid a public court'. Dickens had, she wrote, made the 'absurd proposal' that Catherine should either go abroad or 'keep to her own apartment in his house in daily life, at the same time to appear at his parties still as mistress of the house'.[100]

We cannot be sure how true these allegations are in detail, but we do know that Dickens mentioned Catherine's mental state more than once and that he did get a fright at the thought of the Hogarth family taking the case to the Divorce Court.

Helen Thomson comments on the 'strange conduct' of Georgina, who, 'blinded by the sophistry of her brother-in-law takes his part, and by remaining against the wishes of her parents with him and his daughters, weakens the defence of her sister'. Dickens's 'exaggerated praises of her to the depreciation of his wife' are 'most heart-cruel and unjust'. It should be remembered, she writes, that Catherine had given birth to ten children, often recovering slowly from their births; it was therefore 'natural that she should lean upon the assistance of a sister in the care of her children'; Catherine was nonetheless a loving mother and a good keeper of the house-hold. As for the 'platonic attachment' that Dickens has had the 'bad taste and boldness to profess to a young actress' in his 'foolish and egoistical state-ment': what could the public have to do with his private life? Miss Coutts has been a staunch friend, says Helen Thomson, inviting Catherine to stay with her while matters were being settled. She then quotes from a letter written to her by Catherine herself, expressing her sorrow at parting from the younger children and – contradicting Dickens's account – their sorrow at losing her. Eleven-year-old Sydney was worried that she would be 'very dull and lonely without them', and Charley was 'kind and gentle' towards her. 'I trust by God's assistance', wrote Catherine, 'to be able to resign myself to His will, and to lead a contented if not a happy life, but my position is a sad one.' Finally Helen Thomson points out that though the public 'have made an idol of him', his 'sentimentality and professed benevolence' are mere 'fairy tales'; moreover, she adds, not without schadenfreude, he is the 'third Dickens brother who has deserted his wife'.[101] This is a reference to the doings of the unrepentant Frederick and another brother, Augustus, with whom Dickens's relations were warmer, who had also recently aban-doned his wife before emigrating to America with another woman.[102]

Dickens survived the unwelcome resurrection of his marriage story. He carried on with his readings, revelling in his ongoing love affair with the public and in the money he earned by them – more than £1,000 a month (roughly £100,000 in today's money) after all expenses and deductions, he reckoned. He recognised his debt to Arthur Smith for his 'great zeal' and 'gentle way of dealing with crowds and putting people at their ease'.[103] After the readings were over, in mid-November, he returned to London to begin severing his business contracts with Bradbury and Evans and to take an active part in Edmund Yates's action against the Garrick Club.

The exploits of Dickens's Mr Stryver

In *A Tale of Two Cities*, which Dickens at last began to write early in 1859, having spent 1858 in a constant state of restlessness, mental and physical, there is a minor character, Mr Stryver, who is drawn in remarkable detail. Dickens's anti-hero turned hero, the drunken, cynical, briefless barrister Sydney Carton, 'idlest and most unpromising of men', but enabled by his physical resemblance to Charles Darnay to take the latter's place at the guillotine, is the 'jackal' to his legal boss, the 'lion' Mr Stryver. They work on cases together in their chambers, drinking all night, with Carton doing the work while Stryver reaps the rewards with great success in the courtroom. Mr Stryver's 'florid countenance' is to be seen there every day, 'bursting out of the bed of wigs, like a great sunflower pushing its way at the sun from among a rank garden-full of flaring companions'. Stryver, 'a glib man, and an unscrupulous, and a ready, and a bold', is not gifted at 'extracting the essence from a heap of statements'; this task he delegates to Carton, while his own talents lie in 'shouldering himself (morally and physically) into companies and conversations' with his 'stout, red, bluff' person, 'free from any drawback of delicacy'. In the courtroom he bamboozles juries by 'fitting' his client's case on them 'like a compact suit of clothes'.[104]

This figure is closely modelled on the busy barrister Edwin James. Dickens met him towards the end of the year, when he was employed to represent Yates in his intended suit against the Garrick. James's name was constantly before the public; he was known for acting in court cases which attracted maximum press attention. In June 1858 he had raised a laugh in court while representing Lady Meux in the case brought by her husband's sisters over whether he had been sane at the time of writing his will. He got involved in the Lytton affair in July and August, acting for Bulwer Lytton while appearing to have Rosina's interests at heart. He popped up in Westminster Hall in a Court of the Exchequer case on Monday, 21 June, when, according to the *Weekly Chronicle*, the courtroom was 'densely crowded, great interest being felt in the issue of an action for libel', in which 'Mr Gough, the well-known intemperance lecturer, sought to recover damages against Dr Lees, an advocate of the Maine Liquor Law, for a series of libels, charging the plaintiff with being narcotically and helplessly intoxicated, with getting drunk on drugs, eating opium, &c.'[105] James acted for the plaintiff, Mr Gough, winning the case and ensuring that the jury awarded his client five guineas 'as damages'.[106]

Four days later James was in action once more in Westminster Hall, taking part in an equity case at the Exchequer of Pleas. He represented the plaintiff, a clerk to the Tottenham Local Board of Health, who was claiming breach of contract from a defendant for allegedly appropriating plans and drawings prepared by the plaintiff for supplying Tottenham with 'water and efficient sewerage'. Dickens's brother-in-law Henry Austin, of the Board of Health, was called to give evidence for the defendant, who claimed a right to the plans. This time James was on the losing side; the judge 'showed unmistakably his opinion that such an action should not have been brought', whereupon James promptly accepted the result on his client's behalf, inducing him to relinquish his complaint and pay the defendant £100.[107]

On 23 July James was in York, where, in the aftermath of the Rosina Bulwer Lytton scandal, an inquiry by the Lunacy Commission was getting under way. It concerned Mary Jane Turner, the wife of Charles Turner, who had consigned her to an asylum on Christmas Eve 1857, after an unhappy and turbulent marriage of fourteen years. Mary Jane had been jealous of her husband's suspected affairs with other women, and had attacked him with a poker in 1850. She also claimed that he was poisoning her. On the face of it, this was a difficult case for her counsel to win, but the counsel was Edwin James, who played on the jury's awareness of recent poisoning cases (especially the famous trial in 1856 of William Palmer, in which

James had also played a part) and on the vulnerability of women to spousal abuse. Was a woman to be deemed insane because she was jealous? he asked the jury. Should she be locked up for months in a horrible institution? If the 'fathers, husbands and brothers' who constituted the jury could give their verdict in favour of Mary Jane, they would 'go to their homes with satisfied conscience, and in quietness and peace would lay their heads upon the pillow'.[108] James won the day for Mary Jane.

The newspapers filled their pages with comments on this case and on the general demeanour of the Commissioners of Lunacy, who had won few admirers for their part in the Lytton story. The *Morning Chronicle* complained on 27 July that the Commissioners' annual reports were complacent, always suggesting that everything was *'couleur de rose'* in the nation's asylums. Stung by this, the commission prosecuted the York asylum-keeper who had kept Mary Jane Turner locked up for so long.[109] The next big lunacy case was that of one Laurence Ruck, held at St Clement Inn, Strand, from Monday to Friday, 23–27 August 1858. This time it was the husband who was declared insane by his wife. Once again Edwin James acted on behalf of the alleged lunatic. The jury declared Ruck to be sane, and John Conolly, who had certified him, was found to be in receipt of a retainer by Arthur Stillwell, the owner of the asylum to which Ruck was sent. Both were successfully sued by Ruck the following year.[110]

James's ubiquity in the summer of 1858 stemmed from his most important and most celebrated case of all, the trial in April of Dr Simon Bernard, accused of helping to plan the attempted assassination of Napoleon III. The chief plotter, Felice Orsini, and his co-conspirators were equipped with grenades manufactured in Birmingham, and were assisted by Dr Bernard, a French republican practising medicine in exile in London.[111] The attempt on 14 January 1858 took place as the emperor and empress were going to the Paris opera. Disraeli, at this time in opposition, told his friend Sarah Brydges Willyams the following day that Napoleon III had had 'a narrow escape' from the 'infernal machine', which caused three explosions, killed eight people, and wounded over a hundred.[112] The popular playwright Edward Blanchard noted in his diary on 15 January that he had gone, after work that night, to his club in Clerkenwell, where 'the Emperor's escape from assassination yesterday [was] the general theme of conversation'.[113]

The times soon proved unexpectedly eventful for Disraeli and his Tory colleagues as a direct result of the assassination attempt. Palmerston's Conspiracy to Murder Bill brought down on his head a storm of protest from Liberal politicians and a general public which was not inclined to welcome being told by the French how to run their affairs. The bill was opposed in parliament, lost a vote on 19 February, and three days later Palmerston had resigned and Derby and Disraeli were in power.[114] Dickens was among many observers who were happy to see Palmerston fall for toadying to the French. He told his French friend François Régnier on 20 February that there was 'great excitement here this morning, in consequence of the failure of the Ministry last night, to carry the bill they brought in, to please your Emperor and his troops. I, for one, am extremely glad of their defeat.'[115] Even the queen was not displeased by the attitude of the British people, though she did not welcome another change of government at home as a consequence: 'The Emperor has been so very unwise in all that he has done in France and the insulting language held in France towards this country has so irritated and exasperated the people here, that they would not hear of what they call acting from compulsion.'[116]

In the meantime, however, Simon Bernard had been arrested in London and charged with being an accessory to the murder of the guards who had died in Paris. The Italian conspirators were tried in France; Orsini and one other, Giuseppe Pieri, were sent to the guillotine on 13 March. A very different fate awaited Bernard. His case was heard at the Old Bailey in the week beginning Monday, 12 April; a special commission was required, since the case concerned an act of murder outside Britain.[117] The commission consisted of Lord Campbell, the lord chief justice, who presided, accompanied by a number of luminaries including the lord mayor, the lord chief baron, the recorder of the City of London, and some aldermen, among them David Salomons. M. Gautier of the French embassy was also in attendance, according to an account of the case published in support of Bernard.[118] The attorney general, Sir Fitzroy Kelly, led the prosecution, while Edwin James was the senior member of the team defending Bernard. (By the end of the year Kelly and James were set to go head to head once more over the Garrick Club affair.) The correspondent for *Reynolds's*

Newspaper reported the following Sunday that the court was crowded with both spectators and barristers.[119]

James was in his element when he rose to speak for the defence on Friday, 16 April, the fifth day of the trial. Taking his cue from the public distaste for French bullying and interference, he appealed to the jury to throw out a prosecution which was, he said, essentially a political one brought at the demand of a foreign despot. He began by praising England's history of having 'free shores' and being 'open to exiles from other lands', while the English legal system encouraged the protection of 'the weak against the strong'. The case for the prosecution, he declared, had been fallible; too many witnesses had been unclear or contradictory about matters such as the size of the grenades ordered from the Birmingham factory or the significance of a letter received by Bernard a year before the assassination attempt. His client, he said, did help the conspirators, but in the belief that they intended to 'restore liberty in Italy', not to kill the French emperor. The jury must be sure that Bernard 'was cognisant of, or instigated' the attack on the emperor 'before you consign the prisoner to an English scaffold'. James drew to an elaborate and dramatic close:

> Gentlemen, I have done. To the best of my ability I have discharged my duty towards the unhappy gentleman at the bar. I have discharged it as an English advocate, I believe, ought to have discharged it – fearlessly and conscientiously. Let me urge you to discharge yours also fearlessly, firmly, and conscientiously . . . Tell the prosecutor in this case that the Jury-box is the sanctuary of English liberty . . . Tell him that the verdicts of English Juries are founded on the eternal and immutable principles of justice. Tell him that, panoplied in that armour, no threat of armament or invasion can awe you. Tell him that, though 600,000 French bayonets glittered before you, though the roar of French cannon thundered in your ears, you will return a verdict which your own breasts and consciences will sanctify and approve, careless whether that verdict pleases or displeases a foreign despot.[120]

On the final day, Saturday, 17 April, the judge, Lord Campbell, 'in the presence of one of the most crowded courts ever assembled at the Old

Bailey', summed up the evidence, making it clear that he expected a guilty verdict.[121] At this point Bernard himself addressed the jury. The judge, he said boldly, had been wrong on various matters in his summing up. 'I declare I am not the hirer of assassins'; those who had been in Paris had chosen of their own accord to help Orsini. As for himself and his friends: 'We want only to crush despotism and tyranny everywhere. I have conspired, I will conspire everywhere, because it is my duty, my sacred duty, as of every one; but never, never, will I be a murderer!'[122]

The jury was duly moved to pronounce Bernard not guilty, despite the evidence and the judge's summing up in the opposite direction. According to James Gordon Allan, a barrister of the Inner Temple who printed James's speech for the defence immediately after the trial, 'a vehement burst of applause, which could not be controlled, followed the conclusion of the learned Counsel's speech', which was 'delivered with the greatest oratorical power, and had a thrilling effect upon the audience'.[123] Men, including many of the lawyers present, threw their hats in the air, and women waved their handkerchiefs and bonnets, while the crowd outside cheered.[124] Bernard was not set free immediately, as other indictments of the same kind remained against him, though the attorney general indicated that he had no intention of pursuing them. Bernard was returned to Newgate prison, but Edwin James applied on Tuesday, 20 April for a writ of *habeas corpus* to allow him to be released on bail. At Westminster Hall that afternoon two friends stood bail of £500 each on Bernard's behalf, and he was released to loud cheering.[125] No further action was taken against him.

The prolific chronicler of London life J. Ewing Ritchie remembered the scene after the famous verdict in his book *About London*, published two years later. He described the response of the newspaper boys waiting that day at the publishing office for their papers to be ready for delivery and chatting about the trial's outcome:

[T]heir admiration of the speech of Edwin James was intense. A small enthusiast near me said to another, 'That ere James is the fellow to work 'em; didn't he pitch hin to the hemperor?'

'Yes', said a sadder and wiser boy; 'yes, he's all werry well, but he'd a spoke on t'other side just as well if he'd been paid.'[126]

No doubt James would have done so. As it was, his name was made. Though Friedrich Engels, on reading the reports of the trial, told Marx that he thought James's speech was 'feeble' and 'disjointed', others were impressed by the florid language and obvious appeal to the jury's patriotic feelings.[127] Most newspapers pronounced the prosecution a mistake. *The Times* loftily warned foreign governments that they should be wary of pressing for such cases to be tried in England, where 'our criminal procedure requires conclusive proof' of a kind difficult to acquire.[128] All the papers noted that parliament had rejected the Conspiracy to Murder Bill brought in by Palmerston, and that this had caused the fall of Palmerston's government. The prosecution of Bernard had therefore always been unlikely to succeed in front of an English jury. The *People's Paper* pointed out that the jurors were out for only an hour and twenty minutes that Saturday afternoon before bringing their verdict.[129] *Reynolds's* returned to the topic the following week, stating that cabmen outside Westminster Hall on Tuesday, 20 April fought to have the honour of taking Bernard, now a free man, to his destination.[130] Bernard spoke that evening at Wyld's Reading Room in Leicester Square, a favoured venue for meetings of the powerful group of exiles and English liberals, the Friends of Italy. A French club met there too; on 20 April, Bernard thanked the 'jury of Englishmen' on whom he had relied for justice. The audience applauded him, giving three cheers for Edwin James and another three for the jury.[131]

Bernard's fame was short-lived. By 1862 he had begun to have hallucinations and was confined in an asylum in London, where he died that November.[132] As for James, he became an instant celebrity following his rhetorical success at the Old Bailey. Consequently he was much in demand during the summer of 1858, particularly for difficult, sensational, or in some way controversial cases. When Dickens's solicitors Farrer and Ouvry took on Edmund Yates's action against the Garrick, James was hired as the barrister, because, as Yates remembered in his *Reminiscences*, he 'stood high' at that time 'in popular favour, having recently obtained the acquittal of Dr Bernard'. Yates describes him as a 'fat florid man, with a large hard face', with chambers in the Temple and rooms in Pall Mall:

His practice was extensive, his fees enormous. I had many consultations with him, but found it difficult to keep him to the subject of my
case: he liked talking, but always diverted the conversation into other
channels. One day I took Dickens – who had never seen Edwin James
– to one of these consultations. James laid himself out to be specially
agreeable; Dickens was quietly observant. About four months after
appeared the early numbers of *A Tale of Two Cities*, in which a prominent part was played by Mr Stryver. After reading the description, I
said to Dickens, 'Stryver is a good likeness.' He smiled. 'Not bad, I
think', he said, 'especially after only one sitting.'[133]

James could command huge fees; by 1861 he was apparently earning
£7,000 a year, by which time he was a Liberal MP for Marylebone as well
as a practising barrister. Dickens's intuition that there was something
dodgy about him was to be borne out that year, when James's debts
amounted to £100,000 and he was obliged to retire from the House of
Commons and resign from the Reform Club. At the same time he was in
trouble with his fellow benchers at the Inner Temple for borrowing money
from a defendant while acting for the plaintiff in the same case. He was
disbarred from practising law that summer.[134] As Yates noted later, James
soon left for America, where he denied on oath that he had been struck off
at home, and attempted to practise at the bar in New York. But he 'did no
good' there. 'Six years afterwards he returned to London, called himself a
"jurisconsult", and advised on "shady" cases. He used to be seen walking
the West End in a shabby Inverness cape.'[135]

Disraeli's whitebait dinner

While Yates and Dickens were mulling over the question of taking the Garrick
to court after its decision on 20 July to remove Yates's membership, the main
topic in the newspapers continued to be the Great Stink. In its round-up of
the week's news on Sunday, 18 July the *Era*, like all the other papers, hailed
the parliamentary decision to get on with cleansing the Thames. 'Good News
for the Thames', was its headline, and it chose an extended medical metaphor
as its preferred way of welcoming the agreed plan:

How far the treatment to which the physicians of the Board of Works have submitted the Thames in its prescription of infinitesimal doses of lime, is or was likely to benefit the patient and relieve the public nose, we neither know, and care not in future to inquire, for fortunately for London and the health of her pet patient the medical treatment has been altered . . . and a change of doctors has been decided on . . . The Government, tired of its brief responsibility as consulting physician, has washed its hands, not in, but of the Thames, and made over its treatment, moral and physical, to the Metropolitan Board of Works, and with such ample powers, as are vast enough, we should think, to cleanse an Augean cesspool even more gigantic than the Thames. In plain words, the Metropolitan Board of Works is vested with plenary powers for the purpose of draining the metropolis, suburbs, and city, and carrying the collected sewage to so respectable a distance from the olfactory nerves of the inhabitants, that the most dog-like nostril cannot possibly discover its whereabouts . . . [T]he Board are allowed the space of five years and a half, and a bank account on the national exchequer to the tune of £600,000 a year, to be refunded by a forty years' tax of 3d in the pound on all rateable property. This looks like business . . . Government has certainly done its part of the public duty both well and quickly, and it only remains for the Board of Works to do its share in the same immediate and energetic style.[136]

This neat summary captures the general mood in the press. Though there were still questions and sceptical remarks about the ability of the much-maligned Metropolitan Board of Works to pull together and produce a timely result, there was wide agreement that at last a decision had been made, and it was up to everyone to support it, while keeping a watchful eye on the authorities which had been appointed to the task. On Wednesday, 21 July *The Times* editorial chewed over the subject yet again, declaring that while 'the agency selected' might not be popular, Mr Thwaites and his colleagues must be allowed to get on with it. Not for the first time the paper complained that it had been warning of disaster for at least ten years, and found itself grateful for the horrible hot weeks of June: 'The stench of June was only the last ounce of our burden, or rather it was an accidental flash of light which brought a great fact before our eyes. That hot fortnight did for the sanitary administration of the metropolis what the Bengal mutinies did for the administration of India. It showed us more clearly and forcibly than before on what a volcano we were reposing.'[137]

With parliament tying up the loose ends of legislation before the end of the session, the papers carried out their assessment of the achievements of the Derby ministry. The end of term was to be marked ceremonially by the ritual of cabinet members sailing down the Thames from Westminster to Greenwich, where they partook of the annual 'whitebait dinner'. It was held this year on Saturday, 24 July, and parliament sat right up to that day to clear its collective desk. As the *Illustrated London News* remarked on the 24th, the two houses were 'just about sweeping up the crumbs of legisla-tion'. 'The numerous Committees of Inquiry have closed their labours, even that on the Thames has made its report; and silence reigns in the long corridors on the river front.' (The Lords remained busy, though; their committee rooms looked out, not on the stinking Thames – 'the great sewer of the metropolis' – but on Old Palace Yard in the interior of the building.[138])

While the act to cleanse the Thames received the most notice from the press, there was also praise for the India Act, steered through by Lord Stanley with Disraeli's help. Lord Derby was praised by several papers for standing firm against the attempt by the archbishop of Canterbury, John Sumner, and his fellow lords spiritual, to introduce Christianity to India, now that it was to be governed directly by the British government instead of the now defunct East India Company. Sumner spoke at the third reading of the Government of India Bill on Friday, 23 July, saying he was far from 'desiring any open attempt on the part of Government either to overthrow the false religion with which, unhappily, we have to deal' or to convert the populace wholesale by force or bribery. He did, however, wish to establish that the Bible would be read in schools and that 'the idolatrous rites and festivals of the Hindoos' would be given up. Derby replied with calm authority, as reported in *The Times*:

My lords, after what has fallen from the most rev. prelate, I may be permitted to observe that while I think that due protection ought to be given to the professors of all religions in India, and nothing should be done to discourage the efforts of Christian missionaries in that country, on the other hand I am quite certain that it is essential to the interests, the peace, and the well-being of England, if not also to the very existence of her power in India, that the Government should carefully abstain from doing anything except to give indiscriminate and impartial protection to all sects and all creeds.[139]

Derby was the hero of the hour in the Lords, as Stanley and Disraeli had been in the Commons. *Bentley's Miscellany* in its round-up in August noted that the India Bill had been tricky, with lots of different opinions, though there was general agreement that the East India Company's rule had been disastrous and must be abolished. Disraeli, the magazine said, had succeeded in making the India Bill a national rather than a party matter, and Stanley had introduced 'a large amount of common sense' into the bill.[140] The queen had shown a close interest in its long passage through parliament. On 15 August she encouraged Derby to draft the proclamation for India with due regard for generosity and equality.[141] When the now Viscount Canning became viceroy of India later in the year, she wrote to him acclaiming the 'enormous Empire which is so bright a jewel' in the crown, and which she 'would wish to see happy, contented, and peaceful'. She was glad, she wrote, that the proclamation included freedom of religious worship for Indians.[142]

Other news in the press round-ups included sorrow at the failure again of the attempt to join the Atlantic telegraph cable, and pleasure in its (short-lived) success in August.[143] *Punch* reminded readers on 21 August that the *Great Eastern*, or *Leviathan* as it insisted on calling the doomed vessel, was still stuck at Deptford doing nothing except being a tourist attraction. In 'What to do with the Leviathan', the magazine suggested that 'the whole of the sewage of this dirty London' could be 'emptied into her many holds; and, when all of them are full, let her sail with the cargo right out to sea, and discharge it in the middle of the ocean', where 'no human nostrils are likely to be offended with it'. Since the ship was 'commercially in rather low water, it would not take much to bail her out'. In *Punch's* unkind opinion, Brunel's great ship 'would make a first-rate floating sewer'.[144]

There was praise for the smooth working of the Divorce Act, now being amended to take account of anomalies such as that of Edward Lane's legal

status. The *English Woman's Journal*, begun in March 1858, recorded its
satisfaction with the act and the justice now being given to both 'betrayed
husbands and oppressed wives'.[145] The *Era* reminded readers that the
Divorce Act had been passed the previous year against violent opposition
and grim warnings that society would collapse under the weight of failed
marriages. On the contrary, 'it is found in experience that only those seek
release who are driven by dire necessity'. The number of petitions had not
been huge, the marriage tie had not been taken less seriously than before,
and the act was working well.[146] The treatment of patients in lunatic
asylums also loomed large, as did court cases in which allegations of
insanity were contested. On 27 July the *Morning Chronicle* reported on
the lunacy case of Mary Jane Turner which had opened in York Castle
with Edwin James representing Mary Jane; on the same day the paper
dedicated its editorial to an attack on the 'easy platitudes' and 'soothing
generalizations' offered each year by the Commissioners of Lunacy.
Their reports conceal 'crying wrongs, which, if they were but made
known, would awaken against the perpetrators feelings of public
indignation'.[147]

Surprise was expressed by some newspapers at the relative success of
Derby's minority government in the early months since its arrival in power.
The *Era* in its article 'The Closing Session' on 1 August declared that
Derby's government had 'steadily won the confidence of the country'. It
was remarkable that a Tory government had brought in the 'Jew Bill' where
Liberal leaders had failed to do so. The Thames and India Acts were the
crowning achievement of a brief but eminently successful session.[148] *The
Times* on the following day singled out Disraeli for both praise and criticism: he 'contributed his industry, his resolution, and his oratorical power,
and at the same time entailed on the ministry the suspicion which attaches
to the successful tactician who is supposed, with some reason, to be entirely
exempt from any political prejudices'.[149]

The last remark expresses the general belief that Disraeli was a politician of boundless personal ambition but little party or national loyalty. He
certainly was personally ambitious and not overly scrupulous in his
methods, but he showed during this short session of parliament that he
could also act in the interests of party and country. *The Times* noted that

justice had been done to Baron de Rothschild, India had been sorted out, and the cleansing of the Thames had at long last been decided on – all of these measures owing much to Disraeli. The next session would probably be taken up with the topic of political reform, according to the paper, though the Derby government might at any time fall under 'some unexpected blow', as Palmerston's had done six short months before. If so, *The Times* concluded, Lord Derby could at least claim that he had formed a ministry 'which conducted affairs for several months with tolerable credit and success, notwithstanding the disadvantage of a nominally hostile majority in the House of Commons'.[150]

The whitebait dinner took place on the evening of Saturday, 24 July. Disraeli told Lady Londonderry on that day that he and his colleagues had been working 'morning, noon, & night to close the Session'. He had just come from a Saturday morning sitting of the House of Commons, and a cabinet meeting was about to follow at three o'clock before he could get off to Greenwich at six 'for the fish dinner – the Carnival of Politics'. He was 'so tired', he wrote, that he could 'scarcely guide [his] pen'.[151] He told Sarah Brydges Willyams two days later that the dinner had been eaten 'with a good relish'. 'A great deal of nonsense' had been talked, as is usual, especially 'when you have won the day'.[152] *Punch* marked the event a few days later with a topical poem entitled 'How Father Thames Appeared to the Cabinet, on the Road to the Whitebait Dinner, and What He Said to Them'. The poem names various cabinet members and the opinions and measures with which each is associated – Stanley with India, Bulwer Lytton, rather perversely in the light of recent events concerning him, with 'pleasure', Disraeli with everything:

The sky was blue, the sun was bright,
    Gaily the steamer ploughed her way,
Freighted with hearts as blithe and light
    As schoolboys' on a holiday.
With Youth (as Stanley) at the prow,
    Pleasure (as Bulwer) at the helm,
At top of flood the waves they plough
    That lately threatened to overwhelm.

On to their annual whitebait lark,
   By Wapping's odour-breathing shore . . .
The steamer dashed with Ministères
   (That little thought this day to see),
Triumphant o'er the Session's fears,
   Merry of mood and blithe of blee.

The politicians chat together as they go along the river, discussing topics such as Newdegate's intransigent opposition to allowing Rothschild to take his seat, the Liberals as led by 'Pam, so bravely kept at bay', and the unpopular Board of Works. They cheerfully approach Greenwich, with its famous hospital, when they see a sudden apparition:

So still with joke, and jibe, and jeer,
   The Ministers the way beguiled,
Till Stanley's brow grew less severe,
   And e'en sardonic Dizzy smiled.
And now the Isle of Dogs was past,
   And the Trafalgar rose to view,
When suddenly a cloud was cast,
   That shut the Hospital from view.

(The *Trafalgar* was a Royal Navy ship launched at Woolwich Dockyard in 1841.)

And from the cloud a perfume rose,
   That might be smelt but never sung;
And every member to his nose,
   The guardian bandana flung;
Slowly the cloud took form, and slow
   The perfume to a centre grew,
And on the deck before them, lo!
   A grisly form appeared to view!

A trailing robe of sludge and slime,
   Fell o'er his limbs of muddy green,

And now and then a streak of lime
   Showed where the Board of Works had been;
From out his mouth's mephitic well,
   Poured fetid stench and sulphurous flames,
And – was it sight or was it smell? –
   All there somehow knew Father Thames.

He stood, and breathed, and sick and pale,
   The stoutest, at his breathing, grew;
Quoth he, 'Such visitors I hail:
   My Lords and Commons, how d'ye do?
If any gratitude were here,
   You should have asked me to your feast;
Of all your motley friends this year,
   Thames hath not been the last, or least.

Who . . . thinned full many an awkward House!
   Who sped along the India Bill?
Who huddled up the Jewish claims?
   . . . who but Father Thames?

I lurked behind your terrace wall,
   I breathed athwart your window blind;
Up through your chimneys I would crawl,
   Or through your air-shafts entrance find;
Thanks most to me, the Session's done,
   Your foes have fled; 'tis me they fear:
Mine are the triumphs you have won –
   Yet uninvited I stand here!

Nor this the worst – small charm for me
   In whitebait, or in Moselle cup –
But back to Thwaites and Company,
   Bound hand and foot, you've given me up!
The Board of Works to which I owe
   The poison coursing in my veins,

Henceforward lord it o'er my flow,
   And I must patient drink their drains!

And *you* it is to them have given
   This lordship o'er my banks and bed –
You, in whose service I have striven,
   And stunk and steamed till foemen fled!
Yours is the scheme my course that girds
   With miles of sewer where fever lurks:
London till now, bored by their words,
   Will be bored henceforth by their works!'[153]

The eventful parliamentary session ended on 2 August with the Queen's Speech and the ratifying of all the hard-won legislation. Parliament was prorogued until 19 October, and Disraeli wrote triumphantly to Mrs Brydges Willyams that though 'the last month' had been 'one of almost supernatural labor [*sic*]', it had been remarkably successful. 'Notwithstanding all the disturbance and hostility of the early part of the Session, there has seldom been one in which a greater number of excellent measures have been passed, than the present.'[154] He was off to his Buckinghamshire house at Hughenden to enjoy a rest and to consume the 'fat buck' Queen Victoria sent him on 4 August.[155] He did not expect to have a long break, as there was much to do to prepare for 'the next campaign', which would not be an easy one.[156] He was right. His and Derby's attempt the following session to bring in a Reform Bill was to fail, and their all too brief spell in power would come to an end in June 1859. But not before Disraeli in particular, in the five months during which he had been able to steer various important pieces of legislation through parliament, had impressed a doubtful commentariat and public with his energy and wit.

CHAPTER SEVEN

The Aftermath of the Hot Summer

The fallout from the Garrick Club affair

NEITHER THACKERAY NOR YATES could let go of the petty Garrick Club quarrel. Though Thackeray professed not to care about it in his letter to his American friends the Baxters on 25 August 1858, he had already incorporated another attack on Yates and his journalist friends in the next instalment of *The Virginians*, which he sent to Bradbury and Evans on 5 August for publication on 1 September.[1] 'There are certain lines which must be drawn', writes the narrator haughtily, 'and I am only half pleased, for my part', when young men like 'Tom Garbage, who is an esteemed contributor to the *Kennel Miscellany*', propose 'to join fellowship as brother literary men, slap me on the back, and call me old boy, or by my Christian name'.[2]

On 6 November Yates's friend Sala reached 1 a.m. in his 'Twice Round the Clock' column and singled out Evans's Supper Rooms in Covent Garden, well-known haunt of Thackeray, who had, as Sala points out, immortalised the place as the 'Cave of Harmony' in *The Newcomes*. Sala sets the scene: 'If you wish to see the wits and the journalist men about town of the day, you must go to Evans's about one o'clock in the morning. Then those ineffables turn out of the smoking-rooms of their clubs – clique-clubs mostly – and meet on this neutral ground to gird at one another.'[3] As he had done in his picture of the fashionable club from which one might be excluded for a minor offence, Sala here slyly suggests he is afraid of being lashed out at by Thackeray: 'I should dearly like to draw some pen-and-ink portraits for you of the wits as they sit, and drink, and smoke, at one o'clock in the morning; but I dare not . . . Mr Polyphemus, the novelist, not unfrequently condescends to wither mankind through his spectacles from one of the marble tables.'[4]

Sala wrote to Yates on 7 November, asking, 'Don't you think "Mr Polyphemus" a good name for Thackeray?' It was: as Sala well knew, Thackeray himself had introduced the man-eating giant from Homer's *Odyssey* in his illustrated comic Christmas book of 1850, *The Kickleburys on the Rhine*.[5] In one of his potboiling memoirs written in his sixties, *Things I Have Seen and People I Have Known* (1894), Sala recalled once more that in the Yates affair Thackeray, an 'amiable but too sensitive man of genius', had 'put forth his giant's strength to crush and ruin, socially speaking, a writer many years his junior'.[6]

In the autumn of 1858 it was announced in the press that Yates was to bring a court case against the Garrick. The *Morning Post* obliged its readers on 17 November by going over the whole affair, quoting from Yates's offending *Town Talk* article, from Thackeray's letter to Yates and the latter's reply, from both men's appeals to the committee of the Garrick, and from the committee's demand that Yates apologise to Thackeray. Now, says the paper, Yates has 'instigated an action against the committee for trespass, in refusing to allow him to enter the club'. 'This will raise the important question, as affecting the rights of members generally, whether the club had the right to expel Mr Yates or not.' The *Post* noted that there would be 'a large array of legal talent on both sides'. The attorney general, Sir Fitzroy Kelly, would act for the club, and 'Mr Edwin James, Q.C., is to lead the case on behalf of the plaintiff'.[7]

Dickens involved himself once more as soon as his long summer of readings had come to an end with the final performance in Brighton on Saturday, 13 November. He visited James a week later, then wrote to Thackeray in an attempt to mend matters:

> I find Mr Edwin James's opinion . . . strong on the illegality of the
> Garrick proceeding. Not to complicate this note or give it a formal

appearance, I forbear from copying the opinion; but I have asked to see
it, and I have it, and I want to make no secret from you of a word of
it . . .

Can any conference be held between me, as representing Mr Yates,
and an appointed friend of yours, as representing you, with the hope
and purpose of some quiet accommodation of this deplorable matter,
which will satisfy the feelings of all concerned?[8]

The stiff and awkward tone of this, the insistence that Yates's lawyer knew
best, and the use of the disapproving word 'deplorable' to describe the
quarrel were hardly likely to mollify Thackeray, whose antennae were alert
to the slightest criticism of his behaviour. Dickens intended to help avert
court action, yet he continued in a manner which was bound to make
things worse. He told Thackeray what the latter already knew, namely that
Yates had asked Dickens's advice from the beginning. Making an oblique
reference to the fact that his own marital troubles arose at the same time as
the Garrick business, he explained that Yates had recently 'done me a
manly service I can never forget, in some private distress of mine (generally
within your knowledge), and he naturally thought of me as his friend in an
emergency'. 'I told him that his article was not to be defended', Dickens
continued, 'but I confirmed him in his opinion, that it was not reasonably
possible for him to set right what was amiss, on the receipt of a letter
couched in the very strong terms you had employed.' When Thackeray
appealed to the Garrick Dickens was, he said, 'very sorry to find myself
opposed to you', but he was 'clear that the Committee had nothing on
earth to do with it'.[9] Dickens finished his letter with a reiteration of his
willingness to do his best in the way of mediation though how he can have
imagined he would succeed with these words is difficult to understand.

Thackeray replied two days later, politely, of course, but making it clear
that he was not going to be bullied into conceding that he had been wrong
to pursue the matter. 'I grieve to gather from your letter that you were
Mr Yates's adviser in the dispute between me and him', he wrote disin-
genuously. He insisted that he had done the right thing in referring the
matter to the Garrick committee. And he made it clear that he did not
appreciate the implicit threat that Edwin James would wipe the floor with

the Garrick's defence. Reaching, as always, for the unwritten 'gentlemanly' code of practice, he said he could not conceive 'that the Club will be frightened, by the opinion of any lawyer, out of their own sense of the justice and honour which ought to obtain among gentlemen'. He finished by signing off 'Yours, &c., W.M. Thackeray'.[10] (Yates later claimed that when Dickens showed this letter to John Forster, the latter burst out with 'He be damned, with his "yours, &c."!'[11])

Dickens made no reply to this, though he did send Yates both his own letter and Thackeray's reply, with permission to print them if he wished.[12] Thackeray's hackles were raised once more. He told his correspondent John Blackwood on 2 December that 'Edwin James says' that Dickens 'wrote every word of Yates's letters . . . Isn't it a noble creature?'[13] On 5 December Yates served his writ on the club. Articles against Thackeray appeared in the penny papers that weekend, and he received a letter from his journalist friend Matthew Higgins warning him to 'beware of Edwin James' and the 'scarifying' he would get from him in the witness box.[14] A couple of weeks later Thackeray, having sent Blackwood a copy of Dickens's letter, expostulated about his fellow novelist's hypocrisy and jealousy: 'What pent up animosities and long cherished hatred doesn't one see in the business! "There's my rival, Stab him now, Yates" and the poor young man thrusts out his unlucky paw . . . Send me back the letter of the Great Moralist.'[15] (Thackeray drew a sketch – which he did not publish – of 'The Smiler with the Knife', which showed Yates bowing politely to Thackeray, while holding a knife behind his back.[16])

Things did not quieten down for a while yet. Anny Thackeray reported to a friend towards the end of December 1858 that her father was 'getting disgusted', as 'everybody's been bullying him about his susceptibility'. She passed on Thackeray's scorn at Dickens's remark about Yates having done him a 'manly service'. 'Can't you fancy him & his gusto over Manly Service', she wrote, adding another piece of gossip: 'Papa says the story is that Charley met his Father and Miss Whatsname Whatever the actress out walking on Hampstead Heath.'[17] Charley had by now taken Thackeray's side in the Yates affair, writing a short anonymous piece in *Punch* on 11 December replying to 'The Lounger at the Clubs' (Yates), who had once more attacked the so-called 'gentlemen' of Clubland in the *Illustrated Times* the previous Saturday. 'Really, really, good Mr Lounger', Charley wrote, 'this is rather strong':

> We are ready to believe that you, who, no doubt, belong to all the crack clubs of London, and move, of course, in 'gilded saloons of fashion', are better up in the subject than ourselves, but we must take leave at the same time to protest entirely against . . . the repetition of the old habits of coarse invective and abuse, which we thought had disappeared entirely from our press . . . Let us give you a word of advice, which our respectable old age entitles us to give such a mere boy in periodical literature, as is the *Illustrated Times*. Learn that coarseness is not brilliancy, that slangy vituperation is not wit . . . [and] that a journalist should also be a gentleman.[18]

Even before this piece appeared, relations between father and son can hardly have been other than strained, since Charley annoyed his father by remaining engaged to Frederick Evans's daughter. According to Henry Silver's diary, Dickens found out that Charley was the author of the article, and by mid-January 1859 he had withdrawn Charley's name from the Garrick proposal list because of it.[19] Thackeray shrewdly diagnosed Dickens's behaviour. Dickens's 'quarrel with his wife' had 'driven him almost frantic', he told a friend, William Synge. 'He can't help hating me; and he can't help not being a – you know what I daresay' (meaning, of course, a 'gentleman'). 'He is now quarrelling with his son' by 'withdrawing the lad's name, just as it was coming up for ballot. 'The poor boy is very much cast down at his father's proceedings.'[20]

With the eagerly awaited court case due to begin on Wednesday, 2 February,[21] Yates attacked Thackeray once more, this time with a clever parody of Thackeray's own comic poem 'Ballad of Bouillabaisse'. Yates's poem, published in the *Illustrated Times* on 29 January, and entitled 'Milk and Honey, by W.M. T—k—y', contains the following verses:

> All men alive are rogues and villains,
> All women drabs, all children cursed;

I tell them this, and draw their shillins'
They highest pay when treated worst.

I sneer at every human feeling
Which truth suggests, or good men praise;
The tongue within my cheek concealing,
Write myself 'Cynic' – for it pays![22]

Though Yates's friend Sala congratulated him on the cleverness of these lines, he thought them '*malevolent* and their publication ill judged'. 'Let Polyphemus alone', he counselled. 'A man has no *right* to allow his private feelings to influence his "copy".'[23]

The case never came to court, and the famous Edwin James did not get the chance to 'make mince meat' of Thackeray after all.[24] The Garrick Club claimed that proceedings would have to be taken against its trustees, and since such a case would take place in the notoriously expensive Court of Chancery, Yates had to give it up. It would have cost him £200 or £300. He told a friend on 11 March that the committee had 'got the best of me in my legal proceedings, and my only resource . . . has been the publication of a pamphlet'.[25] This was the self-exculpatory – and in places self-pitying – *Mr Thackeray, Mr Yates, and the Garrick Club*, in which Yates set down all the details of the affair and his part in it. Anny Thackeray told William Synge on 6 March that 'an abusive pamphlet' was coming out instead of the lawsuit, and she hoped that Thackeray would leave things at that. 'We are begging our Jupiter to keep in his thunder & not even read it & as he has taken to paying great attention to what we say lately perhaps he won't.'[26]

Thackeray does seem to have dropped it at last, though he asked a friend to lend him a copy of Yates's pamphlet, and he defended his initial action against Yates in a semi-shamefaced letter of 12 March 1859 to Charles Kingsley, saying he felt rather sorry for him and blaming Dickens. 'Scores of the pennyaline [*sic*] fraternity have written on [Yates's] side' and have made out that Dickens tried to be a peacemaker, when in fact he 'dictated Yates's letters to me' and made him 'go to law'.[27] The newspapers had heard that Bulwer Lytton and the Irish novelist Charles Lever were to be asked to give evidence on Yates's behalf, to prove that Yates had done no more – a lot less, in fact – in the way of attacking the work of others than Thackeray had in his unflattering parodies of their novels which appeared as 'Punch's Prize Novelists' in *Punch* in 1847.[28] Bulwer Lytton had been parodied in April 1847 in the short story 'George de Barnwell, by Sir E.L.B.L.BB.LL.BBB.LLL., Bart' – Rosina would have appreciated the joke on the name – which opens pretentiously, 'In the Morning of Life the Truthful wooed the Beautiful and their offspring was Love.' Disraeli, too, got the treatment in 'Codlingsby, by D. Shrewsberry, Esq.', which played on the title of Disraeli's 'Young England' novel *Coningsby* (1844), and exaggerated Disraeli's already elaborate romanticising of Judaism.[29] Thackeray too had heard that Bulwer Lytton was to be invited to give evidence; he told Blackwood in December 1858 that he believed Dickens was, as usual, involved. Bulwer Lytton, he said, had been 'applied to (by my indefatigably kind friend Dickens I suppose)'.[30]

(That the Yates affair continued to rankle with Thackeray is shown by the fact that an essay published in the *Cornhill Magazine* in November 1863, only a month before his death, contains yet another veiled reference to the Garrick Club affair. Entitled 'Strange to Say, On Club Paper', the piece complains of the 'tattle' of 'Club gossips and loungers'. 'I've seen literary fellows at Clubs writing their rubbishing articles', 'literary vagabonds' ready to 'stab a reputation' or 'tell any monstrous falsehood'.[31])

In January 1859 the *Sheffield and Rotherham Independent* was among the provincial newspapers which picked up the news of the expected court case between Yates and the Garrick. 'A considerable interest will be attached to the trial', it wrote, 'as it is understood that the line of cross-examination of Mr Thackeray is to deduce from his earlier works – long ago ignored, if not repudiated – sins against good taste exceeding those of which Mr Yates stands accused in the court of letters'.[32]

The same paper expressed its mock sorrow on 2 April that the trial would not, after all, take place:

The *quid nuncs* are deprived of a rare treat, but literature is saved from being a subject of scorn . . . The admirers of Thackeray must ever regret that he thought it worth his while to be moved by the scribbling of the

editor of 'Town Talk' into writing a letter which was undoubtedly a
mistake. The part played by Mr Yates needs no comment, still less does
the pamphlet he has circulated, giving his version of the affair.[33]

Yates's pamphlet goes over the whole sorry business in detail. He
complains that Thackeray was intentionally 'arrogant and offensive'
towards him, and insists that Thackeray had committed at least as many
'errors' in taste in his youthful writings as he, Yates, had done at the tender
age of twenty-six the previous summer. He blames the Garrick Club for
finding a means to stop his suit by turning it into a Chancery matter:
'That I, a young man with the world before me, could possibly survive
long in a tilting-match with a rich Club and a dozen or two of not poor
individuals . . . representing it . . . I suppose to be as plain to my readers as
to the Garrick Club Committee.' He finishes by asking his readers to
'judge for themselves' what would have happened 'if Mr Thackeray had
addressed me with any temper or generosity'.[34]

Yates always felt his life had been unfairly blighted by this intense storm in
a teacup. He repeated his complaints in his *Recollections and Experiences*,
published in 1884, long after the deaths of most of those involved, going
so far as to claim that the 'whole affair was a struggle for supremacy, or an
outburst of jealousy, between Thackeray and Dickens', and that 'my part
was merely that of the scapegoat or shuttlecock'.[35] He continued to work
in the Post Office until 1872, and he also pursued his rather rackety career
in journalism, where he endured mixed fortunes, now doing well out of
editorships, now getting on the wrong side of the libel laws, and on one
occasion appearing in the bankruptcy court, though he was relatively well
off on his death in 1894.[36]

Dickens kept up the friendship, publishing stories by Yates in his new
weekly paper, *All the Year Round*, discussing his pamphlet about the Garrick
quarrel with him,[37] and commiserating with him on the death of his
mother in August 1860. One reason for Dickens's fondness for Yates was
his admiration for Elizabeth Yates, who had played the part of Nancy in
her husband's adaptation of *Oliver Twist* at the Adelphi in 1839. He wrote
in melancholy vein after her death that his memory of her was 'a part of

my youth no more capable of restoration than my youth itself'.[38] When Yates got into financial difficulties in 1868 Dickens wrote encouragingly, 'You are quite young enough, and have a sufficiently free stage before you, to play the play out yet to everybody's satisfaction.'[39] Yates could not avoid appearing in the bankruptcy court that summer, whereupon Henry Silver noted in his *Punch* diary, 'How the Shade of Thackeray would chuckle.'[40] Yates never forgot his youthful disgrace at the hands of the novelist he had most admired when growing up.[41] He told a correspondent in 1889 that his expulsion from the Garrick had been the best-known thing about him all his life. 'Think of being "expelled" from a club, as tho' one had been a card-sharper, a cheat, a thief, a braggart about women!'[42]

As for Edwin James, whose talents were not, after all, to be displayed in this high-profile case, he was not short of work. *The Times* records lawsuits almost daily during January and February 1859 in which he was active: there were libel cases, a case of false imprisonment, one of alleged abduction and seduction of a minor, and many more. In the midst of all this James found time to stand as the Liberal candidate in a by-election for the borough of Marylebone. He addressed the electors at a meeting on 21 February, declaring that he was a sincere reformer and, if elected, 'would advocate a large and liberal extension of the franchise'. James was elected on 25 February, and on 1 March was already participating in a debate in the House of Commons.[43] He continued to be successful until 1861, when his huge debts and an inquiry into his conduct by the Inner Temple brought an end to his career in London.

Dickens and Thackeray did not correspond or converse again. They coincided at Drury Lane Theatre in May 1861 and shook hands but did not speak. Thackeray reported to a friend that he had no desire to make up the quarrel; he had 'found Dickens out', and knew that 'poor Yates' was only 'the mouthpiece' in the Garrick Club affair.[44] He and Dickens met again by chance in the lobby of the Athenaeum Club on Pall Mall in May 1863. According to Henry Silver's diary, they shook hands and tears came to Dickens's eyes when he saw how ill Thackeray looked.[45] They saw one another once more, in the same club, in December 1863; a week later, on Christmas Eve, Thackeray died, aged fifty-two, of a stroke.[46] Dickens attended the funeral and was asked by George Smith, publisher of the

Cornhill Magazine, of which Thackeray had been the editor, to write an appreciation of his old rival.

As he told Wilkie Collins in January 1864, he would have 'gladly excused' himself from the task, but felt he had to write a few pages in tribute:

> Thus I have tried . . . to avoid the fulsome and injudicious trash that has been written about him in the papers,[47] and delicately to suggest the two points in his character as a literary man that were bad for the literary cause . . . You can have no idea of the vile stuff that has been written: the scribes particularly dwelling on his having been 'a gentleman', 'a great gentleman', and the like – as if the rest of us were of the tinker tribe.[48]

Though the last phrase betrays once again Dickens's sense of being looked down on by Thackeray, he managed to write an extremely gracious piece, 'In Memoriam', which appeared in the *Cornhill* in February 1864. Calling Thackeray his 'old comrade and brother in arms', he tells the story Thackeray himself had told at the dinner preceding the opening of the Royal Academy exhibition in May 1858, shortly before the rift between them occurred. Naturally he makes no mention of the quarrel in his essay. They first met nearly twenty-eight years ago, Dickens writes, when Thackeray 'proposed to become the illustrator of my earliest book'. They became friendly (though Dickens does not say they became 'friends'), and Dickens saw many examples of Thackeray's 'genial, natural, cordial, fresh, and honestly impulsive' nature. 'We had our differences of opinion. I thought that he too much feigned a want of earnestness, and that he made a pretence of undervaluing his art' (the 'two points in his character' Dickens notes in his letter to Collins), but when they had discussions on the subject, Thackeray often ended them with a laugh. With the Yates affair no doubt in mind but taking care not to point to it directly, Dickens adds that 'in the reckless vivacity of his youth, his satirical pen' had sometimes 'gone astray or done amiss', but he had often asked forgiveness for the fault. Dickens merely touches on the writings, which he could not truly admire; he praises Thackeray's 'subtle acquaintance with the weaknesses of human nature', his 'delighted playfulness as an essayist', and 'his mastery over the English language'. The short piece ends with a memory of the 'bright wintry day, the last but one of the old year', when Thackeray was buried in Kensal Green cemetery with 'a great concourse of his fellow-workers in the Arts' in attendance.[49]

Given their temperaments and backgrounds, and the inevitable rivalry between them as the two giants of fiction in the 1840s and 1850s, the two men could never have been close friends. Nonetheless, the unnecessary estrangement of 1858 surely happened because each was coping with difficulties that hot summer, especially Dickens. Both tried to 'police the gossip' about themselves, to avoid public humiliation, and to use newspapers to 'manage' their reputations.[50] Neither can be said to have been entirely successful in these endeavours. Though the Garrick was the arena in which the cause of their estrangement occurred, and though its committee sided with Thackeray, the club continued to take pride in the membership of both writers. Today a portrait of Dickens by Charles Fullwood, copied from Daniel Maclise's famous 1839 picture in the National Portrait Gallery, looks across the room at a drawing of Thackeray by Samuel Lawrence.[51]

Success and embarrassment for Dickens

When Dickens gave the final performance of his first grand reading tour in Brighton on Saturday, 13 November 1858, G.A. Sala was in town, hiding from his London creditors. He heard that 'the great Panjandrum' was coming and that he had already 'banked £5,000'; after the readings he reported that they had 'of course' been 'tremendous hits'. 'Town Hall crammed on each occasion.'[52] After his triumphant progress, Dickens lost no time in ensuring that he distanced himself and his writings from his old friends and publishers Bradbury and Evans. On 27 November he drafted a letter for Forster to present to the firm declaring that he intended to discontinue publication of *Household Words* in six months' time, and asking if they were 'disposed to treat with Mr Dickens for the sale to him of your interest in the work'.[53] They rejected his offer of £1,000 for their share of the copyright, but Dickens went ahead with his plan to print the

last number of *Household Words* on 28 May 1859, by which time he had
already begun publishing his replacement weekly, *All the Year Round*,
which – to Forster's astonishment and horror – he had originally intended
to call *Household Harmony*. He gave way rather ungraciously to his friend's
objection that this might be an unfortunate title given the nature of the
events of summer 1858 which had led to the demise of *Household Words*.[54]

Bradbury and Evans tried to stop him through legal proceedings, but
had to concede defeat in May 1859, when an auction of *Household Words*
took place, which Dickens won by having Arthur Smith buy the journal
and its stock on his behalf.[55] Dickens's implacable hostility to the firm, and
especially to Frederick Evans, was explained by the latter to Henry Silver at
a *Punch* dinner in February. It all went back to the ill-advised personal
statement Dickens printed in *Household Words* on 12 June 1858. Silver
recorded Evans's account of the split. Dickens had persuaded his old friend
and publisher to be a trustee for Catherine in the separation arrangements,
but resented the fact that Evans did not publish the statement in *Punch*.[56]

Evans's reward for reluctantly agreeing to Dickens's pressing request to
represent Catherine was thus to make himself into Dickens's worst enemy.
He and Bradbury made a financial loss out of the break with Dickens,
though they exacted some revenge by printing a frank statement, 'Mr
Charles Dickens and His Late Publishers', alongside the twentieth number
of Thackeray's still-ongoing novel, *The Virginians*, in June 1859.[57] Here
the publishers describe the friendly relations they had enjoyed with
Dickens until he printed his personal statement 'on the subject of his
conjugal difficulties' in *Household Words* the previous June. The public
disclosure of his problem took most people by surprise, they say, 'and was
notoriously the subject of comments, by no means complimentary to Mr
Dickens himself, as regarding the taste of this proceeding'. To their surprise,
a friend told them that Dickens intended to break off relations with them
because they had not printed the statement in *Punch*,

> in other words, because it did not occur to Bradbury and Evans to
> exceed their legitimate functions as proprietors and publishers, and to
> require the insertion of statements on a domestic and painful subject in
> the inappropriate columns of a comic miscellany . . . [T]he grievance

of Mr Dickens substantially amounted to this, that Bradbury and Evans did not take upon themselves, unsolicited, to gratify an eccentric wish by a preposterous action.[58]

In July 1859 Bradbury and Evans started another weekly paper, *Once a Week*, to rival *All the Year Round*. By the end of 1859 both papers were attempting to woo the new candidate for Great English Novelist, George Eliot. The 'unknown' pseudonymous author found immediate critical acclaim and financial success with *Adam Bede*, published in February 1859. Her partner G.H. Lewes had corresponded regularly from Germany over the summer of 1858 with her publisher John Blackwood, sending news of progress on the novel, which he teasingly called 'the Bedesman' in allusion to Beadsman, the horse which famously beat Lord Derby's Toxopholite in the 1858 Derby.[59]

With *Adam Bede* seen as the great literary publishing event of the year 1859, George Eliot became a target for rival publishers, including Bradbury and Evans and Dickens's new publishers Chapman and Hall (to whom he was in fact returning, having left them for Bradbury and Evans fifteen years earlier after a disagreement over their handling of *Martin Chuzzlewit*). Lewes noted in his journal on 15 November that Frederick Evans and the editor of *Once a Week*, Samuel Lucas, had asked him if George Eliot – now generally known to be Lewes's partner Marian Evans – would consider publishing her next novel (*The Mill on the Floss*, already half written and being negotiated for by Blackwood) in their paper, assuring him that they would pay more than Blackwood, no matter how much he might offer. The previous day Dickens, who greatly admired *Scenes of Clerical Life* and *Adam Bede*, had written to ask if she would publish a story in *All the Year Round* the following year, assuring her that she could name her terms.[60] Not liking to tie herself to deadlines, and feeling she owed loyalty to Blackwood, George Eliot declined both offers. According to Edmund Yates's memoirs, when literary London was asking who this 'George Eliot' could be, Dickens joked that it was either Bradbury or Evans, 'but I do not think that it is Bradbury'.[61]

By this time Dickens had published *A Tale of Two Cities* in his paper; it was followed in November 1859 by the first instalment of Wilkie Collins's

The Woman in White. Though *A Tale of Two Cities* was reasonably well received, it was not the most popular of Dickens's writings. He himself noted that the work, concerning the violent upheavals of the French Revolution, was a novel not of characterisation, but rather of plot. He told Forster in August 1859 that he had intended to write 'a *picturesque* story'; 'I fancied a story of incident might be written . . . pounding the characters out in its own mortar, and beating their interests out of them.'[62] The people in the novel serve the plot rather than having interesting inner lives. In the case of Dr Manette, whose mind has gone after almost eighteen years of incarceration in the Bastille, Dickens told Collins in October 1859 that 'the peculiarity of the Doctor's character, as affected by his imprison- ment' rendered it 'quite out of the question to put the reader inside of him' in the way a writer might do for other characters.[63] Of these the drunken self-loathing lawyer Sydney Carton is a psychologically credible figure, though still primarily a tool of the melodramatic plot, while Lucie Manette, the young woman with whom both Darnay and Carton are in love, is a mere cipher, a golden-haired girl whose only role is to be a loving daughter and eventually a loving wife.

Dickens went on to write two great novels with protagonists who bear the intolerable burden of self-loathing and a guilty conscience, *Great Expectations* (1860–1) and *Our Mutual Friend* (1864–5), followed by his dark murder story *The Mystery of Edwin Drood*, which remained unfinished at his death in June 1870. From autumn 1860 he lived mainly in Gad's Hill, spending nights in London above the offices of *All the Year Round* and presumably also with Ellen in one or other of the houses he rented for her and her mother over the years. He probably spent time with her in France too, for he often went there for a few days at a time without specifying to his correspondents what he planned to do.[64] It was his misfortune – and hers – that, having decided that his priority was to retain the respect of the public, he could not live openly with the woman he had chosen. (By contrast, Lewes and Marian Evans enjoyed an enduring and loving relationship, though they suffered – Marian partic- ularly – disapproval and ostracism from some friends and family.) Dickens covered his tracks so carefully that Ellen disappears from view for some years in the 1860s.[65]

While he went on earning money from his books and from doing more reading tours, including one in America in 1867–8, he also had many demands on his purse from members of his family, some of whom also caused him to fear yet more scandal. His two surviving daughters, Mamie and Katey, gave him pleasure, Mamie because she settled into the role of sensible unmarried daughter and joint organiser of the household with Georgina Hogarth, and Katey because she was clever and charming. A talented artist, in July 1860 she married Wilkie Collins's younger brother, the Pre-Raphaelite artist Charles. The union was not exactly to Dickens's taste, but he accepted her choice and gave her a wedding breakfast at Gad's Hill. The boys were a different matter. No fewer than six of his seven sons disappointed him in one way or another. (Harry, the second youngest, was the exception: he succeeded in getting into Cambridge to read mathematics and became a successful lawyer and, in due course, Sir Henry Dickens.)

Their father wrote frankly to friends of his troubles with them, his attempts to find them suitable appointments, his disappointment when they failed, and, above all, his irritation with them for racking up debts which he was obliged to pay until he lost patience completely. In March 1862 his Lausanne friend William de Cerjat received a letter containing a round-up of their doings. The oldest, Charley, had 'married not particularly to my satisfaction' (that is, to the hated Frederick Evans's daughter Bessie), had gone into business in the City, 'and will do well if he can find continuous energy'.[66] His doubts about Charley went back to the boy's childhood and youth. Dickens had told Angela Burdett-Coutts in January 1854, when Charley had just turned seventeen, that he had inherited from his mother, along with 'tenderer and better qualities', 'an indescribable lassitude of character'.[67]

As the boys grew up he discovered a similar lack of energy or willpower in several of them. Though he was proud of his second son Walter's exploits in India, he tells de Cerjat in 1862 that Walter 'spends more than he gets and has cost me money and disappointed me'. Two years later Dickens had to pay off Walter's debts after the boy's death in Calcutta, in December 1863, only days after Thackeray's. Walter had stopped writing home after being told by his father that he would not continue to pay his debts.[68]

He was twenty-two. In 1862, as Dickens tells de Cerjat, his third son, Frank, is working for him in the office of *All the Year Round*. Two years later Frank joined the Bengal Mounted Police. Alfred, born in 1845, 'a good steady fellow, but not at all brilliant, is educating expensively for engineers or artillery', Dickens writes. Eventually Alfred became a land agent in Australia. After his father's death Alfred wrote of his shock and sorrow, and also of the 'one unfortunate incident of our father's life', his 'separation from our mother'. 'We their children always loved them both equally', and 'not one word of the subject *ever* passed from the lips of either father or mother'. 'Of the causes which led to this unfortunate event', which had occurred when Alfred was twelve, 'we know no more than the rest of the world.'[69]

Ploughing on with his list, Dickens reaches his fifth son and seventh child, Sydney, aged fifteen in 1862, whom he describes as 'a born little sailor' and already a midshipman at Bermuda. Sydney would go on to trouble his father more than any of the others; he wrote from Vancouver Island in 1869, where he was a second lieutenant on HMS *Zealous*, telling his father that if he refused to pay his debts the result would be 'utter ruination'. Dickens replied that he would not be received in Gad's Hill on his next return to England.[70] The other two are still at school in 1862. Harry is 'very bright and clever'; the youngest, Edward, having just turned ten at the time of this letter to de Cerjat, is given no character or prediction by Dickens at this point.[71] A few years later, when Edward was fifteen, Dickens wrote to his schoolmaster to suggest that his son drop Latin and learn subjects likely to be more useful to him when he leaves school to join Alfred in Australia. Dickens bemoans Edward's 'lack of application and continuity of purpose' and says he has 'tried to trace it up to its source', by which he once more means Catherine.[72]

Charley, who displeased his father with his choice of wife in November 1861, further displeased him by becoming a partner in a papermaking company alongside Bessie's brother Frederick Evans Jr. When the company failed in 1868 Dickens fumed about 'Charley's connexion with this precious Paper Mill Company; against which . . . I wrote him a letter of warning when it first loomed in the Evans atmosphere. It is coming to irretrievable bankruptcy, smash, and ruin.'[73] (Sala wrote jauntily to Yates in August 1868,

'So young Charles D *has* gone smash.'[74]) In response to this disaster Charley 'staggers back', wrote Dickens with despairing humour, 'with a family of five children in the present and fifty in the future, on the parental shoulder'.[75] However, Charley avoided bankruptcy and the following year Dickens, who had by now accepted his son's wife – despite her hated maiden name – and was fond of his grandchildren, gave Charley the job of running *All the Year Round*. His excellent colleague Wills was retiring due to ill health after twenty years of supporting Dickens's journalism and discreetly acting as go-between for his messages to Ellen. Charley was 'a very good man of business', Dickens told Macready, 'and evinces considerable aptitude in sub-editing work', despite having made 'a terrible Mess of his paper-making'.[76]

Dickens's two black sheep brothers died before him. Augustus succumbed to consumption in Chicago in October 1866. 'Poor fellow!' wrote Dickens, who had helped to support his brother's abandoned wife since he left her in February 1857.[77] Augustus had used his famous name to try to involve Dickens in his foolish business ventures and had generally been an embarrassment.[78] Fred, much the more troublesome of the two, was divorced by his wife Anna in 1859 on grounds of adultery and desertion. She had told her sister as early as 1852 that Fred was 'violent & disgusting' in his treatment of her, calling her an unfit companion, and even threatening to get medical advice which would justify his stopping her from pursuing an artistic career.[79] Sir Cresswell Cresswell of the Divorce Court granted the separation in July 1859, having ordered Fred to pay alimony. Fred gave up his job at the War Office and disappeared without keeping up his payments to Anna.[80] He died on 20 October 1868 in the northern town of Darlington, a useless wreck. It was 'a wasted life', Dickens told John Forster; he sent Charley to Darlington to organise the funeral.[81] Fortunately the London press paid no attention to the news, though a few northern newspapers picked it up from Fred's local paper, the *Darlington Times*.[82] In London Sala, who shared Fred's problem with alcohol, noted in a letter to his friend Yates of 26 October the sad details of Fred's life and death:

> I suppose you have heard that Fred Dickens is dead. And I suppose he was a bad egg; but assuredly a most miserable life he had led since

1858. One hundred and twenty pounds a year superannuation from the War Office and out of that £60 per ann. set aside by the Divorce Court as alimony for his wife, and £20 by the Bankruptcy Court for his creditors. F.D.'s habitual breakfast was a penny bun and a glass of gingerbeer. The remainder of his diet was mainly gin; cold. He couldn't smoke; he had no taste for reading: in fact he had no taste for anything save Van John and three card loo [card games]: luxuries not altogether attainable on a net income of £40 per ann. Poor devil.[83]

In June 1870 Dickens died of a stroke at Gad's Hill, aged fifty-eight. He had exhausted himself with months of reading in America and a final set of performances in St James's Hall in London, which came to a premature end in mid-March. Despite being in poor health, he had insisted on continuing to give his particularly fatiguing performances of Nancy's murder from *Oliver Twist*; Ellen attended one of these on 21 January.[84] In March the first instalment of *Edwin Drood* was published to acclaim and huge sales, at which Dickens was overjoyed.[85] The country mourned his death, and he received a funeral service in Westminster Abbey. In his will he left £1,000 to Ellen, who continued to live quietly, marrying a young schoolmaster, George Robinson, in 1876. Dickens had no last words for Catherine other than that he wished to record that she had received an annual income of £600 from him, 'while all the great charges of a numerous and expensive family have devolved wholly upon myself'. He could not bring himself to be gracious towards her, and his children may well have felt uncomfortable at the words 'expensive family'.[86]

More admirably he demanded in his will that his friends should 'on no account make me the subject of any monument, memorial, or testimonial whatever. I rest my claims to the remembrance of my country upon my published works.'[87] He had used almost the same words when expressing his disapproval of the plan for a statue of Shakespeare to be commissioned in 1864, with one suggestion being that it should adorn Bazalgette's brand new Thames Embankment. 'I dread the notion of a statue', he told Hepworth Dixon in January 1864, 'shiver and tremble at the thought of another graven image in some public place'. 'I believe that Shakespeare has left his best monument in his works, and is best left without another.'[88]

Dickens did not know it, but his old adversary Thackeray had given vent to the same feeling in one of the last letters he wrote before his death. On 17 December 1863 he told George Smith that he had received 'a circular about the Shakespeare business'. 'I think the scheme is bosh.'[89]

The end of the Robinson case

In November 1858, four months after the judges had adjourned the Robinson divorce case in order to await the expected amendment to the Divorce Act which would allow Edward Lane to give evidence as a witness, the case came to court again. Since the adjournment on 3 July Lane had quietly continued with his hydropathic practice at Moor Park. Among his loyal patients was Darwin, who spent a week there from 25 October, noting once more that his visit improved his health. 'Moor Park did me wonderful good', he told Hooker on 2 November; 'I walked one day 4½ miles! with only a few rests!'[90] The case resumed on 26 November, when Lane was formally dismissed from the suit and sworn in as a witness. Sir Alexander Cockburn was in the chair. Lane answered questions from both Isabella's and Henry's lawyers about his relations with her and the entries in her diary. He declared the former to have been in no way inappropriate, let alone adulterous. As for the diary, it was 'utterly and absolutely false – a tissue of romances from beginning to end, as far as they implicated me in anything improper'. The court could not resolve the question of whether Isabella was of sound mind when she wrote the diary (which Henry's counsel sought to prove) or under delusions related to her menopausal state (the line pursued by Isabella's counsel). Cockburn adjourned the case once more, without fixing a date for its renewal.[91]

Darwin, working with urgency to finish *Origin of Species* – though he still called it his 'abstract' in a letter to Wallace in January 1859[92] – took himself off to Moor Park once more on 5 February. Halfway through his two-week stay he told W.D. Fox that he was feeling better. 'We are a very pleasant party here', he wrote, '& are very comfortable, & I am glad to say that not one of Dr Lane's patients has given him up & he gets fresh new ones pretty regularly.'[93] By the time he returned to Moor Park in May – when among his leisure reading was *Adam Bede*, which he described as 'excellent', telling Hooker that 'entire rest & the douche & Adam Bede have together done me a world of good'[94] – the Robinson case had returned to court for the last time.

The three original divorce judges – Cresswell, Wightman, and Cockburn – were present when the case resumed on 2 March 1859. Cockburn summed up, beginning by describing the case as 'peculiar and remarkable in its character and circumstances'. Since the diary was the only evidence, it could not be used to 'establish the criminality of the co-respondent Dr Lane', which was the reason why the court had adjourned the previous summer in order to take advantage of the forthcoming amendment to the Divorce Act. The court now had to decide whether through the admission by Isabella in her diary 'a case of adultery was made out which entitled the petitioner to the redress he sought', or whether, with Lane dismissed as a co-respondent and acquitted of guilt, 'the suit against the wife must not of necessity fail'. The judges, Cockburn said, so far agreed with Henry Robinson's lawyers as to believe that his wife was not insane, but they did not think that the diary disclosures amounted to a confession of actual adultery, however suggestive of intimacy they might appear. It simply could not be proved that she and Lane had committed adultery. The case was therefore dismissed, though Cockburn expressed regret at Henry Robinson's position, with his separation granted earlier by the Ecclesiastical Court but no full divorce settlement available to him. He remained 'burdened with a wife who had placed on record the confession of her misconduct' or at least 'of unfaithful thoughts and unchaste desires'. Nonetheless, the court could not find legal proof of adultery 'in the incoherent statements of a narrative so irrational and untrustworthy as that of the respondent'. Though the judges had decided against Henry's petition, they decreed that Isabella, having independent means, must pay her own costs.[95] According to the report in The Times, Cockburn and Wightman retired from the court after this judgment, while Sir Cresswell Cresswell continued with the other cases scheduled for a hearing that day. The very next one was Dickens v. Dickens, a stage in the case being brought by Anna Dickens against the impecunious Fred which was finally resolved in her favour in July.[96]

Lane survived the scandal unscathed. In 1860 he moved with his family, including his mother-in-law Lady Drysdale, to another handsome establishment, already well known for its water-cure treatments, Sudbrook Park near Richmond in Surrey, closer to London than Moor Park and containing one of the first Turkish baths in Britain.[97] Isabella became estranged from her friends and family. She rented a cottage and took in lodgers. Her youngest son chose to live with her rather than with his father when he left school in 1861. Henry finally succeeded in divorcing Isabella in 1864. His hired agents had found her with a man in a hotel room in London in June 1863; the man was a tutor she had employed to teach the boys French in 1855. Henry was now free to marry again, which he did in 1865.[98]

The Robinson case, coming right at the beginning of the jurisdiction of the new Divorce Court and containing such unprecedented elements as to require the law to be amended to accommodate it, touched many people outside the immediate family circles of the Lanes, the Drysdales, and the Robinsons. Through Lane's profession patients like Darwin became involved, if only by watching from the sidelines as the case took its protracted course, from the hot June days of 1858 to the final decision in March 1859. At a time when the new Medical Act, designed to regulate and improve the profession, was finally passing into law, the standing of the medical profession itself was threatened, as both conventional and alternative practitioners realised, by the possibility that women would accuse doctors of improprieties when they attended their female patients. And the whole question of what constituted lunacy, particularly in women of a certain age, was being raised at the same time as the Robinson case, with many stories reaching the public ear about incarcerations of inconvenient spouses and the accompanying scrutiny of the efficiency of the Lunacy Commission. One writer who quickly exploited the subject's potential for fiction was Wilkie Collins. *The Woman in White*, with its plotting by the wicked husband Sir Percival Glyde to put his wife in an asylum in order to claim her fortune, began serialisation in Dickens's new paper *All the Year Round*, succeeding *A Tale of Two Cities* in November 1859.

Darwin triumphant

Darwin's main concern after the sad death of his son, and the excitement (and anxiety) of Wallace's letter and the reading of his and Wallace's work to the Linnaean Society, was to regain health by holidaying with his family, before returning to Down on 13 August 1858 to get on with his work on natural selection. Despite recognising the need to publish something soon if he wanted to be sure of receiving the recognition he craved, he had not yet decided to print his major findings in one volume, thinking that he would first of all extend the short pieces introduced by Lyell and Hooker on 1 July into 'a long abstract on my notions about Species & Varieties, to be read in parts' before the Linnaean Society at its subsequent meetings and then printed in its journal. 'My bigger Book will not be out for some two or three years', he wrote to the naturalist Thomas Campbell Eyton from the Isle of Wight on 4 August 1858.[99] Slowly and in a way reluctantly he came to the idea that the long abstract *would* in fact be his 'big book' on the subject, and that it would be published by a mainstream publisher (in the event the respected firm of John Murray) rather than in a specialist journal, where it would be read only by fellow scientists. As he frequently told his correspondents, he was a slow worker; in addition, his diffidence and fear of upsetting his wife and many devout friends contributed to the snail's pace at which he moved while finally coming to realise what had to be done.

The modest papers by Darwin and Wallace, harbinger of one of the greatest landmarks in the progress of science, not only received no press attention after their presentation to the Linnaean Society on 1 July; when they were published in the *Proceedings* of the society in August, they attracted no notice then either. The next event in the scientific world was the meeting in Leeds of the British Association for the Advancement of Science (BAAS) in September. Darwin was listed in the press as being one of the likely attendees, but on 1 September he wrote to John Phillips, the assistant general secretary of the association, saying his health would not permit him to take over as president of the zoological section for the occasion; indeed, he would not be able to travel to Leeds to attend the meeting.[100] Darwin only ever attended three BAAS meetings, at Southampton in 1846, at Oxford in 1847, and at Glasgow in 1855.[101] His home-loving character and increasingly poor health kept him away from such gatherings, though he always heard all about them from his more active friends Hooker and Huxley. The latter looked forward eagerly to attending; in a letter of

5 September to Hooker he 'rejoiced' that Wallace had moved Darwin nearer to publication of his work, which Huxley was confident would effect 'a great revolution' and bring in 'an English epoch in science and art'. 'Shall I have a row with the great O. there?' he asked, referring to Richard Owen, president of the BAAS and a man who was determined, as Darwin pointed out after the publication of *Origin of Species* in November 1859, that there would be 'only one cock of the walk!'[102]

As had been the case at the Linnaean Society meeting in July, so now in September neither Darwin nor Wallace (still toiling in the Malay Archipelago) was present to promote the theory of natural selection. According to the *Illustrated London News*, more than 1,660 members did attend.[103] Owen presided magisterially. *The Times* gave generous coverage to the event, which began on Thursday, 23 September and closed the following Wednesday, and the weekly *Athenaeum* printed a long account on 16 October. Darwin was mentioned once or twice by speakers, including a Dr Wright, who spoke in Section D (zoology and botany), the section Darwin had been asked to chair. Wright quoted Darwin and his friend William Tegetmeier on bees' cells.[104]

Owen gave his presidential speech in Leeds Town Hall on the first evening. *The Times*, reporting the event the following day, noted that his speech was 'a very prolix document, which occupied full three hours in its delivery'. The paper's summary of what Owen had to say includes a reference to the most interesting and up-to-date elements of his speech, namely Owen's firm support for statistical and sanitary science. It also quotes the opening of the speech, which places God firmly at the helm of all scientific progress and the BAAS as God's favoured servant. The aim of the association, Owen said, was 'the knowledge of the laws of nature' and the application of those laws so as to 'advance the wellbeing of society and exalt the condition of mankind'. God, he said, had 'given to mankind a capacity to discover and comprehend the laws by which His universe is governed'.[105] Lest anyone should worry about the proven fact that species can become extinct, Owen assured them that this presented no problem for religion since 'creation ever compensate[es] for extinction'.

The Rev. Dr William Hook, vicar of Leeds, took encouragement from this to claim in his speech of thanks that science, instead of being the opponent of religion, is really 'the handmaid of Christianity'. *The Times* reported his words:

> People were beginning to see that the philosopher might carry out his researches into the secrets of nature fearless of consequences and regardless of results; and that, at the same time, the theologian, with equal tenacity and boldness, could assert the facts of revelation, since the author of nature and the author of revelation was the same blessed Being. They might also rest assured that the facts of science were reconcilable with the facts of Scripture.[106]

Though it is to be expected that a clergyman would make such claims, the fact that Owen also spoke so frequently and freely about God in the context of science is a reminder of how far apart he, Britain's leading light in the scientific establishment, was from Darwin, whose work was conceived and expressed in a fundamentally different form. Little wonder that Darwin had no appetite to join in with such discussions, or that he was so apprehensive about the storm his own work would cause not only among the general public but also among leading scientists. Owen had read the Darwin–Wallace papers in the *Proceedings* of the Linnaean Society. He devoted two paragraphs of his mammoth speech to them, neither praising nor criticising, but simply summarising. Of Wallace's essay he says merely that it shows how 'deviations from type may either tend to the destruction of a variety, or to adapt a variety to some changes in surrounding conditions, under which it is better calculated to exist, than the type-form from which it deviated'. He quotes a paragraph from Darwin on variation in dogs and foxes, prefacing the extract with a faintly praising remark: 'Mr Charles Darwin had previously to Mr Wallace illustrated this principle by ingenious suppositions, of which I select the following.'[107] If he saw that something new and important was afoot, that, as Huxley predicted, the Darwin–Wallace hypothesis would cause a revolution in science, he certainly did not let on.

While his fellow scientists exchanged their views in Leeds, Darwin laboured on 'most steadily' at his 'abstract', as he still called his work – though by 6 October, as he told Hooker, it was growing to book length.

'You cannot imagine what a service you have done me in making me make this abstract', he wrote, 'for though I thought I had got it all clear, it has clarified my brains much, by making me weigh relative importance of the several elements.'[108] On the same day Wallace wrote from Ternate in the Moluccas to both his mother and Hooker, telling the first how gratified he was by the approval Darwin, Lyell, and Hooker had shown for his work and how he expected to acquire 'the assistance of these eminent men' on his return to London in a few years' time. He meant their much-needed support in the business of trying to make a living in science by having his observations published and being given grants for further research. The letter to Hooker was his reply to the news sent in early July about the reading of his and Darwin's papers at the Linnaean Society; he expressed his gratitude to Hooker and Lyell for making the arrangements and voluntarily declared that Darwin's pieces had 'secured to him a claim to priority'.[109]

In their correspondence all three – Darwin, Hooker, and Wallace – as well as Huxley were exercised at this time about the future of the nation's natural history collections, which were stuck in the limited confines of the British Museum building, despite being added to all the time. Owen devoted the last part of his Leeds speech to the subject. It was his hope that a completely new museum could be built to accommodate the collections. Scientists were being asked to sign appeals and memoranda to the government, and specifically to Disraeli as chancellor of the Exchequer.

In his speech Owen pleaded with the government, particularly with Disraeli, though not by name. Having mentioned the great 'practical results' which had come from scientific successes such as the steam engine, the lightning conductor, the electric telegraph, and anaesthetics in surgery, he spoke grandly and with prospective flattery of a putative 'far-seeing Finance Minister', by whom 'the man of Science will be regarded with a favourable eye, not less for the unlooked-for streams that have already flowed, but for those that may in future arise, out of the applications of the abstract truths to the discovery of which he devotes himself'.[110] Owen's plan was to have a dedicated building, superintended by him. His wish was to be fulfilled finally with the Alfred Waterhouse-designed Natural History Museum, which opened in South Kensington in 1881, and which remains

Owen's greatest claim to fame, outlasting and outdoing his achievements in science. Though Darwin signed the memorandum making the case for a new building, which was addressed to the government by Britain's leading scientists in November 1858, he took a dim view of Disraeli as its recipient. 'I cannot put much faith in a memorial[,] even if signed by every real man of science, having much influence at least with such a poor creature as B. Disraeli', he wrote to Huxley on 1 December.[111]

By April 1859 the first part of *Origin of Species* was finished and Darwin had sent it to John Murray. In July he was at Dr Lane's establishment at Moor Park once more, trying to get up some strength. He wondered how many copies Murray intended to print.[112] The first print run was 1,250, but since all the copies sold out on the first day of publication in November, a second run of 3,000 was printed off in December.[113] He had told Murray only a few weeks earlier, on 10 September, that on advice from friends he had finally decided to drop the word 'abstract' or 'essay' from his title. The most important word in what was still a 'rather too long' title was 'Species'.[114] Darwin was sure of Hooker's and Huxley's admiration and support, though Hooker himself confessed that it took him fourteen years after first reading Darwin's 1844 fragment to accept his views completely.[115] Lyell, though a good friend and mentor, never became a complete convert to the theory of natural selection. He wrote kindly but not enthusiastically after reading his presentation copy of *Origin*:

> I have just finished your volume, and right glad I am that I did my best with Hooker to persuade you to publish it without waiting for a time which probably could never have arrived, though you lived to the age of a hundred . . .
>
> It is a splendid case of close reading and long sustained argument throughout so many pages, the condensation immense, too great perhaps for the uninitiated, but an effective and important preliminary statement.[116]

Lyell's chief worry was the problem Darwin's theory posed for humanity, since if one were to accept the hypothesis in the case of other animals and of plants, one would have to accept it in 'the case of Man', and 'all the consequences must follow'.[117] As late as 1863 Darwin told Hooker of his disappointment that Lyell had not yet 'spoken out on Species'.[118]

As for Owen, Darwin knew he would attack the book. He told Wallace in a letter of 9 August 1859 that 'Owen, I do not doubt, will bitterly oppose us; but I regard this very little, as he is a poor reasoner'.[119] It was tactful and generous to say 'us' here in connection with the theory of natural selection, though in the same letter he once more stakes his claim to independent thinking. He reiterates his disagreement with Wallace, expressed in a letter of December 1857, over 'colonisation of *oceanic islands*'; while Wallace believed that islands got their flora and fauna from previously existing land connections, Darwin thought that the dispersal of seeds and eggs by wind, water, or birds caused the colonisation of islands.[120]

He wrote again to Wallace a few days before the official publication date of 24 November, saying that Murray was sending Wallace his copy.[121] 'God knows what the public will think.' Lyell 'does not seem' to be a convert, though Hooker is, and Darwin hopes Huxley will approve; if he does, 'I shall be content.' Darwin's timidity and apprehension about the likely reception of the work were partly a result of his isolation; as he confessed to Wallace, 'I have not seen one naturalist for 6 or 9 months owing to the state of my health.'[122] He had to wait until May 1860 to receive Wallace's supportive reply.

Meanwhile responses came in letters to him and in reviews. The clergyman, novelist, and amateur scientist Charles Kingsley was one of the first to thank Darwin for his presentation copy. He wrote on 18 November, honestly expressing his respectful disagreement. The book '*awes* me', he wrote, 'both with the heap of facts, & the prestige of your name, & also with the clear intuition, that if you be right, I must give up much that I have believed & written'. He agrees with Darwin about the variation and extinction of species: 'I have long since, from watching the crossing of domesticated animals & plants, learnt to disbelieve the dogma of the permanence of species.' He even thinks he can reconcile Darwin's views with his religious faith:

I have gradually learnt to see that it is just as noble a conception
of Deity, to believe that he created primal forms capable of self

development into all forms needful pro tempore & pro loco [for the time and place], as to believe that He required a fresh act of intervention to supply the lacunas w[hic]h he himself had made. I question whether the former be not the loftier thought.[123]

Darwin was not offended by this response, but rather heartened. He asked Kingsley if he could quote from the letter in the historical sketch of writings on evolution which he was preparing in December 1859 for the second printing.[124]

On 5 December Marian Evans, or Marian Lewes, as she liked to be known, told a correspondent that she and Lewes had been reading *Origin*. Her response was a little grudging, largely because she felt that Lewes, a writer of popularising books on science, was not appreciated by other writers on the subject, though he and Darwin corresponded amicably about each other's work. She saw that Darwin's book 'makes an epoch, as the expression of his thorough adhesion, after long years of study, to the Doctrine of Development', but she thought it lacked sufficient 'illustrative facts'. Nonetheless, it would 'have a great effect in the scientific world, causing a thorough and open discussion of a question about which people have hitherto felt timid'.[125] Another intelligent lay person, Friedrich Engels, commented enthusiastically to Karl Marx, though he noted disparagingly that Darwin, not being a German thinker, was no theorist:

> Darwin, by the way, whom I'm reading just now, is absolutely splendid. There was one aspect of teleology that had yet to be demolished, and that has now been done. Never before has so grandiose an attempt been made to demonstrate historical evolution in Nature, and certainly never to such good effect. One does, of course, have to put up with the crude English method.[126]

Marx agreed, echoing in his many references to Darwin Engels's criticism of what appeared to them the 'unphilosophical' nature of Darwin's argument, but grasping the connections to be made between Darwin's interpretation of natural history and his own of social history. He told a German friend in 1861 that Darwin's work was 'most important'; it 'suits my purpose in that it provides a basis in natural science for the historical class struggle', though 'one does, of course, have to put up with the clumsy English style of argument'.[127] The chief philosophical difference between Marx and Darwin was that Marx was a determinist who interpreted history in terms of inevitable progress. In 1866 he welcomed a now-forgotten French book on the origin and transformations of the human and other species, preferring it to Darwin's work on the grounds that 'progress, which Darwin regards as purely accidental, is essential here on the basis of the earth's development'.[128]

Darwin's English friends and supporters soon started responding to *Origin*. Hooker called the book 'glorious' in an optimistic letter of 21 November. 'What a mass of close reasoning on curious facts & fresh phenomena – it is capitally written & will be very successful.'[129] Darwin's brother Erasmus thought it 'the most interesting book I have ever read'; he wrote discerningly and gratifyingly that he could 'only compare it to the first knowledge of chemistry, getting into a new world or rather behind the scenes'.[130] Huxley, on whose positive judgment Darwin depended and who Darwin knew would review *Origin* in at least one newspaper or periodical, wrote on 23 November to say that the work had made a great impression on him, and that he was 'prepared to go to the Stake if requisite' in support of it, though he disagreed with one or two points, including Darwin's view that evolution has always been gradual, that Nature has never made 'jumps'. But Darwin has 'earned the lasting gratitude of all thoughtful men', while 'considerable abuse & misrepresentation' is 'in store for you'. Darwin should not worry, for he, Huxley, who later called himself 'Darwin's bulldog', would go into battle: 'As to the curs which will bark & yelp – you must recollect that some of your friends at any rate are endowed with an amount of combativeness which (though you have often & justly rebuked it) may stand you in good stead. I am sharpening up my claws & beak in readiness.'[131]

Huxley was surprised and delighted to be asked to write a review in *The Times*. He told Hooker gleefully that he had sent Darwin a cartoon of himself as a prize-fighter with Hooker 'holding the bottle'. As for the review, 'I wrote it faster than I ever wrote anything in my life. The last column nearly as fast as my wife could read the sheets. But I was thoroughly in the humour and full of the subject . . . I earnestly hope it may have made some of the educated mob, who derive their ideas from the *Times*, reflect. And whatever they do, they *shall* respect Darwin.'[132]

Darwin was thrilled with this review, which was published on 26 December. He had a 'strong suspicion', he told Hooker, that it was by Huxley, 'but I never heard that he wrote in [*The*] *Times*. It will do grand service, especially as so nobly soaring above religious prejudices.'[133] To Huxley himself he wrote on the same day in unusually high spirits, teasingly wondering who the author of this review might be and praising him for his perspicacity and expertise:

> [He] is a literary man & German scholar. He has read my Book very attentively; but what is very remarkable, it seems that he is a profound naturalist . . . [H]e writes & thinks with quite uncommon force & clearness; & what is even still rarer his writing is seasoned with most pleasant wit . . . Who can it be? Certainly I should have said that there was only *one* man in England who could have written this essay & that *you* were the man. But I suppose I am wrong, & that there is some hidden genius of great calibre. For how could you influence Jupiter Olympus ['Jupiter' was a common nickname for *The Times*] & make him give 3½ columns to pure science? The old Fogies will think the world will come to an end.[134]

Huxley's review reveals that his strategy for getting Darwin's views accepted, or at least not rejected out of hand, is to begin with the general statement that new speculations in science are coming faster than ever before, and that each needs careful testing and criticising. He explains that the hypothesis offered by Darwin, 'the eminent Naturalist before us', is 'as vast as it is novel'. It 'may or may not be sustainable hereafter; it may give way to something else', but in any case it must be tested properly. Huxley faces head-on the 'controversy which is coming' as a result of Darwin's book, but insists that only the test of science is appropriate. He discusses briefly the idea of the variation of species, and singles out, as Darwin deftly does in the early chapters of *Origin*, the familiar human activity of breeding animals such as pigeons or dogs in order to capitalise on the most useful features of each species. If man can breed variations in or out of domestic species, why might not nature do the same in the wild, over a long period of time? He notes that others have written about evolution and tried to explain it, from Lamarck to 'such dreamers as the author of *Vestiges*' (a remark about Robert Chambers's book, which Huxley had reviewed with what he later regretted as 'needless savagery'[135]). Darwin's history is then related – how he belongs to a distinguished scientific family, how he went on his circumnavigatory voyage and published some of the results of his research, and how he has been working on the current book for over twenty years. 'No living naturalist and anatomist has published a better monograph than that which has resulted from his labours.'[136]

Huxley describes the theory of natural selection, calling it 'an ingenious hypothesis' which 'gives a reason for many anomalies in the distribution of living beings in time and space'. Whether the theory is absolutely true is still to be discovered:

> Goethe has an excellent aphorism defining that state of mind which he calls '*Thätige Skepsis*' – active doubt. It is doubt which so loves the truth that it neither dares rest in doubting, nor extinguish itself by unjustified belief; and we commend this state of mind to students of species ... Mr Darwin abhors a vacuum ... The path he bids us follow professes to be not a mere airy track, fabricated of ideal cobwebs, but a solid and broad bridge of facts. If it be so, it will carry us safely over many a chasm in our knowledge, and lead us to a region free from the snares of those fascinating but barren Virgins, the Final Causes, against whom a high authority has so justly warned us. 'My sons, dig in the vineyard', were the last words of the old man in the fable [by Aesop]; and, though the sons found no treasure, they made their fortunes by the grapes.[137]

So ends Huxley's clever and lively article. The quotation from Goethe is the evidence Darwin found of his being a 'German scholar'; Huxley had taught himself German as a young man. He is careful not to be too enthusiastic about Darwin's work, partly because he had some honest disagreements about details, and partly because he judged it would be easier to persuade people to give Darwin a hearing if he did not appear too much of a partisan, though from this point on it was Huxley's explicit intention to be just that. In the essay he wrote for Darwin's son Frank's edition of his father's *Life and Letters*, published in 1887, entitled 'The Reception of the "Origin of Species" ', Huxley remembered being cautious at first, then thinking, 'How extremely stupid not to have thought of that!', adding, 'I suppose Columbus' companions thought much the same when he made the egg stand on end.' The Darwin–Wallace papers of July 1858, and 'still more' the *Origin* of November 1859, 'had the effect of the flash of light which, to a man who has lost himself on a dark night, suddenly reveals a road which, whether it takes him straight home or not, certainly goes his way.'[138] When Huxley reviewed *Origin* at greater length and in more detail in the radical quarterly the *Westminster Review* in April 1860, he introduced another striking metaphor for the effect of *Origin*: 'Extinguished theologians lie about the cradle of every science as the strangled snakes beside that of Hercules.' Darwin thought this sentence 'splendid'.[139]

Darwin was fortunate in his friends, and he needed to be. Negative responses came thick and fast. Most difficult for Darwin was his wife's distress, partly at the book itself, and partly at the reaction of theologians and religious readers; he told W.B. Carpenter on 3 December 1859 that the 'odium theologicum much pains all one's female relations'.[140] Emma was particularly upset by the letter Darwin received from Adam Sedgwick, professor of geology at Cambridge. Sedgwick declared that he had read the book with more pain than pleasure, and some parts of it 'with absolute sorrow' because he thought them 'utterly false & grievously mischievous'. 'Many of your wide conclusions are based upon assumptions which can neither be proved nor disproved.' Worst of all, Darwin does not explicitly exclude mankind from his scheme, though he chooses animal and plant species to illustrate his theory. The question of humanity exercises Sedgwick:

> There is a moral or metaphysical part of nature as well as a physical. A man who denies this is deep in the mire of folly. Tis the crown and glory of organic science that it *does* thro' *final cause*, link material to moral . . . You have ignored this link . . . you have done your best in one or two pregnant cases to break it. Were it possible (which thank

God it is not) to break it, humanity in my mind, would suffer a damage that might brutalize it – & sink the human race into a lower grade of degradation than any into which it has fallen since its written records tell us of its history.

Finally, 'I greatly dislike the concluding chapter' because of the 'tone of triumphant confidence in which you appeal to the rising generation' and 'prophesy of things not yet in the womb of time'.[141] Sedgwick attacked *Origin* a few months later in a review in the *Spectator* and a speech to the Cambridge Philosophical Society, by which time Hooker, though confessing that he thought Darwin had 'pressed his hypothesis too far', insisted to a correspondent that it was 'the "Book of the Day" '. He thought poorly of the 'senseless howl' of many reviewers in articles full of 'ignorant prejudice' and 'mere twaddle'.[142]

The great Richard Owen wrote his review in the famous quarterly periodical, the *Edinburgh Review*. He never admitted to being its author, which is hardly surprising given that Darwin's book is reviewed alongside a number of other works, including Owen's own new book, *Palaeontology*, a French translation of one of his previous books, and his lengthy presidential address to the British Association for the Advancement of Science in Leeds in September 1858. He repeatedly quotes his unacknowledged self against Darwin, whose theory of natural selection is described as 'mere hypothesis'.[143] Darwin wrote to his publisher Murray on 9 April 1860 asking if he had read this. 'I am thrashed in every possible way to the full content of my bitterest opposers. The article is very venomous, & is manifestly by Owen. I wish for auld lang syne's sake he had been a little less bitter.'[144] To Hooker he wrote amusedly of the *Edinburgh* review that some of his relations 'say it cannot *possibly* be Owen's article, because the Reviewer speaks so very highly of Prof. Owen. Poor dear simple folk!'[145]

By May 1860 Darwin had received Wallace's letter acknowledging receipt of *Origin*. The letter is lost, but Wallace jotted down some notes in February 1860 after reading the work, and these survive. He calls the work 'admirable' and says it agrees absolutely with his own essay written two years earlier and sent to Darwin. In stark contrast to Owen, however, he responds to reading Darwin with complete honesty. 'His work touches upon & explains in detail many points which I had scarcely thought upon', and 'many of his facts & explanations in Geographical distribution are also quite new to me & of the highest interest'.[146] He clearly wrote in this vein to Darwin, who thanked him on 18 May for his letter of 16 February:

> You must let me say how I admire the generous manner in which you speak of my Book: most persons would in your position have felt some envy or jealousy. How nobly free you seem to be of this common failing of mankind. But you speak far too modestly of yourself; you would if you had had my leisure [have] done the work just as well, perhaps better, than I have done it.[147]

The 1860 meeting of the British Association took place in Oxford, from 27 June to 4 July. Given what we know of his habits and health, not to mention his sensitivity to criticism, it seems highly unlikely that Darwin would have wished to attend the first meeting of his fellow scientists since the publication of his controversial work. Sure enough, he found he could not attend. He told Lyell on 25 June 1860 that he had 'given up Oxford'. His stomach had 'utterly broken down' and he was about to go to Edward Lane's new hydropathic establishment, Sudbrook Park, in the hope of getting the usual respite.[148] In his absence the most famous row in Victorian science broke out, not directly between Huxley and Owen, as might have been expected, but more spectacularly between Huxley and a supporter of Owen's, the bishop of Oxford Samuel Wilberforce (known universally as 'Soapy Sam').[149]

As had been the case at the Linnaean Society and British Association meetings in 1858, so now in September 1860 neither of the two heroes of natural selection was present. Instead, Huxley and Hooker spoke up when Darwin came under fire. Hooker wrote excitedly to Darwin on Monday, 2 July about events the previous Thursday, 28 June: 'Huxley & Owen had a furious battle over Darwin's absent body at Section D [the botanical and zoological section], before my arrival'. Huxley had been 'triumphant – you & your book forthwith became the topics of the day'.[150]

On the Saturday Hooker impatiently sat through a mass of 'flatulent stuff' until Wilberforce 'got up & spouted for half an hour with inimitable spirit ugliness & emptiness & unfairness' before a huge crowd of between '700 & 1000 people, for all the world was there to hear Sam Oxon'. 'I saw he was coached up by Owen & knew nothing & he said not a syllable but what was in the Reviews – he ridiculed you badly & Huxley savagely – Huxley answered admirably & turned the tables. Then Hooker himself asked to speak:

> I smashed him amid rounds of applause – I hit him in the wind at first shot in 10 words taken from his own ugly mouth – & then proceeded to demonstrate in as few more 1 that he could never have read your book & 2 that he was absolutely ignorant of the rudiments of Bot. Science . . . Sam was shut up – had not one word to say in reply & the meeting *was dissolved forthwith* leaving you master of the field after 4 hours [*sic*] battle.[151]

Though Hooker thus took much of the credit to himself, others put the rout down mainly to Huxley's brilliant repartee when Soapy Sam apparently asked him whether he claimed his descent from a monkey through his grandfather or his grandmother. Huxley told a friend in September 1860 that he had replied that he would 'rather have a miserable ape for a grandfather' than a man 'possessed of great means of influence & yet who employs' that influence 'for the mere purpose of introducing ridicule into a grave scientific discussion'.[152] Many years later he recalled that he had been so astonished at how ignorant the bishop of Oxford showed himself to be that he muttered to the man next to him, 'The Lord hath delivered him into mine hands', then stood up and 'let [himself] go'.[153]

From Sudbrook Park Darwin responded to Hooker's account with a mixture of melancholy and pleasure:

> I have been very poorly with almost continuous bad headache for 48 hours, & I was low enough & thinking what a useless burthen I was to myself & all others, when your letter came & it has so cheered me. Your kindness & affection brought tears into my eyes. Talk of fame, honour, pleasure, wealth, all are dirt compared with affection . . . [N]ow that I hear that you & Huxley will fight publicly (which I am

sure I never could do) I fully believe that our cause will in the long run prevail. I am glad that I was not at Oxford, for I sh[oul]d have been overwhelmed, with my stomach in its present state.[154]

He wrote to Huxley too: 'I honour your pluck; I would as soon have died as tried to answer the Bishop in such an assembly.'[155]

Darwin's chronic ill health never left him. He tried many alleged remedies, and in 1865 he wrote down his symptoms for Dr John Chapman, old friend and journalist colleague of Marian Evans and Lewes, publisher of the *Westminster Review,* and the inventor of an ice-bag which he claimed could cure a number of ailments, including those suffered by Darwin.[156] Now aged fifty-six, Darwin wrote that he had endured for twenty-five years 'extreme spasmodic daily & nightly flatulence', occasional vomiting, which was 'on two occasions prolonged during months', singing in the ears, shivering, and half-fainting. He could not walk more than half a mile and was always tired.[157] Over the years Darwin tried among other things calomel, cinnamon, potassium bicarbonate, aloe, bitters, phosphate of iron, chalk, magnesia, and various purgatives, as well as making frequent visits to hydropathic establishments, including Edward Lane's.[158] Nothing gave him lasting relief, though he lived to the age of seventy-three, dying of heart failure in April 1882. Modern medical diagnoses range from physical causes – perhaps from germs picked up during the voyage of the *Beagle* – to psychological or psychosomatic ones, traced usually to Darwin's alleged anxiety as a boy to please his formidable father.[159]

Like Dickens twelve years before, Darwin was deemed important enough to be buried in Westminster Abbey. One of the pallbearers was Alfred Russel Wallace. In his autobiography Wallace quotes the obituary in *Nature* by Huxley, which he thinks the 'most discriminating and most beautiful' of the many tributes to Darwin. Huxley had written:

One could not converse with Darwin without being reminded of Socrates. There was the same desire to find some one wiser than himself; the same belief in the sovereignty of reason; the same ready humour; the same sympathetic interest in all the ways and works of men. But instead of turning away from the problems of nature as wholly insoluble, our modern philosopher devoted his whole life to attacking them in the spirit of Heraclitus and Democritus.[160]

As ever, Huxley had found a fitting analogy to place Darwin's importance in the history of science and of knowledge generally. He wrote in a letter to a colleague that Darwin had 'a clear rapid intelligence, a great memory, a vivid imagination, and what made his greatness was the strict subordination of all these to his love of truth'.[161]

Darwin himself would not have claimed as much. In the autobiography he wrote for his children in 1876 he notes that he was slow at school and not thought clever: 'I believe that I was considered by all my masters and by my Father as a very ordinary boy, rather below the common standard in intellect.'[162] Even after finding his métier, he never felt he could express himself 'clearly and concisely', though he believes that this 'has had the compensating advantage of forcing me to think long and intently about every sentence'.[163] He admits that he could not learn to speak another language, and though he likes music and poetry, he has no aptitude for them.[164] (This seems to have been true of the whole Darwin–Wedgwood family; Gwen Raverat remembered that all of her aunts and uncles – Darwin's children – except Frank were 'benevolently philistine', regarding the arts 'as the inessential ornaments of Life'.[165])

Darwin continues with his description of his failings. 'I have no great quickness of apprehension or wit which is so remarkable in some clever men, for instance Huxley.' His memory meanwhile 'is extensive, yet hazy'. Finally, he analyses, as he might do in the case of an animal or plant species, his characteristics and the conditions in which he has existed:

My habits are methodical, and this has been of not a little use for my particular line of work. Lastly, I have had ample leisure from not having to earn my own bread. Even ill-health, though it has annihilated several years of my life, has saved me from the distractions of society and amusement.

Therefore, my success as a man of science, whatever this may have amounted to, has been determined, as far as I can judge, by complex and diversified mental qualities and conditions. Of these the most important have been – the love of science – unbounded patience in long reflecting over any subject – industry in observing and collecting facts – and a fair share of invention as well as of common-sense. With such moderate abilities as I possess, it is truly surprising that thus I should have influenced to a considerable extent the beliefs of scientific men on some important points.[166]

Strikingly, when he came to write *his* autobiography thirty years later, Alfred Russel Wallace assessed his own talents in similar terms and with equal modesty. He too contrasts himself with Huxley; he possesses, he writes, none of Huxley's 'fiery energy and intense power of work'. Like Darwin he notes that he has no ear for music, no facility in learning languages, and – more problematically for a naturalist – not much talent for drawing. Nor does he have a good verbal memory, and he regrets 'the total absence of wit or humour, paradox or brilliancy, in my writings',[167] though here he surely underestimates himself. His account of his eight years away, published in 1869 under the title *The Malay Archipelago: The Land of the Orang-utan, and the Bird of Paradise. A Narrative of Travel, with Studies of Man and Nature*, is lively and proved lastingly popular. If he does not write wittily, he can certainly paint a vivid verbal picture of the singular experiences he has had in remote places. On his return to England in March 1862 from his long trip, he notified the secretary of the Zoological Society that he had safely brought back the two live birds of paradise he had bought in Singapore seven weeks earlier, describing in detail the almost impossible task he had performed in getting them home. He recounts the difficulties of finding suitable food for them *en route*. 'Bananas they had till Suez & melons at Malta.' '*Cockroaches* they are excessively fond of & I managed to get them fairly regularly till leaving Bombay.' In the middle of the Red Sea he resorted, nervously, to giving them hard-boiled eggs, 'which they are very fond of but which I doubt agreeing with them for long'. He reassures his correspondent that the birds have survived the long journey north and the increasingly low temperatures 'wonderfully'. He has succeeded in bringing live birds of paradise to Europe for the first time, and he writes simply, 'I hope they will be glorious.'[168]

Wallace never claimed to be the originator of the theory of natural selection. On the contrary, he wrote at every turn, both privately and publicly, of Darwin's genius and claim to priority. While in Ternate in December 1860 he told his correspondent Henry Bates how much he admired *Origin*: 'I could never have *approached* the completeness of his book, – its vast accumulation of evidence, its overwhelming argument, & its admirable tone & spirit.' Darwin had created 'a new science & a new Philosophy, & I believe that *never* has such a complete illustration of a new branch of human knowledge been due to the labours & researches of a single man'.[169]

After his return to England in 1862 and up to his death in 1913 Wallace published books on the geographical distribution of animals, while his best-known work was *Darwinism*, published in 1889. When the Darwin Medal was instituted by the Royal Society in 1890, Wallace was the first winner, with Hooker following in 1892 and Huxley in 1894.[170] He surprised friends by turning to spiritualism in the 1860s, as did other free thinkers, including Robert Chambers and Darwin's cousin Hensleigh Wedgwood. For them evolutionary theory did not exclude religious faith, but confirmed their belief that higher forms of life would continue to evolve in the spiritual realm after death.[171] Wallace also became involved in social and political issues, including land nationalisation and women's suffrage. He was a prominent figure when the Linnaean Society marked the fiftieth anniversary of its seminal, though at the time unnoticed, meeting of 1 July 1858. The fittingly named 'Darwin–Wallace Celebration' took place on 1 July 1908 in the Institution of Civil Engineers in Great George Street, Westminster, the Linnaean Society's rooms in Burlington House not being big enough to hold the large gathering of scientists who attended. Present were several members of the Darwin family, including Darwin's son Frank, now a fellow of the Royal Society; representatives from the Danish, Swedish, and German embassies; and all the current leaders of natural history, including the zoologist Sir Ray Lankester and Darwin's cousin the geneticist Francis Galton, who both received medals at the event.

The president, Dr Dukinfield Scott, opened the proceedings by noting that they were commemorating the first time the 'now classic term' natural selection was used. He was delighted to say that of Darwin's original supporters and friends Wallace himself and Hooker, now Sir Joseph Hooker, were present. The oldest of Darwin's supporters, Lyell, had died in 1875, and the youngest, Huxley, in 1895. Wallace was the first recipient of the Darwin–Wallace Medal bearing the head of Darwin on one side and that of Wallace on the other, which had been specially struck for the occasion.[172] Hooker was presented with the second medal, then Galton and Lankester stepped up for theirs. The latter praised Huxley as 'the great and beloved teacher, the unequalled orator, the brilliant essayist, the unconquerable champion and literary swordsman' that he undoubtedly was.[173] The German ambassador collected a medal on behalf of Professor Ernst Haeckel of Jena University, the leading proponent of Darwinism in Germany. Darwin himself had noted in his autobiography in 1876 that his work had borne fruit especially among German scholars. 'In Germany', he wrote, 'a catalogue or bibliography on "Darwinismus" has appeared every year or two.'[174]

In his speech of thanks for his medal Hooker told his audience how the special meeting of 1 July 1858 had come about by the death of Robert Brown and the coincidental arrival in Darwin's letterbox of the essay from Wallace, and how, Darwin being ill, he and Lyell had undertaken to arrange for the papers of both men to be read. Lankester spoke of the subsequent work of the Abbé Mendel, which took the study of evolution forward. Nonetheless, he said, 'the main lines of the theory of Darwin and Wallace remain unchanged'; indeed, 'the more it is challenged by new suggestions and new hypotheses', the more brilliantly 'does the novelty, the importance, and the permanent value' of the work of the two men 'shine forth as the one great and epoch-making effort of human thought on this subject'.[175] On receiving his own medal Wallace said simply that he and Darwin had come to the idea of natural selection independently, but that the idea had occurred to Darwin twenty years earlier and he had been working patiently on it for that time, whereas he, Wallace, had merely had a 'flash of insight' which he sketched within a week in February 1858. He was proud to have shared this insight and to have explained and elucidated the theory in his own work, but to Darwin, 'my honoured friend and teacher', belonged the praise.[176]

Epilogue

The year in pantomime

EVERY LONDON THEATRE PRESENTED a pantomime over the Christmas and New Year period. Theatre-goers could choose from the famous houses in the West End – the two long-established patent theatres Drury Lane and Covent Garden, along with the Haymarket, the Adelphi on the Strand, the Princess's Theatre on Oxford Street, and the Lyceum just off the Strand. Poorer Londoners patronised smaller theatres, often attached to pubs, in unfashionable parts of the capital; there was Highbury Barn in the north, the Grecian Saloon, the Effingham Saloon and the Britannia Theatre in the East End, and the Royal Surrey Theatre on the south bank of the Thames. Rather as everyone, rich and poor, went to Epsom on Derby Day, so pantomime was for everyone too. Edward Harvey, a young postman whose diary survives, attended the cheap theatres in east London, the Britannia in Hoxton, where he lived and did his rounds, the Standard in Shoreditch, and the Grecian on Old Street.[1] At the other end of town Victoria and Albert took their children to Drury Lane or commissioned a pantomime to be played for them in Windsor Castle. Many theatres relied on the few weeks from Boxing Day to the end of January to ensure financial survival. The number of pantomimes performed had increased, as had the number of theatres to accommodate them, after the passing of the

Theatre Regulation Act of 1843, which removed the monopoly on presenting plays with dialogue previously enjoyed exclusively by the two patent theatres.[2]

Pantomimes, which up to the passing of the act had been slapstick knockabouts with comic songs and fairy scenes, were now able to add dialogue, often in the form of puns, rhyming couplets, and running commentaries on current affairs. In terms of scenery and spectacle, they became ever more elaborate, as new kinds of lighting and stage machinery came into use, especially for the high point of the show, the transformation scene, in which ordinary characters from the first part turned into the traditional figures of the harlequinade – the young lovers Harlequin and Columbine, the lecherous old Pantaloon, the boastful Scaramouche, and the silly boy Pierrot.[3] By the late 1850s the transformation scene itself had become the main talking point. The two most successful purveyors of Christmas entertainment were the writer Edward Blanchard and the scene painter William Beverley, who produced ever more extravagant effects. His work on Blanchard's *Robin Hood* at the Theatre Royal, Drury Lane, in December 1858 drew gasps of admiration when the transformation scene unfolded. In the opinion of the *Athenaeum* reviewer on 1 January 1859, the scene was 'one of Mr Beverley's best'; 'representing the Fairies' Retreat, it is a moving and unfolding piece of mechanical work, which develops into an ever-changing prospect of extraordinary brilliancy and beauty'.[4] The writer in the *Era* agreed, marvelling at the sight of 'the trees of Porcelain created with golden branches, which constitute the foreground, opening in the centre and unfolding a vista, through which a torrent of living water is seen sporting and tumbling over a precipitous incline of rockwork . . . This vast scenic effort will, no doubt, be the talk of the metropolis for some time to come.'[5] Drury Lane, which seated 3,000 people, was difficult to fill all the year round, and so relied on a successful pantomime to keep its proprietor solvent.[6]

In addition to the astounding transformation scenes and other startling effects, such as a revolving stage at the Princess's Theatre, where *The King of the Castle; or, Harlequin Prince Diamond and the Princess Brightness* was playing,[7] the pantomimes made sport of the main events of the preceding year. Topical allusions, jokes, and puns abounded. Naturally nothing was said, since nothing was known, about the new direction being taken in evolutionary theory, but some of the more visible advances in science and technology featured widely, as did the Great Stink and the plans to solve it.

Brunel's great ship, usually referred to as the *Leviathan*, the Atlantic telegraph cable, and Donati's Comet were popular topics. Blanchard's *Robin Hood* combines the comet and the cable with the hot summer weather in a scene in which the character 'The Year 1858' speaks:

I have no long tail like my friend the Comet.
I've been a curious year with splendid weather,
But not I think a bad sort altogether.
Observe the world round which you may be able
Perhaps to notice runs the Electric Cable.[8]

C.J. Collins's *Harlequin Father Thames; or, The River Queen and the Great Lord Mayor of London*, one of the best of the year's shows, includes a song about the Atlantic Cable:

And now the line has once been laid,
Let's hope the splice will soon be made,
By which once more from shore to shore
The flash shall fly to yankee land,
The work completed by the band
Who sailed in the Agamemnon.[9]

Of the many pantomimes which allude to Brunel's *Great Eastern*, Blanchard's other production for the 1858–9 season, *Harlequin and Old Izaak Walton; or, Tom Moore of Fleet Street, the Silver Trout, and the Seven Sisters of Tottenham*, produced at Sadler's Wells, plays on the change of name and the desperate plea for a new owner during the summer. A man crosses the stage with a board which first reads 'The Leviathan for sale', then changes to 'The Great Eastern for Sail & Steam'.[10] Thomas Mowbray's *Harlequin Master Walter; or, The Hunchback Nunky and the Little Fairies* at the Royal Soho Theatre also mentions the change of name and the fact that the ship, 'a goodly boat', has been, without money to finish fitting her out, 'rather difficult to get afloat'.[11] As if foreseeing the joint success in 1866 of the Atlantic Telegraph and the *Great Eastern*, George Conquest's *Harlequin Guy Faux* at the Grecian Saloon in Hoxton plays on the idea that the two innovations are alike in seeking to cover a larger area than had been achieved before. In this pantomime Antiope, the Amazonian queen, says she would invade England if she could get there. 'I'd engage the Leviathan, but she isn't fitted.' Meanwhile Electricity offers to send a message to History: 'Let me convey it, then no time is lost, / In half of no time half the world is crossed.'[12]

Passing fads and fancies and sensational news stories from 1858 found their way on to the stage too, as might be expected. The new Divorce Act gets some mention, though no individual cases are highlighted. The year's great fashion story features frequently. Crinolines crop up everywhere, exploited for their visual value and the chance to joke about the 'hoop de dooden do'. As we have seen, Amy Robsart is saved by her crinoline in *Kenilworth* at the Strand Theatre. W.E. Sutor's *Harlequin and the Forty Thieves; or, Ali Baba and the Fairy Ardinella*, playing at the Queen's Theatre, also exploits the craze for crinolines, as does Blanchard's *Robin Hood* at Drury Lane with its topical reference to the extra-wide dimensions of the brand new building of its rival patent theatre Covent Garden, the 'famous mansion' where 'e'en crinoline finds room for its expansion'. W. Cusnie's *Tit, Tat, Toe* at the Effingham Saloon in Whitechapel alludes to the fact that the craze was embraced by all classes of society; it features a simple farmer's daughter who comes back from London 'the pink of fashion, all dressed in Crynoline'.[13]

The year's popular entertainments are given the nod. Mowbray's *Harlequin Master Walter* includes a character whose singing is described as 'worse than Christy's Minstrels'. The comic business at the end of *Robin Hood* includes a board reading, 'Wanted a partner who understands Horse taming', followed by ostlers coming on stage with broomsticks and shouting 'Cruiser'. *Red Riding Hood* at Covent Garden featured two horses driving the wicked baron's carriage in tandem; one grows restive, and breaks away from the harness, only calming down when it is shown James Rarey's card, after which it lies down as if tamed.[14] *Harlequin Guy Faux* at the Grecian Saloon is one of several pantomimes to connect horse taming with 'wife taming' and the new Divorce Court. In *Harlequin and Old Izaak Walton* two placards appear in succession, one advertising the 'Yankee Horse Taming Establishment', the other the 'Wife Taming Establishment 1858'. As the *Era* reviewer notes, this Sadler's Wells offering embraces 'all the principal topics of the past year' – the comet, the Atlantic Cable, the art of horse taming, a theme which is 'improved upon by the Clown showing the art of taming a wife, a hint to husbands in need of it', all of which brings much laughter and applause.[15] In *Harlequin Father Thames* at the Royal Surrey Theatre the Clown helps a couple to meet and get married, then displays a door inscribed 'Office of the New Divorce Court now open'. *Tit, Tat, Toe* has the Fairy Queen rejoice in the new act, especially on behalf of women:

> You're right, the poor now have a chance, however low their station,
> If they can't knock their heads together, they have a separation.
> And should the men desert us, we're better off than many.
> An order from the Beak we get, and stick to every penny.
> And should they offer any threat, make any fuss or bother,
> We get a cheap divorce – are free –
>
>   . . . Yes free to try another.

Among the serious events of 1858 the India Act attracts some attention, following on from the frequent allusions to the Sepoy rebellion in the previous year's pantomimes. Buckstone's *Undine; or, Harlequin and the Spirit of the Waters* at the Haymarket finishes in a palace in Delhi with an allegory of the inauguration of the British Empire in India, which had formally taken place on 1 November.[16] In *Harlequin and Old Izaak Walton* Blanchard waves a cheeky farewell to the rotten old East India Company. An 'East Indian Nabob' comes on stage with a ticket reading 'The Hon East India Company', knocks on the door of the government office, and has his umbrella stolen from him by the clown, who tells him punningly, 'Your reign is over'. He is then soaked by 'The Victoria Extinguisher'.

The most topical topic of all was the Great Stink of the summer. Old Father Thames is the main character in several of the pantomimes, which bring verbal and visual ingenuity to the subject, and many whose titles do not mention the state of the Thames aim at least a passing swipe at the top news item of the scorching summer. *Harlequin and the Forty Thieves* at the Queen's Theatre makes much of the 'odour of the river' and the notion that its water is more poisonous than strychnine, a favourite subject of the previous year's pantomimes, after the Madeleine Smith poisoning case of summer 1857. So does *Harlequin Master Walter*, in which the wicked Sir Rowland, wishing to get rid of two young children, says he can easily buy poison for three pence an ounce, but 'Thames Water does as well', and is free.

Two of the most successful shows are set on or beside the Thames. Blanchard's *Harlequin and Old Izaak Walton* opens in 'the muddy mountains of Old Father Thames'. He himself is 'in a very bad state surrounded by four mudlarks [boys who collected items from the river at low tide] bearing large smelling bottles' and attended by four physicians named 'Parliament', 'The Press', 'Town Talk', and 'Public Opinion'. There are bottles labelled 'Deodorising Powder', 'Disinfecting Fluid', 'Lime', and 'Whitewash', the last of which is an indication that this pantomime has a sharp edge to its fun. The much criticised Board of Works is here represented as a doctor drawn along by snails and fussing about the cost of curing Old Father Thames. The medicines do not work, and Father Thames exclaims: 'I must be put to rights, / At present I'm the shockingest of sights. / Away with all of you, od's shrimps and frogs! / Hence throw your physic to the Isle of Dogs.'

As its title suggests, the most thoroughgoing critique of the state of the Thames comes in Collins's *Harlequin Father Thames*. More than any other pantomime, it attracted the blue pencil of William Donne, the examiner of plays in the Lord Chamberlain's Office. Whole passages of dialogue concerning parliament, the Board of Works and its personnel, as well as Sir Benjamin Hall and Alderman David Wire, recently elected as the lord mayor of London, were struck out on the grounds that they attacked public figures too directly. Any attempt to represent members of the royal family was prohibited, and a few of the plays were reprimanded for trying to smuggle in scenes representing Victoria and Albert's second son, Prince Alfred, as a midshipman, Alfred having joined the navy, aged fourteen, in the summer.[17] *Harlequin Father Thames* was one of the culprits; Donne demanded that the scene in which Prince Alfred 'rolls up his Trowsers and dances a hornpipe' be expunged.[18] Many passages mentioning cabinet ministers and other public figures by name also attracted his disapproval, as did too political a treatment of the Great Stink, though some things do seem to have got past him, such as the passage in *Tit, Tat, Toe* discussing the act allowing Jews to sit in the House of Commons and praising 'Little Lord John Russell' for his efforts on that issue.

The title character of *Harlequin Father Thames*, revealed in the opening scene at Waterloo Bridge 'at night' and at low tide, wears 'an immense beard' and carries his trident. He addresses the scavengers 'grubbing about' his muddy banks, punning freely on the geographical conjunction of the Thames and the Houses of Parliament: 'My house of Commons are the *common Sewers*. / With my favour they have great pretence / As common Sewers produce us common *scents*.' The sewers enter, 'allegorically represented', and are greeted by Father Thames as follows:

> . . . it's from you that I get my supplies.
> Each morning liberally you pour down
> Into my stream from every part of town.
> Go summon in the *Peers* from all the Bridges;
> This day I will confirm their privileges.

The wordplay on 'peers' (as in members of the House of Lords) and 'piers' (as in support structures on bridges) displeased the censor. When Westminster Bridge enters, much of his speech is ordered to be cut, including the following lines:

> Why there my liege indeed you speak aright.
> I am in a most miserable plight.
> I am you know the oldest of the *peers*
> And bending 'neath the heavy weight of years.
> Pray burden me no more with jokes to crack.

Father Thames replies: 'Why lately you had *Hall* upon your back', to which Westminster Bridge responds (critically): 'Yes so I had[;] in him lies all my guilt. / He should have seen me long ago *re-built*. / But he was rude – the rudest of all planners . . .' Chelsea Bridge comes on next, complaining that 'Sir Ben Hall denounced my toll', which means, as Father Thames, points out, that 'Big Ben is now without a *toll*' (punning on the recently cast chimes for the parliamentary clock named after Hall). Chelsea Bridge announces: 'That for a *cracked* joke may do very well / I meant the *Gentleman* and not the *Bell*.'

All these speeches were crossed out by the censor.

The play continues relentlessly with its sanitation theme; Father Thames is reluctant to agree to have new intercepting sewers to clean him up. Those empowered by parliament to set about organising the work – the chairman of the Board of Works (Thwaites) and various aldermen on the committee – are seen getting drunk and raucous in a pub with Father Thames rather than getting on with the job. The censor demands the deletion of much of this scene, and also that of a song, 'I'm a Wire, I'm a Wire', in which the name of the lord mayor of London is connected with the Atlantic Cable.

Despite the censor's attentions, enough carnivalesque satire of the authorities seems to have remained in the actual production of *Harlequin Father Thames* for the *Era* critic to single it out for praise as a hard-hitting 'sanitary epic' and one of the best pantomimes in recent years. It went down well with its 'crowded' audiences at the Royal Surrey too, with its 'strictures on city and corporate abuse; the Board of Works and its half measures; Commissioners of Sewers; and other popular themes of the day; and all given with a freedom and harmless energy that, while rendering each subject extremely amusing, elicits unbounded laughter and enjoyment from the audience, who relish, with unmistakable delight, every blow aimed at public and familiar abuse'.[19]

One hot summer's consequences

While the humour of the pantomimes may be lost on the page, the spectacle they presented to audiences was clearly extraordinary, with their scores of characters – both human and allegorical – taking to the stage, their frequent changes of scene and costume, talking bridges and sewers, and elaborate effects such as muddy rivers turning into crystal caverns and forests and fountains sprouting up suddenly before the eyes of astonished audiences. In terms of the themes chosen to characterise the year just passed, these were naturally the ones which had most preoccupied the press and public during the year. There were the trivial or ephemerally popular attractions – the Christy Minstrels, the Great American Horse Tamer, and the new widths achieved by the ongoing fashion for the crinoline. Then there were the innovative and exciting events which held promise of future progress: the semi-successful laying of the Atlantic telegraph cable, the sight of Donati's Comet (and the fact that photography had progressed enough to capture it), the magnitude and tribulations of the *Great Eastern*.

Beyond the scope of topical theatrical entertainments lay more far-reaching events which had their origin in the hot summer of 1858. These included the matters consuming criminal and civil courts, especially those relating to the very first examples coming to court under the life-changing new law of divorce. Not unrelated to marriage and divorce settlements was the flush of cases involving asylums and the remit of the Lunacy Commission. Some results lay further in the future, the chief example being the progress in medicine following the passing of the Medical Act, which began the process of putting medicine on a proper professional footing and paved the way for better medical education and greater equality of opportunity for doctors. Though the tortuous procedure by which Baron de Rothschild was at last enabled to take his seat in the House of Commons affected only him, his brother, and David Salomons in the first few years, it marked, alongside the little-noticed act to abolish the property qualification hitherto required of prospective MPs, further progress in the history of political reform from the great Reform Act of 1832 to the arrival of universal suffrage in the early twentieth century.

As the pantomimes record, the most significant public event was the Great Stink, which finally, in the hottest of June days, brought about the hugely important sanitary measures for the world's largest city. Not only was the Thames cleansed over the next decade, but the whole city was structurally, infrastructurally, and visibly improved by the Thames embankments which carried Bazalgette's sewers and their burden of sewage while at the same time easing road traffic from the congested Strand, embracing the new underground railway system, and enhancing the look of London above ground. The whole modernisation of the city which was now undertaken took longer than the five-and-a-half years Disraeli envisaged for the Thames when pushing through the act in July 1858, and cost more than the £3 million he estimated for the job. On the other hand, the work which was eventually completed was well worth the time and money spent. By 1865 the Victoria and Chelsea Embankments on the north side of the river and the Albert Embankment on the south were under construction – 52 acres having been reclaimed from the river to create them – and 82 miles of sewers had been laid. The total cost in the end was just over £4 million for the main drainage and £2.5 million for the embankments, with more spent on enhancing parks, gardens, streets, and bridges.[20]

After Bazalgette's death in 1891 the *Illustrated London News* reminded Londoners what the city had been like 'before those vast undertakings of the Metropolitan Board of Works, the system of Main Drainage and the magnificent Thames Embankment, which had contributed so much to sanitary improvement and to the convenience and stateliness of this immense city'.[21]

Bazalgette himself recalled not long before his death that he got 'the most credit for the Thames Embankment, but it wasn't anything like such a job as the drainage':

> The fall in the river isn't above three inches a mile; for sewage we want a fall of a couple of feet and that kept taking us down below the river and when we got to a certain depth we had to pump up again. It was certainly a very troublesome job. We would sometimes spend weeks in drawing out plans and then suddenly come across some railway or canal that upset everything, and we had to begin all over again. It was tremendously hard work.[22]

The vital part of the construction, the intercepting sewers which improved public health by safely removing the ever-enlarging city's ever-increasing sewage, was invisible and therefore received less consideration than the above-ground grandeur of the embankments.

If Disraeli's expert steering of the Thames Bill through parliament was the greatest political and public achievement of summer 1858, with long-lasting consequences for the inhabitants of London and for engineering and construction generally, the greatest individual and private success belonged to Darwin. His work had been taking shape as it were subterraneously for twenty years, and might have gone on like that for many more years, if it had not been for his receiving out of the blue a letter and some notes from a colleague on the other side of the world which caused him to set about making his theory public by finally completing and publishing *On the Origin of Species*. His upheaval in June 1858 remained hidden from public sight, with only a handful of firm friends aware of the likely storm to come when his work appeared above ground the following year.

For Disraeli summer 1858 was the time of his triumphant arrival as a politician to be reckoned with, a man wielding political power at last; for Darwin it was a critical moment when he faced up to his desires and difficulties, as well as his responsibility to give to the public the findings of his researches.

By nature Darwin was as private a man as Disraeli was a flamboyantly public one. Between these two extremes was Dickens, indisputably a public man by virtue of his remarkable literary success. He was also by nature a showman, a man who enjoyed being in the spotlight, whether acting in plays, performing magic tricks at children's parties, or giving dramatic readings from his novels. In 1858, however, he was desperate to deflect attention away from his relationship with Ellen Ternan and his shabby treatment of his wife. For such a clever man, he acted foolishly, losing his head in those hot summer months, and unnecessarily drawing attention to his miserable private life by printing his personal statement about the separation from Catherine and demanding that his adoring readers accept his nobility and truthfulness just when he was most equivocating. Of these three great Victorians, Dickens experienced the least successful or promising time in 1858. He wrote no novel and enjoyed no steady happiness. But his reputation did not suffer much, he drank in the overwhelming success of his new venture of countrywide public readings, and two years after the dreadful summer of 1858 he began *Great Expectations*, his greatest novel and one which presents, with the astuteness of bitter personal experience, the inner life of an unhappy man who, recognising and regretting his mistakes, bears his burden of guilt as best he can.

For all three men the hot summer of 1858 presented new challenges, as it did also for others in the public eye, among them Thackeray, Sir Edward and Rosina Bulwer Lytton, Isabella and Henry Robinson and Dr Edward Lane, Lord Derby and his son Lord Stanley, Brunel and Bazalgette, Queen Victoria as India came under direct British rule, Alfred Russel Wallace on his distant travels, London journalists like Yates and Sala and the *Punch* set, the lawyer Edwin James, artists of contemporary life like Frith and Egg, and the rising star in English fiction, George Eliot. The interactions and connections between these people were sometimes unexpected, as, for example, the friendship between the retiring Darwin and the inadvertently scandalous Edward Lane, or the hearing of Frederick Dickens's divorce proceedings in the same court and on the same day as the final judgment in the case of Isabella Robinson. There is also the coincidence in May and June of Bulwer Lytton and his friend Dickens making allegations of madness about their respective wives, the provocative and hysterical Rosina and the unfortunate and stoical Catherine. These people, along with many Londoners who had no particular claim to fame, were touched in different ways and to different degrees by the public events of the summer, while the events themselves, from the decision about rectifying the catastrophic state of the Thames to parliamentary legislation on political representation, foreign affairs, divorce, and medicine, were in turn affected by the increasing power of the press to influence outcomes. Nowhere was this more clearly shown than in the matter of the fetid Thames, about which the newspapers kept up a constant howl of protest. The backdrop to London living, especially along the banks of the capital's river, was the unprecedented, lasting, and oppressive summer heat.

Endnotes

Chapter One: 1858 in history

1. John Lothrop Motley to his wife, 20 June 1858, *The Correspondence of John Lothrop Motley*, ed. George William Curtis, 2 vols (London, 1889), vol. 1, p. 271.
2. G.M. Trevelyan, *British History in the Nineteenth Century (1782–1901)* (London, 1922), p. 292.
3. Charles Darwin, *On the Origin of Species by Means of Natural Selection, or the Preservation of Favoured Races in the Struggle for Life*, ed. John Burrow (Harmondsworth, 1968), pp. 53–63. This edition reproduces the first edition, with 'An Historical Sketch' added. For the immediate success of Chambers's *Vestiges of Creation*, the intelligent work of a scientific amateur, of which Darwin is respectfully critical, see James A. Secord, *Victorian Sensation: The Extraordinary Publication, Reception and Secret Authorship of 'Vestiges of the Natural History of Creation'* (London, 2000).
4. *The Autobiography of Charles Darwin*, ed. Nora Barlow (London, 1958), pp. 76–7.
5. Ibid., p. 72.
6. See Bill Luckin, *Pollution and Control: A Social History of the Thames in the Nineteenth Century* (Bristol, 1986), Stephen Halliday, *The Great Stink of London: Sir Joseph Bazalgette and the Cleansing of the Victorian Capital* (Stroud, 1999) and *The Great Filth: The War against Disease in Victorian England* (Stroud, 2007), Michelle Allen, *Cleansing the City: Sanitary Geographies in Victorian London* (Athens, Ohio, 2008), and Lee Jackson, *Dirty Old London: The Victorian Fight against Filth* (New Haven, Connecticut, 2014).
7. See Adrian Vaughan, *Isambard Kingdom Brunel: Engineering Knight-Errant* (London, 1991), and R. Angus Buchanan, *The Life and Times of Isambard Kingdom Brunel* (London, 2002).
8. See A.R. Bennett, *London and Londoners in the Eighteen-Fifties and Sixties* (London, 1924), and Gillian Cookson, *The Cable: Wire to the New World* (Stroud, 2012).
9. See Jay M. Pasachoff, Roberta J.M. Olson and Martha L. Hazen, 'The Earliest Comet Photographs: Usherwood, Bond, and Donati 1858', *Journal for the History of Astronomy*, vol. 27 (1996), pp. 129–45.
10. G.A. Sala, *Twice Round the Clock, or Hours of the Day and Night in London* (London, 1859), reprint edited by Philip Collins (Leicester, 1971), p. 164. The work was first published serially in the journal *Welcome Guest* from May to November 1858 For the history of photography

in London, see Gavin Stamp, *The Changing Metropolis: Earliest Photographs of London 1839–1879* (Harmondsworth, 1984).

11. *The Birthplace of Podgers*, in *Lacy's Acting Edition*, vol. 35 (1858), and *Your Likeness – One Shilling!*, in ibid., vol. 36 (1858).

12. Edward A. Copland, *Photography for the Many*, number 11 (1858), pp. 25, 29.

13. Richard Owen, *President's Address to the British Association for the Advancement of Science*, 1858, Internet Archive, p. 62.

14. Ibid., pp. 97, 98, 102. See also Donald J. Olsen, *The Growth of Victorian London* (London, 1976).

15. For assessments of Chadwick's career, see S.E. Finer, *The Life and Times of Sir Edwin Chadwick* (London, 1952), and Christopher Hamlin, *Public Health and Social Justice in the Age of Chadwick: Britain 1800–1854* (Cambridge, 1998).

16. The work of the 'nightsoil men', of 'mudlarks' (collectors of debris from the Thames foreshore at low tide), and of 'toshers' (scavengers in the sewers) was brought to the public's attention by Henry Mayhew in his articles during 1849 and 1850 for the *Morning Chronicle*, reprinted in 1851 as *London Labour and the London Poor*; see the selected edition by Robert Douglas-Fairhurst (Oxford, 2010).

17. See Martin Daunton, 'London's "Great Stink" and Victorian Urban Planning', BBC History (2004).

18. For Snow's career and the late appreciation of his discovery, see Peter Vinten-Johansen et al., *Cholera, Chloroform, and the Science of Medicine: A Life of John Snow* (Oxford, 2003). See also Halliday, *The Great Stink*, pp. 129–37, and David S. Barnes, *The Great Stink of Paris and the Nineteenth-Century Struggle against Filth and Germs* (Baltimore, Maryland, 2006), pp. 9–10, 243–4.

19. Owen, *President's Address*, pp. 102, 104, 105.

20. Ibid., p. 105.

21. Snow, 'Cholera and the Water Supply', *The Times*, 26 June 1856.

22. See 'Health of London', *Era*, 27 June 1858.

23. See Halliday, *The Great Stink*, pp. 61–9.

24. Dante Gabriel Rossetti to Robert Brough, 7 July 1858, *The Correspondence of Dante Gabriel Rossetti*, ed. William E. Fredeman, 10 vols (Woodbridge, 2002–10), vol. 2, p. 219.

25. *The Times*, 3 July 1858 (quoting the *Globe*). The temperature in Hyde Park on 30 June was given in *The Times* on 2 July 1858.

26. Edwin Lankester, 'The Silver Thames', *Athenaeum*, 17 July 1858. For Lankester's career, see Mary P. English, *Victorian Values: The Life and Times of Dr Edwin Lankester, MD, FRS* (London, 1990).

27. *Punch*, vol. 35 (24 July 1858), p. 33. For cartoons featuring Father Thames, see *Punch*, vol. 35 (3 and 10 July 1858), pp. 5, 15.

28. Editorial, *The Times*, 21 July 1858.

29. Karl Marx, 'Lord Palmerston', *People's Paper*, 22 October 1853, *Marx–Engels Collected Works*, 50 vols (London, New York, Moscow, 1975–2005), vol. 12, p. 345.

30. Ibid., vol. 12, p. 346.

31. Dickens, speech to the Administrative Reform Association, 27 June 1855, *The Speeches of Charles Dickens*, ed. K.J. Fielding (Hemel Hempstead, 1988), pp. 198n, 199, 200.

32. See *ODNB* entry for Clanricarde.

33. *Punch*, vol. 34 (23 January 1858), p. 35.

34. *Illustrated London News*, vol. 32 (27 February 1858), p. 201.

35. Prince Albert, memorandum, 4 September 1858, *The Letters of Queen Victoria: A Selection from Her Majesty's Correspondence between the Years 1837 and 1861*, ed. A.C. Benson and Viscount Esher, 3 vols (London, 1907), vol. 3, pp. 381–2.

36. Marx, 'The Attempt upon the Life of Bonaparte', *New York Daily Tribune*, 22 February 1858, *Marx–Engels Collected Works*, vol. 12, p. 458.

37. Sir George Grey to Lord John Russell, 2 February 1858, *The Later Correspondence of Lord John Russell 1840–1878*, ed. G.P. Gooch, 2 vols (London, 1925), vol. 2, p. 225.

38. Sir James Graham to Lord John Russell, 4 February 1858, ibid., vol. 2, p. 226.

39. 'The Derby Ministry', *Bentley's Miscellany*, vol. 43 (April 1858), p. 331.

40. Lord Stanley, journal, 21 February 1858, *Benjamin Disraeli Letters*, ed. J.A.W. Gunn, M.G. Wiebe, Michel W. Pharand et al., 10 vols so far (Toronto, 1982–), vol. 7 (2004), p. 124n.

41. See the summary of his career in Robert Blake, *Disraeli* (London, 1966), pp. 757–66.

42. Disraeli, the 'Mutilated Diary' for 1833, see Thea Van Dam, *My Dearest Ben: An Intimate Glimpse into the World of Benjamin Disraeli, his Family and the Women in his Life – through their Letters*, Buckinghamshire Papers, number 16 (Aylesbury, 2008), p. 47.

43. Disraeli to Lord Derby, 22 February 1858, *Letters*, vol. 7, p. 124.

44. See William Flavelle Monypenny and George Earle Buckle, *The Life of Benjamin Disraeli*, new and revised edition, 2 vols (London, 1929), vol. 1, pp. 1520ff.

45. Joseph Irving, *The Annals of Our Time: A Diurnal of Events, Social and Political, Home and Foreign, from the Accession of Queen Victoria, June 20, 1837, to the Peace of Versailles, February 28, 1871*, new revised edition (London, 1880), p. 510.

46. Disraeli to Queen Victoria, 12 March and 24 June 1858, *Letters*, vol. 7, pp. 142, 215.

47. Disraeli to Queen Victoria, 24 June 1858, ibid., vol. 7, pp. 215–16.

48. 'The Closing Session', *Era*, 1 August 1858.

49. See W.D. Jones, *Lord Derby and Victorian Conservatism* (Oxford, 1956), pp. 238–40.

50. 'Prorogation of Parliament', *The Times*, 3 August 1858.

51. See Stephanie J. Snow, *Blessed Days of Anaesthesia: How Anaesthetics Changed the World* (Oxford, 2008).

52. For Wakley see John Hostettler, *Thomas Wakley: An Improbable Radical* (Chichester, 1993). For medical reform in the nineteenth century see Ivan Waddington, *The Medical Profession in the Industrial Revolution* (Dublin, 1984); Dorothy Porter and Roy Porter (eds), *Doctors, Politics and Society: Historical Essays* (Amsterdam, 1993); W.F. Bynum, *Science and the Practice of Medicine in the Nineteenth Century* (Cambridge, 1994); Vivian Nutton and Roy Porter (eds), *The History of Medical Education in Britain* (Amsterdam, 1995); Michael J.D. Roberts, 'The Politics of Professionalization: MPs, Medical Men, and the 1858 Medical Act', *Medical History*, vol. 53 (January 2009), pp. 37–56.

53. See Waddington, *The Medical Profession*, pp. 53–4, 96–107.

54. 'The Doctors and their Bills', *Punch*, vol. 34 (12 June 1858), p. 235.

55. See Waddington, *The Medical Profession*, pp. 107–11.

56. *Hansard*, vol. 127, col. 1092, 3 June 1853.

57. Dickens, 'The Murdered Person', *Household Words*, vol. 14 (11 October 1856), p. 290.

58. [Charles Egan], *A Handy Book on the New Law of Divorce and Matrimonial Causes, and the Practice of the Divorce Court* (London, 1860), pp. 6–7.

59. *Hansard*, vol. 145, col. 486, 19 May 1857.

60. Ibid., vol. 142, col. 406, 20 May 1856.

61. *Crim. Con. Gazette*, vol. 2 (1839), p. 75, quoted in Lawrence Stone, *Road to Divorce, England 1530–1987* (Oxford, 1990, paperback 1992), p. 366. Stone's is the most comprehensive study of the history of divorce in England.

62. Stone, *Road to Divorce*, p. 357, *A Handy Book*, p. 8.

63. Michael Slater, *Charles Dickens* (New Haven, Conn. and London, 2009, paperback 2011), p. 67.

64. *Morning Chronicle*, 11 October 1836, reprinted in Charles Dickens, *Sketches by Boz*, ed. Dennis Walder (Harmondsworth, 1995), pp. 110–12. See also Slater, *Charles Dickens*, p. 33.

65. Charles Dickens, *David Copperfield* (1850), chap. 23.

66. Caroline Norton, *A Letter to the Queen on Lord Chancellor Cranworth's Marriage and Divorce Bill* (1855), p. 154. For Caroline Norton's life see Diane Atkinson, *The Criminal Conversation of Mrs Norton* (London, 2012).

67. *Hansard*, vol. 147, cols 1021, 1073, 4 August 1857; col. 1996, 21 August 1857; col. 2036, 24 August 1857.

68. Rosina Bulwer Lytton conducted a campaign against her husband, often in novels, including *The World and his Wife: or, A Person of Consequence*, which she published in May 1858.

69. *Morning Chronicle*, 12 January 1858.
70. *Punch*, vol. 34 (9 January 1858), p. 11, and vol. 35 (6 November 1858), p. 184.
71. See *Hansard*, vol. 145, col. 532, 19 May 1857.
72. Letters of Dr John Lee, May–June 1858, MS 2876, Lambeth Palace Library.
73. For a full account of the case see Kate Summerscale, *Mrs Robinson's Disgrace: The Private Diary of a Victorian Lady* (London, 2012).
74. Dickens to Forster, 30 January 1858, *The Letters of Charles Dickens*, Pilgrim Edition, ed. Madeleine House, Graham Storey, Kathleen Tillotson et al., 12 vols (Oxford, 1965–2002), vol. 8, p. 511.
75. See George Curtis to Thackeray, 17 June 1858, *The Letters and Private Papers of William Makepeace Thackeray*, ed. Gordon N. Ray, 4 vols (Cambridge, Mass., 1945–6), vol. 4, p. 92; John Blackwood to G.H. Lewes, 23 May 1858, *The George Eliot Letters*, ed. Gordon S. Haight, 9 vols (New Haven, Conn., 1954–5, 1978), vol. 2, p. 458.
76. See *Trollope: The Critical Heritage*, ed. Donald Smalley (London, 1969), pp. 71–2, 73, 76.
77. For George Eliot's life and career see Rosemary Ashton, *George Eliot: A Life* (London, 1996, reprinted 1997).
78. See George Eliot, *Adam Bede* (1859), chap. 17; John Blackwood to George Eliot, 30 January 1857, *The George Eliot Letters*, vol. 2, p. 291; Dickens to John Forster, ?mid-April 1857, *Letters*, vol. 8, p. 317.
79. The triptych is in Tate Britain. For the symbolism see Susan P. Casteras, *Images of Victorian Womanhood in English Art* (London, 1987), pp. 61–3.
80. Thomas Carlyle to Jane Carlyle, 15 July 1857, and to John Carlyle, 28 January 1858, and Jane Carlyle to Mary Russell, 19 November 1857, *The Collected Letters of Thomas and Jane Welsh Carlyle*, Duke–Edinburgh Edition, ed. C.R. Sanders, K.J. Fielding, Clyde de L. Ryals et al., 42 vols so far (Durham, North Carolina, 1970–), vol. 32, p. 188, vol. 33, pp. 173, 120.
81. See Rosemary Ashton, *Thomas and Jane Carlyle: Portrait of a Marriage* (London, 2002, reprinted 2003), chaps 14 and 15.
82. *Annual Register* (1858), p. 90; *Bentley's Miscellany*, vol. 43 (May 1858), p. 441.
83. See Richard D. Altick, *The Shows of London* (Cambridge, Mass. and London, 1978), p. 411.
84. For details of Frith's painting and career see Aubrey Noakes, *William Frith: Extraordinary Victorian Painter* (London, 1978), and Mary Cowling, *The Artist as Anthropologist: The Representation of Type and Character in Victorian Art* (Cambridge, 1989).
85. *Comic Songs and Recitations forming Mr Merryman's Magazine of Miscellaneous Mirth* (1840).
86. G.A. Sala, *Gaslight and Daylight, with Some London Scenes They Shine Upon* (London, 1859), p. 384.
87. See Roger Mortimer, *The History of the Derby Stakes* (London, 1962).
88. See Dickens, *Letters*, vol. 3, pp. 581–2n.
89. Dickens to Thomas Chapman, ?28 June 1846, *Letters*, vol. 4, pp. 576–7, and to Richard Watson, 21 July 1849, ibid., vol. 5, p. 580.
90. Disraeli to Lady Londonderry, 16 September 1857, *Letters*, vol. 7, p. 67.
91. Disraeli to Sarah Disraeli, 8 March 1838, ibid., vol. 3, p. 33.
92. Disraeli to Sarah Disraeli, ?13 February 1839, ibid., vol. 3, p. 143.
93. See Darwin to Joseph Hooker, 26 May 1859, *The Correspondence of Charles Darwin*, ed. Frederick Burkhardt et al., 22 vols so far (Cambridge, 1985–), vol. 7, p. 300; to Hooker, 18 April 1860, ibid., vol. 8, p. 163; and to Hooker, 27–28 September 1865, ibid., vol. 13, p. 246.
94. See, for example, Darwin to Charles Lyell, 9 August 1838, *Correspondence*, vol. 2, p. 98; to Mary-Anne Herbert, 5 May 1842, ibid., vol. 2, p. 318; and to Hooker, 25 September 1853, ibid., vol. 5, pp. 155–6.
95. Darwin to Hooker, 10 December 1864, ibid., vol. 12, p. 459.
96. Disraeli, *Tancred*, 3 vols (1847, reprinted 1864), vol. 1, pp. 225–6.
97. See Barbara Black, *A Room of His Own: A Literary-Cultural Study of Victorian Clubland* (Athens, Ohio, 2012), pp. 59–63.

98. Darwin, *Autobiography*, pp. 34–5.

99. Blake, *Disraeli*, pp. 81–2, 88–9, 435.

Chapter Two: May 1858

1. 'Banquet at the Royal Academy of Arts', *The Times*, 3 May 1858.

2. See *ODNB* entry for David Salomons.

3. 'Banquet at the Royal Academy of Arts', *The Times*, 3 May 1858.

4. See Slater, *Charles Dickens*, pp. 68–9, and Thackeray, *Letters and Private Papers*, vol. 1, p. cxxi. For a fictionalised account of the relationship between Dickens and Seymour, which criticises the part played by Dickens in the tragedy, see Stephen Jarvis, *Death and Mr Pickwick* (London, 2014).

5. Dickens, *Speeches*, p. 262.

6. Thackeray, *Letters and Private Papers*, vol. 4, p. 392; Dickens to Thackeray, 28 April 1858, *Letters*, vol. 8, p. 551.

7. See *Athenæum*, 1 and 8 May 1858, *Illustrated London News*, 8 May 1858, and *Era*, 30 May 1858.

8. Rossetti to William Bell Scott, *c.* 21 June 1858, *Correspondence*, vol. 2, p. 213.

9. Dickens, *Speeches*, pp. 246–53.

10. See Dickens to Wilkie Collins, 21 March 1858, *Letters*, vol. 8, p. 535.

11. See Slater, *Charles Dickens*, pp. 426–7, 435–6.

12. Francesco Berger, *Reminiscences, Impressions and Anecdotes* (London, 1913), pp. 19, 24.

13. Ibid., p. 22.

14. Queen Victoria, journal, 4 July 1857, online at http://www.queenvictoriasjournals.org, vol. 43, p. 202.

15. Dickens to Frederick Evans, 16 March 1858, *Letters*, vol. 8, p. 533.

16. Slater, *Charles Dickens*, pp. 461–8.

17. 'Mr Charles Dickens', *The Times*, 16 April 1858.

18. 'Mr Charles Dickens and "The Cricket on the Hearth" ', *Era*, 2 May 1858.

19. Ibid.

20. Dickens to Angela Burdett-Coutts, 9 May 1858, *Letters*, vol. 8, p. 558.

21. See Michael Slater, *Dickens and Women* (London, 1983), pp. 145–6.

22. See Dickens, *Letters*, vol. 8, pp. 558–60n.

23. For a history of the journalistic activities on Wellington Street, see Mary L. Shannon, *Dickens, Reynolds, and Mayhew on Wellington Street: The Print Culture of a Victorian Street* (Farnham, 2015).

24. See Slater, *Charles Dickens*, pp. 471, 587; Lillian Nayder, *The Other Dickens: A Life of Catherine Hogarth* (Ithaca, New York, 2011), pp. 245, 285, 287.

25. See *Macready's Reminiscences, and Selections from his Diaries*, ed. Sir Frederick Pollock, 2 vols (London, 1875); Tracy C. Davis, 'Actresses and Prostitutes in Victorian London', *Theatre Research International*, vol. 13 (1988), pp. 221–34.

26. Dickens to Wilkie Collins, 2 August 1857, *Letters*, vol. 8, p. 394.

27. Dickens to Frank Stone, 17 August 1857, and to Angela Burdett-Coutts, 5 September 1857, ibid., vol. 8, p. 412 and n., p. 433 and n. See also Claire Tomalin, *The Invisible Woman: The Story of Nelly Ternan and Charles Dickens* (London, 1990).

28. Dickens to Angela Burdett-Coutts, 5 September 1857, *Letters*, vol. 8, pp. 432–3.

29. Dickens to Wilkie Collins, 29 August 1857, ibid., vol. 8, p. 423.

30. See Andrew Lycett, *Wilkie Collins: A Life of Sensation* (London, 2014).

31. Dickens to John Forster, 3 September 1857, *Letters*, vol. 8, p. 430; Slater, *Charles Dickens*, p. 375.

32. Dickens to the Hon. Mrs Richard Watson, 7 December 1857, *Letters*, vol. 8, p. 488; see also Dickens to Lady Duff Gordon, 23 January 1858, ibid., vol. 8, p. 508.

33. See Dickens to Georgina Hogarth, 15 September 1857, ibid., vol. 8, p. 447 and n.

34. Dickens and Collins, 'The Lazy Tour of Two Idle Apprentices', chap. 5, *Household Words*, 31 October 1857, reprinted in *Dickens' Journalism*, ed. Michael Slater, 4 vols (London, 1994–2000), vol. 3, p. 471.
35. Dickens to Wilkie Collins, 21 March 1858, *Letters*, vol. 8, p. 536.
36. Dickens to Angela Burdett-Coutts, 19 May 1858, ibid., vol. 8, p. 565.
37. Catherine Dickens to Angela Burdett-Coutts, 19 May 1858, ibid., vol. 8, p. 565n.
38. Dickens to Angela Burdett-Coutts, 19 May 1858, ibid., vol. 8, p. 565.
39. Dickens to Macready, 28 May 1858, ibid., vol. 8, p. 570.
40. See Michael Slater, *The Great Charles Dickens Scandal* (New Haven, Conn. and London, 2012), chap. 1.
41. Thackeray to his mother, early June 1858, *Letters and Private Papers*, vol. 4, p. 86.
42. See *The Times*, 21 May and 24 June 1858.
43. Ibid., 20 May 1858.
44. See *Racing Times,* 17 May 1858, and *St James's Chronicle*, 20 May 1858.
45. J. Ewing Ritchie, *Here and There in London* (1859), pp. 99, 101.
46. *Era*, 16 May 1858.
47. 'The Great Derby Extravaganza', *Racing Times*, 17 May 1858.
48. *Punch*, vol. 34 (22 May 1858), p. 212.
49. For a clear analysis of the very complicated India question, see Jones, *Lord Derby and Victorian Conservatism*, pp. 234–7.
50. Dickens to Angela Burdett-Coutts, 4 October 1857, *Letters*, vol. 8, p. 459.
51. Dickens to Cavendish Spencer Boyle, 5 February 1858, ibid., vol. 8, p. 516.
52. Thomas Carlyle to John Strachey, 13 September 1857, *Collected Letters*, vol. 33, p. 81.
53. Marx, 'The Indian Revolt', *New York Daily Tribune*, 16 September 1857, *Marx–Engels Collected Works*, vol. 15, pp. 353–6.
54. William Howard Russell, *My Diary in India, in the Year 1858–9*, 2 vols (1860), vol. 1, p. 356.
55. Lord Ellenborough's dispatch to Lord Canning, 19 April 1858, quoted in Irving, *Annals of Our Time*, p. 518.
56. Lord Ellenborough to Queen Victoria, 10 May 1858, *Letters of Queen Victoria*, vol. 3, p. 358.
57. Memorandum by Prince Albert, 16 May 1858, ibid., vol. 3, p. 367.
58. Disraeli to Queen Victoria, 21 May 1858, *Letters*, vol. 7, pp. 189–90.
59. Disraeli's speech at Slough, 26 May 1858, reported in the *Era*, 30 May 1858.
60. *Disraeli's Reminiscences*, ed. Helen M. Swartz and Marvin Swartz (London, 1975), p. 113.
61. Lord Derby to Queen Victoria, 23 May 1858, *Letters of Queen Victoria*, vol. 3, p. 369.
62. The *Era* described Palmerston and Russell as 'two Artful Dodgers', 9 May 1858.
63. See R.L. Leonard, *Nineteenth-Century British Premiers: Pitt to Rosebery* (New York, 2008), p. 227.
64. Disraeli to Queen Victoria, 19 April 1858, *Letters*, vol. 7, p. 170.
65. Disraeli to Sarah Brydges Willyams, 22 May 1858, ibid., vol. 7, p. 191.
66. *Bentley's Miscellany*, vol. 44 (July 1858), p. 3.
67. 'Public Dinner to the Chancellor of the Exchequer', *Era*, 30 May 1858; see also *The Times*, 27 May 1858, and Irving, *Annals of Our Time*, p. 520.
68. Irving, *Annals of Our Time*, p. 521.
69. 'House of Lords, Monday 31 May', *The Times*, 1 June 1858.
70. Irving, *Annals of Our Time*, p. 521.
71. See Joseph S. Meisel, 'Humour and Insult in the House of Commons: The Case of Palmerston and Disraeli', *Parliamentary History*, vol. 28, part 2 (2009), pp. 238–9, 244.
72. John Lothrop Motley to his wife, 6 June 1858, *Correspondence*, vol. 1, p. 249.
73. Benjamin Disraeli, *Sybil, or the Two Nations* (1845), book 4, chap. 14.
74. See Patrick Leary, *The 'Punch' Brotherhood: Table Talk and Print Culture in Mid-Victorian London* (London, 2010), p. 42.
75. Leonard, *Nineteenth-Century British Premiers*, pp. 271–6; Disraeli, *Letters*, vol. 7, pp. xx, 51.

76. For Disraeli's relationships with men and references to homosexuality in his novels and in Lady Lytton's writings, see William Kuhn, *The Politics of Pleasure: A Portrait of Benjamin Disraeli* (London, 2006).

77. See Daisy Hay, *Mr and Mrs Disraeli: A Strange Romance* (London, 2015), p. 111.

78. Nathaniel Parker Willis, *Pencillings by the Way* (New York, 1852), quoted in Hay, *Mr and Mrs Disraeli*, p. 49.

79. See Kuhn, *The Politics of Pleasure*, pp. 168, 169.

80. See Patrick Waddington, *Turgenev and England* (New York, 1981), p. 67.

81. See Hay, *Mr and Mrs Disraeli*, pp. 134, 171–2, 214.

82. Ibid., p. 248.

83. For examples of cases continuing from 1857 or requiring refinement before returning before the new court, see *The Times*, 12 and 18 January, 10 February, 3 March, 17 April, 1 May 1858.

84. See Summerscale, *Mrs Robinson's Disgrace*, pp. 111–12, and the *ODNB* entries for Cresswell, Wightman, and Cockburn.

85. *ODNB* entry for Sir Cresswell Cresswell.

86. See *The Times*, 6 May 1858.

87. *Manchester Times*, 15 May 1858.

88. See Summerscale, *Mrs Robinson's Disgrace*, pp. 138, 260; *St James's Chronicle*, 13 May 1858; *Era*, 16 May 1858.

89. 'The New Divorce Court', *Era*, 16 May 1858.

90. *The Times*, 13 May 1858.

91. Ibid., and Disraeli, *Letters*, vol. 7, pp. 127–8n.

92. See, for example, Disraeli to Delane, 25 February 1858, ibid., vol. 7, pp. 129–30.

93. Lord Derby to Disraeli, 25 February 1858, ibid., vol. 7, p. 129n.

94. Disraeli to Bulwer Lytton, 24 February 1858, ibid., vol. 7, p. 127.

95. See Leslie Mitchell, *Bulwer Lytton: The Rise and Fall of a Victorian Man of Letters* (London and New York, 2003).

96. Rosina Bulwer Lytton, *The World and his Wife: or, A Person of Consequence*, vol. 1, p. 19.

97. Ibid., vol. 1, p. 33.

98. For letters complaining of her publisher, see, for example, Rosina to Rebecca Ryves, 8 March 1858, *The Collected Letters of Rosina Bulwer Lytton*, ed. Marie Mulvey-Roberts, 3 vols (London, 2008), vol. 3, p. 32.

99. Rosina Bulwer Lytton, *Very Successful!*, 3 vols (1856), vol. 1, p. ix.

100. Ibid., vol. 1, p. 284, vol. 2, pp. 58, 61, 76.

101. Ibid., vol. 2, pp.178–9.

102. Ibid., vol. 2, pp. 181, 187, vol. 1, p. 166.

103. Rosina Bulwer Lytton to Lord Derby, 23 February 1858, *Collected Letters*, vol. 3, p. 23.

104. Rosina Bulwer Lytton to Lord Stanley, 23 February 1858, ibid., vol. 3, pp. 25–6.

105. Rosina Bulwer Lytton to Lord Lyndhurst, 23 February 1858, ibid., vol. 3, pp. 26–7. For Lyndhurst's life, and particularly his relationship with Lady Sykes and Disraeli, see Dennis Lee, *Lord Lyndhurst, the Flexible Tory* (Niwot, Colorado, 1994).

106. *Disraeli's Reminiscences*, pp. 118–19.

107. See *Hansard*, passim, summer 1856 and summer 1857; Lee, *Lord Lyndhurst*, pp. 244, 247.

108. *Disraeli's Reminiscences*, p. 120.

109. *Fraser's Magazine*, vol. 18 (August 1838), pp. 195–6, and Gordon N. Ray, *Thackeray: The Uses of Adversity (1811–1846)* (London, 1955), pp. 270–1.

110. See *The Poems of Tennyson*, ed. Christopher Ricks (New York, 1969), pp. 736–9 and n.

111. *Disraeli's Reminiscences*, pp. 61–2.

112. Ibid., p. 65.

113. Rosina Bulwer Lytton to Rebecca Ryves, 2 March 1858, *Collected Letters*, vol. 3, p. 28.

114. See Dickens to Bulwer Lytton, 9 May 1851, *Letters*, vol. 6, pp. 379–80 and n.

115. See, for example, Dickens to his solicitor Frederic Ouvry, 26 May 1858, ibid., vol. 8, p. 568.

116. Dickens to William Charles Macready, 7 June 1858, ibid., vol. 8, p. 579 and n.
117. John Forster to Frederic Ouvry, 21 May 1858, in K.J. Fielding, 'Dickens and the Hogarth Scandal', *Nineteenth-Century Fiction*, vol. 10 (June 1955), p. 65.
118. Legal copy of George Hogarth's statement, ibid., p. 68.
119. Dickens to Arthur Smith, 25 May 1858, *Letters*, vol. 8, p. 568.
120. Dickens to Herbert Watkins, 31 May 1858, ibid., vol. 8, p. 576.
121. *The Times*, 3 June 1858.
122. Queen Victoria, journal, 27–31 May 1858, online at http://www.queenvictoriasjournals. org, vol. 45, pp. 219–22.
123. See Disraeli to Lord Derby, 25 May 1858, and to Bulwer Lytton, 30 May 1858, *Letters*, vol. 7, pp. 196, 198.
124. 'The Exhibition of the Royal Academy', *Era*, 30 May 1858.
125. 'The Leviathan', ibid.
126. 'The Atlantic Telegraph', *St James's Chronicle*, 8 June 1858.
127. See Darwin to his wife Emma, 25 April 1858, and to Joseph Hooker, 6 May 1858, *Correspondence*, vol. 7, pp. 80, 89.

Chapter Three: June 1858, part I

1. Charles Darwin to Joseph Hooker, 3 June 1858, *Correspondence*, vol. 7, p. 98.
2. Darwin to William Tegetmeier, 5 June 1858, and Erasmus Darwin to Charles Darwin, 8 June 1858, ibid., vol. 7, pp. 98, 100–102.
3. A search through *The Times* Digital Archive for the year 1858 yields only three brief entries on Darwin.
4. Darwin to Hooker, 10 August 1858, *Correspondence*, vol. 7, p. 148.
5. Darwin to Hooker, 11 January 1844, ibid., vol. 3, p. 2.
6. Darwin to Asa Gray, 5 September 1857, ibid., vol. 6, p. 447.
7. Ibid., vol. 7, pp. 15, 17, 20, 27, 36.
8. Leonard Huxley, *Life and Letters of Sir Joseph Dalton Hooker*, 2 vols (London, 1918), vol. 1, p. 495.
9. See *Bromley Record*, vol. 1 (1 June and 1 July 1858), pp. 1, 7.
10. Ibid., vol. 1 (1 June 1858), p. 3.
11. See Tori Reeve, *Down House: The Home of Charles Darwin* (London, 2009, reprinted 2011), pp. 16, 21, 36; R.B. Freeman, *Charles Darwin: A Companion* (Folkestone, 1978), p. 126.
12. For Huxley's life and career, see Leonard Huxley, *Life and Letters of Thomas Henry Huxley*, 2 vols (London, 1900), Cyril Bibby, *Scientist Extraordinary: The Life and Scientific Work of Thomas Henry Huxley 1825–1895* (London, 1972), and Paul White, *Thomas Huxley: Making the 'Man of Science'* (Cambridge, 2003).
13. Darwin, *Autobiography*, p. 106.
14. Ibid., p. 101.
15. Sir Charles Lyell to Darwin, 15 March 1863, *Life, Letters and Journals of Sir Charles Lyell, Bart., ed. by his sister-in-law Mrs Lyell*, 2 vols (London, 1881), vol. 2, p. 366.
16. Freeman, *Charles Darwin*, pp. 169–70; *ODNB* entry for Huxley.
17. Leonard Huxley, *Life and Letters of Thomas Henry Huxley*, vol. 1, pp. 91, 96.
18. Alfred Russel Wallace, *My Life: A Record of Events and Opinions* (London, 1908), p. 45.
19. Ibid., pp. 143–4, 146.
20. Ibid., p. 168.
21. Ibid., pp. 175, 177, 194–5; Alfred Russel Wallace to his mother, 30 September 1854, *Alfred Russel Wallace: Letters from the Malay Archipelago*, ed. John van Wyhe and Kees Rookmaaker (Oxford, 2013), pp. 21–2.
22. *Letters from the Malay Archipelago*, p. 125 and n. For Wallace's career see also Peter Raby, *Alfred Russel Wallace: A Life* (London, 2001), Ross A. Slotten, *The Heretic in Darwin's Court: The Life of Alfred Russel Wallace* (New York, 2004), and Michael A. Flannery, *Alfred Russel Wallace: A Rediscovered Life* (Seattle, Washington State, 2011).

23. Wallace to Henry Walter Bates, 4 January 1858, *Letters from the Malay Archipelago*, p. 146.
24. Wallace to Bates, 25 January 1858, ibid., p. 148.
25. Wallace to Samuel Stevens, 15 May 1857, ibid., pp. 127, 128.
26. Wallace, *My Life*, p. 183.
27. Darwin, memorandum, December 1855, *Correspondence*, vol. 5, pp. 510–11, 521–2n.
28. Darwin to Wallace, 1 May 1857, ibid., vol. 6, p. 387.
29. Ibid.
30. Wallace to Darwin, 27 September 1857, *Letters from the Malay Archipelago*, p. 132.
31. Darwin to Wallace, 22 December 1857, *Correspondence*, vol. 6, pp. 514–15.
32. Darwin to Syms Covington, 18 May 1858, ibid., vol. 7, p. 95. For a fictionalised account of Covington's life in Australia, see Roger McDonald, *Mr Darwin's Shooter* (London, 1998).
33. See Darwin, *Autobiography*, p. 124.
34. See Darwin to William Darwin Fox, 8 May 1858, *Correspondence*, vol. 7, p. 90.
35. Darwin to Hooker, 8 June 1858, ibid., vol. 7, p. 102.
36. Dickens to Daniel Maclise, [11 June 1858], *Letters*, vol. 8, p. 584.
37. 'Mr Charles Dickens Reading "Little Dombey" at St Martin's Hall', *Illustrated London News*, vol. 33 (31 July 1858), p. 100.
38. See Slater, *Charles Dickens*, p. 463.
39. Dickens, *Dombey and Son* (1846–8), chap. 16.
40. See Martin Hewitt, *The Dawn of the Cheap Press in Victorian Britain: The End of the 'Taxes on Knowledge' 1849–1869* (London, 2014).
41. Dickens's statement, *The Times*, 7 June 1858; *Household Words*, 12 June 1858.
42. See Dickens to Frederic Ouvry, 2 June 1858, and to William Macready, 7 June 1858, *Letters*, vol. 8, pp. 577 and n., 579–80 and n.
43. Dickens to William Holman Hunt, 13 and 20 April 1858, ibid., vol. 8, pp. 543 and n., 548 and n.
44. *St James's Chronicle*, 8 June 1858.
45. *Era*, 13 June 1858.
46. *Court Circular*, 12 June 1858, and *Reynolds's Newspaper*, 13 June 1858; both articles are quoted in part in Fielding, 'Dickens and the Hogarth Scandal', pp. 71–2.
47. William Henry Wills to Frederic Ouvry, 14 June 1858, ibid., p. 71.
48. See Shannon, *Dickens, Reynolds, and Mayhew on Wellington Street*, p. 28.
49. Carlyle to Ralph Waldo Emerson, 2 June 1858, *Collected Letters*, vol. 33, p. 233.
50. *The Life and Reminiscences of E.L. Blanchard, with Notes from the Diary of Wm. Blanchard*, ed. Clement Scott and Cecil Howard, 2 vols (London, 1891), vol. 1, p. 198.
51. Thackeray to his mother, early June, *Letters and Private Papers*, vol. 4, p. 87.
52. G.H. Lewes, journal, 14 June 1858, MS George Eliot / George Henry Lewes Collection, Beinecke Rare Book and Manuscript Library, Yale University.
53. For Dickens's itinerary, see *Letters*, vol. 8, pp. 752–3.
54. Queen Victoria, journal, 4, 5, and 8 June 1858, online at http://www.queenvictoriasjournals.org, vol. 45, pp. 228, 234.
55. *The Times*, 7 June 1858.
56. See Edmund Yates, *Recollections and Experiences*, 2 vols (London, 1884), vol. 1, p. 227; Altick, *The Shows of London*, pp. 475–7.
57. Disraeli to his wife, *Letters*, vol. 7, p. 200; for the temperature report see *The Times*, 10 June 1858.
58. *The Times*, 11 June 1858.
59. See ibid., 8 June 1858.
60. Disraeli to Bulwer Lytton, [8 June 1858], *Letters*, vol. 7, p. 201.
61. Rosina Bulwer Lytton, *A Blighted Life: A True Story* (London, 1880); see also David Lytton Cobbold, *A Blighted Marriage: The Life of Rosina Bulwer Lytton, Irish Beauty, Satirist and Tormented Wife, 1802–1882* (Knebworth, 1999).
62. For a detailed summary of election day in Hertford, see Sarah Wise, *Inconvenient People: Lunacy, Liberty and the Mad Doctors in Victorian England* (London, 2012), pp. 223–6.

63. Carlyle to Jane Carlyle, 11 July 1858, *Collected Letters*, vol. 34, p. 30.

64. Rosina Bulwer Lytton to Rebecca Ryves, 11 June 1858, *Collected Letters*, vol. 3, p. 70; *The Times*, 9 June 1858.

65. Earl of Lytton, *The Life of Edward Bulwer Lytton, first Lord Lytton*, 2 vols (London, 1913), vol. 2, p. 269.

66. See James A. Davies, *John Forster: A Literary Life* (Leicester, 1983), pp. 40, 41. The journalist Thornton Hunt called Forster 'the beadle of the universe', see Alethea Hayter, *A Sultry Month: Scenes of London Literary Life in 1846* (London, 1966, reprinted 1992), p. 163.

67. Mitchell, *Bulwer Lytton*, p. 63.

68. Rosina Bulwer Lytton to Rebecca Ryves, 12 June 1858, *Collected Letters*, vol. 3, p. 72.

69. Rosina Bulwer Lytton to Frederick Hale Thomson, 15 June 1858, ibid., vol. 3, p. 76.

70. For a number of cases dating from 1858, see Wise, *Inconvenient People*, pp. 252–81.

71. 'Commission of Lunacy', *The Times*, 18 June 1858.

72. See *The Times* account in the article 'Commission of Lunacy', 11 June 1858.

73. For monetary values then and now, see Slater, *Charles Dickens*, p. xviii, and http://www.measuringworth.com.

74. See *ODNB* entry for Sir Henry Meux and reports in *The Times* on 9, 10, 11, 18, and 21 June 1858.

75. *People's Paper*, 19 June 1858. For Edwin James's career, see *ODNB*. See also Wise, *Inconvenient People*, p. 274.

76. Rosina Bulwer Lytton to Rebecca Ryves, 11 June 1858, *Collected Letters*, vol. 3, p. 70.

77. Carlyle to his brother John, 12 June 1858, *Collected Letters of Thomas and Jane Welsh Carlyle*, vol. 33, p. 240.

78. Carlyle to Forster, 17 June 1858, ibid., vol. 33, pp. 242–3.

79. Queen Victoria, journal, 13 June 1858, online at http://www.queenvictoriasjournals.org, vol. 45, p. 238.

80. Disraeli to Sarah Brydges Willyams, 16 June 1858, *Letters*, vol. 7, p. 205.

81. See *Morning Chronicle*, 1 June 1858.

82. See Ritchie, *Here and There in London*, p. 11; *ODNB* entry for Lord Chelmsford (previously Sir Frederick Thesiger); Disraeli, *Letters*, vol. 7, pp. 205–6n.

83. *Liverpool Mercury*, 2 June 1858.

84. Lord Derby to Lord Carnarvon, Carnarvon Papers, vol. 9, Add MS 60,765, British Library.

85. *Weekly Chronicle*, 19 June 1858.

86. See 'Pestilential State of the Thames', *Era*, 20 June 1858.

87. 'The State of the Thames', *People's Paper*, 3 July 1858.

88. *Theatrical Journal*, 23 June 1858.

89. 'The Weather and the Wigs', *Weekly Chronicle*, 19 June 1858.

90. See P.D. Edwards, *Dickens's 'Young Men': George Augustus Sala, Edmund Yates, and the World of Victorian Journalism* (Aldershot, 1997).

91. For Sala's life and career see his *ODNB* entry, and Ralph Straus, *Sala: The Portrait of an Eminent Victorian* (London, 1942). For details of the circulation of cheap newspapers in 1855–8 see Richard Altick, *The English Common Reader: A Social History of the Mass Reading Public, 1800–1900* (Columbus, Ohio, 1957, reprinted 1988), pp. 394–5.

92. Sala, *Twice Round the Clock*, pp. 95, 98, 100–101, 193.

93. G.A. Sala to Edmund Yates, [December 1858], *Letters of George Augustus Sala to Edmund Yates*, ed. Judy McKenzie (University of Queensland Victorian Fiction Research Guide, 1993), p. 53.

94. Ibid., pp. 25, 32–3, 143, 148, 327, 333.

95. G.A. Sala, *The Life and Adventures of George Augustus Sala, Written by Himself*, 2 vols (London, 1895), vol. 1, p. 381.

96. 'Gossip of the Week', *Reynolds's Newspaper*, 20 June 1858; Sala to Yates, [31 January 1859], *Letters of Sala to Yates*, p. 59.

97. 'The Lounger at the Clubs', *Illustrated Times*, vol. 6 (12 June 1858), p. 415.

98. Yates, *Recollections and Experiences*, vol. 2, p. 2.

99. See Guy Boas, *The Garrick Club 1831–1947* (London, 1948), p. 41.

100. Yates, *Recollections and Experiences*, vol. 1, pp. 218–19.

101. Yates, 'Literary Talk', *Town Talk*, 12 June 1858.

102. Thackeray to Mrs Baxter, 23 April 1858, *Letters and Private Papers*, vol. 4, p. 80.

103. Yates, *Town Talk*, 12 June 1858.

104. Yates, *Recollections and Experiences*, vol. 2, pp. 9–10.

105. See Thackeray's diary, 3 January–23 September 1858, *Letters and Private Papers*, vol. 4, pp. 390–4.

106. Thackeray to Yates, 13 June 1858, *Letters and Private Papers*, vol. 4, pp. 89–90.

107. Ibid., vol. 4, pp. 90–1n.

108. Yates, *Recollections and Experiences*, vol. 2, p. 18.

109. Dickens to Yates, 15 June 1858, *Letters*, vol. 8, p. 588; for 'My dear Edmund', see the letter of 8 June 1858, ibid., vol. 8, p. 581.

110. Yates to Thackeray, 15 June 1858, *Letters and Private Papers of William Makepeace Thackeray*, vol. 4, pp. 91–2.

111. Yates, *Recollections and Experiences*, vol. 2, pp. 15–16.

112. Thackeray to Bulwer Lytton, 21 June 1853, *Letters and Private Papers*, vol. 3, p. 278.

113. Thackeray to the committee of the Garrick Club, 19 June 1858, *Letters and Private Papers*, vol. 4, pp. 93–4.

114. Thackeray to Charles Dickens Jr, 15 June 1858, Gordon N. Ray, *Thackeray: The Age of Wisdom (1847–1863)* (London, 1958), p. 477, n. 20.

115. See James C. Whorton, *The Arsenic Century: How Victorian Britain was Poisoned at Home, Work and Play* (Oxford, 2010), pp. 262–70.

116. *Punch*, vol. 34 (12 June 1858), p. 233.

117. *The Times*, Editorial, 'An Extraordinary Meeting at St James's-hall', 12 June 1858.

118. Queen Victoria to her daughter Vicky, 14 June 1858, *Dearest Child: Letters between Queen Victoria and the Princess Royal*, ed. Roger Fulford (London, 1964), p. 113. Vicky had got married, aged seventeen, on 25 January 1858.

119. *Punch*, vol. 35 (24 July 1858), p. 35; see also ibid., vol. 35 (9 October and 27 November 1858), pp. 147, 217.

120. J. Ewing Ritchie, *The London Pulpit* (London, 1858), pp. 47–8.

121. Basil F. Clarke, *Parish Churches of London* (London, 1966), pp. 185–6.

122. 'The Lounger at the Club', *Illustrated Times*, vol. 6 (19 June 1858), p. 431.

Chapter Four: June 1858, part II

1. 'To the Editor', *The Times*, 16 June 1858.

2. See, for example, a report from Berkhamsted in Hertfordshire, ibid., 18 June 1858.

3. *Bromley Record*, vol. 1 (1 July 1858), p. 8.

4. National Meteorological Library and Archive, https://library.metoffice.gov.uk/M10326UK/OPAC/Details/Record.aspx?BibCode=5660244 3.

5. *Hansard*, vol. 150, cols 2157–89, 16 June 1858.

6. Disraeli to Sarah Brydges Willyams, 16 June 1858, *Letters*, vol. 7, p. 204 and n.

7. *The Times*, 19 June 1858.

8. B.W. Richardson, memoir of John Snow in Snow, *On Chloroform and Other Anaesthetics: Their Action and Administration* (London, 1858), pp. xli–xliv.

9. Ibid., p. xxii.

10. The authorities in Paris continued to subscribe to the miasma theory until well into the 1880s: see Barnes, *The Great Stink of Paris*, and Colin Jones, *Paris: Biography of a City* (London, 2004), pp. 338–9.

11. *Builder*, vol. 16 (26 June 1858), p. 445.

12. *The Times*, 18 June 1858.

13. 'Pestilential State of the Thames', *Era*, 20 June 1858.
14. 'To the Editor', *The Times*, 18 June 1858.
15. *Illustrated London News*, vol. 32 (26 June 1858), p. 626; *Times* editorial, 29 June 1858; Luckin, *Pollution and Control*, p. 17; Allen, *Cleansing the City*, p. 57.
16. See Halliday, *The Great Filth*, pp. 75–6; Allen, *Cleansing the City*, pp. 57–8.
17. *Annual Register* (1858), p. 111.
18. Carlyle to Joseph Neuberg, 21 June 1858, *Collected Letters*, vol. 33, p. 246.
19. E.L. Blanchard, diary, 23 June 1858, *Life and Reminiscences*, vol. 1, p. 199.
20. John Ruskin to his father, 25 June 1858, *John Ruskin: Letters from the Continent 1858*, ed. John Hayman (Toronto, 1982), p. 58.
21. Motley to his wife, 20 June 1858, *Correspondence*, vol. 1, pp. 271, 269.
22. Letter to the editor of *The Times*, 21 June 1858. For the arguments between the crown and the City of London over ownership of the Thames foreshore, see Luckin, *Pollution and Control*, pp. 143–4.
23. John Simon and Edward Headlam Greenhow, *Papers Relating to the Sanitary State of the People of England*, June 1858, House of Commons Parliamentary Papers Online, pp. iii–iv.
24. See Royston Lambert, *Sir John Simon (1816–1904) and English Social Administration* (London, 1963), pp. 50–51.
25. See 'Return of the Number of Select Committees appointed in the Session of 1857–8', House of Commons Parliamentary Papers Online, p. 749.
26. See Disraeli, *Letters*, vol. 7, p. 214n.
27. Queen Victoria, journal, 23 June 1858, online at http://www.queenvictoriasjournals.org, vol. 45, p. 254.
28. Disraeli to Queen Victoria, 24 June 1858, *Letters*, vol. 7, p. 215.
29. Ibid., vol. 7, p. 216n.
30. *The Times*, 26 June 1858.
31. Report from the select committee on the River Thames, 17 July 1858, House of Commons Parliamentary Papers Online, pp. 252–85.
32. *The Times*, 26 June 1858.
33. See *ODNB* entry for Thwaites.
34. See Halliday, *The Great Filth*, p. 205.
35. *People's Paper*, 5 June 1858.
36. 'No Coat, No Justice', ibid., 26 June 1858.
37. Alfred Smee, letter to the editor of *The Times*, 26 June 1858; *Illustrated London News*, vol. 32 (26 June 1858), p. 631; *Era*, 27 June 1858.
38. 'Londoners, Look to Your River!', *Era*, 27 June 1858.
39. Darwin to Lyell, 26 June 1858, *Correspondence*, vol. 7, p. 119.
40. Darwin to Hooker, 23 June, to W.D. Fox, 24 and 27 June, and to Lyell, 25 June 1858, ibid., vol. 7, pp. 115–19.
41. See Queen Victoria, journal, 19, 21, 22, 23, 24 June 1858, online at http://www.queen victoriasjournals.org, vol. 45, pp. 251–9.
42. Queen Victoria, journal, 26 June 1858, ibid., vol. 45, p. 258.
43. See the list of subscribers to Rarey's book, *The Times*, 19 April 1858.
44. *Punch*, preface to vol. 34 (January–June 1858), p. iii; *How I Tamed Mrs Cruiser, by Benedict Cruiser, M.M. (Married Man), and now H.H. (Happy Husband)*, ed. George Augustus Sala, with Illustrations by Phiz [Hablot Knight Browne] (London, 1858).
45. Queen Victoria to Vicky, 29 June 1858, *Dearest Child*, p. 118.
46. Queen Victoria, journal, 28 June 1858, online at http://www.queenvictoriasjournals.org, vol. 45, p. 260.
47. 'Queen of the River', *Punch*, vol. 35 (10 July 1858), p. 20.
48. *Weekly Chronicle*, 19 June 1858, p. 5.
49. See Buchanan, *The Life and Times of Isambard Kingdom Brunel*, p. 123.
50. Thomas Wright, *Some Habits and Customs of the Working Classes, by a Journeyman Engineer* (London, 1867), pp. 251–60.

51. Isambard Kingdom Brunel to John Scott Russell, 2 October 1855, Buchanan, *Life and Times*, p. 121.
52. *The Times*, 18 and 20 April 1858; see also Vaughan, *Isambard Kingdom Brunel*, p. 257.
53. Buchanan, *Life and Times*, p. 123.
54. See *The Times*, 2, 4, 5, 7, 11, 16, and 17 December 1857; Carlyle to John Carlyle, 7 December 1857, *Collected Letters*, vol. 33, p. 128.
55. Vaughan, *Isambard Kingdom Brunel*, p. 258; *ODNB* entry for Henry Thomas Hope.
56. Buchanan, *Life and Times*, p. 128.
57. Ibid., pp. 127–32; Vaughan, *Isambard Kingdom Brunel*, pp. 260–69.
58. See *ODNB* entry for Robert Howlett.
59. Irving, *Annals of Our Time*, p. 524.
60. See *The Times*, 3 July 1858.
61. *Athenaeum*, 3 July 1858, p. 24.
62. 'Advice in Hot Weather', *Punch*, vol. 35 (3 July 1858), p. 9.
63. Princess Royal to Queen Victoria, 24 July 1858, *Dearest Child*, p. 124.
64. Gwen Raverat, *Period Piece: A Cambridge Childhood* (London, 1952), p. 260.
65. See Lucy Johnston with Marion Kite and Helen Persson, *Nineteenth-Century Fashion in Detail*, V&A Publications (London, 2005), p. 128.
66. See Norah Waugh, *Corsets and Crinolines* (New York, 1954, reprinted 2004), pp. 79, 93.
67. 'Philosophy and Fashion', *Punch*, vol. 48 (6 May 1865), p. 181.
68. Mary Anne Disraeli to Sarah Brydges Willyams, 24 April 1856, Hay, *Mr and Mrs Disraeli*, p. 181.
69. Elizabeth Gaskell, 'The Cage at Cranford', *All the Year Round*, vol. 10 (28 November 1863), pp. 332–6.
70. 'Every Lady her own Perambulator', *Punch*, vol. 31 (23 August 1856), p. 77.
71. 'Crinolineomania. Treated pathologically by Dr Punch', ibid., vol. 31 (27 December 1856), p. 253.
72. 'Effect of Crinoline on Parties' and 'Crinoline in the Studio', ibid., vol. 32 (7 February and 2 May 1857), pp. 57, 177.
73. 'A Wholesome Conclusion', ibid., vol. 34 (6 February 1858), p. 54; 'Crinoline in the Slums', ibid., vol. 35 (10 July 1858), p. 17; 'New Omnibus Regulation', ibid., vol. 35 (2 October 1858), p. 133.
74. 'The Theatre of Crinoline', ibid., vol. 34 (29 May 1858), p. 221.
75. 'The Opening of the New Opera House, Covent-garden', *Builder*, vol. 16 (22 May 1858), pp. 345–7.
76. See Bennett, *London and Londoners*, p. 75.
77. Examples are quoted in Denis Pellerin and Brian May, *Crinoline: Fashion's Most Magnificent Disaster* (London, 2016), pp. 24, 54, 154–6.
78. 'Perversion of Crinoline', *People's Paper*, 10 July 1858.
79. *Athenaeum*, 1 January 1859, p. 24.
80. The British Library catalogue lists eleven items under the title 'Hoop de dooden do' from 1850 to the 1870s.
81. 'Hoop de dooden doo. A fashionable ballad', *Punch*, vol. 34 (5 June 1858), p. 229.
82. *Illustrated Times*, vol. 6 (26 June 1858), p. 446; see also *People's Paper*, 17 July 1858.
83. Jane Carlyle to Thomas Carlyle, 5 September 1864, *Collected Letters*, vol. 41, p. 7.
84. Summerscale, *Mrs Robinson's Disgrace*, p. 63.
85. Darwin to Lyell, 13 April 1857, *Correspondence*, vol. 6, p. 377.
86. Darwin to Hooker, 29 April 1857, ibid., vol. 6, p. 384.
87. Darwin to W.D. Fox, 30 April 1857, ibid., vol. 6, pp. 385–6.
88. Darwin to his son William, 13 May 1857, ibid., vol. 6, pp. 394–5.
89. See Summerscale, *Mrs Robinson's Disgrace*, pp. 20, 27–9, 61.
90. Rosanna Ledbetter, *A History of the Malthusian League 1877–1927* (Columbus, Ohio, 1976), p. 58.
91. See *ODNB* entry for Charles Drysdale.

92. Charles Drysdale, 'Tobacco and the Diseases It Produces', *The Times*, 25 September 1878.

93. [George Drysdale], *Physical, Sexual, and Natural Religion, by a Student of Medicine* (London, 1855), pp. 53–4.

94. See E. Royston Pike, *Human Documents of the Victorian Golden Age (1850–1875)* (London, 1967), p. 338. See also Angus McLaren, *Birth Control in Nineteenth-Century England* (London, 1978).

95. See Charles Gibbon, *The Life of George Combe*, 2 vols (London, 1878), vol. 2, pp. 215, 298; George Combe, journal, 10 October 1850 and 25 May 1851, MS George Combe Papers, National Library of Scotland.

96. Summerscale, *Mrs Robinson's Disgrace*, pp. 55–6.

97. Ibid., pp. 8–10, 132.

98. Ibid., pp. 106–7, 131–2.

99. Ibid., pp. 114ff., 254–5; Summerscale's account of the trial is drawn from daily reports in the newspapers and from the first volume of *Reports of Cases Decided in the Court of Probate and in the Court for Divorce and Matrimonial Causes*, ed. M.C.M. Swabey, T.H. Tristram et al., 4 vols (London, 1858–65).

100. 'Court for Divorce and Matrimonial Causes', *The Times*, 16 June 1858.

101. Ibid.

102. Summerscale, *Mrs Robinson's Disgrace*, pp. 156–7.

103. *The Times*, 17 June 1858.

104. *People's Paper*, 19 June 1858.

105. 'Crim. Con. and Hydropathic Love', *Era*, 20 June 1858.

106. Ibid., 22 June 1858; Summerscale, *Mrs Robinson's Disgrace*, pp. 172–5.

107. Summerscale, *Mrs Robinson's Disgrace*, pp. 81–6. The quotations are from the more scurrilous newspapers and the *Reports of Cases*; the journal itself has disappeared.

108. *Daily News*, 23 June 1858. For a discussion of the discriminatory remarks about women in the newspaper reports of the Robinson case, see Janice M. Allan, 'Mrs Robinson's "Day-book of Iniquity": Reading Bodies of/and Evidence in the Context of the 1858 Medical Reform Act', in *The Female Body in Medicine and Literature*, ed. Andrew Mangham and Greta Depledge (Liverpool, 2011), pp. 169–81.

109. 'Classified Advertisements', *The Times*, 29 May 1854.

110. *British Medical Journal*, vol. 80 (10 July 1858), pp. 561–2.

111. Summerscale, *Mrs Robinson's Disgrace*, pp. 181–3.

112. Ibid., pp. 163–4.

113. Ibid., p. 167.

114. Ibid., p. 168.

115. Darwin to Fox, 24 June 1858, *Correspondence*, vol. 7, p. 116.

116. Darwin to Hooker, 23 June 1858, ibid., vol. 7, p. 115.

117. See ibid., vol. 6, p. 386, n. 5.

118. Darwin to Hooker, 25 June 1857, ibid., vol. 6, p. 416.

119. See Darwin to Fox, 3 October 1856, ibid., vol. 6, p. 238. For Annie Darwin see Randal Keynes, *Annie's Box: Charles Darwin, his Daughter, and Human Evolution* (London, 2001).

120. Darwin to Hooker, 30 October 1857, *Correspondence*, vol. 6, p. 476.

121. Darwin to Lyell, 18 June 1858, ibid., vol. 7, p. 107.

122. For a dismissal of the suggestion by some commentators that Darwin was less than candid about the date on which he received Wallace's communication, and that he may have borrowed the idea of divergence from Wallace, see the editors' Introduction to volume 7 of Darwin's *Correspondence*, pp. xvii–xix, and the lengthy note to Darwin's letter, ibid., vol. 7, p. 108. The editors of Wallace's *Letters from the Malay Archipelago* also dismiss the accusation against Darwin, pp. xv–xvi, as does Darwin's most recent biographer Janet Browne, *Charles Darwin: The Power of Place* (London, 2002), pp. 16, 501, n. 17.

123. Darwin to his son William, 20 June 1858, *Correspondence*, vol. 7, p. 113.

124. Darwin to Fox, 24 June 1858, ibid., vol. 7, p. 116.
125. Darwin to Lyell, 25 June 1858, ibid., vol. 7, pp. 117–18.
126. See ibid., vol. 8, p. 600 (Appendix VII).
127. Darwin, *Autobiography*, pp. 86–7.
128. Ibid., p. 87n.
129. Darwin to Wallace, 22 December 1857, *Correspondence*, vol. 6, p. 515.
130. Darwin, *Autobiography*, p. 130.
131. Darwin to Lyell, 26 June 1858, *Correspondence*, vol. 7, p. 119.
132. Darwin to Hooker, 29 June 1858, ibid., vol. 7, p. 121.
133. Wallace, *My Life*, pp. 201, 203; Wallace to Philip Sclater, 31 March 1862, *Letters from the Malay Archipelago*, p. 283 and n.
134. Hooker and Lyell to the Linnaean Society, 30 June 1858, Darwin, *Correspondence*, vol. 7, pp. 122–3.
135. Ibid., vol. 7, p. 123.
136. Darwin to Hooker, 29 June 1858, ibid., vol. 7, p. 122.
137. Ibid., vol. 7, p. 121.

Chapter Five: July 1858

1. 'Register of Burials in the Parish of Downe in the County of Kent in the Year 1858', Bromley Local Studies Library.
2. Darwin to W.D. Fox, 6 July 1858, *Correspondence*, vol. 7, p. 129.
3. Darwin, journal, ibid., vol. 7, p. 504 (Appendix II).
4. Darwin's memorial on the death of Charles Waring Darwin, ibid., vol. 7, p. 521 (Appendix V).
5. See Keynes, *Annie's Box*, pp. 225–6. Keynes is the only biographer of Darwin to notice that Charles Waring Darwin's funeral took place on the same day as the Linnaean Society meeting.
6. Henrietta Lichfield (ed.), *Emma Darwin: A Century of Family Letters*, 2 vols (London, 1915), vol. 2, p. 162.
7. See Darwin to Hooker, 16 May 1858, *Correspondence*, vol. 7, p. 94. Darwin's next visit to London was on 19 October 1858, ibid., vol. 7, p. 504 (Appendix II).
8. Darwin to Hooker, 5 and 13 July 1858, ibid., vol. 7, pp. 127–8, 129.
9. Darwin, *Autobiography*, pp. 103–4.
10. Hooker's speech, *The Darwin–Wallace Celebration held on Thursday 1 July 1908 by the Linnaean Society of London* (London, 1908), p. 15.
11. Ibid.
12. For the list of those attending the meeting, see *Darwin–Wallace Celebration*, p. 83.
13. Darwin to W.B. Carpenter, 18 November 1859, and to Hooker, 20 November 1859, *Correspondence*, vol. 7, pp. 378, 382.
14. The information about the order of items on the agenda comes from *Darwin–Wallace Celebration*, pp. 85–6.
15. Darwin to Hooker, 13 July 1858, *Correspondence*, vol. 7, p. 130.
16. 'Abstract of Darwin's Theory', ibid., vol. 7, pp. 508–9 (Appendix III; original letter to Asa Gray, 5 September 1857, ibid., vol. 6, pp. 448–9).
17. Wallace, *My Life*, pp. 189–90.
18. See *ODNB* entry for Malthus.
19. Darwin, *Autobiography*, p. 120.
20. Wallace, *My Life*, pp. 190–91.
21. 'Wallace's Essay on Variation', Darwin, *Correspondence*, vol. 7, p. 514 (Appendix IV).
22. Darwin, *On the Origin of Species*, ed. John Burrow, p. 117.
23. 'Wallace's Essay on Variation', Darwin, *Correspondence*, vol. 7, pp. 516–18.
24. Hooker's speech in 1908, *Darwin–Wallace Celebration*, p. 15.
25. Darwin, *Autobiography*, p. 122.

26. See *ODNB* entry for Samuel Haughton.
27. Wallace to his mother and to Hooker, 6 October 1858, *Letters from the Malay Archipelago*, pp. 180, 181.
28. Wallace to Bates, 4 January 1858, ibid., p. 147.
29. Wallace, *My Life*, p. 194.
30. Huxley to Hooker, 5 September 1858, *Life and Letters*, vol. 1, p. 159.
31. Ibid., vol. 1, p. 171.
32. Darwin to W.D. Fox, 21 July 1858, *Correspondence*, vol. 7, p. 138.
33. See Darwin to his publisher John Murray, 10 September 1859, ibid., vol. 7, p. 331.
34. Darwin, *Autobiography*, p. 124.
35. Darwin's journal, *Correspondence*, vol. 7, p. 504 (Appendix II).
36. 'Court for Divorce and Matrimonial Causes', *The Times*, 5 July 1858.
37. Ibid.
38. Darwin to W.D. Fox, 21 July 1858, *Correspondence*, vol. 7, p. 138.
39. Letters to the editor of *The Times*, 8 July 1858.
40. See Disraeli, *Letters*, vol. 7, p. 219 and n., and Queen Victoria to Bulwer Lytton, 24 July 1858, *Letters of Queen Victoria*, vol. 3, p. 376.
41. Rosina Bulwer Lytton to Rebecca Ryves and to Frederick Hale Thomson, 12 June 1858, *Collected Letters*, vol. 3, pp. 72–4.
42. Rosina Bulwer Lytton to Thomson, 15 June 1858, ibid., vol. 3, pp. 75–6.
43. Rosina Bulwer Lytton to Thomson, 20 June 1858, ibid., vol. 3, p. 85.
44. See *ODNB* entries for Hill and Conolly.
45. Advertisement for Wyke House, *The Times*, 4 December 1856.
46. Rosina Bulwer Lytton, *A Blighted Life*, p. 34.
47. See Wise, *Inconvenient People*, pp. 227–8, 426–7.
48. Rosina Bulwer Lytton to Rebecca Ryves, 29 June, 4 and 5 July 1858, *Collected Letters*, vol. 3, pp. 92, 95–6, 98.
49. The pamphlet is in the archives at Knebworth, Lytton's country estate; a copy is also held by the National Library of Scotland, see Thomas and Jane Welsh Carlyle, *Collected Letters of Thomas and Jane Welsh Carlyle*, vol. 34, p. 25, where the title page is reproduced.
50. See Mitchell, *Bulwer Lytton*, pp. 62–3.
51. See *ODNB* entry for Joseph Levy.
52. Jane Carlyle to Thomas Carlyle, 12 July 1858, *Collected Letters*, vol. 34, pp. 37–9.
53. Ibid., vol. 34, p. 39.
54. Carlyle to Jane Carlyle, 14 July 1858, ibid., vol. 34, pp. 43–4.
55. *Daily Telegraph*, 15 July 1858.
56. *The Times*, 14 July 1858.
57. 'Lady Bulwer Lytton', *The Times*, 19 July 1858.
58. See Summerscale, *Mrs Robinson's Disgrace*, p. 158.
59. Marx, 'Imprisonment of Lady Bulwer-Lytton', *New York Daily Tribune*, 4 August 1858, *Marx–Engels Collected Works*, vol. 15, pp. 599, 600–601.
60. Rosina Bulwer Lytton to Edwin James, 5 August 1858, *Collected Letters*, vol. 3, p. 111.
61. Rosina Bulwer Lytton to Robert Lytton, 27 August and 3 November 1858, ibid., vol. 3, pp. 117, 121, 122.
62. Rosina Bulwer Lytton to the earl of Shaftesbury, 25 October 1858, ibid., vol. 3, pp. 118–19.
63. Rosina Bulwer Lytton, *A Blighted Life*, pp. 38, 39, 43, 55.
64. *The Times*, 20 July 1858.
65. Hill's notes, quoted in Wise, *Inconvenient People*, pp. 232–3.
66. Robert Gardiner Hill, letter to the editor of *Freeman's Journal and Daily Commercial Advertiser*, 23 July 1858.
67. See Wise, *Inconvenient People*, pp. 244–5.
68. Ibid., p. 247.
69. 'The Lounger at the Clubs', *Illustrated Times*, vol. 7 (17 July 1858), p. 42.

70. Mitchell, *Bulwer Lytton*, p. 213.
71. Disraeli to Lytton, 20 December 1858, *Letters*, vol. 7, p. 294.
72. Lytton to Disraeli, 22 December 1858, ibid., vol. 7, p. 294n.
73. Disraeli to Lord Derby, 1 January 1859, ibid., vol. 7, p. 308.
74. Disraeli to Queen Victoria, 22 March 1859, ibid., vol. 7, p 347.
75. See ibid., vol. 7, p. 358 and n.
76. Even Disraeli's most prominent biographer, Robert Blake, devotes only a dozen pages of his 800-page biography to the Derby–Disraeli ministry of 1858–9, and makes no mention at all of the Great Stink or Disraeli's achievements in relation to it.
77. 'Parliamentary Committee: The State of the River Thames'. *The Times*, 1 July 1858.
78. Editorial, ibid.
79. 'The Thames and the House', letter to the editor, ibid., 2 July 1858.
80. 'The Thames', letter to the editor, ibid.
81. *Illustrated London News*, vol. 33 (3 July 1858), p. 11.
82. *Punch*, vol. 35 (3 July 1858), p. 5.
83. Ibid., p. 7.
84. 'The Thames and its Doctors', *Era*, 4 July 1858.
85. *The Times*, 10 July 1858.
86. 'State of the Thames: Parliamentary Committee', ibid., 14 July 1858.
87. Disraeli to Queen Victoria, 8 July 1858, *Letters*, vol. 7, p. 220.
88. *Hansard*, vol. 151, col. 1508, 15 July 1858.
89. Michael Faraday, letter to the editor of *The Times*, 9 July 1855.
90. See Halliday, *The Great Filth*, pp. 132, 135.
91. See Halliday, *The Great Stink*, p. 43, and 'Pestilential State of the Thames', *Era*, 20 June 1858.
92. 'Liberty and Tranquillity. The Seine and the Thames', *People's Paper*, 10 July 1858. For Paris's sanitation problems see Barnes, *The Great Stink of Paris*.
93. *Hansard*, vol. 151, cols 1510–15, 15 July 1858.
94. Ibid., cols 1522–3.
95. See Halliday, *The Great Filth*, p. 205.
96. *Hansard*, vol. 151, cols 1525–6, 15 July 1858.
97. Ibid., cols 1532, 1536–7.
98. Ibid., cols 1538–40.
99. 'Purification of the Thames', *Illustrated London News*, vol. 33 (24 July 1858), p. 72.
100. 'Sketches in Parliament', ibid., p. 88.
101. *Punch*, vol. 35 (17 July 1858), p. 22.
102. Marx to Engels, 29 March 1858, *Marx–Engels Collected Works*, vol. 40, p. 295.
103. Marx to Engels, 15 July 1858, ibid., vol. 40, pp. 328–41. For the original letter in German, see *Marx–Engels Werke*, 39 vols (Berlin, 1956–68), vol. 29, pp. 340–42.
104. Engels to Marx, 16 July 1858, *Marx–Engels Collected Works*, vol. 40, pp. 332 and 619.
105. Marx to Engels, 28 January and 8 August 1858, ibid., vol. 40, pp. 258, 336; for his articles see ibid., vol. 15, pp. 453–8, 510–14, 533–8, 602–6. For Marx's life in London see Rosemary Ashton, *Little Germany: Exile and Asylum in Victorian England* (Oxford, 1986).
106. Queen Victoria, journal, 4 July 1858, online at http://www.queenvictoriasjournals.org, vol. 45, p. 266.
107. Ibid., 17 and 18 July 1858, vol. 45, pp. 280, 281.
108. *Hansard*, vol. 150, col. 2241, 17 June 1858.
109. Disraeli to Queen Victoria, 8 July 1858, *Letters*, vol. 7, p. 219.
110. See Waddington, *The Medical Profession*, pp. 123–5.
111. 'Parliamentary Intelligence', *St James's Chronicle*, 20 May 1858.
112. 'Topics of the Week', *Era*, 11 July 1858.
113. 'The Triumph of Moses', *Punch*, vol. 35 (10 July 1858), p. 12.
114. 'Punch's Essence of Parliament', ibid., vol. 35 (24 July 1858), p. 23.

115. 'Notes of the Week', *Illustrated London News*, vol. 33 (17 July 1858), p. 57.
116. For an account of the final toing and froing between Lords and Commons over the Oaths Bill, see Disraeli, *Letters*, vol. 7, pp. 212–13n.
117. 'Baron Rothschild and the House of Commons', *Era*, 1 August 1858. See also Niall Ferguson, *The World's Banker: The History of the House of Rothschild* (London, 1998), p. 548.
118. 'Gossip of the Week', *Reynolds's Newspaper*, 1 August 1858.
119. W. Cusnie, *Tit, Tat, Toe: The Three Butcher Boys; or, Harlequin Old Father Thames and Mephistopheles*, licensed for performance at the Effingham Saloon on 27 December 1858, Lord Chamberlain's Plays, Add MS 52,977D, British Library.
120. 'Sketches in Parliament', *Illustrated London News*, vol. 33 (24 July 1858), p. 88.
121. Thomas Aspden, *Historical Sketches of the House of Stanley, and Biography of Edward Geoffrey, 14th Earl of Derby* (London, 1877), pp. 40, 41.
122. Lord Derby's speech in the House of Lords, 1 March 1858, see Jones, *Lord Derby and Victorian Conservatism*, p. 231.
123. Editorial, *The Times*, 7 June 1858.
124. Ibid., 11 June 1858.

Chapter Six: July–August 1858

1. Irving, *Annals of Our Time*, p. 522.
2. George Hodder, *Memories of My Time, including Personal Reminiscences of Eminent Men* (London, 1870), p. 277.
3. Thackeray to his mother, 7 January 1848, *Letters and Private Papers*, vol. 2, p. 333.
4. For an excellent discussion of the talk at the *Punch* table, see Leary, *The 'Punch' Brotherhood*, especially chap. 4.
5. Ibid., p. 81.
6. Thackeray to James Wilson, late May 1858, *Letters and Private Papers*, vol. 4, p. 83.
7. Anny Thackeray to Amy Crowe, late December 1858, *Anne Thackeray Ritchie: Journals and Letters*, ed. Lillian F. Shankman, Abigail Burnham Bloom, and John Maynard (Columbus, Ohio, 1994), p. 58.
8. Thackeray to the committee of the Garrick Club, 19 June 1858, *Letters and Private Papers*, vol. 4, pp. 93–4.
9. Yates to the committee of the Garrick Club, 19 June 1858, ibid., vol. 4, p. 94.
10. Alexander Doland to Yates, 19 June 1858, ibid., vol. 4, pp. 94–5.
11. Undated fragment of a letter from Dickens to Thackeray, June 1858, *Letters*, vol. 8, p. 591.
12. Yates to the committee of the Garrick Club, 23 June 1858, Thackeray, *Letters and Private Papers*, vol. 4, pp. 95–6.
13. Doland to Yates, 26 June 1858, ibid., vol. 4, p. 97.
14. Minutes of the Garrick Club committee, 3 April 1858, quoted in Leary, *The 'Punch' Brotherhood*, p. 97.
15. Thackeray, *The Virginians*, number 9 (1 July 1858), quoted in *Letters and Private Papers*, vol. 4, p. 98n.
16. Yates to the committee of the Garrick Club, 1 July 1858, ibid., vol. 4, p. 98; Yates, *Recollections and Experiences*, vol. 2, p. 23.
17. See Silver, *Punch* diary, 1 September and 21 October 1858, 2 March 1859, Add MS 88937/2/13, British Library; for some of these instances, see Leary, *The 'Punch' Brotherhood*, pp. 30, 38.
18. Percival Leigh, 'Liberties of the Press', *Punch*, vol. 35 (3 July 1858), p. 7.
19. Editorial, *Critic*, 3 July 1858, p. 347; quoted in Leary, *The 'Punch' Brotherhood*, p. 102.
20. Dickens to Yates, 6 July 1858, *Letters*, vol. 8, p. 595.
21. Dickens to W.H. Russell, 7 July 1858, ibid., vol. 8, pp. 600–601.

22. Yates to the committee of the Garrick Club, 10 July 1858, Thackeray, *Letters and Private Papers*, vol. 4, p. 103.
23. Thackeray to the chairman of the general meeting of the Garrick Club, 10 July 1858, ibid., vol. 4, pp. 101–2. The editor of Thackeray's letters, Gordon N. Ray, adds in a footnote that the letter was not sent, but Leary found the letter in the Garrick Club minute book, see *The 'Punch' Brotherhood*, p. 100 and n.
24. John Blackwood to Thackeray, 9 July 1858, Ray, *Thackeray: The Age of Wisdom*, pp. 285, 477n.
25. See Thackeray to Lytton, 21 June 1853, *Letters and Private Papers*, vol. 3, p. 278, and to Dickens, 11 June 1847, ibid., vol. 2, p. 299.
26. Shirley Brooks, quoted in Ray, *Thackeray: the Age of Wisdom*, p. 280.
27. Silver, *Punch* diary, 12 August 1863, Add MS 88937/2/13, British Library.
28. Leary, *The 'Punch' Brotherhood*, p. 101.
29. Dickens to Charley Dickens, ?10–12 July 1858, and to the committee of the Garrick Club, 12 July 1858, *Letters*, vol. 8, pp. 602, 603.
30. Thackeray, *Letters and Private Papers*, vol. 4, p. 105n.
31. Thackeray, diary, 12 July to 17 August 1858, ibid., vol. 4, pp. 393–4.
32. Frank Fladgate to Thackeray, 27 July 1858, ibid., vol. 4, p. 107.
33. Minutes of the Garrick Club meeting, 20 July 1858, quoted in Leary, *The 'Punch' Brotherhood*, p. 101 and n.
34. Dickens to J. Palgrave Simpson, 23 July 1858, *Letters*, vol. 8, p. 611.
35. Yates, *Mr Thackeray, Mr Yates, and the Garrick Club. The Correspondence and Facts* (London, 1859), pp. 10–11; see also *Recollections and Experiences*, vol. 2, p. 28.
36. See Dickens, *Letters*, vol. 8, pp. 752–3.
37. Dickens to Yates, 21 August 1858, ibid., vol. 8, p. 631.
38. 'The Garrick Club – Thackeray and Yates – A Tempest in a Teacup', *Reynolds's Newspaper*, 1 August 1858.
39. Sala, *Twice Round the Clock*, pp. 211, 213–14; the number containing 'The Fashionable Club' was published in *Welcome Guest* at the end of July or beginning of August 1858.
40. See Ruskin to his father, 24 July 1858, *Letters from the Continent*, p. 99.
41. Thackeray to the Baxters, 25 August 1858, *Letters and Private Papers*, vol. 4, pp. 109–10.
42. 'Mr Thackeray and the Garrick Club', *Reynolds's Newspaper*, 22 August 1858.
43. 'The Row at the Garrick Club', ibid.
44. 'The Garrick Club', ibid., 29 August 1858.
45. Dickens to Yates, 21 August 1858, *Letters*, vol. 8, p. 631.
46. Dickens to William de Cerjat, 7 July 1858, ibid., vol. 8, pp. 597–8.
47. Ibid., vol. 8, pp. 596–7, 598.
48. Deed of Separation, 4 June 1858, see Nayder, *The Other Dickens*, pp. 254–5.
49. Dickens to Catherine Gore, 31 May 1858, *Letters*, vol. 8, p. 574.
50. Dickens to John Leech, 31 May 1858, ibid., vol. 8, p. 575.
51. Charley Dickens to Dickens, 10 May 1858, ibid., vol. 8, p. 575n.
52. Dickens to Catherine Dickens, 4 June 1858, ibid., vol. 8, p. 578.
53. Dickens to Charley Dickens, ?10–12 July 1858, ibid., vol. 8, p. 602.
54. Charley Dickens to Catherine Dickens, 13 July 1858, ibid., vol. 8, p. 602n.
55. See Nayder, *The Other Dickens*, p. 257.
56. Dickens, *Letters*, vol. 8, p. 603n.
57. Dickens to Frederick Evans, 22 July 1858, ibid., vol. 8, p. 608.
58. Slater, *Charles Dickens*, p. 465.
59. See Tomalin, *The Invisible Woman*, pp. 111, 113, 116–17.
60. Ibid., pp. 121, 127, 170, 172; Slater, *Dickens and Women*, pp. 209–10, and *The Great Charles Dickens Scandal*, pp. 173–4.
61. *Athenaeum*, 18 December 1858.
62. See *The Times*, 14 March 1859, and *Era*, 13 March 1859.

63. See Malcolm Morley, 'The Theatrical Ternans', a series of ten articles published in *The Dickensian*, vols 54–7 (January 1958–January 1961). Morley's collection of Haymarket playbills is in the V&A Theatre and Performance Archive, Blythe House, Kensington Olympia. These give the parts which Ellen was billed to play, though some newspaper advertisements and reviews name her sister Maria instead; this was the case with *Out of Sight, Out of Mind* in August 1859.

64. See Dickens, *Letters*, vol. 8, pp. 752–3 (Appendix H).

65. See Slater, *Charles Dickens*, pp. 461–4.

66. Dickens to Georgina Hogarth, 5 August 1858, *Letters*, vol. 8, p. 617.

67. *Chambers's Exeter Journal*, 7 August 1858, ibid., vol. 8, p. 617n.

68. Dickens to Mamie Dickens, 7 August 1858, ibid., vol. 8, p. 619.

69. Dickens to Yates, 11 August 1858, ibid., vol. 8, p. 623 and n.

70. Dickens to Collins, 11 August 1858, ibid., vol. 8, p. 623.

71. See Dickens to Collins, 12 February and 13 April 1856, ibid., vol. 8, pp. 53, 86–7.

72. Dickens to Collins, 11 August 1858, ibid., vol. 8, p. 623.

73. Dickens to Mamie Dickens, 12 August 1858, ibid., vol. 8, p. 625.

74. Dickens to Anne Cornelius, 17 August 1858, ibid., vol. 8, p. 627.

75. Dickens to Georgina Hogarth, 20 August 1858, ibid., vol. 8, p. 629.

76. Dickens to Angela Burdett-Coutts, 23 August 1858, ibid., vol. 8, p. 632.

77. Watkins took the photograph on 17 June 1858, see ibid., vol. 8, pp. 576n, 607n.

78. Dickens to Georgina Hogarth, 25 August 1858, ibid., vol. 8, p. 637.

79. Dickens to Mamie Dickens, 28 August 1858, ibid., vol. 8, p. 641.

80. Dickens to Frederick Dickens, 12 December 1856, ibid., vol. 8, p. 236 and n. See also Slater, *Charles Dickens*, pp. 281, 325.

81. Dickens to Frederick Dickens, 5 February 1857, *Letters*, vol. 8, p. 275.

82. Frederick Dickens to Dickens, 7 February 1857, ibid., vol. 8, p. 277n.

83. Dickens to Georgina Hogarth, 29 August 1858, ibid., vol. 8, p. 644.

84. See 'Law Intelligence', *Daily News*, 27 July 1859.

85. Dickens to T.J. Thompson, 8 November 1858, *Letters*, vol. 8, p. 699.

86. Dickens to T.J. Thompson, 22 November 1858, ibid., vol. 8, p. 706.

87. Dickens to Arthur Smith, 25 May 1858, *Letters*, vol. 8, p. 568.

88. See ibid., vol. 8, p. 648n.

89. Dickens to Anne Cornelius, 11 October 1857, ibid., vol. 8, p. 465.

90. Dickens, 'Violated Letter', 25 May 1858, ibid., vol. 8, p. 740.

91. Henry Morley to Mary Anne Sayer, early December 1851, in Henry Solly, *The Life of Henry Morley* (London, 1898), pp. 200–1.

92. Dickens, 'Violated Letter', 25 May 1858, *Letters*, vol. 8, p. 741.

93. Statement by Mrs Hogarth and Helen Hogarth, 29 May 1858, ibid., vol. 8, p. 742.

94. 'The Dickens Domestic Affair', *New York Daily Tribune*, 16 August 1858, ibid., vol. 8, p. 648n.

95. *Morning Star*, 30 August 1858, *Morning Chronicle* and *Morning Herald*, 31 August 1858, and *Daily Telegraph*, 2 September 1858; see Dickens, *Letters*, vol. 8, pp. 648n, 746n.

96. Dickens to Frederic Ouvry, 5 September 1858, Dickens, *Letters*, vol. 8, p. 648.

97. Dickens to Wilkie Collins, 6 September 1858, ibid., vol. 8, p. 650.

98. Elizabeth Barrett Browning, letter of 11 July 1858, see Dickens, *Letters*, vol. 8, p. 597n.

99. Elizabeth Barrett Browning, letter of 5 October 1858, ibid., vol. 8, pp. 648–9n.

100. Helen Thomson to Mrs Stark, 30 August 1858, ibid., vol. 8, p. 746.

101. Ibid., vol. 8, pp. 478–9.

102. See Slater, *The Great Charles Dickens Scandal*, p. 501.

103. Dickens to Angela Burdett-Coutts, 27 October 1858, *Letters*, vol. 8, p. 689.

104. Dickens, *A Tale of Two Cities* (1859), ed. George Woodcock (Harmondsworth, 1980), pp. 117, 110, 104.

105. 'Extraordinary Libel Case', *Weekly Chronicle*, 26 June 1858.

106. Ibid.
107. 'Board of Health Actions', *Builder*, 3 July 1858.
108. Report in the *Standard*, 26 July 1858; for an account of the case see Wise, *Inconvenient People*, pp. 252–64.
109. Wise, *Inconvenient People*, pp. 265–6.
110. Ibid., pp. 271–7; *Daily News*, 24 August 1858; *The Times*, 24 June 1859.
111. See *ODNB* entry for Simon Bernard.
112. Disraeli to Sarah Brydges Willyams, 15 January 1858, *Letters*, vol. 7, p. 114.
113. Blanchard, *Life and Reminiscences*, vol. 1, p. 190.
114. Disraeli, *Letters*, vol. 7, p. 120n.
115. Dickens to François Régnier, 20 February 1858, *Letters*, vol. 8, p. 522.
116. Queen Victoria to her daughter Vicky, 20 February 1858, *Dearest Child*, p. 54.
117. For details of the arrangements at the trial see Irving, *Annals of Our Time*, pp. 516–17.
118. Bernard, *Life of Dr Simon Bernard, with Judgment and Extracts from the Press on his Trial* (London, 1858), p. 10. See also Irving, *Annals of Our Time*, p. 516.
119. 'A Day at the Old Bailey during Dr Bernard's Trial', *Reynolds's Newspaper*, 18 April 1858.
120. Edwin James, *Speech of Edwin James, Esq., One of Her Majesty's Counsel, in Defence of Dr Simon Bernard, delivered at the Central Criminal Court, on Friday, the 16th of April, 1858, revised and edited by James Gordon Allan, of the Inner Temple, Esquire, Barrister at Law* (London, 1858), pp. 5, 17, 22, 29.
121. Bernard, *Life of Dr Simon Bernard*, p. 13.
122. Ibid.
123. James Gordon Allan's note in James, *Speech of Edwin James, Esq.*, p. 30.
124. See Simon Bernard's own pamphlet recounting the trial, *The Life and Extraordinary Trial of Simon Bernard, for conspiring to assassinate in the French Empire, with Important Disclosures* (London, 1858), p. 8.
125. Bernard, *Life of Dr Simon Bernard*, p. 15.
126. J. Ewing Ritchie, *About London* (London, 1860), pp. 9–10.
127. Engels to Marx, 22 April 1858, *Marx–Engels Collected Works*, vol. 40, p. 309.
128. 'The Acquittal of Dr Bernard', *The Times*, 20 April 1858; see also the *Morning Post*, 20 April 1858.
129. 'Trial of Dr Bernard', *People's Paper*, 24 April 1858.
130. 'Liberation of Dr Bernard', *Reynolds's Newspaper*, 25 April 1858.
131. James, *Speech of Edwin James, Esq.*, p. 22. Wyld is probably James Wyld, the cartographer who exhibited a huge globe in Leicester Square in the 1850s.
132. See *ODNB* entry for Simon Bernard.
133. Yates, *Recollections and Experiences*, vol. 2, pp. 31–2.
134. *ODNB* entry for Edwin James.
135. Yates, *Recollections and Experiences*, vol. 2, p. 133 and n.
136. 'Good News for the Thames', *Era*, 18 July 1858.
137. Editorial, *The Times*, 21 July 1858.
138. 'Sketches in Parliament', *Illustrated London News*, vol. 33 (24 July 1858), p. 88.
139. 'Parliamentary Intelligence', *The Times*, 24 July 1858.
140. 'The Results of the Session', *Bentley's Miscellany*, vol. 44 (August 1858), p. 217.
141. Queen Victoria to Lord Derby, 15 August 1858, *Letters of Queen Victoria*, vol. 3, p. 379.
142. Queen Victoria to Viscount Canning, 2 December 1858, ibid., vol. 3, p. 389.
143. See *Illustrated London News*, vol. 33 (31 July 1858), p. 111, and *Era*, 8 August 1858.
144. *Punch*, vol. 35 (21 August 1858), p. 80.
145. 'The Working of the New Divorce Bill', *English Woman's Journal*, vol. 1 (1 July 1858), p. 339.
146. 'Domestic Differences', *Era*, 25 July 1858.
147. 'Commission of Lunacy – Private Asylums' and Editorial, *Morning Chronicle*, 27 July 1858.
148. 'The Closing Session', *Era*, 1 August 1858.

149. 'The Session', *The Times*, 2 August 1858.
150. Ibid.
151. Disraeli to Lady Londonderry, 24 July 1858, *Letters*, vol. 7, pp. 220–21.
152. Disraeli to Sarah Brydges Willyams, 26 July 1858, ibid., vol. 7, pp. 222–3.
153. 'Father Thames', *Punch*, vol. 35 (31 July 1858), p. 47.
154. Disraeli to Sarah Brydges Willyams, 26 July 1858, *Letters*, vol. 7, p. 222.
155. Disraeli to Sarah Brydges Willyams, 5 August 1858, ibid., vol. 7, p. 225.
156. Ibid., vol. 7, p. 223.

Chapter Seven: The aftermath of the hot summer

1. See Thackeray, diary, 5 August 1858, *Letters and Private Papers*, vol. 4, p. 393.
2. *The Virginians*, number 11, see ibid., vol. 4, pp. 109–10n.
3. Sala, *Twice Round the Clock*, ed. Collins, pp. 333, 344.
4. Ibid., pp. 344–5.
5. Sala to Yates, 7 November 1858, *Letters*, pp. 44 and 46n.
6. Sala, *Things I Have Seen and People I Have Known*, 2 vols (London, 1894), vol. 1, p. 3.
7. 'Mr Thackeray and Mr Edmund Yates – The Garrick Club', *Morning Post*, 17 November 1858.
8. Dickens to Thackeray, 24 November 1858, *Letters*, vol. 8, pp. 707–8.
9. Ibid., vol. 8, p. 708.
10. Thackeray to Dickens, 26 November 1858, *Letters and Private Papers*, vol. 4, p. 118.
11. Yates, *Recollections and Experiences*, vol. 2, p. 36n.
12. Dickens to Yates, *c.* 28 November 1858, *Letters*, vol. 8, p. 711.
13. Thackeray to Blackwood, 2 December 1858, Ray, *Thackeray: The Age of Wisdom*, p. 285.
14. Thackeray to Anny and Minny Thackeray, 4 December 1858, *Letters and Private Papers*, vol. 4, p. 121.
15. Thackeray to Blackwood, 12–15 December 1858, Ray, *Thackeray: The Age of Wisdom*, p. 286.
16. Thackeray, 'The Smiler with the Knife', reproduced in *Letters and Private Papers*, vol. 4, facing p. 102.
17. Anny Thackeray to Amy Crowe, late December 1858, *Journals and Letters*, p. 58.
18. Charles Dickens Jr, 'The Offence is Rank', *Punch*, vol. 35 (11 December 1858), p. 239.
19. Henry Silver, diary, 19 January 1859, Ray, *Thackeray: The Age of Wisdom*, p. 288.
20. Thackeray to William Synge, *c.* mid-January 1859, ibid., pp. 288–9.
21. See Thackeray, *Letters and Private Papers*, vol. 4, p. 131n.
22. *Illustrated Times*, 29 January 1859; Ray, *Thackeray: The Age of Wisdom*, p. 289.
23. Sala to Yates, 31 January 1859, *Letters*, p. 59.
24. Thackeray to Synge, mid-January 1859, Ray, *Thackeray: The Age of Wisdom*, p. 288.
25. See Thackeray, *Letters and Private Papers*, vol. 4, p. 131n.
26. Anny Thackeray to William Synge, 6 March 1859, *Journals and Letters*, p. 73.
27. Thackeray to Charles Kingsley, 12 March 1859, *Letters and Private Papers*, vol. 4, pp. 134–5.
28. See Ray, *Thackeray: The Age of Wisdom*, p. 290, and Thackeray, *Letters and Private Papers*, vol. 4, p. 131n.
29. Thackeray, 'Punch's Prize Novelists', *Punch*, April–October 1847, reprinted in *Miscellaneous Contributions to 'Punch' 1843–1854*, ed. George Saintsbury, vol. 8 of *The Oxford Thackeray*, 17 vols (Oxford, 1908).
30. Thackeray to John Blackwood, 12–15 December 1858, Ray, *Thackeray: The Age of Wisdom*, p. 290.
31. Thackeray, 'Strange to Say, On Club Paper', *Cornhill Magazine*, vol. 8 (November 1863), pp. 638, 639.
32. *Sheffield and Rotherham Independent*, 29 January 1859.
33. Ibid., 2 April 1859.

34. Yates, *Mr Thackeray, Mr Yates, and the Garrick Club*, pp. 5, 12, 15.

35. Yates, *Recollections and Experiences*, vol. 2, p. 32.

36. See *ODNB* entry for Yates.

37. See Dickens to Yates, 19 February 1859, *Letters*, vol. 9, p. 30.

38. Dickens to Yates, 23 September 1860, ibid., vol. 9, pp. 315–16.

39. Dickens to Yates, 12 May 1868, ibid., vol. 12, p. 107.

40. Ibid., vol. 12, p. 107n.

41. See the whole chapter devoted to his desire to be like Thackeray's Pendennis, *Recollections and Experiences*, vol. 1.

42. Yates to Herman Merivale, 25 May 1889, Thackeray, *Letters and Private Papers*, vol. 4, pp. 133–4n.

43. See *The Times*, 18 and 26 January, 10, 17, 21, 24 February, 1 and 12 March 1859.

44. Thackeray to Whitwell Elwin, May 1861, Ray, *Thackeray: The Age of Wisdom*, p. 312.

45. Henry Silver, diary, 27 May 1863, ibid., pp. 404–5.

46. See Dickens's tribute to Thackeray, 'In Memoriam', *Cornhill Magazine*, vol. 9 (February 1864), p. 129.

47. See, for example, James Hannay in the *Edinburgh Evening Courant* and an editorial in the *Daily News*, quoted in Dickens, *Letters*, vol. 10, p. 347n.

48. Dickens to Collins, 25 January 1864, *Letters*, vol. 10, pp. 346–7.

49. Dickens, 'In Memoriam', *Cornhill Magazine*, vol. 9 (February 1864), pp. 129, 130, 132.

50. See the excellent chapter on the Garrick Club affair in Leary, *The 'Punch' Brotherhood*, pp. 79–109.

51. Information from Marcus Risdell, former art curator at the Garrick Club. See also Geoffrey Ashton, *Pictures in the Garrick Club: A Catalogue* (London, 1997).

52. Sala to Yates, 7 and 15 November 1858, *Letters*, pp. 44, 52.

53. Dickens to Forster for Messrs Bradbury and Evans, 27 November 1858, *Letters*, vol. 8, p. 711.

54. Dickens to Forster, 24 and ?25 January 1859, ibid., vol. 9, p. 15.

55. See Slater, *Charles Dickens*, pp. 469–75.

56. Henry Silver, diary, 2 February 1859, quoted in Leary, *The 'Punch' Brotherhood*, p. 89.

57. See Leary, *The 'Punch' Brotherhood*, p. 168, and Dickens, *Letters*, vol. 8, p. 608n.

58. Bradbury and Evans, 'Mr Dickens and His Late Publishers', printed in newspapers including *Trewman's Exeter Flying Post*, 2 June 1859.

59. See John Blackwood to Lewes, 7 June 1858, and Lewes to Blackwood, 9 June, 19 July, and 16 August 1858, *The George Eliot Letters*, vol. 2, pp. 463, 464, 469, 474.

60. Dickens to Lewes, 14 November 1859, *Letters*, vol. 9, p. 160; Lewes, journal, 15 November 1859, and George Eliot, journal, 18 November 1859, *The George Eliot Letters*, vol. 3, pp. 204, 205.

61. Yates, *Recollections and Experiences*, vol. 2, p. 167.

62. Dickens to Forster, 25 August 1859, *Letters*, vol. 9, pp. 112–13n.

63. Dickens to Wilkie Collins, 6 October 1859, ibid., vol. 9, p. 127.

64. See Slater, *Charles Dickens*, pp. 498, 511–12, 527.

65. See Tomalin, *The Invisible Woman*, especially the chapter entitled 'Vanishing into Space', and Slater, *The Great Charles Dickens Scandal*, p. 174.

66. Dickens to William de Cerjat, 16 March 1862, *Letters*, vol. 10, p. 53.

67. Dickens to Angela Burdett-Coutts, 14 January 1854, ibid., vol. 7, p. 245.

68. See Dickens to Angela Burdett-Coutts, 12 February 1864, ibid., vol. 10, pp. 355–6.

69. Alfred Dickens to G.W. Rusden, 11 August 1870, ibid., vol. 12, pp. 734–5.

70. Sydney Dickens to Dickens, 19 March 1869, and Georgina Hogarth to Annie Fields, 18 June 1872, in Nayder, *The Other Dickens*, pp. 280–1 and n.

71. Dickens to de Cerjat, 16 March 1862, *Letters*, vol. 10, p. 53.

72. Dickens to the Rev. John Taylor, 4 May 1867, ibid., vol. 11, pp. 362–3.

73. Dickens to Janet Wills, 26 June 1868, ibid., vol. 12, p. 139.

74. Sala to Yates, 18 August 1868, *Letters*, p. 114.

75. Dickens to James Fields, 7 July 1868, *Letters*, vol. 12, p. 149.
76. Dickens to Macready, 20 July 1869, ibid., vol. 12, p. 378.
77. Dickens to W.H. Wills, 21 October 1866, ibid., vol. 11, p. 257.
78. See Dickens to his brother Alfred's wife Helen, 13 November 1859, ibid., vol. 9, p. 159.
79. Anna Dickens to Christiana Thompson, ?10 January 1852, in Nayder, *The Other Dickens*, p. 222.
80. See Dickens to T.J. Thompson, 6 January 1859, *Letters*, vol. 9, p. 6 and n.
81. Dickens to Forster, 24 October, and to Henry Morley, 21 October 1868, ibid., vol. 12, pp. 208, 206.
82. See *York Herald*, 24 and 31 October 1868, *Manchester Times* and *Preston Guardian*, 31 October 1868.
83. Sala to Yates, 26 October 1868, *Letters*, p. 116.
84. See Slater, *Charles Dickens*, p. 608.
85. Ibid., pp. 608–9.
86. Dickens's Last Will and Testament, 12 May 1869, *Letters*, vol. 12, p. 732.
87. Ibid.
88. Dickens to Hepworth Dixon, 15 January 1864, ibid., vol. 10, p. 341.
89. Thackeray to George Smith, 17 December 1863, ibid., vol. 10, p. 341n.
90. Darwin to Hooker, 2 November 1858, *Correspondence*, vol. 7, p. 181.
91. See *The Times*, 27 November 1858; Summerscale, *Mrs Robinson's Disgrace*, pp. 190–99.
92. Darwin to Wallace, 25 January 1859, *Correspondence*, vol. 7, p. 241.
93. Darwin to W.D. Fox, 12 February 1859, ibid., vol. 7, p. 247.
94. Darwin to Hooker, 26 May 1859, ibid., vol. 7, p. 300 and n.
95. See 'Court for Divorce and Matrimonial Causes', *The Times*, 3 March 1859.
96. Ibid.; see also *Daily News* and *Morning Post*, 27 July 1859.
97. See Summerscale, *Mrs Robinson's Disgrace*, p. 211. For the importance of Sudbrook Park in the history of hydropathy, see Richard Metcalfe, *The Rise and Progress of Hydropathy in England and Scotland* (London, 1906).
98. Summerscale, *Mrs Robinson's Disgrace*, pp. 217–20.
99. Darwin to Thomas Campbell Eyton, 4 August 1858, *Correspondence*, vol. 7, p. 145.
100. Darwin to John Phillips, 1 September 1858, ibid., vol. 7, p. 153.
101. See Freeman, *Charles Darwin*, pp. 101–2.
102. Huxley to Hooker, 5 September 1858, *Life and Letters of Charles Darwin*, vol. 1, pp. 159–60; Darwin to Huxley, 28 December 1859, *Correspondence*, vol. 7, p. 459.
103. 'Notes of the Week', *Illustrated London News*, vol. 33 (25 September 1858), p. 284.
104. *Athenaeum*, 16 October 1858, p. 492.
105. 'The British Association', *The Times*, 24 September 1858.
106. Ibid.
107. Owen, *President's Address*, pp. 91, 92.
108. Darwin to Hooker, 6 October 1858, *Correspondence*, vol. 7, p. 165.
109. Wallace to his mother and to Hooker, 6 October 1858, *Letters from the Malay Archipelago*, pp. 180, 181.
110. Owen, *President's Address*, p. 107.
111. Darwin to Huxley, 1 December 1858, *Correspondence*, vol. 7, p. 214.
112. Darwin to John Murray, 25 July 1859, ibid., vol. 7, p. 319.
113. See Darwin to Murray, 31 August 1859, and to J. de Quatrefages de Bréau, 5 December 1859, ibid., vol. 7, pp. 327 and n., 416.
114. Darwin to Murray, 10 September 1859, ibid., vol. 7, p. 331.
115. See Hooker, *Life and Letters*, vol. 1, p. 520.
116. Lyell to Darwin, [November] 1859, *Life, Letters, and Journals*, vol. 2, p. 325. The editor of Lyell's correspondence dates this letter 3 October, but Darwin had not received his own advance copies of *Origin* at that date, so Lyell could not have received his so early.
117. Ibid.
118. Darwin to Hooker, 24 February 1863, *Correspondence*, vol. 11, p. 173.

119. Darwin to Wallace, 9 August 1859, ibid., vol. 7, p. 324.

120. See ibid., vol. 7, p. 324n.

121. For the official publication date of *Origin* and the list of men to whom presentation copies were sent out early in the month, see ibid., vol. 7, pp. 533–6 (Appendix VIII).

122. Darwin to Wallace, 12 November 1859, ibid., vol. 7, p. 375.

123. Charles Kingsley to Darwin, 18 November 1859, ibid., vol. 7, pp. 379–80.

124. See Darwin to John Lubbock, 14 December 1859, and to W.D. Fox, 25 December 1859, ibid., vol. 7, pp. 433, 449.

125. George Eliot to Barbara Bodichon, 5 December 1859, *The George Eliot Letters*, vol. 3, p. 227. For Lewes's writings on science and relations with other scientific men, see Rosemary Ashton, *G.H. Lewes: A Life* (Oxford, 1991).

126. Engels to Marx, 11 or 12 December 1859, *Marx–Engels Collected Works*, vol. 40, p. 551.

127. Marx to Ferdinand Lassalle, 16 January 1861, ibid., vol. 41, pp. 246–7.

128. Marx to Engels, 7 August 1866, ibid., vol. 42, p. 304. See Gareth Stedman Jones, *Karl Marx: Greatness and Illusion* (London, 2016), p. 567. The French work was Pierre Trémaux, *Origine et Transformations de l'Homme et des autres Êtres* (Paris, 1865).

129. Hooker to Darwin, 21 November 1859, *Correspondence*, vol. 7, p. 383.

130. Erasmus Darwin to Darwin, 23 November 1859, ibid., vol. 7, p. 390.

131. Huxley to Darwin, 23 November 1859, ibid., vol. 7, p. 391.

132. Huxley to Hooker, 31 December 1859, *Life and Letters*, vol. 1, p. 177. The letter to Darwin has been lost.

133. Darwin to Hooker, 28 December 1859, *Correspondence*, vol. 7, p. 457.

134. Darwin to Huxley, 28 December 1859, ibid., vol. 7, p. 458.

135. See Huxley's essay, 'The Reception of the "Origin of Species"', written for *The Life and Letters of Charles Darwin*, ed. Francis Darwin, 3 vols (London, 1887), printed in *Life and Letters of Thomas Henry Huxley*, vol. 1, p. 168.

136. Huxley, 'Darwin on the Origin of Species', *The Times*, 26 December 1859.

137. Ibid.

138. Huxley, 'The Reception of the "Origin of Species"', in *Life and Letters of Charles Darwin*, vol. 1, p. 170.

139. Darwin to Huxley, 14 April 1860, *Correspondence*, vol. 8, p. 160 and n.

140. Darwin to W.B. Carpenter, 3 December 1859, ibid., vol. 7, p. 412.

141. Adam Sedgwick to Darwin, 24 November 1859, ibid., vol. 7, pp. 396, 397.

142. Hooker, letters of May 1860, *Life and Letters*, vol. 1, pp. 513, 514.

143. [Richard Owen], review of *Origin of Species* and other works, *Edinburgh Review*, vol. 111 (April 1860), pp. 487–532. See Nicolaas A. Rupke, *Richard Owen: Victorian Naturalist* (New Haven, Conn. and London, 1994), pp. 238–40.

144. Darwin to John Murray, 9 April 1860, *Correspondence*, vol. 8, p. 152.

145. Darwin to Hooker, 18 April 1860, ibid., vol. 8, p. 162.

146. Wallace, note, February 1860, *Letters from the Malay Archipelago*, p. 209.

147. Darwin to Wallace, 18 May 1860, *Correspondence*, vol. 8, pp. 219–20.

148. Darwin to Lyell, 25 June 1860, ibid., vol. 8, pp. 265–6.

149. See *ODNB* entry for Wilberforce; he acquired the nickname after behaving equivocally over the appointment to the bishopric of Hereford in 1847.

150. Hooker to Darwin, 2 July 1860, Darwin, *Correspondence*, vol. 8, p. 270.

151. Ibid., vol. 8, pp. 270–71.

152. Huxley to F. Dyster, 9 September 1860, quoted in *ODNB* entry on Huxley. See Huxley, *Life and Letters*, vol. 1, pp. 184–5, for reports of Huxley's speech by various members of the audience.

153. Huxley to Francis Darwin, 27 June 1891, *Life and Letters*, vol. I, p. 188; for various accounts of the encounter, see ibid., vol. 1, pp. 179–87.

154. Darwin to Hooker, 2 July 1860, *Correspondence*, vol. 8, p. 272.

155. Darwin to Huxley, 3 July 1860, ibid., vol. 8, p. 277.

156. For Chapman's career see Rosemary Ashton, *142 Strand: A Radical Address in Victorian London* (London, 2006).

157. Darwin, note written for John Chapman, 20 May 1865, *Correspondence*, vol. 13, pp. 481–2 (Appendix IV).

158. Editors' notes, ibid., vol. 13, p. 484.

159. A number of biographies of Darwin focus on his health, some offering physical, others psychological diagnoses; among the latter see Ralph Colp, *To Be an Invalid: The Illness of Charles Darwin* (Chicago and London, 1977), and John Bowlby, *Charles Darwin: A Biography* (London, 1990).

160. Wallace, *My Life*, p. 238.

161. Huxley to George Romanes, 9 May 1882, *Life and Letters*, vol. 2, p. 39.

162. Darwin, *Autobiography*, p. 28.

163. Ibid., pp. 136–7.

164. Ibid., pp. 27, 138.

165. Raverat, *Period Piece*, p. 188.

166. Darwin, *Autobiography*, pp. 140, 144–5.

167. Wallace, *My Life*, pp. 375, 116–17.

168. Wallace to Philip Sclater, 31 March 1862, *Letters from the Malay Archipelago*, pp. 283–5.

169. Wallace to Bates, 24 December 1860, ibid., p. 239.

170. See Freeman, *Charles Darwin: A Companion*, p. 83.

171. For an interesting discussion of the ideas of evolutionary spiritualists see Sherrie Lynn Lyons, *Species, Serpents, Spirits, and Skulls: Science at the Margins in the Victorian Age* (Albany, New York, 2009).

172. See *The Darwin–Wallace Celebration*, pp. 1–3.

173. Ibid., p. 29.

174. Darwin, *Autobiography*, p. 123.

175. *The Darwin–Wallace Celebration*, p. 32.

176. Ibid., pp. 6–11.

Epilogue

1. See *A Postman's Round 1858–1861: Selected Extracts from the Diary of Edward Harvey*, ed. Richard Story with an Introduction by Tony Mason, University of Warwick Library Occasional Publications, number 10 (Coventry, 1982), p. 19.

2. See Jeffrey Richards, *The Golden Age of Pantomime: Slapstick, Spectacle and Subversion in Victorian England* (London, 2015), p. 2.

3. Ibid., pp. 6–7, 35–6.

4. 'Pantomimes', *Athenaeum*, 1 January 1859.

5. 'Christmas Pantomimes and Burlesques', *Era*, 2 January 1859.

6. Richards, *The Golden Age of Pantomime*, p. 158.

7. See 'The Christmas Entertainments', a preview of the season's pantomimes, *Era*, 26 December 1858.

8. E.L. Blanchard, *Robin Hood*, licensed for performance at the Theatre Royal, Drury Lane, on 27 December 1858, Lord Chamberlain's Plays, Add MS 52,977J, British Library.

9. C.J. Collins, *Harlequin Father Thames; or, The River Queen and the Great Lord Mayor of London*, licensed for performance at the Royal Surrey Theatre on 27 December 1858, Lord Chamberlain's Plays, Add MS 52,977B, British Library.

10. E.L. Blanchard, *Harlequin and Old Izaak Walton; or, Tom Moore of Fleet Street, the Silver Trout, and the Seven Sisters of Tottenham*, licensed for performance at Sadler's Wells on 27 December 1858, Lord Chamberlain's Plays, Add MS 52,977I, British Library.

11. Thomas Mowbray, *Harlequin Master Walter; or, The Hunchback Nunky and the Little Fairies*, licensed for performance at the Royal Soho Theatre on 27 December 1858, Lord Chamberlain's Plays, Add MS 52,977Y, British Library.

12. George Conquest, *Harlequin Guy Faux*, licensed for performance at the Grecian Saloon on 27 December 1858, Lord Chamberlain's Plays, Add MS 52,977F, British Library.

13. W.E. Suter, *Harlequin and the Forty Thieves; or, Ali Baba and the Fairy Ardinella*, licensed for performance at the Queen's Theatre on 27 December 1858, Lord Chamberlain's Plays, Add MS 52,977S, British Library; W. Cusnie, *Tit, Tat, Toe, The Three Butcher Boys; or, Harlequin Old Father Thames and Mephistopheles*, licensed for performance at the Effingham Saloon on 27 December 1858, Lord Chamberlain's Plays, Add MS 52,977D, British Library.

14. See 'Christmas Pantomimes and Burlesques', *Era*, 2 January 1859.

15. Ibid.

16. John Buckstone, *Undine; or, Harlequin and the Spirit of the Waters*, licensed for performance at the Theatre Royal, Haymarket, on 27 December 1858, Lord Chamberlain's Plays, Add MS 52,977V, British Library.

17. See Queen Victoria, journal, 21 July 1858, online at http://www.queenvictoriasjournals. org, vol. 45, p. 283.

18. For instructions for omissions from *Harlequin Father Thames*, see 'Register of Lord Chamberlain's Plays', vol. 2 (1852-65), Add MS 53,703, British Library. The censor also objects to passages in *Harlequin Master Walter*, *Robin Hood*, and *Tit, Tat, Toe*. In his notes to *Tit, Tat, Toe* the censor, William Donne, wrote on 20 December 1858; 'The Rule is that a Pictorial representation is permitted, but members of the Royal Family must not be represented on the Stage by male or female performers.' For censorship in the theatre see John Russell Stephens, *The Censorship of English Drama 1824–1901* (Cambridge, 1980).

19. 'Christmas Pantomimes and Burlesques', *Era*, 2 January 1859.

20. See Halliday, *The Great Stink*, pp. 144, 182–3.

21. *Illustrated London News*, vol. 98 (21 March 1891), p. 368.

22. Bazalgette, interview with *Cassell's Saturday Journal*, August 1890, quoted in Halliday, *The Great Stink*, p. 183.

Select Bibliography

Manuscript and archive sources

Beinecke Rare Book and Manuscript Library, Yale University (George Eliot / George Henry Lewes Collection)

British Library (Carnarvon Papers; Lord Chamberlain's Plays; Register of Lord Chamberlain's Plays; Henry Silver's *Punch* Diary)

Bromley Local Studies Library (Burial Register)

Lambeth Palace Library Archives (Tait Papers)

Met Office National Meteorological Archive, Exeter

National Library of Scotland (George Combe Papers)

V&A Theatre and Performance Archive, Blythe House, Kensington Olympia (Haymarket Theatre playbills)

Online sources

19th-Century British Library Newspaper Archive

BBC History Online

Hansard Online

Illustrated London News Historical Archive

Internet Archive

Old Bailey Online

Parliamentary Papers Online

Queen Victoria's Journals Online

The Times Digital Archive

Newspapers, magazines and periodicals

All the Year Round

Annual Register

Athenaeum

Bentley's Miscellany

British Medical Journal

Bromley Record
Builder
Chambers's Exeter Journal
Cornhill Magazine
Court Circular
Daily News
Daily Telegraph
Edinburgh Review
English Woman's Journal
Era
Fraser's Magazine
Freeman's Journal and Daily Commercial Advertiser
Household Words
Illustrated London News
Illustrated Times
Liverpool Mercury
Manchester Times
Morning Chronicle
Morning Herald
Morning Post
New York Daily Tribune
Observer
People's Paper
Preston Guardian
Punch
Racing Times
Reynolds's Newspaper
St James's Chronicle
Sheffield and Rotherham Independent
The Standard
Theatrical Journal
The Times
Town Talk
Trueman's Exeter Flying Post
Weekly Chronicle
York Herald

Books and articles

Allan, Janice M., 'Mrs Robinson's "Day-book of Iniquity": Reading Bodies of/and Evidence in the Context of the 1858 Medical Reform Act', in *The Female Body in Medicine and Literature*, ed. Andrew Mangham and Greta Depledge, Liverpool, 2011, pp. 169–81.
Allen, Michele, *Cleansing the City: Sanitary Geographies in Victorian London*, Athens, Ohio, 2008.
Altick, Richard D., *The English Common Reader: A Social History of the Mass Reading Public, 1800–1900*, Columbus, Ohio, 1957, reprinted 1988.
—*The Shows of London*, Cambridge, Mass. and London, 1978.
Ashton, Geoffrey, *Pictures in the Garrick Club: A Catalogue*, London, 1997.
Ashton, Rosemary, *142 Strand: A Radical Address in Victorian London*, London, 2006.
—*George Eliot: A Life*, London, 1996.
—*G.H. Lewes: A Life*, Oxford, 1991.
—*Little Germany: Exile and Asylum in Victorian England*, Oxford, 1986.
—*Thomas and Jane Carlyle: Portrait of a Marriage*, London, 2002.
Aspden, Thomas, *Historical Sketches of the House of Stanley, and Biography of Edward Geoffrey, 14th Earl of Derby*, London, 1877.

Atkinson, Diane, *The Criminal Conversation of Mrs Norton*, London, 2012.

Barnes, David S., *The Great Stink of Paris and the Nineteenth-Century Struggle against Filth and Germs*, Baltimore, Maryland, 2006.

Bennett, A.R., *London and Londoners in the Eighteen-Fifties and Sixties*, London, 1924.

Berger, Francesco, *Reminiscences, Impressions and Anecdotes*, London, 1913.

Bernard, Simon, *The Life and Extraordinary Trial of Simon Bernard, for Conspiring to Assassinate in the French Empire, with Important Disclosures*, London, 1858.

—*Life of Dr Simon Bernard, with Judgment and Extracts from the Press on his Trial*, London, 1858.

Bibby, Cyril, *Scientist Extraordinary: The Life and Scientific Work of Thomas Henry Huxley 1825–1895*, London, 1972.

Black, Barbara, *A Room of His Own: A Literary-Cultural Study of Victorian Clubland*, Athens, Ohio, 2012.

Blake, Robert, *Disraeli*, London, 1966.

Blanchard, Edward Leman, *The Life and Reminiscences of E.L. Blanchard, with Notes from the Diary of Wm. Blanchard*, ed. Clement Scott and Cecil Howard, 2 vols, London, 1891.

Boas, Guy, *The Garrick Club 1831–1947*, London, 1948.

Bowlby, John, *Charles Darwin: A Biography*, London, 1990.

Brake, Laurel and Marysa Demoor (eds), *The Lure of Illustration in the Nineteenth Century: Picture and Press*, London, 2009.

Briggs, C.F. and A. Maverick, *The Story of the Telegraph and a History of the Great Atlantic Cable*, New York, 1858.

Browne, Janet, *Charles Darwin: The Power of Place*, London, 2002.

Buchanan, R. Angus, *The Life and Times of Isambard Kingdom Brunel*, London, 2002.

Bynum, W.F., *Science and the Practice of Medicine in the Nineteenth Century*, Cambridge, 1994.

Carlyle, Thomas and Jane Welsh Carlyle, *The Collected Letters of Thomas and Jane Welsh Carlyle*, ed. C.R. Sanders, K.J. Fielding, Clyde de L. Ryals et al., 42 vols to date, Durham, North Carolina, 1970–.

Casteras, Susan P., *Images of Victorian Womanhood in Victorian Art*, London, 1987.

Cesarani, David, *Disraeli the Novel Politician*, London, 2016.

Clarke, Basil F.L., *Parish Churches of London*, London, 1966.

Cobbold, David Lytton, *A Blighted Marriage: The Life of Rosina Bulwer Lytton, Irish Beauty, Satirist and Tormented Wife, 1802–1882*, Knebworth, 1999.

Colp, Ralph, *To Be an Invalid: The Illness of Charles Darwin*, Chicago and London, 1977.

Cookson, Gillian, *The Cable: Wire to the New World*, Stroud, 2012.

Copland, Edward A., *Photography for the Many*, London, 1858.

Cowling, Mary, *The Artist as Anthropologist: The Representation of Type and Character in Victorian Art*, Cambridge, 1989.

Darwin, Charles, *The Autobiography of Charles Darwin*, ed. Nora Barlow, London, 1958.

—*The Correspondence of Charles Darwin*, ed. Frederick Burkhardt et al., 22 vols so far, Cambridge, 1985–.

—*The Life and Letters of Charles Darwin*, ed. Francis Darwin, 3 vols, London, 1887.

—*On the Origin of Species by Means of Natural Selection, or the Preservation of Favoured Races in the Struggle for Life*, ed. John Burrow, Harmondsworth, 1968.

Darwin, Emma, *A Century of Family Letters*, ed. Henrietta Litchfield, 2 vols, London, 1915.

The Darwin–Wallace Celebration held on Thursday 1 July 1908 by the Linnaean Society of London, London, 1908.

Daunton, Martin, 'London's "Great Stink" and Victorian Urban Planning', *BBC History*, 2004.

David, Saul, *The Indian Mutiny: 1857*, London, 2002.

Davies, James A., *John Forster: A Literary Life*, Leicester, 1983.

Davis, Tracy C., 'Actresses and Prostitutes in Victorian London', *Theatre Research International*, vol. 13 (1988), pp. 221–34.

Dickens, Charles, *A Tale of Two Cities*, London, 1859.

—*David Copperfield*, London, 1850.

—*The Letters of Charles Dickens*, ed. Madeleine House, Graham Storey, Kathleen Tillotson et al., 12 vols, Oxford, 1965–2002.

—*The Speeches of Charles Dickens*, ed. K.J. Fielding, Hemel Hempstead, 1988.

Disraeli, Benjamin, *Benjamin Disraeli Letters*, ed. J.A.W. Gunn, M.G. Wiebe, Michel W. Pharand et al., 10 vols so far, Toronto, 1982–.

—*Disraeli's Reminiscences*, ed. Helen M. Swartz and Marvin Swartz, London, 1975.

—*Sybil, or the Two Nations*, London, 1845.

—*Tancred*, London, 1847.

[Drysdale, George], *Physical, Sexual, and Natural Religion, by a Student of Medicine*, London, 1855.

Edwards, P.D., *Dickens's 'Young Men': George Augustus Sala, Edmund Yates, and the World of Victorian Journalism*, Aldershot, 1997.

[Egan, Charles], *A Handy Book on the New Law of Divorce and Matrimonial Causes, and the Practice of the Divorce Court*, London, 1860.

Eliot, George, *The George Eliot Letters*, ed. Gordon S. Haight, 9 vols, New Haven, Conn., 1954–5, 1978.

English, Mary P., *Victorian Values: The Life and Times of Dr Edwin Lankester, MD, FRS*, London, 1990.

Ferguson, Niall, *The World's Banker: The History of the House of Rothschild*, London, 1998.

Field, Henry M., *History of the Atlantic Telegraph*, New York, 1867.

Fielding, K.J., 'Dickens and the Hogarth Scandal', *Nineteenth-Century Fiction*, vol. 10 (June 1955), pp. 64–74.

Finer, S.E., *The Life and Times of Sir Edwin Chadwick*, London, 1952.

Flanery, Michael A., *Alfred Russel Wallace: A Rediscovered Life*, Seattle, Washington, 2011.

Freeman, R.B., *Charles Darwin: A Companion*, Folkestone, 1978.

Gibbon, Charles, *The Life of George Combe*, 2 vols, London, 1878.

Halliday, Stephen, *The Great Filth: The War against Disease in Victorian England*, Stroud, 2007.

—*The Great Stink of London: Sir Joseph Bazalgette and the Cleansing of the Victorian Capital*, Stroud, 1999.

Hamlin, Christopher, *Public Health and Social Justice in the Age of Chadwick: Britain 1800–1854*, Cambridge, 1998.

Harrington, N.H. and Edmund Yates, *Your Likeness – One Shilling!*, in *Lacy's Acting Edition*, vol. 36 (1858).

Harvey, Edward, *A Postman's Round 1858–1861: Selected Extracts from the Diary of Edward Harvey*, ed. Richard Story with an Introduction by Tony Mason, University of Warwick Library Occasional Publications, number 10, Coventry, 1982.

Hay, Daisy. *Mr and Mrs Disraeli: A Strange Romance*, London, 2015.

Hayter, Alethea, *A Sultry Month: Scenes from London Literary Life in 1846*, London, 1966, reprinted 1992.

Hewitt, Martin, *The Dawn of the Cheap Press in Victorian Britain: The End of the 'Taxes on Knowledge' 1849–1869*, London, 2014.

Hodder, George, *Memories of My Time, including Personal Reminiscences of Eminent Men*, London, 1870.

Hollingshead, John, *The Birthplace of Podgers*, in *Lacy's Acting Edition*, vol. 35 (1858).

Hostettler, John, *Thomas Wakley: An Improbable Radical*, Chichester, 1993.

Huxley, Leonard, *Life and Letters of Sir Joseph Dalton Hooker*, 2 vols, London, 1918.

—*Life and Letters of Thomas Henry Huxley*, 2 vols, London, 1900.

Irving, Joseph, *The Annals of Our Time: A Diurnal of Events, Social and Political, Home and Foreign, from the Accession of Queen Victoria, June 20, 1837, to the Peace of Versailles, February 28, 1871*, new revised edition, London, 1880.

Jackson, Lee, *Dirty Old London: The Victorian Fight Against Filth*, New Haven, Conn., 2014.

James, Edwin, *Speech of Edwin James, Esq., One of Her Majesty's Counsel, in Defence of Dr Simon Bernard, delivered at the Central Criminal Court, on Friday, the 16th of April, 1858, revised and edited by James Gordon Allan, of the Inner Temple, Esquire, Barrister at Law*, London, 1858.

Jarvis, Stephen, *Death and Mr Pickwick*, London, 2014.

Johnston, Lucy (with Marion Kite and Helen Persson), *Nineteenth-Century Fashion in Detail*, London, 2005.

Jones, Colin, *Paris: Biography of a City*, London, 2004.

Jones, W.D., *Lord Derby and Victorian Conservatism*, Oxford, 1956.

Keynes, Randal, *Annie's Box: Charles Darwin, his Daughter, and Human Evolution*, London, 2001.

Kuhn, William, *The Politics of Pleasure: A Portrait of Benjamin Disraeli*, London, 2006.

Lambert, Royston, *Sir John Simon (1816–1904) and English Social Administration*, London, 1963.

Leary, Patrick, *The 'Punch' Brotherhood: Table Talk and Print Culture in Mid-Victorian London*, London, 2010.

Ledbetter, Rosanna, *A History of the Malthusian League 1877–1927*, Columbus, Ohio, 1976.

Lee, Dennis, *Lord Lyndhurst, the Flexible Tory*, Niwot, Colorado, 1994.

Leonard, R.L. *Nineteenth-Century British Premiers: Pitt to Rosebery*, New York, 2008.

Luckin, Bill, *Pollution and Control: A Social History of the Thames in the Nineteenth Century*, Bristol, 1986.

Lycett, Andrew, *Wilkie Collins: A Life of Sensation*, London, 2014.

Lyell, Sir Charles, *Life, Letters and Journals of Sir Charles Lyell, Bart., ed. by his sister-in-law Mrs Lyell*, 2 vols, London, 1881.

Lyons, Sherrie Lynn, *Species, Serpents, Spirits, and Skulls: Science at the Margins in the Victorian Age*, Albany, New York, 2009.

Lytton, Earl of, *The Life of Edward Bulwer Lytton, First Lord Lytton*, 2 vols, London, 1913.

Lytton, Rosina Bulwer, *A Blighted Life: A True Story*, London, 1881.

—*The Collected Letters of Rosina Bulwer Lytton*, ed. Marie Mulvey-Roberts, 3 vols, London, 2008.

—*Very Successful!*, London, 1856.

—*The World and his Wife: or, A Person of Consequence*, London, 1858.

Macready, William Charles, *Macready's Reminiscences, and Selections from his Diaries*, ed. Sir Frederick Pollock, 2 vols, London, 1875.

McDonald, Roger, *Mr Darwin's Shooter*, London, 1998.

McLaren, Angus, *Birth Control in Nineteenth-Century England*, London, 1978.

Marx, Karl and Friedrich Engels, *Marx–Engels Collected Works*, 50 vols, London, New York, and Moscow, 1975–2005.

—*Marx–Engels Werke*, 39 vols, Berlin, 1956–68.

Mayhew, Henry, *London Labour and the London Poor*, ed. Robert Douglas-Fairhurst, Oxford, 2010.

Meisel, Joseph S., 'Humour and Insult in the House of Commons: The Case of Palmerston and Disraeli', *Parliamentary History*, vol. 28, part 2 (2009), pp. 228–45.

Metcalfe, Richard, *The Rise and Progress of Hydropathy in England and Scotland*, London, 1906.

Mitchell, Leslie, *Bulwer Lytton: The Rise and Fall of a Victorian Man of Letters*, London and New York, 2003.

Monypenny, William Flavelle and George Earle Buckle, *The Life of Benjamin Disraeli*, new and revised edition, 2 vols, London, 1929.

Morley, Malcolm, 'The Theatrical Ternans', *The Dickensian*, vols 54–7 (January 1958–January 1961).

Mortimer, Roger, *The History of the Derby Stakes*, London, 1962.

Motley, John Lothrop, *The Correspondence of John Lothrop Motley*, ed. George William Curtis, 2 vols, London, 1889.

Mussell, James, *The Nineteenth-Century Press in the Digital Age*, London, 2012.

Nayder, Lillian, *The Other Dickens: A Life of Catherine Hogarth*, Ithaca, New York, 2011.

Noakes, Aubrey, *William Frith: Extraordinary Victorian Painter*, London, 1978.

Norton, Caroline, *A Letter to the Queen on Lord Chancellor Cranworth's Marriage and Divorce Bill*, London, 1855.

Nutton, Vivian and Roy Porter (eds), *The History of Medical Education in Britain*, Amsterdam, 1995.

Olsen, Donald J., *The Growth of Victorian London*, London, 1976.

Owen, Richard, *President's Address to the British Association for the Advancement of Science*, London, 1858.

The Oxford Dictionary of National Biography (ODNB).

Pasachoff, Jay M., Roberta J.M. Olsen, and Martha M. Hazen, 'The Earliest Comet Photographs: Usherwood, Bond, and Donati 1858', *Journal for the History of Astronomy*, vol. 27 (1996), pp. 129–45.

Pellerin, Denis and Brian May, *Crinoline: Fashion's Most Magnificent Disaster: A History of the Crinoline Dress from Victorian Times to the Present Day, Seen through Stereo Photography, Illustrated Magazines and other Ephemera*, London, 2016.

Pike, E. Royston, *Human Documents of the Victorian Golden Age (1850–1875)*, London, 1967.

Porter, Dorothy and Roy Porter (eds), *Doctors, Politics and Society: Historical Essays*, Amsterdam, 1993.

Raby, Peter, *Alfred Russel Wallace: A Life*, London, 2001.

Raverat, Gwen, *Period Piece: A Cambridge Childhood*, London, 1952.

Ray, Gordon N., *Thackeray: The Age of Wisdom (1847–1863)*, London, 1958.

—*Thackeray: The Uses of Adversity (1811–1846)*, London, 1955.

Reeve, Tori, *Down House: The Home of Charles Darwin*, London, 2009, reprinted 2011.

Richards, Jeffrey, *The Golden Age of Pantomime: Slapstick, Spectacle and Subversion in Victorian England*, London, 2015.

Ritchie, Anne Thackeray, *Chapters from Some Memoirs*, London, 1894.

—*Journals and Letters*, ed. Lillian F. Shankman, Abigail Burnham Bloom and John Maynard, Columbus, Ohio, 1994.

Ritchie, J. Ewing, *About London*, London, 1860.

—*Here and There in London*, London, 1859.

—*The London Pulpit*, London, 1858.

Roberts, Michael J.D., 'The Politics of Professionalization: MPs, Medical Men, and the 1858 Medical Act', *Medical History*, vol. 53 (January 2009), pp. 37–56.

Rossetti, Dante Gabriel, *The Correspondence of Dante Gabriel Rossetti*, ed. William E. Fredeman, 10 vols, Woodbridge, 2002–10.

Rupke, Nicolaas A., *Richard Owen: Victorian Naturalist*, New Haven, Conn. and London, 1994.

Ruskin, John, *Letters from the Continent 1858*, ed. John Hayman, Toronto, 1982.

Russell, Lord John, *The Later Correspondence of Lord John Russell 1840–1878*, ed. G.P. Gooch, 2 vols, London, 1925.

Russell, William Howard, *My Diary in India, in the Year 1858–9*, 2 vols, London, 1860.

Sala, G.A., *Gaslight and Daylight, with Some London Scenes They Shine Upon*, London, 1859.

—*How I Tamed Mrs Cruiser, by Benedict Cruiser, M.M. (Married Man), and now H.H. (Happy Husband)*, ed. George Augustus Sala, with Illustrations by Phiz, London, 1858.

—*Letters of George Augustus Sala to Edmund Yates*, ed. Judy McKenzie, University of Queensland Victorian Research Guide, 1993.

—*The Life and Adventures of George Augustus Sala, Written by Himself*, 2 vols, London, 1895.

—*Things I Have Seen, and People I Have Known*, 2 vols, London, 1894.

—*Twice Round the Clock, or Hours of the Day and Night in London*, London, 1859.

Secord, James A., *The Extraordinary Publication, Reception and Secret Authorship of 'Vestiges of the Natural History of Creation'*, London, 2000.

Shannon, Mary L., *Dickens, Reynolds, and Mayhew on Wellington Street: The Print Culture of a Victorian Street*, Farnham, 2015.

Simon, John and Edward Headlam Greenhow, *Papers Relating to the Sanitary State of the People of England*, London, 1858.

Slater, Michael, *Charles Dickens*, New Haven, Conn. and London, 2009, paperback 2011.

—*Dickens and Women*, London, 1983.

—*The Great Charles Dickens Scandal*, New Haven, Conn. and London, 2012.

Slotten, Ross A., *The Heretic in Darwin's Court: The Life of Alfred Russel Wallace*, New York, 2004.

Smalley, Donald (ed.), *Trollope: The Critical Heritage*, London, 1969.

Snow, John, *On Chloroform and Other Anaesthetics: Their Action and Administration*, with a memoir by B.W. Richardson, London, 1858.

Snow, Stephanie J., *Blessed Days of Anaesthesia: How Anaesthetics Changed the World*, Oxford, 2008.

Solly, Henry, *The Life of Henry Morley*, London, 1898.

Stamp, Gavin, *The Changing Metropolis: Earliest Photographs of London 1839–1879*, Harmondsworth, 1984.

Stedman Jones, Gareth, *Karl Marx: Greatness and Illusion*, London, 2016.

Stephens, John Russell, *The Censorship of English Drama 1824–1901*, Cambridge, 1980.

Stone, Lawrence, *Road to Divorce, England 1530–1987*, Oxford, 1990.

Straus, Ralph, *Sala: The Portrait of an Eminent Victorian*, London, 1942.

Summerscale, Kate, *Mrs Robinson's Disgrace: The Private Diary of a Victorian Lady*, London, 2012.

Swabey, M.C.M., T.H. Tristram et al., *Reports of Cases Decided in the Court of Probate and in the Court for Divorce and Matrimonial Causes*, 4 vols, London, 1858–65.

Tennyson, Alfred, *The Poems of Tennyson*, ed. Christopher Ricks, New York, 1969.

Thackeray, William Makepeace, *The Letters and Private Papers of William Makepeace Thackeray*, ed. Gordon N. Ray, 4 vols, Cambridge, Mass., 1945–6.

—*The Oxford Thackeray*, ed. George Saintsbury, 17 vols, Oxford, 1908.

Tomalin, Claire, *The Invisible Woman: The Story of Nelly Ternan and Charles Dickens*, London, 1990.

Trevelyan, G.M., *British History in the Nineteenth Century (1782–1901)*, London, 1922.

Van Dam, Thea, *My Dearest Ben: An Intimate Glimpse into the World of Benjamin Disraeli, his Family and the Women in his Life – through their Letters*, Buckinghamshire Papers, number 16, Aylesbury, 2008.

Vaughan, Adrian, *Isambard Kingdom Brunel: Engineering Knight-Errant*, London, 1991.

Victoria, Queen, *Dearest Child: Letters between Queen Victoria and the Princess Royal*, ed. Roger Fulford, London, 1964.

—*The Letters of Queen Victoria: A Selection from Her Majesty's Correspondence between the Years 1837 and 1861*, ed. A.C. Benson and Viscount Esher, 3 vols, London, 1907.

Vinten-Johansen, Peter et al., *Cholera, Chloroform, and the Science of Medicine: A Life of John Snow*, Oxford, 2003.

Waddington, Ivan, *The Medical Profession in the Industrial Revolution*, Dublin, 1984.

Waddington, Patrick, *Turgenev and England*, New York, 1981.

Wallace, Alfred Russel, *Letters from the Malay Archipelago*, ed. John van Wyhe and Kees Rookmaaker, Oxford, 2013.

—*My Life: A Record of Events and Opinions*, London, 1908.

Waugh, Norah, *Corsets and Crinolines*, New York, 1954, reprinted 2004.

White, Jerry, *London in the Nineteenth Century*, London, 2007.

White, Paul, *Thomas Huxley: Making the 'Man of Science'*, Cambridge, 2003.

Whorton, James C., *The Arsenic Century: How Victorian Britain was Poisoned at Home, Work and Play*, Oxford, 2010.

Willis, Nathaniel Parker, *Pencillings by the Way*, New York, 1852.

Wilson, Ben, *Heyday: Britain and the Birth of the Modern World*, London, 2016.

Wise, Sarah, *Inconvenient People: Lunacy, Liberty and the Mad Doctors in Victorian England*, London, 2012.

Wright, Thomas, *Some Habits and Customs of the Working Classes, by a Journeyman Engineer*, London, 1867.

Yates, Edmund, *Mr Thackeray, Mr Yates, and the Garrick Club: The Correspondence and the Facts*, London, 1859.

—*Recollections and Experiences*, 2 vols, London, 1884.

Index